POWER IN THE CITY

Frederick M. Wirt

POWER IN THE CITY

DECISION MAKING IN SAN FRANCISCO

Published for the Institute of Governmental Studies,
University of California, Berkeley, by the

UNIVERSITY OF CALIFORNIA PRESS
BERKELEY · LOS ANGELES · LONDON

University of California Press
Berkeley and Los Angeles, California
University of California Press, Ltd.
London, England
Copyright © 1974, by
The Regents of the University of California
ISBN 0–520–02654–3
Library of Congress Catalog Card Number: 73–90662
Printed in the United States of America

Contents

Acknowledgments

This study began just as I completed research on the impact of federal laws and a changing economy upon a county in the Mississippi Delta. Both studies were motivated by a single inquiry: How has the nature of contemporary community life been altered by forces currently beating upon the local walls? As removed as sophisticated San Francisco and bucolic Panola County are—in distance, climate, history, resources, social structure (and cuisine)—they also demonstrate surprising similarities in their reactions to recent national events. While different in the complexity of their response to those events, both are alike in their inescapable necessity to respond. Those responses are filtered and conditioned by differences in their history, group life, and so on. But the sultry rural Delta and cool urbane San Francisco are as one in having to reverberate to the fact of their membership in a national system of governance and economics now being swept by massive social and political changes. It is thus the theme of this book that San Francisco, while a very special city in its beauty, shares much with other cities of the nation—and indeed, with dusty Delta hamlets.

I was stimulated to initiate this project, encouraged to continue in the face of intervening studies and other professional ventures, and supported financially by Eugene C. Lee, Director of the Institute of Governmental Studies, University of California at Berkeley. Through the Institute, he provided salary support and institutional resources, while personally he gave emotional reinforcement at every stage. It was a high honor to have been part of an organization which seeks to provide such a quality linkage between scholarship and public policy needs in American government. It was even better to have had the friendship and advice of Gene Lee.

When I turn to list the many others who have contributed to this book, I fear to forget some because so many were involved. Those thirty-four "knowledgeables" of this city who, in successive interviews provided insights and information, are not identified for reason of our agreement to keep their names confidential. But others can be mentioned and appreciated.

Through several drafts of this manuscript I have benefited immensely from those reviewers who saved me from sin and error in matters of fact, interpretation, and style. Eugene Lee had the fortitude to read two drafts, while Morton Baratz and Willis Hawley reviewed the penultimate draft. Portions of this book relevant to their expertise were reviewed by observers ranging from academia to City Hall to the city's group life: Walton Bean; William Dauer; Robert Dolan; Sid Gardner; Chester Hartman; Lenneal Henderson, Jr.; Victor Jones; T. J. Kent; John McGloin, S. J.; Robert Mendelson; Thomas Miller; and Stanley Scott.

Others opened doors to officials, as did Eugene Lee, Victor Jones, and Stanley Scott, or to data sources. Here I acknowledge the enormous assistance of the staff of the Institute of Governmental Studies Library: head librarians Barbara Hudson and Jack Leister, and on a day-to-day basis Karen Chase and Dorothy Simpson, who never once shuddered when I popped out of my office with yet *another* request. Librarians at the Bancroft collection on the Berkeley campus served this book fully and enthusiastically over several years. Librarians for the morgues of the San Francisco *Chronicle* and *Examiner* served it equally well.

Innumerable officials of this city's agencies made available their reports and even raw data. Especially helpful in this respect was Frank Quinn of the Board of Elections for providing the precinct data of several chapters. Too, he, along with others, provided the impressionistic data on ethnic location shown in Figure 5. Like so many others, Mr. Quinn is a walking history of this city, and the professor learned much from him.

Special research assistance was provided by the many scholars cited in this book, but direct assistance came from several students mentioned at the appropriate places in the footnotes. However, William Zinn was especially valuable in several instances, while Sandy Wirt did a thorough check of my footnotes for love of father and ten-speed bicycle. The interviews of Patricia Gallagher in the Irish community were both sensitive and sensible.

Many secretaries worked over this writing, but Jane Burton, as with my other books, typed and retyped the bulk of the work. Special assistance came from Laura Justus on typing and from Hariet Nathan on citations. Hazel Karnes of the IGS staff was always there to help me out with the innumerable niggling details involved in putting an idea on paper.

Even then, however, it took special editorial assistance to get this effort into readable form. Eugene Lee has performed that task through all the drafts. Gladys Castor of the University of California Press staff entered at a critical moment and made my style and prose flow more clearly. William McClung, editor of the Press, is especially appreciated for having the patience and hopefully good judgment to publish this work.

Not all these people agree that what I have written is correct in fact, interpretation, or style. But all these should be held blameless for what appears hereafter, for such sins as there may be are mine alone. Yet I think all agree that this "cool, grey city of love" has not been denied its beauty and special feeling in anything written here. For they, like so many millions of Americans tired and frustrated, if not frightened, by most of our urban places, agree with the aphorism current in the early 1970s, "There may be no heaven, but somewhere there is a San Francisco."

FREDERICK M. WIRT
February, 1974
Columbia, Maryland

PART 1

THE CITY AS CONCEPT AND HISTORY

The winds of the Future wait
At the iron walls of her Gate,
And the western ocean breaks in thunder,
And the western stars go slowly under,
And her gaze is ever West
In the dream of her young unrest.
Her sea is a voice that calls,
And her star a voice above,
And her wind a voice on her walls—
My cool, grey city of love.

GEORGE STERLING

I may not be a competent judge, but this much I will say. That I have seen purer liquors, better segars, finer tobacco, truer guns and pistols, larger dirks and bowie knives, and prettier courtezans, here in San Francisco, than in any other place I have ever visited; and it is my unbiased opinion that California can and does furnish the best bad things that are obtainable in America.

HINTON R. HELPER,
The Land of Gold, 1855

CHAPTER 1

An Overview:
The Politics of Pluralism

INTRODUCTION

Of Time and the City

A city is a time machine, displaying signs of the past if we but look for them. One obvious sign is the old building or monument, focusing present attention on past events that shaped the city. Less evident are special signs of thinking and acting, patterns of value and behavior rooted in choices made in earlier days on the basic questions of how people should live. Whatever their form, though, these signs tell us that a modern city exists because of the past.[1] In this urban time machine there always lies a set of values to be found in the manner of its decision making. Clearly the forms by which we are governed reflect traditional values amid modern problems. Our ancestors' values are manifest in constitutions and charters found at all levels of American government. These political contracts, so dear to our people, bind the present to the past in agreement over basic, continuing values such as protection of freedom, defense of interests, and suspicion of power. While Americans may not revere the past, aside from giving lip service to patriotism, they live in a political system inherited from that past.

The past is but one of the many forces outside a city's wall that shape events inside it. National law increasingly affects local policies, and the conditions of the national economy constantly limit the options open to localities in their allocation of capital. The constitution and laws of the state, as well as its economic policies, affect the procedures, content, and quality of services to urban citizens. In all these forces there is a potential—and often a reality—for diluting urban autonomy, despite the rhetoric of "local control."

I wish to examine the nature of these external influences upon a special city. Of course, each city has some special quality, at least for its citizens; but for San Francisco, the city most loved by Americans according to polls, that special quality centers around its visual beauty. So dominant is this quality that its inhabitants—whether hard-bitten politicians, bitter ethnic leaders, cosmopolitan bankers, or ordinary citizens—proudly call San Francisco "The City." Even those from other parts of the Bay Area and for long reaches up the flanking valleys refer to it in their own home towns in this way.

Despite the special aesthetic feelings this city generates in residents and visitors alike, San Francisco is in many respects representative of all cities. It has its politics and its decisional processes just as any other city has. Unfortunately, most works on San Francisco concentrate on its past and its beauty[2] and rarely treat its current politics. It is in keeping with this preoccupation with the city's past that the most recent political era given full analysis was that of Boss Abe Ruef, jailed a few years after the 1906 earthquake for the usual charge—corruption.[3] There are excellent volumes on the politics of other major American cities; even some small cities, like New Haven, Connecticut, have provoked voluminous writing. The present work, therefore, undertakes the description of the contour of San Francisco's modern political reality.

Problems in Defining a City

A city has many dimensions, and not all of these are visible. Legally, a city is a public corporation with a definite geographical limit. To the Census Bureau and the legal code, it is a thing of aggregates—population, borders, responsibilities, and so on. But it also has an emotional context. It is one thing to a young, white, middle-class couple who fall in love amid the visual beauty of the beach, park, and view of the Bay. It is yet something else to a poor, black family living on the outskirts of the city in Hunter's Point and who rarely visit the inner city's tourist attractions. The latter group may live within the city, yet lack any emotional identification with it. They are in, but not of, the city. Others far removed hold it in warm memory for an earlier and happier experience. They are of, but not in, the city.

This difficulty in defining a city is compounded by the fact that its influence may extend beyond its legal boundaries. Any city influences the economy of the surrounding area it services beyond its legal limits. Every city reaches out for different lengths with its retail commerce, wholesale trade, commutation, or newspaper circulation.[4] The last can extend for hundreds of miles; San Francisco's newspapers circulate far up and down central California. Furthermore, if there are major financial and commercial centers in a city, decisions made there reach to the state, the nation, and even the world. Decisions by central offices of petroleum, banking, and trading firms located in San Francisco often influence citizens in Saudi Arabia, Tokyo, and La Paz more than they may influence residents of the city. Because this study could not possibly encompass all the influences the city has on the greater metropolitan area, the state, the nation, or the international scene, it will focus first on the city as it is defined legally.

The city will also be defined as a complex set of transactions, or exchanges, among its citizens. In a real sense, this definition literally treats this city in much the way that the first city operated. We do not know the location or time in world history of those dawn cities, although the best estimate is 5,000 years ago and roughly at the same time along the Indus and Yellow rivers. But when cities do emerge in records, they are seen as places where people are exchanging things—goods, ideas, protections, and so forth. As Aristotle noted 2,500 years ago, people formed cities to live and stayed there to live well. Both purposes imply the function of exchange.

This transactional character, found today in even the smallest town, varies with the city's inhabitants. The mere size of population may well account for more variation in urban policy and structure than any other factor.[5] In "the big city" there is an almost uncountable variety of patterns of exchange. The transformation of our nation from rural to urban represented also a transition from homogeneity to heterogeneity, from the comforting uniformity of the farmstead to the frightening variety of a New York or a San Francisco. These urban qualities arise because the bringing together of such diversity has also meant an increase in the volume and variety of transactions among people. The content of these transactions is found in many sources—ordinances, elections, sales receipts, library circulation, labor strikes, riots, and so forth. Characteristic of each transaction is the exchange by one person or group with another for something material or symbolic that contributes to the safety, income, or respect of each.

Individual needs, resources, and preferences constitute the raw materials for transactions within a city, and obviously the larger the city, the larger the combinations of transactions. American communities differ widely in their needs, preferences, and resources, with a consequent diversity in their policy programs.[6] Community needs will vary with size; for example, most small towns have little need for police homicide squads. Community resources are also a matter of size; the small town could hardly afford the homicide squad even if it needed it. Furthermore, the greater the size, the greater the pool of judgments about what is valuable, so that preference is another factor that also accounts for diversity; in a small town there is likely to be general agreement that a homicide squad is unnecessary.

This variety in city resources and programs suggests also the variety of perspectives one may bring to bear on city life. In this study, I will use many perspectives—economic, sociological, historical—befitting the multifaceted qualities of urban life. But the pivot on which such analyses turn will be political, namely, the operations of local decision making and the impact on it of influences from outside the city walls.

Politics and the Political System

In the politics and political system of San Francisco, we can see the processes by which its public and private decisions are made. Implicit or explicit, the term "politics" involves the element of dissension—conflict over both ends and means within community life. Elections are the most familiar method of resolving such conflict, but the scope of politics is not limited to electoral politics. With a community split by disagreement over goals—substantive or procedural, fundamental or casual, long- or short-term—the methods by which such disagreements are met or resolved may range from peaceful to violent. Disagreements arise out of the various economic, religious, or cultural stresses within a society. These external stresses generate demands on the political system,[7] whose members struggle to resolve (or block) them by producing new public policies which, in turn, feed back upon the subsystem originally generating the stresses. (See Appendix I.) In this way the political system is intimately tied to other systems of society from which stress may arise.

Characteristically, the political system permits the conversion into public policy of some private demands and ignores others because political authorities regard some demands as more important than others. This political system does not operate in an ad hoc fashion each time a demand is thrust upon it; rather, it is institutionalized. That is, it has a history of implementing certain values by procedures which, over time, come to be accepted as the authoritative and reasonable ways of performing; and this history influences the process of converting contemporary demands into policy. In one sense, local governments are urban time machines which "can be thought of as storage places for memories, recorded in their files or carried in the minds of their specialized personnel." [8]

Even if the political system has a certain stability, it exists in a community in which change is also characteristic. The forces for change are constantly renewed by recurring demands on the political system which challenge old decisions about the distribution of income or other resources. But the basic stability of institutions in the processing of issues continues to exist even in the constant conflict over obtaining resources or regulating interests. The resolution of many of these issues may in time reshape the very institutions themselves, and the goals of the community may then be better served; such was the impact of the Progressive urban reform at the turn of this century. On other occasions, although institutions may not change, their personnel may be replaced by those more sensitive to new configurations of resources and interests; this has occurred over the last century through the entrance of new ethnic groups into urban politics.

These concepts of politics and the political system, sharing elements from both the past and the present, guide my inquiry into the decision-making processes of San Francisco. They require one to look beyond elections to the characteristic patterns of processing issues that exist in other political forums such as councils, agencies, and courts. They also require an understanding of the linkage between this public arena and the "private" systems of the community, whose stresses generate the demands which are the stimuli of politics. One must also understand that the stresses generated by changes within the community never arise and never are settled entirely *within* the community. To some degree, local politics is influenced by events and forces outside the city, and any analysis of "community power" that does not estimate the force of outside constraints tells us little about the community. These concepts, then, frame a process of decision making over a range of issues—some unresolvable, some being resolved, some suppressed—which represent the accumulation of many demands on the political system.

This introduction to the concepts guiding this study of San Francisco should be paired with some preliminary overview of the private and public political systems of the city.

THE POLITICAL SYSTEM OF SAN FRANCISCO TODAY:
AN OVERVIEW

My point of departure is an explanation of how this study will proceed. However, while such an explanation of methodology may be of special interest to scholars of community politics, its technical aspects usually distract lay readers. To accommodate both audiences, I have provided in Appendix I an essay on the methods used here. But I think both groups will find rewarding some overview of what they are about to experience, without its detracting from subsequent findings. Therefore, the rest of this chapter will summarize the decision-making system of San Francisco as it has operated in recent years. This overview follows roughly the sequence of chapters to come, but its style is more casual and its observations more sweeping. Most of the major themes are touched on without the scope and depth of later analysis. With most of the actors removed in this overview, I will emphasize only the contours of the arena of decisions.

Private and Public Decision Making

Because men are not angels, as James Madison once noted, some form of government is a necessity; but from our earliest history, the makers of American charters have been almost obsessed by fears of too much government. The Platonic method of controlling arbitrary power by recruiting only moral men has had limited practicality in our societies. It is Aristotle who informs the American political tradition: the dividing of power so that no one gets too much, the setting of power against power, ambition against ambition, and interest against interest. The hope is that, in this way, "Nobody gets everything, nobody gets nothing, everybody gets something."

Few American cities have embraced this traditional principle more enthusiastically than San Francisco. Here, public decision making proceeds amid such fragmentation of power that the traditional principle has sometimes come to its logical end, powerlessness. But sometimes it can operate successfully when the challenge arises, and in some areas of decision making much that is routine operates success-fully, albeit quietly. Sometimes the process is blocked by divergent interest groups, and at other times success is achieved without fric-tion; some groups win much, and many win much less; winners of one period are compelled to share power in another period. So there is no single process of how decisions are made in San Francisco.

Political decisions of wide community scope are my main focus in this book; but private organizations also make decisions affecting the city's people, and these, too, reflect the total decisional context. In that private corner of the system, there is no single "establish-ment," but rather a Big Establishment and a Small Establishment. The money available to each is not the sole factor that distinguishes their effects on community decision making. The Big Establishment is peopled by financial and industrial capitalists and managers whose interests run far beyond the Bay Area to the nation and the world. The Small Establishment is centered on financial interests that ex-tend only to the Bay Area, and particularly to the city itself. There-fore, the Big Establishment has little interest in San Francisco politics or its government, whereas many in the Small Establishment focus on it with perseverance and enthusiasm. Of course, both have ma-terial interests at stake in local government, but the Big Establish-ment can afford to bide its time, while the Small Establishment has a more immediate commitment. Both, however, cooperate on cul-tural, civic, and generally nonpolitical matters.

One might postulate that it is this constellation of private interests that makes many, if not most, of the decisions concerning resources and values in this community. But there is a complex little world of power on this famed peninsula. Establishments disagree on many matters; new groups are constantly coming into power, and outside forces increasingly add their voices. So the private power groups are not alone in the city, and government often has to deal with many of the problems that result from these private decisions. Local govern-ment may have little to do with the origins of such problems; it may not help in the takeoff, but only in the flight—and often only when cries of "Mayday!" fill the air.

Parties as an Agent of Power

One aspect that needs to be explored is the role of political parties. To anyone accustomed to the frenetic party politics of the East, the party politics of California cities must seem mystifying, if only because of their absence. Like the dog in the Sherlock Holmes story, they are important because they do *not* bark. One finds traces of their presence in party leader titles and in announcements of committee meetings. But such spoor lead to nothing at all.

The evanescent nature of California's local political parties is a result of the state's distinctive nonpartisan political culture. Its central features are a distrust of politics and politicians and a magical belief that if you give something a different name, you can change its essential quality, like the Victorians calling chicken breast "white meat." But instituting local nonpartisanship did *not* make local politicians and local politics vanish. It only shifted their operations into informal procedures, for the tasks of party life still get done: nominating, getting out the vote, presenting issues, governing. The result in San Francisco has been the shifting of patterns of partisan activity, often in a nonpartisan garb.

It was not always so. During and for a while after the New Deal, the Irish totally dominated Democratic politics; but in the period after World War II their grasp began to loosen. Today, both parties reveal a high degree of factionalism, and it is not uncommon to see interparty coalitions on behalf of candidates or issues. Among the Democrats there had been hopes in the late 1950s that the California Democratic Council (CDC) would permanently consolidate and lead a liberal movement. Indeed, old CDC members in the 1960s controlled the party's central committee in the county (identical with the city, as the two are consolidated). But the fervor generated by Adlai Stevenson had diffused into a turbulent mosaic of factions in conflict over symbolic and material issues.

In all this confusion, party structure, predictably, is only a thing of paper. There is no cadre of precinct workers except that provided by each candidate, and the candidate also does his own fund raising. There is a central committee, but no one seems to know why its control is important. In ostensibly nonpartisan elections, it doesn't endorse candidates; formally this would be illegal, and informally there would be the fear of driving away Republican support. While the committee does take stands on some issues, these are seldom, if ever, publicized. In this world of form without substance, not unlike the smile of Alice's Cheshire cat, the struggles to control the central committee seem meaningless, a mark of the politician's propensity to grab any loose marbles lying around.

In this context of invisible parties an election is much like the start of those long-distance races where everybody is on his own, eyes straight ahead, and there's a considerable amount of jostling in the pack. Candidates raise their own funds, rarely coalesce with other candidates in a slate, and strive earnestly to reach across party and ethnic lines. With a number of candidates for all offices, running at large with no runoffs (except for mayor, beginning in 1975), the process is symbolized by the local practice of slapping hundreds of election posters on buildings, fences, and poles all over the city. By election day the city is a kaleidoscope of jarring, confusing, and possibly self-defeating posters.

One consequence of such partyless politics is reminiscent of what scholars once found in some Southern politics. Because the party does not bind its candidates to a common program, temporary coalitions of voters support a given candidate but fall away by the next election, thereby rendering impossible any accountability for programs. Elected at large, a candidate cannot be certain what combination of neighborhood interest most clearly supports him. He may know the neighborhoods from which he got his votes and he may know which groups endorsed him, but he cannot be certain which ones actually voted for him. As the parties have no internal discipline, they cannot provide any clear-cut image of responsibility for the voters, and they cannot impose a sense of purpose on their members' commitment to policies or programs. Even if the parties were to attempt some standard of responsibility, the structural obstacles embodied in the city charter are immense.

The Cage of Authority

In 1932 the voters approved a charter whose primary purpose was to prevent widespread corruption. It succeeded admirably. Indeed, the charter divided the power and structure of government into so many pieces that if officials wanted to be corrupt, it would hardly be worth their while. But the price for achieving this honesty was to make those who govern San Francisco impotent, to rob them of coordinated instruments for meeting emergent urban problems. The cover of a League of Women Voters' volume fully caught the essence of the city's government. A Calder-like mobile has figures frozen in midair and interconnected in inexplicable ways by wildly zooming lines. A mobile is a thing of beauty, but hardly functional.

To control corruption, members of a legislative board of supervisors are elected in off years and at large in a part-time office for

staggered terms. Further to close off the gates of temptation, they
are prohibited from intervening in administrative affairs. Too, innumerable boards and commissions, designed to maximize citizen participation—long before the recent interest in "participatory democracy"—exercise powers independent of the mayor, except that he
appoints them. Basically, the mayor has few formal powers short of
appointment and budget making, and even these are limited.

Administrative power is split among a mayor, a chief administrative officer, a comptroller, boards and commissions, and an entirely independent school board. The charter also mandates rigid
and extensive civil service and merit systems, fiercely guarded by
city employee unions and regularly sweetened by referenda. The personnel system is so frozen by the city charter that ordinary personnel
changes, like adding one more police sergeant to the lists, require a
referendum. The weight of city employees in local elections brings
pressure on the supervisors to increase their salaries and provide other
benefits.

To the constraints on governing imposed by the formal partitioning
of power, the charter adds popular limits found in the frequent use
of the referendum for matters small and great. For every time even
the most minor charter change—often only administrative—is required, there must be a referendum. Though only a tiny minority of
San Franciscans understand the minutiae of these proposals, at every
election, where the turnout rate is usually high, they are confronted
with ten to twenty of them.

On the national level, the accumulated price of such fractionated
decision making would be considerable. Even on the municipal level,
the price San Francisco pays is the lack of decision making. When
the successful outcome of policy must rest on the agreement of so
many private groups and public authorities, the power of one component to block any action is magnified. Over time, consequently,
only minor policy adjustments are possible, but it is highly doubtful
whether these add up to an adequate response to deep and widespread community problems. Instead, the bulk of public policy is
made by clerks beyond the reach of the electorate. Each of these can
affect only small sections of the government, but cumulatively their
little decisions make up the totality of public policy. What San
Francisco has, then, is government by clerks. Moreover, the central
drift of the pattern of these decisions can best be characterized as

nondecision. And the decision *not to act* has as much public consequence as the decision *to act*.

The Mayor as a Centralizing Authority

In this context, the position of mayor is what he makes it by the force of his character and personality. He may define his role as that of chief greeter for the city, and considering the flow of the world's notables through this port, he could well fill his time. If he has higher ambitions, he can play the role of rising politico, spending time in Sacramento or Washington. That also requires him to build a firm local base and record, which few have been able to do, given the fragmented context of city politics. All mayors try out another role to some degree, that of community quarterback. This is the effort to coordinate, stimulate, and articulate a program to deal with community problems. But again, given the segmented urban life, the mayor is usually much like a quarterback in a sandlot game, where the huddle argues and votes on each play, and there are many penalties for delay of the game.

Joseph Alioto, the mayor after 1967, entered office with a splash, clearly trying to rise above these limited roles without ignoring them. He has worn many hats, those of ceremonial shaman, public relations officer, carrier of some authority, worrier about crucial urban problems, target of contenders in the urban struggle. Keenly aware of the charter and the political limitations of his office, Alioto has used to the utmost that power which may ultimately be the prime one for all executives, public and private—the power to persuade others to find a satisfactory compromise among contending groups. Such is the potential in the mayor's office in San Francisco, and perhaps in most, if not all, cities in America.

Yet another potential lies in one's reputation as a rising politico. Like many other mayors, from the day of his election Alioto was surrounded by expectations of higher things politically. This attracted some local power holders who simply like to be associated with future governors or senators. But this role also exacts a price in the time and energy it takes away from the city. Administrators are more likely to move when the mayor leans on them persuasively and continually, a likelihood diminished when time must be spent considering his political future. Whatever this role may have done for the mayor's future, it limited his power to persuade.

The role of rising politico, then, probably offers little help to a mayor of San Francisco in strengthening his persuasiveness and imposing some programmatic unity on the city. The charter's restraining cage makes it difficult to construct a convincing record as administrator which could be trumpeted about the state. Reciprocally, the resources needed to work hard toward future political eminence diminish his influence in the city administration.

Major Issues on the Public Agenda

In this context of power fragmentation, coalition, and diffusion, major issues are fought out. In the 1960s and later, two issues were predominant. One was the "politics of profit," the other the "politics of deference." The former revolves around the enormous effort to construct office and residential highrises in the commercial district of San Francisco. In places where ships were once deserted by the forty-niners seeking gold in the Sierra, there now rear many-storied buildings on filled-in land. The cityscape had been characteristically marked by a gently rolling quality, but in the 1960s all that changed. Skyscrapers now jut up in tight formation in the Montgomery Street financial district through the efforts of the city's leaders to maintain its position as "the financial capital of the West." National corporations poured in to construct, work, and reside in these highrises as San Francisco became linked increasingly to a "Pacific Rim" international economy.

San Francisco also became the focus of the vision which business leaders had of a regional economy, with the city as an administrative and entertainment center. A mass regional transit system was planned as the means for sucking in and out each day the thousands of white-collar commuters necessary for San Francisco's role in this economy, just as highrise office buildings provided the worksites for them. In this major decision, business and political leaders were joined by unions, ethnic minorities, and the mass media, as well as by voters who supported almost every referendum that fostered the local government's share of this vision. By the early 1970s the city was transformed, not merely in visual perspective, but in the coalition of interests that agreed on this urban goal.

Of course, there was opposition to all this construction, especially from those who saw the result as a "Manhattanization" of their beloved city. Conservationists objected to landfill operations (and increasingly won their battles); architects and urban designers complained about the inferior aesthetic qualities of the buildings (and increasingly lost that battle); economists questioned whether the city's municipal costs for highrises would not exceed the revenue they could be expected to return (that battle's outcome is unknown); radicals condemned the economic-political combination that stimulated the program; and those who were once favorably situated objected to destruction of their prized views of the Bay. For many of these, another vision of the city was foremost: a small town of beauty and grace, fabled in a romantic past, ordered in style and manner. Theirs was a vision of a paradise lost.

The second major issue in San Francisco politics revolved around ethnic conflict. There were many material struggles involved here, but at heart this was not a politics of profit, as it was with highrises. Rather, it was much more a "politics of deference," the effort to achieve recognition of a group's worth in the urban and national scheme of values. That struggle runs through all the city's social institutions, past and present. It was visible in the efforts of Germans, Irish, and Italians to achieve recognition in church, government, business, schools, and status circles of an earlier San Francisco, or in the equivalent efforts of black, brown, red, and yellow citizens in the new city. The earlier battles had led to success for later generations of Germans, Irish, and Italians—the "arrived" minorities.

But the contemporary struggle of the "arriving" minorities for recognition has not met with the same success. The federal government has been responsible for most of the impetus for change on the local scene, with legislation, court orders, and various supportive resources. One result has been that new political cadres have been recruited and trained in the intricacies of local politics, so that the former quiescence of Negroes, Latin-Americans, Orientals, and Indians has become the turbulent challenge of blacks, Chicanos, Asians, and Native Americans. The change in self-designation is symbolic in many ways besides the obvious one of augmenting group morale. It symbolizes also a new outlook on the local political system and on the opportunities to participate in its rewards or to "get a piece of the action." These arriving groups learned in the 1960s what had taken the already arrived minorities many decades to master: the means of obtaining political power.

This politics of deference is distinguished from that of profit in ways other than their respective symbolic and material differences. The ethnic contest does not engage as many elements of the local society of San Francisco as does the politics of the highrise, although it is tending that way. Another difference lies in the crucial fact that not all urban sectors merge in a supportive coalition, as they did with the highrises. Rather, by its very nature, this is a politics of dissimilar interests. The arriving minorities are asking for redistribution of existing material resources, jobs, income, schooling, health, safety, as ways to achieve the central resource of deference. In one sense, one is a politics of expansion, the other a politics of redistribution, and each must necessarily employ different decision-making processes.

External Influences on Local Decision Making

A major new element in San Francisco's political system is the new force of external power on local decision making. Studies of community power since the 1950s have paid little attention to the local effects of those decisions made elsewhere in higher private and governmental levels. But in the 1960s San Francisco and other cities began feeling the impact of this greater external involvement. The Great Society and its successors in urban policy brought the federal government into many activities in the city and provided new issues, resources, and actors in expansive as well as redistributive politics. The volume of that new external input and its qualitative requirements have been great and the consequences significant. More attention has to be given to how this external force has altered the basic nature of community power in this and other cities.

For example, the schools have been dramatically affected by court orders against segregation, and their curricula and teacher training have been influence by federal legislation providing school aid. Across a wide sweep of other local programs—welfare, safety, transportation, and similar city services—local government now runs on large amounts of federal financial fuel. The impetus that federal law gave to arriving ethnic groups has changed the political system in ways that can never be reversed. Federal plans intersect other local interests, too, in ways not yet fully realized. Local governance has created new offices for federal relationships almost overnight, and new knowledge has been gathered for such negotiations; the city even maintains its own diplomat in Washington for such purposes. The "federal presence" is manifest in local agencies big and small and on issues both significant and trivial. All this external influence works to affect local autonomy and the potential "power structure" in ways that need to be analyzed in the study of urban affairs.

The "feds" are not, however, the only external constraint upon local autonomy. Numbers of regional organizations sprang up during the 1960s, in San Francisco and elsewhere, to develop and apply a broader perspective to the particularism and parochialism of local government. Some of these regional units are only advisory, operating by local consensus, gently prodding by raising local perspectives. Others provide a regional service, such as rapid transit; San Francisco is one of the three counties to participate in the first new rapid transit system in a half-century in this nation. Yet other regional organizations carry bigger sticks, especially in environmental controls, a response to the pollution crisis of the 1960s. These organizations can compel local systems to clean their air and water and purify their sewage, and prevent them from destroying the bay and the ocean beaches. No one knows where this new development will go. Again, however, as regional organizations operate in the early 1970s, they are another external influence on local decision making.

Finally, among those outside forces the power of the state continues to grow. Local government everywhere operates within a network of mandates, options, taxes, and services that the state requires and that necessarily limit local autonomy. In recent decades there have developed increasing signs of greater specification, broader mandates, and more varied objectives in state ties to localities. Many of these arise from local stimuli, but not all localities want these new burdens, and not all local people agree on them. Again, the full weight of this external influence on local decision making needs to be taken into account by students of "power structures."

Nor is it only governmental agencies that work on local affairs from the outside. In the private realm of American life, one can detect signs of the effect on the local scene of decisions made elsewhere. That is most visible in San Francisco and other places in the spurt of highrise construction during the 1960s. While many local groups welcomed this program eagerly, they did not have the option to accept or reject it until private capital centers first decided to move there and build. Of similar effect are decisions by national trade unions, which restrict what local unions can do and how they will have an impact on the local economy. Also, no city is immune from the multitude of incremental decisions made throughout the nation which create economic booms and busts; thus, no wall kept out higher food prices during the early 1970s in San Francisco or any other local community.

The omnipresent national force of professionalism also permeated

San Francisco's borders. Professional definitions of work, competency, procedures, and other aspects of social endeavor have been so closely married to private and governmental organizations that separation is no longer even thought of. However, the poor challenged many of these accepted behavior patterns during the programs of the 1960s. Long-accepted notions of "qualified" teachers, of "professional" behavior by lawyers, doctors, and social workers, of "competencies" that could be measured by testing—all came under attack.

But, ironically, whether such contests were won by the professionals or their challengers, the dominating factor was external influence. The professionals have everywhere grafted their norms of behavior and values on constitutions, statutes, and court decisions. When they win locally, they do so because of outside power. When they lose locally to new claimants, it is again outside power which led to the loss, for victories were possible because of such instruments as legal aid services, federal enforcement of national law, and national movements for improving the life conditions of consumers, the poor, and minorities. These are nationalized efforts which penetrate the local scene—new, large of scope, and binding upon local autonomy.

History as a Local Constraint

While these are the outside dimensions, yet another force constrains the local scene, that of history. The reference here is not to the romantic history that fills so much of the popular writing on San Francisco. Rather it is to that history which actually contained violent, exploitative, bigoted, and corrupt elements, alongside more praiseworthy features. I cannot cover every aspect of that side of the city's history, but can explore only those actions and decisions of the past which have shaped current thinking and practices in decision making.

I noted earlier the revulsion against past urban corruption, which created the constraints of the present governing charter. There was also the statewide revulsion of the Progressive movement which achieved legislation that structured party activity. These historical movements shape the nature of the present-day partisan struggle in local affairs. The very essence of San Francisco was set early by forces outside its control. The gold found in the Sierras was several hundred miles away, but its discovery created a city where months before there stood only a hamlet on a sandy cove. The mining and processing of gold converted the city into an entrepôt, a commercial center, middleman in the economic life of the state and region, and this function prevailed through later mining and agricultural booms. History played another role when Chinese immigration created a major political conflict with the Irish workers. A national mobilization of workers and federal law in the 1930s achieved a dominance for labor which made it a power in the city decades later. The Great Depression sapped the city's economy, and World War II pumped it; the needs of shipbuilders around the bay during that war also attracted thousands of blacks, who are now a power in the city. And the postwar evolution of a Pacific economy fastened on San Francisco as its center.

All of these represent major historical events that have shaped the city's decision making and policy life. Some have been continuing, such as the influences of being an entrepôt, the Progressive tradition, and the migration of blacks. Others were not tangibly ongoing but have left images on the minds of those who participated in local affairs. These images were passed on to create for later eras the insubstantial, almost mystical, political ethos. Such lingering touches of people long dead are seen in the anathema of partisanship in nonpartisan elections, the suspicion of elected officials, and the deference to trade unions.

This book, then, views the city as a set both of deposits from the past and of contemporary forces contending over limited resources. In this context, decision making reflects in part a local element, in configurations of power and privilege, in coalitions of mutual benefit, and in institutions which channel the struggle. But decision making is also viewed as operating against constraints that are not always visible. Some come out of the past to affect current affairs, for example, by setting some options as possible and others as unthinkable. Other constraints, from outside San Francisco, affect matters whose scope can be wide or narrow and whose source can be private or governmental. In all this, my object is not merely to examine one city, no matter how favored it has been by nature, history, and visitors. It may be, as San Franciscans proclaim, that their city is truly unique among American cities. But if I can demonstrate that in this most special and beautiful city there is much that one can also find elsewhere, then much will have been learned about, not "The City," but the city in American life.

CHAPTER

The People and Their History

Because history has its effect, what San Francisco has been must be known if we are to understand what it is today. That rich and complex tale must be condensed here and added to throughout the book. The focus here is on the economic transactions that have made and sustained the city since 1848, and on the life opportunities which its people and their resources have shaped. The historical conditions of these transactions and opportunities created community problems, thus leading to stress and then to demands on the political system. There is a solid although complex line from history to economic transactions and life opportunities to stress to decision making; if one is interested in the last, he must begin with the first. These elements of the bay city are provided in this chapter as a backdrop for later analysis.

AN ECONOMIC HISTORY

In the evolution of this Bay Area, San Francisco itself has played different roles. It has evolved from a fog-blown, sandy cove called Yerba Buena—transshipping goods between the gold fields and the world—into the still fog-blown financial and cultural center of the West—"everybody's favorite city." [1]

Trading Post to Entrepôt

In its early history San Francisco was little known or cherished. In light of its current tourist attraction, it is ironic that early explorers along the West Coast repeatedly failed to find the bay because its

20

opening was so often cloaked with fog. Once found by a surprised
Spanish explorer, the peninsula was settled with a fort and a mission
in 1776. The limited fur trade in the eighteenth century grew in the
nineteenth century as New England traders sought cowhides
("Yankee dollars") for shoe factories. But they saw this area as
simply one of a number of outposts for their great clippers. Prior to
1848 it was not sought out by settlers moving west, most of whom
turned north to Oregon, where the green valleys were more like those
of the East than were the searing valleys and chilly coasts of the
California country.

All of this changed with the discovery of gold several hundred
miles away in the Sierra. Where trade had been conducted by a few
Boston men, now thousands came to San Francisco to live off the
transfer of gold from the ground to the nation's banks. There is
much romanticism about those decades. Later generations, for reasons
of conscience, profit, or parochialism, placed filters against the bright
glare of those raw, brawling people. A contemporary, prominent
San Franciscan wryly noted in a refrain:

> They're San Franciscans of the Nob Hill crowd,
> Of course they're wealthy and of course they're proud.
> Their names only show a few slight signs
> Of inelegant beginnings in the placer mines.[2]

Those early San Franciscans shaped their local society and economy in ways that continued to be influential. For gold—and later
silver, cattle, and grain—made the city into an entrepôt, a middleman in the nation's economy. Its people did not make goods; instead
they transferred them. That exchange function was established early,
and in most respects it has persisted. How that began can only be
briefly told here, but it sets the force of history which affects the city
even today.

In the two decades after the gold discovery, the Bay Area became
a warehouse for the economy of the state. Here were stored and sold
the miners' needs, middlemen between the shovel and the bullion.
But those goods had also to be moved up to the Sierra, and the
ore down and out to the world, an enormous trade based on the
sands and mud of the cove that became San Francisco. From 1848,
when the first deep-sea vessel hove to in this cove, long wharves
were built out into the bay to reach these ships, exact extensions
of the city's few streets, as figure 1 demonstrates. Those wharves,

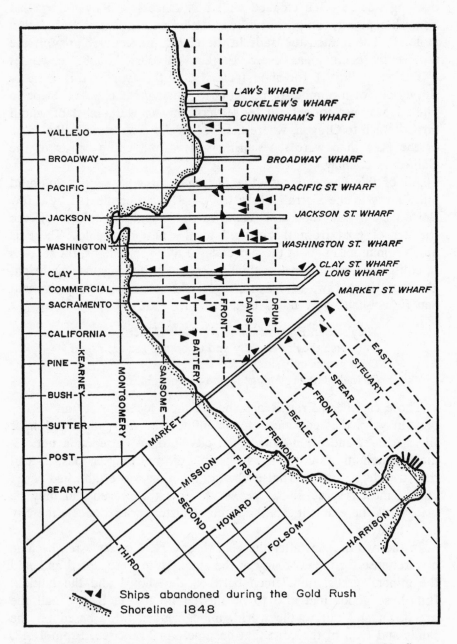

Fig. 1. Past and present along the Embarcadero—1850s and 1972. Source: San Francisco *Sunday Examiner and Chronicle,* May 14, 1972, p. A27.

by their convenience for trade, attracted even more ships to the bustling settlement just inside the Golden Gate.

But San Francisco was more than just a dumping place for goods brought halfway around the world. Incoming deep-draft vessels loaded their goods onto shallow-draft river boats which went from the bay up to Sacramento or Stockton, transshipping there to even lighter boats for the run to the gold fields. In effect, then, gold mining was but a few score miles from a waterhead which ran back 400 miles to San Francisco, about the distance from Boston to Washington. As a consequence, as James Vance notes: "In much the same way that the California Gold Rush finally made capital relatively plentiful in the United States, it made money available, as if overnight, to set up a city's business structure. More than perhaps any other American city, San Francisco had money to burn, both figuratively and, too frequently, literally." [3]

In the process, land uses were shaped by commercial and social pressures. Thus, warehousing was accompanied by the financing of the stored goods, and at first these two economic functions lived side by side on the waterfront. But commercial functions moved them out; as early as 1841 the Hudson's Bay Company had a primitive trading post on the waterfront. Other traders appeared later, in abandoned ship hulks, then in shanties, and finally in full-scale buildings. But behind them came the "dealers in intangibles—mine expectations, land titles, capital, and credit," [4] who financed the state's bonanzas in gold, silver, railroads, and wheat. These users pushed the stores and warehouses back from the shoreline so as to form a new financial district, like those to be found at mid-century only in Boston, New York, and Philadelphia. Here, too, a stock market emerged early, its saloon location paralleling the coffeehouse origins of the London exchanges. Wholesaling activity split off early, with fresh produce in one location (where it remained until 1963) and less perishable goods elsewhere. The point is that these various early business districts set down lines which became the modern pattern.*

Much of the same is true for housing. While residential areas bordering the business district in 1850 have since yielded to other land uses, the residential pattern of combining social with geographical stratification has continued. That is, wealthy residents seek the

---

* This has never been a city of much industry. Some was there early, related primarily to mining, but even then began the continuing trend of its movement to other communities bordering the bay.

highlands while the less wealthy deposit themselves in layers down the hills to the shores of bay or ocean, where an occasional rich view creates a rich neighborhood. In the century between, new subdivisions have appeared, land use catering to special ethnic, economic, or status groups.

Time and the Outside World Set the City

Over these decades of the nineteenth century, the inner city was sensitive to the economy outside its walls, and that external force—which originally made it—has never lost its influence. Strikes of silver in Nevada lodes, the opening of the Central Valley to wheat growing in the 1860s, the depressions of the 1870s and 1890s, the investment opportunities occasioned by construction of transcontinental railroads, the influx of Chinese as laborers on those tracks, the development of large-scale banking to finance these developments in mining, agriculture, and transportation—in all of these, San Francisco either played a central part or was shaken by them, or both. One reason was the size of the place: one in four Californians at the turn of the century were San Franciscans, and Los Angeles was a placid town of only 6,000 in 1870 when there were about 150,000 in the city by the bay.

Much of San Francisco's influence was attributable to the concentration of capital and labor there, which generated resources and influence throughout the economy of the West. The result was enormous political influence. The demands of banks and railroads on the state and city political systems for privilege and profit were inescapable, albeit heavily corruptive. Some labor demands, such as those arising out of the fear of cheap, Chinese competition, generated effective results in San Francisco and Sacramento. But always capital dominated, particularly railroad capital, which, in the hands of men like Leland Stanford, almost literally owned legislators and governors. But in all this, San Francisco echoed a union of capital and government that existed all across America in that pre-Progressive era, which was condoned, even in its endemic corruption, by public opinion. And, like the Progressive revolt elsewhere, when reform did come, it struck directly at the root—the corruption of too-great power in the hands of railroads.

A graphic display of that sensitivity of San Francisco to extramural events before World War I is provided in figure 2. This relates its imports and exports—a clear indicator of the exchange nature of an urban area—to those of the nation in the first half-century. In the earliest decades, this city's ratio is not congruent with that of the nation because of the bonanzas in mining and wheat. But thereafter the fit becomes much closer, although still unmatched for short periods. Depressions and prosperity that were felt nationwide also echoed here, although sometimes not in the same year.

From 1849 to World War I, all of these activities, only lightly sketched here, provided a historical conditioning that also shaped much of the visual city for subsequent years.[5] Its heart remained in the area of its origin, close to the bay where early vessels had anchored. Even the street pattern laid out in 1847 was not revised much when it was restored after the 1906 earthquake. Lands excluded in 1920 from commercial or residential development—such as military installations and parks—were the same as those a half-century earlier. Newer strip commercial developments were already in place, radiating along the main lines of travel established by the early electric trolleys, which here as elsewhere expanded the population and housing sites.[6] Older residential areas had pretty well stabi-

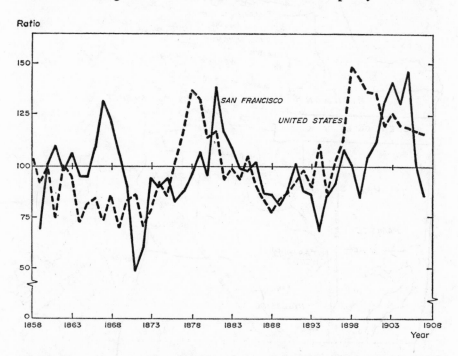

Fig. 2. Export-import ratios, San Francisco and the United States, 1858–1907. Source: Annual reports of the San Francisco Chamber of Commerce.

lized, although even then there was immense demand for the available housing, partly because of the amount of land preempted by the military, and partly because of poor topography or soil for housing construction. The downtown business district in 1919 had set into much the shape it still has. Commerce and manufacturing, always in conflict over land use at the foot of Market Street, plus growing financial institutions, had by then demarcated their various land sectors in the city, seen in figure 3.

Two decades later, in 1937, the urban structure was much the same. But the salient quality of that period was the new availability of easier transportation, which here, as elsewhere, spread housing out further, both within the city and to nearby areas. As with the trolley car decades earlier, ease of transportation generated new housing, and housing realtors generated pressures to provide new access routes. Automobiles enabled San Franciscans to live farther west toward

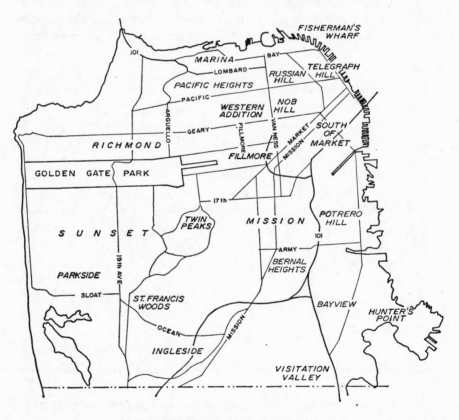

Fig. 3. Neighborhoods in San Francisco.

the ocean or south down the peninsula. The westward surge was made possible in part by the 1920s breakthrough of tunnels in hills once blocking movement. At the very end of these decades, the Golden Gate Bridge to the north and the Bay Bridge to the east set the foundation of suburban flight in later years.

In the downtown central business district, commerce had won out over industry in the use of land. Yet, adjoining areas which had once been heavily commercial became increasingly residential, and new commercial uses of "Auto Row" along Van Ness Avenue emerged after 1921. Transit lines stimulated more commercial development in other major centers throughout the city, but particularly in its now-filling western sections, which reached toward the ocean. As a result, much of the vacant, nonmilitary land was disappearing under the housing spread.

If we step ahead another decade to 1947, we find that the commercial, industrial, and housing vectors of the economy remained largely in place. But growth had taken place in the interstices, particularly in the west and south. By 1947 the force of history had exhausted vacant land, but there were still some alterations in its specific uses. Zoning and planning had come to control rational land use more fully. Commercial usage downtown had shifted south of Market Street under the impetus of the Bay Bridge approaches and the transit terminal. Commercial subcenters began to develop outside this core, along westwarding Geary Boulevard, in the Sunset district and west of Twin Peaks, and at Fisherman's Wharf. Some of these served specialized requirements of ethnic groups and others met the demands of a growing number of tourists. More important, the historical forces that had segmented land use into neighborhoods made these neighborhoods a vital element of the city's social structure. As one analyst noted: "Aided by topography and the street pattern which has been influenced by topography, the local shopping centers in San Francisco have become oriented to community districts and to neighborhoods. . . . To a degree probably unsurpassed in any large city in the United States, the shopping centers are focal points for residents of the immediately surrounding area." [7]

These decades from 1900 to World War II show again not merely this constricting land use reflecting the effect of past decisions, but also the impact of outside forces on the city's economy. In figure 4 we see its movement, which echoes national trends—the World War I stimulus, recession in the early 1920s followed by prosperity,

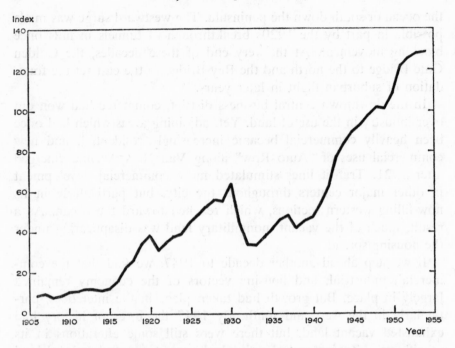

Fig. 4. San Francisco Business Activity Index, 1906–1954. Source: San Francisco Chamber of Commerce. Freight car movements, department store retail sales, electrical energy sales, and bank debits in San Francisco 1947–1949. Monthly average = 100 index number. Prior to 1921 index based on bank clearings only.

the Great Depression, World War II recovery, and the subsequent prosperity. The congruence is not complete though, as the Depression came a little later here, and its incidence seems less severe than elsewhere. But the match overall is impressive evidence of extramural influences.

The quarter-century after World War II is the focus of much of the following chapters, so I need not detail here the rise of San Francisco as a major capital center in the West and the intense construction of highrises. The bulk of the latter were concentrated in 10 percent of the area; they housed numerous banking, insurance, brokerage, realty, and law firms in the area north of Market Street bounded by Van Ness Avenue, Nob Hill, and the Embarcadero. These highrises are visible symbols of what seems a new role for San Francisco but is really the current shape of the older exchange function that created the city. They merely illuminate the fact that the city accounts for almost two-thirds of the metropolitan area's finance, insurance, and real estate employment, and almost half of the employment in transportation, communications, utilities, and services.[8] Indeed, the service sector employs the largest number of San Franciscans, a growth spurred by a large demand for business services and the need to accommodate the increasing number of visitors. (By 1965, San Francisco received 71 percent of the tourist money in the Bay Area.)

While economic life still reverberates to the basic rhythm of those capital firms whose towers dominate the skyline, the shipping activity which first turned Yerba Buena into a major city remains a steady but diminished contributor to its income and job structure.[9] San Francisco has the West Coast's most numerous foreign banking firms, consulates, chambers of commerce, and trade agencies, and the most domestic import-export firms and steamship lines and headquarters. The total tonnage into the docks on the Embarcadero and China Bay is not impressive, but it is very valuable; in 1964, sixty-seven public piers saw imports only one-fortieth the volume of New York's, but four times New York's in per ton evaluation. San Francisco's trade today, as in the past, faces the Pacific; most of its exports and about half of its imports go to the Far East.[10] Yet the port is in trouble for failure to adapt modern cargo-handling techniques. In the late 1960s, partly to overcome this decline in trade, city officials convinced the state legislature to return the port to local management, the politics of which are discussed in chapter 8.

The purpose of this rough sketch of 125 years of San Francisco's history as an exchange system was to make several points. In turning to the decisional context of the present era, we must understand the constraints imposed by past decisions and the external world. We have seen here that from its emergence on the national scene it has been shaped by external factors into a commercial entrepôt and then a major capital center; clearly it has been sensitive to national economic currents while generating regional currents of its own. That history of influence as a commercial and financial center must be explored for its consequences for the local decisional field. That is, these influences constitute historically received "givens" with consequences for the city's political system that are the objects of this study. One of the "givens" is the way the urban land use has developed with remarkably little change in this century. Those are past decisions unaltered through time which set the relationship of space to the economy and to people's lives—where they work and live. More needs to be known about these people, however, and how they provide another background factor for the study.

THE PEOPLE OF THE CITY

A city is not merely a complex of economic exchanges. It is first a place where people live and work in the manifold experiences of their lives. What the small town was for so long in American history —the forum of most human life—the city and its suburbs have become in our time. Only part of these experiences are caught in the census reports; like crowd snapshots in a narrow time frame, they show little of the individual and only some of the crowd. Thus, they say little about how many hate or love their town, although the mobility data are suggestive. They do not show how a city impinges on the senses or how it generates feelings. Yet census reports are the best data available for highlighting some aspects of citizens' lives in San Francisco. We employ them to suggest the kinds of problems that enter the context of community decision making as a result of many people living in different—sometimes opposing—styles and of their multiple transactions which underlie urban society.

Such organization in this or any other city is a mosaic of life styles. The variety is not merely a matter of money or education. It goes beyond to such simple aspects as the way people relax or to more complex aspects such as their relationship to family and community. Those who drink Scotch on Nob Hill or beer on Hunter's Point, watch the Giants at Candlestick Park or fellow Italians at bocce ball, attend mass every day or worship under the silver dome of the First Baptist Church, and look down on the Golden Gate from on high while others rarely see it—these suggest the living mosaic of any city.

The Ethnic City

San Francisco has its own human mosaic, which many find distinctive. That special quality is traceable to the many foreign-born who have shaped the city's life style from the first. In later chapters the roles of the most and the least influential in this decisional context will be detailed. But for now a sketch is necessary to set one of the dimensions of history which shape the political system.

At the turn of the century, 30 percent of San Franciscans had been born abroad, and as late as 1970 that figure was still as high as

21.6 percent. When we add to that those born here of foreign parents, the figure is 44.3 percent of all San Franciscans in 1970, third highest in the nation behind New York and Boston, and a large minority of the entire state's foreign-born. Most are European in origin. The largest percentage of foreign stock in 1970 were from Italy (9.2), Germany (6.2), Ireland (5.3), the United Kingdom (4.5), and about 4 percent each from Canada and Russia. Every ninth San Franciscan in 1970 was a person of Spanish descent; unlike those in Los Angeles, however, most were not from Mexico but from Central America. Almost one in eleven was Chinese in 1972 estimates, almost doubled since 1960, while other Asians, Filipinos, and Japanese were over half the Chinese proportion.[11]

But these people of foreign stock have not been fixed like pictures in a museum; rather, they have been in constant change in the space and society of the city. We can see some of this flux in figure 5 where the city is portrayed in terms of ethnic movement over time. In the beginning, as later, the affluent could afford hilltop residences close to the northern and northeastern shores. However, workers, primarily Irish and Chinese in the first decades and Irish and Italians later, did cluster on one height—Telegraph Hill—although most of these lived closer to the North Beach docks. That hill, now the site of expensive apartment houses, was once a slum hill, as poet Wallace Irwin depicted it in another era:

> O Telygraft Hill she sits proud as a queen
> And the docks lie below in the glare
> and th'bay runs beyant 'er all purple and green
> Wid th'ginger-bread island out there,
> And the ferry boats toot at owld Telygraft Hill,
> And th'Hill it don't care if they do
> While the Bradys and Caseys av Telygraft Hill
> Joost sit there enj'yin' the view.
>
> For the Irish they live on the top av it,
> And the Dagos they live on the base av it,
> And every tin can in the knowledge av man,
> Is scattered all over the face av it,
> Av Telygraft Hill, Telygraft Hill,
> Nobby owld, slobby owld Telygraft Hill.

At the close of the nineteenth century, many Irish moved south of Market Street to homes along the new trolley lines. Behind them

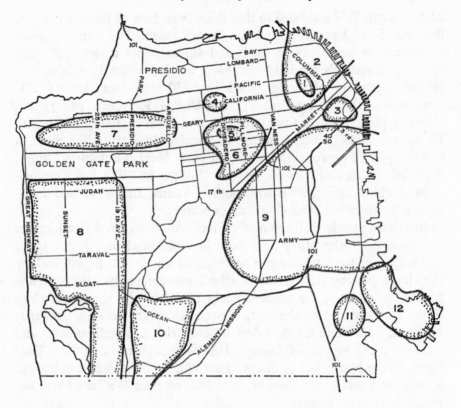

Fig. 5. Ethnic group movement in San Francisco.
KEY
1. Chinatown.
2. North Beach. Originally Irish, then Italian from late 1880s, now influx of Chinese.
3. Greek.
4. Japanese until 1941.
5–6. Fillmore area. Inset Jewish until 1950. Area became black beginning in 1940.
7. Irish and Jewish since 1920. Increasingly Chinese now.
8. Developed since 1930. Heavily varied ethnic mix.
9. Mostly Irish, to 1930 close to Market Street, and to 1920 closer to the bay. Italian close to Market 1915–1955. Since 1940 Spanish-surname, particularly south of Valencia.
10. Once mixed white ethnic, more black since 1945.
11. Maltese and Basque.
12. Hunter's Point and Potrero Hill. Heavily black since 1940.

in North Beach the Chinese stayed, as most of them do today, while the Irish were replaced by the Italians. The latter in time followed the Irish "south of Market" and the two mixed, although not always socially, until they were pulled away by affluence and availability of better housing on the ocean side of the peninsula. Immigrants with Spanish names moved behind them to the south of Market, giving the area today its distinctive Hispanic quality and hinting at a succeeding generation's move out and up.

The city has always had a scatter of smaller ethnic groups, some of which are indicated in figure 5. Illustrative are East Indians south of Market, Maltese and Basques in the southeast and up behind the honky-tonk of Broadway, Japanese southeast of the army's Presidio, Jews in a few blocks of the Western Addition, and Greeks near the upper end of Market Street. After the end of World War II the Chinese began to move out of their ghettos to blocks north of Golden Gate Park, although the highly publicized Chinatown still remains as a tourist attraction, home of the most recent and most disadvantaged aliens. But one small group has increased enormously in recent decades. In 1940 there were only 4,800 blacks, but wartime labor recruitment in the South pulled many others to the naval shipyards at Hunter's Point. As table 1 shows, blacks by 1950 had increased by seven times, almost doubled that by 1960, and by 1972 were an estimated one in seven of San Franciscans.

Since some of the political strains generated by this ethnic mix will be considered later, it is sufficient here to note that this ethnic diversity has been the cause of continuing friction in the community

TABLE 1

San Francisco's Racial Composition, 1940–1972

	1940	1950	1960	1972
Total Pop.	634,536	775,357	740,316	685,600
White (%)	94.8	89.4	81.6	69.4
Black (%)	0.8	5.6	10.1	14.1
Asian* (%)	3.6	3.9	6.2	10.5
Filipino (%)	...	...	1.7	3.8

SOURCES: For 1940 and 1950, *San Francisco: Characteristics* (Institute for Urban Research, San Francisco State College, n.d.). For 1960, *San Francisco Business* (Chamber of Commerce periodical), March 1966 (estimate). For 1972, *Weekly Bulletin*, San Francisco Public Health Dept., Nov. 13, 1972 (estimate).

* Chinese and Japanese.

since its beginning. Feelings were particularly intense against the Australians in the 1850s (crimes of the "Sydney Ducks" led to vigilante action), the Chinese in the 1870s (one mayoral candidate for the Workingmen's party promised to kill Chinese whose cheap labor threatened Irish workers), and the Japanese in the panic-inspired evacuation to concentration camps in World War II. In San Francisco, as in most big cities, blacks now generate fears among older ethnic groups. There is evidence of an ethnic politics of different goals and styles distinguished by whether the group has established its claim to recognition or is still struggling to do so. Also, while no comprehensive ethnic history of the city has been written, enough signs exist that the dominant ethnic groups in each era, for their own political and economic enhancement, have exploited newly emerging groups. While its past and present images emphasize ethnic variety and "melting-pot" harmony, there is much in the city's history to confirm the variety but question the harmony.

The Life-Style City

But there are other aspects to a person besides the land of his birth or his skin color. These aspects, no less interesting because less colorful, do tell a story of differences, and these differences create a potential for community conflict and hence political conflict. Thus, there are differences in styles of family life and in what aspects of society are incorporated into them. Most obvious, of course, are differences in the degree of socioeconomic rewards. Such variety in San Francisco for the decades around World War II has been shown by Robert C. Tryon, who early in the 1950s demographically isolated clusters of census tracts into "neighborhoods." [12] The citizens of each were more similar on thirty-three measurements than those in other neighborhoods. These measurements were condensed into three life-style syndromes—quality of family life, degree of assimilation, and amount of socioeconomic resources, education, and so forth. In effect, these three factors not only assembled the mosaic of San Francisco but when plotted over time, demonstrated its stability. Two decades after his study the details may have altered, but observers agree that there still remains these life-style reservations where dwellers freely choose and follow their distinctive preferences in social existence.

From Tryon's graphing, seen in figure 6, these neighborhoods can be visualized as clusters existing in social space. The three life-style measures form the axes of a spherical map, the mix of each neighbor-

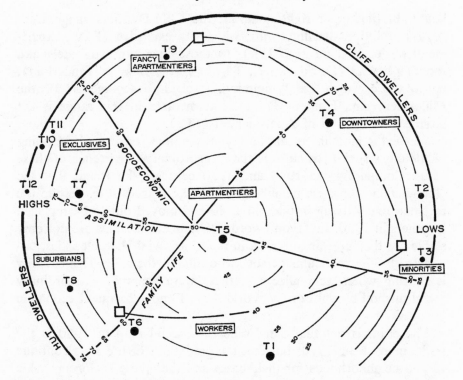

Fig. 6. Spherical configuration showing the structure of twelve social areas of the Bay Area before World War II.

hood on these three dimensions positions it on this map as a dot, and the size of the dot represents roughly the size of the neighborhood. Generally, those on the right side are low on the three measures and those on the left are high. By such analysis, those in the upper right-hand quadrant are more likely to live in multiple-residence houses (thus Cliff Dwellers), and those in the lower left quadrant are more likely to live in single-residence homes (or Hut Dwellers).

All of this depicts neighborhoods familiar in any city. The Exclusives, which account for several varieties of social areas (T10–T11), are estate and mansion neighborhoods (e.g., Pacific Heights). The Suburbians (T8) are lower on the socioeconomic scale but, like the Exclusives, are high in assimilation and family life styles (e.g., the Sunset). These slide off into Workers (T6, T1—e.g., the Outer Mission), which fade into different types of Minorities (T2–T3), as seen earlier in figure 5. Somewhere along this scale neighborhoods fade gradually from the Exclusive's estate to the Worker's modest house. In the upper right quadrant the Cliff Dwellers range from those in multiple-dwelling units, which are exclusive (Fancy Apart-mentiers, T9—as on Nob Hill), to those in run-down hotels and rooming houses (Downtowners, T4—as in the Mission Tenderloin), on to those which are "slumming, stacked-up tenements" of the Minorities (e.g., Hunter's Point). Intermediate in this range is the large average group of Apartmentiers (T5).

Maybe the most important of Tryon's findings for an understanding of the city's social structure is the extraordinary persistence of these areas. Comparing the 1940 and 1950 censuses, he found that the characteristics of these neighborhoods had changed little, despite the fact that many living in them in 1940 had moved out to be replaced by others in 1950. In Tryon's words, "Urban social areas are not only stable but they appear to persist in their bio-social characteristics, un-affected by the particular persons who inhabit them." [13] This stability is striking when we realize that these were years of extraordinary social turmoil brought on by World War II and subsequent economic changes.

The point is not that San Francisco's social map of 1950 is the social map of the 1970s but that the gradations of life style continue to find neighborhoods for their bases and that these sociogeographic units are the basic constituents of community political life. This phe-nomenon is not merely a San Francisco experience, for in other cities, too, neighborhoods are way stations for persons holding or moving up different rungs of the life-style ladder. In this city and elsewhere, there is a repeated pattern of working-class districts, filled at one time by one ethnic group, being invaded later by another group, as the former with newfound affluence seeks to enjoy the fruits of labor by moving elsewhere. Samuel Lubell has graphically described for New York City this movement up "the tenement trail." [14] We have also seen signs of this in figure 5, where the city's Italians and Irish danced a great social reel, clockwise from North Beach to the south of Market, and thence to the ocean districts, and in 1970 out to suburbia. Today such shifts are also found among those groups generally less well regarded; later-generation Chinese, blacks, and Spanish move toward the ocean's middle-class neighborhoods. Areas once peopled by working-class Irish and Italians south of Market are now the homes of working-class Spanish-speaking and blacks.

There is a political dimension to this neighborhood pattern, which will be shortly demonstrated, showing that where no political party exists to organize and transmit fragmented demands on the political system, other agencies appear to perform these tasks. This is the "neighborhood association," so vital to the city's community politics.[15]

The Working City

Until recently San Francisco was a workingman's city, not so much for industry as for other labor—for example, construction (it had burned severely several times even before the 1906 disaster) and craft workers (including printers—San Francisco is a major publishing center). But the ocean had dominated occupations in the city as it had dominated other developments. Longshoremen, shipbuilders, chandlers, marine engineers—the job structure reflected a port status during the gold rush and still does today. Although workers built a briefly powerful political movement in the 1870s, San Francisco did not earn its reputation as a "good labor town" until after the Depression. Early in the New Deal, a strike by longshoremen precipitated a bloody shoot-out in the streets, which left many dead and wounded. Now, however, organized labor is powerful in the polity and economy. When the Port of San Francisco was returned to the city from the state recently, one of the appointees to its governing body was Harry Bridges, president of the Longshoremen's Union, and other labor representatives serve on similar municipal agencies, public and private.

But these historical strokes on the canvas of the city must be laid alongside a more modern one. The tour guide focuses on the past, on Fisherman's Wharf and Chinatown, but is blind to the present, the highrise offices and apartments. He may point out the great bridges spanning the bay as if they were of the past, though they were built only in the late 1930s. Yet over them flow daily the thousands of commuters to those office buildings, a major new element in urban life.

For this is now a white-collar city, not a city of sailors, Irish hod carriers, and Chinese coolies. It is a very long time since spotters on Telegraph Hill signaled to the downtown wharves the arrival of clipper ships, and a very long time, too, since men seeing these signals shouted, "Men needed along the shore!"—men later to be called longshoremen. This has become a city of lawyers, computer operators, proprietors, creditors, salespersons, and clerks in the burgeoning national corporation headquarters. White-collar occupations engaged 44 percent of the population in 1950, 52 percent by 1960, and 61 percent by 1970. The growth of such job opportunities (50,000 new jobs during the 1960s), as well as the famed Bay Area living, brought large numbers of migrants; in the twenty-one cities over 500,000 in population in 1960, only Seattle had a larger percentage of migrant population (17 percent). The children of the Joads of *The Grapes of Wrath* did not all stay in the fruit fields of the Central Valley, for many moved into white-collar niches in San Francisco. These jobs paid comparatively well, and in 1960 only Los Angeles had a larger proportion of high-income residents, and only two large cities had smaller shares of low-income residents. In turn, this affluence has made this a very expensive city in which to live. For example, of the ten major American cities, in 1950 San Francisco ranked ninth in its rent prices, seventh in 1960, and second by 1965; for the cost of living index on all items including rent, by 1965 it was the first in the nation.[16]

As in other cities, many people enter San Francisco to work by day and leave at night to sleep elsewhere. During the 1960s there was a 50 percent increase in automobiles entering daily, and a 75 percent increase in those crossing the Golden Gate Bridge from affluent suburbs in mushrooming Marin County. Despite this outflow —or maybe contributing to it—there was an extraordinary demand on available housing in the city, enough to produce the lowest occupancy rate in the nation. More people in the Bay Area are now using the suburbs for family life, and San Francisco for jobs and entertainment, than before the growth of suburbia. As in many other cities, many kinds of workers seek livelihood in the urban center; yet many, maybe most, do not live there. For some the reason is lack of housing and the resulting high rentals. Some may cite other reasons for living elsewhere, such as crime, fear of blacks, high taxes, or congestion. Thus, there exists the contradiction of many who identify with the city and desire to live in it, and yet who do not. Despite all of the extraordinary publicity about San Francisco, the population has declined since 1950.

Considering the events after 1960, it is important to recall that, despite its wealth and romanticized glamor, there is another San Francisco—that of the poor. The contradiction is exemplified by storied Chinatown, which, as someone has noted, may be the only poverty area in America that is a tourist attraction. Here and in the Spanish-speaking Mission District or black Hunter's Point or the

Fillmore District, census reports provide for romantic San Francisco the same dreary record to be found in any American city—poverty distributed by ethnicity. For brown less than white, black less than brown, and possibly yellow less than black, the city's rewards cascade down from the affluent peaks of white Nob Hill and Pacific Heights to the deprived colored valleys of the city.

The census tracts in 1970 showed better family median income for the Spanish-speaking ($10,180) than for blacks ($7,942). Only 6.8 percent of the former had families living below the poverty level, but it was a grim 21.1 percent among blacks (and 4.1 percent for the city as a whole). The percentage differential between blacks and whites in 1970 is also striking: in high school graduates, 48.5 versus 61.8; in unemployment, 6.5 versus 5.3; in personal median income, $7,676 versus $10,503; and in the percentage below poverty level, 21.1 versus 9.9.

The details of this other San Francisco, unseen by the tourist even in Chinatown, were buried before 1960 in census reports on the unnumbered private lives of those afflicted. But during the 1960s, depressing and ignored facts came to light in the drama of city politics, here and elsewhere, generating a new phase of the city's history (see chapter 10). As a major consequence, however, some of life's opportunities opened for some of these other San Franciscans. Whereas in 1960 the black baseball superstar Willie Mays was refused a house because of his color, and thirty-four of every thirty-five apartments were banned to blacks (the other was in the ghettos), by the early 1970s overt discrimination of this kind was little evident. Other factors, however, such as chronic low income and limited schooling, effectively barred many of the "new" ethnic groups from the city's affluence.[17]

SOCIAL DEMANDS AS POLITICAL INPUTS

This chapter has introduced the concepts that what the city of San Francisco has become as a place to live and work was shaped by past and external events. It was created by outsiders, first the Spanish and then those who flooded in for the gold rush. Its economy was also created by outside forces—gold and silver strikes, wheat booms, and railroads. Its basic transactional quality as an entrepôt, set by its port location, is still vital to its contemporary exchange functions. Prosperity and depression in the larger nation have affected the local business cycle, just as recent national events affecting minorities reverberated in these streets. Decisions that were to make San Francisco a major financial center by 1970 came from elsewhere in the nation, just as the success of labor here came only when New Deal legislation provided a national legal basis for it. The treatment of disadvantaged minorities by the more favored echoed the cycles experienced elsewhere, with results that influence the city's politics even today. However, the distinctions here between past and present, or local and national, are not all that sharp. Details of these influences from the past and the outside will fill subsequent chapters, but here the emphasis has been on creating an awareness of their operations.

Another concept raised here suggests the tie between social diversity and the political system. All visitors to San Francisco are struck by its contrasts and by the new perspectives around the corner or over the hill. What is true physically exists also in the social context within which San Franciscans work and live. We have seen this variety in the development in this chapter of the city's social ecology, economy, and demography.

But social contrasts are not merely picturesque; they are the generator of private and public conflicts within a community. In the nation and its cities, and particularly in San Francisco, Americans are a various people despite some recent lamenting of their conformity. There are substantial differences in income, education, occupation, religion, and ethnicity.[18] Such differences can mean competition, and in an American society where individualism is a basic credo, the linkages among difference, competition, and conflict are very short. The exact form of this conflict depends on different conditions of heterogeneity, group tension, and insecurity, as well as on the existence of social channels for blocking or siphoning off intergroup conflict.

How Americans and San Franciscans have channeled conflict arising out of group differences is a varied story. They have sometimes used the crudest violence—the disadvantaged against the disadvantaged, as with unemployed Irish workers against the Chinese in the 1870s; the disadvantaged against the advantaged, as in labor strikes of the 1930s; or the advantaged against the disadvantaged, as in the city's early vigilante committees.[19] But the reaction to social differentiation can take other forms than the violent. One of these is the political process, with its characteristic adjustment of clashing interests. In these terms, while many social and economic differences may exist in the city, with an attendant competition for scarce values and resources, competition may not generate conflict. Barriers to conflict exist within each group; not all of its members may be conscious of what the differences are, who their competitors are, or what needs to be done. However, when these differences become conscious, personal, and group-based, latent competition is transformed into concrete social conflict. This, in turn, may be—and in the American experience often has been—transferred into the political arena. Such transference takes the form of demands that some public agency extend or protect values against encroachment by others.

In the social order of San Francisco, there are many socioeconomic bases with a potential for dividing citizens and hence for generating conflict. There are conflicts among capital development interests seeking to secure the scarce land for highrise construction, a consequence of the struggle to convert the city into a major financial and administrative center. As we shall see later, that internal conflict among capital interests—business and labor—became a three-way contest by the politicization of San Franciscans concerned with conservation and distressed that highrises would block views and change the city's contours. There also exist among the ethnic groups a number of potential generators of conflict, rooted in status or life style—such as different religions, courtship patterns, skin colors, recreations. These would be adequate bases for conflict even if there were not yet others, rooted in economic and political concerns—a share of the job market, influence in political parties and with elected officials, and insistence that the schools provide children with equal resources.

The demographic conditions noted earlier mark the potential existence of even more conflicts. When life styles are frozen to a particular neighborhood, efforts by "outsiders" to move in have regularly generated such defenses as restricted covenants, zoning, and the use of police. Here, the social struggle is transferred to the governmental arena. The demands of the young, the middle-aged, and the old are not all of a kind; illustrative is the resistance by the old against taxation to pay for the education of the young. The tolerance of sexual and ideological deviance which accompanies increasing education may well bring the views of a heavily white-collar population into contrast with those of different background and persuasion. Unless a code of tolerance develops, conflict can become manifest and deep.[20] Even more basically, those well established in the institutions of capital and politics very often conflict with the aspirations of those less well established, who want "the good old days" to start immediately.

This book deals primarily with how such problems of conflicting demands, generated by social stress, were handled by the decision-making processes of this community from the middle 1960s onwards. Some of these decisions in their origin and solution are private, such as the many private decisions that increased the city's rent level drastically after 1960. Others, however, occasionally spill over into the channels of public decision because mechanisms for private resolution are flooded by demands beyond their control. Whether the private groups come to the arena seeking arbitration or rescue (or both), the public-private interrelation must be kept in mind.

Whatever the stress that generates the political process, that process has many arenas and aspects. The search for decisional patterns in any community requires examination of several possibilities. The analytic framework employed here directs us to a prior consideration of the agencies that transmit demands into the political system. Two of these are the subjects of the next chapters, the "power structure" and political parties. With these we turn from the focus of this chapter on the social context of the city's political system to the conduits into that system.

PART II

CHANNELS TO THE POLITICAL SYSTEM

Multitudes, multitudes in the valley of decision
JOEL 3:14

The "Power Structure" and Popular Will

To this point we have emphasized the diversity of the economic and social structures of San Francisco. Such variety constitutes the raw social material for local politics, for it indicates the multiple preferences of San Franciscans concerning how public and private resources should be distributed. As in other cities, this community distributes its rewards and penalties quite unequally among its citizens. That unequal distribution contributes to social conflict, some of which is transmitted into the political system. Two major transmission channels are the "power structure" and the party system. In any study of a local political system the interactions of these two and their links to the community must be understood. A primary function of the two is to transmit demands into the political system. Business community demands are expressed through the "power structure," and the demands of the electorate are transmitted through the party system. Whatever the dispute over the nature of power structures in the United States, all observers find them restricted to a small segment of the local population in which business values are influential. Parties, on the other hand, despite the small number of activists who manage them, serve to channel more diverse demands from a wider range of citizens. The mutual relationships between power structures and parties may take several forms. Depending on place and time, one system may check the other, the two may share parallel interests, or one may dominate the other.

Part II portrays the experience in San Francisco with these two channels, in this chapter on the power structure and the next on parties and elections. A close link between the two exists in San Francisco because of the special and heavy use of the ballot for decisions on issues of local government. A study of that device can tell us much about the success or constraints of the power structure, and can also serve as a bridge to a study of election for public office in the next chapter.

Research into the community power structure in other American cities provides many guides to the San Francisco inquiry. That literature has dealt mainly with three queries: What is power? How is it discovered? What accounts for the differences in its composition and actions that have been found? [1] More recently, observers have raised the ancient question central to Aristotle's *Politics:* What difference does it make for citizens *how* a community makes decisions? [2] However, the focus of prior research has been more narrow—what is the interaction between local leaders and citizens? A final query is raised in this book: What is the influence of an increasingly centralized national society on local power? If local decisions are increasingly determined outside the community, and if outside sources create new local groups, the result could be the breakdown of closed local power structures, which would also make the local institutions of decision making irrelevant. It is the last two questions—concerning the quality of urban life and the interdependence of national and local currents —which are the main themes throughout this book.

The study of community power structures is not as simple as it seems at first glance. The concept is vague, its measures are not always agreed on, the evidence drawn from many such studies provides no easy explanation or description, and the value of this evidence is subject to debate. Much of the debate has dealt with questions of methods of research. But these, like questions of the nature of power and explanations of what has been found, are not treated here; specialists may refer to the Appendix for such considerations. Because of many such problems, this study of San Francisco combines different methods of analysis. It examines the degree of agreement among holders of governmental and private positions concerning the patterns of influence they see about them. The issues selected for analysis are those which they report to involve the most time and resources of the community. However, to complement these perceptions by knowledgeable individuals, indeed, to check them, certain hard data

are presented in this chapter and certain issues and groups are analyzed in later chapters. In short, I will look at actual cases of community conflict which observers believe tell most about how decisions
are usually made in the city. But along the way, data I have generated
independently of these informants will test those perceptions. By these
means, there is a greater chance of presenting the worlds of power
and influence, of decisions and nondecisions, of issues and values, as
these are experienced and judged by those most active in them. The
reasons for and limits of this methodology are expanded on in the
Appendix.

PERCEPTIONS OF DECISIONAL PROCESSES

Power Models

Ascertaining from knowledgeable individuals some picture of the
processes working about them is difficult, because many of them
have little reason to think in such conceptual terms. Such participants
know that surviving in a turbulent environment from day to day is
no minor victory; but little time exists for reflection on the meaning
of it all. In order to protect and advance one's interests under such
conditions, high value is placed on reacting to events. This reactive
stance depends less on a comprehensive framework of judgment than
on particular criteria based on experience. While one can build up
the implicit model such persons have in mind by drawing out and
reflecting on their experiences in decision making—as will be done
throughout this book—it is also possible to take a complementary
route. This is to offer knowledgeable individuals a set of alternative
models of decision making from which to choose.

This set was constructed from studies of other communities, with
each model embodying common dimensions found to be relevant elsewhere, e.g., the number of groups—one, few, or many—participating
in decision making; the number of groups that were successful; and
the duration of their success. Previous studies have treated these three
dimensions, and it is the variation among combinations of the three
that has been much debated.

Five models of community power patterns have appeared most
often. At one extreme is the community where only one group consistently and for some time decides—or suppresses—all issues. Other
groups merely support this Stable Dominant Group. In this category
are studies demonstrating power in the hands of an old family, a
business cabal, or a political boss. It is the X family of the Lynds'

Middletown, the merchants of Floyd Hunter's "Regional City," and Boss Crump of Memphis.[3]

In a second model, no one group permanently dominates. Rather, a cluster of several groups regularly prevails against other more numerous and scattered groups, whose interests get little hearing. While these two clusters disagree on policy outputs, both accept the legitimacy of the way things work. As with the first model, this Stable Dominant Constellation—Consensual is still an enduring combination, but power is now more diffused because more than one group are consistent winners. It appeared in the corrupt sharing of power by business and political dominants recorded by Lincoln Steffens at the turn of the century in *The Shame of the Cities.* It is also found in small towns where old and new wealth have intermarried, for example, the union in status and marriage of agricultural and commercial-industrial families in William Faulkner's stories of the not-so-fictional Snopses and Compsons.

A third model is distinguished because those not in the winning constellation question the legitimacy of the whole process. Where such a Stable Dominant Constellation—Dissentious exists, a break from the past—possibly from outside the community—has changed the perceptions and evaluations of the regular losers. Clearly, the civil rights awakening of Southern blacks after the *Brown* Supreme Court decision in 1954 constituted such a break. By 1970 this altered context had brought to innumerable southern communities a new set of resources and actors in local politics.[4] The northern counterpart of this development came in the 1960s and at this writing is running fully, with consequences to be explored later.

A fourth model suggested by these three dimensions has not one but many groups participating in decision making; here there are two variants. In one, the Occasional Coalition, one combination of groups wins more consistently than others, but it also loses often enough to rob it of any permanency. In this class are large cities in which a combination of Chamber of Commerce, mayor, and professional civil service is more often successful than not.[5] Another possibility exists, however, a Temporary Coalition, where no single group or combination wins regularly enough to demonstrate any cohesion over time. Rather, each issue is typically resolved (accepted or blocked) by a coalition existing only for this issue and falling out again when other issues generate different combinations. Urban prototypes of this model exist in some new suburbs, where political parties or other partisan groups have not yet emerged as carriers of demands.[6]

Observers' View of Power Models

These five models, rooted in American community experience, were offered to knowledgeable observers of the San Francisco scene, who were asked for their judgment as to the most applicable. Table 2 contains thumbnail sketches of the five types presented to these observers, and their responses.

TABLE 2

Selection by Knowledgeable Individuals of Characteristic
Decision-making Process in San Francisco in 1968

Description of Process	N
(1) Although there seem to be a lot of groups involved in making decisions, in reality one of the groups makes all the decisions, with the others going along with the important one.	0
(2) Although there seem to be a lot of groups involved in making decisions, in reality there is a permanent majority of the groups who makes all the decisions, and a minority of groups who never makes decisions. This permanent majority and minority disagree on policies but agree on the general rightness of the system as a whole.	1
Between (2) and (3).	2
(3) Same as (2), except permanent majority and minority disagree not only on policies, but the minority questions the rightness of the system as a whole.	1
(4) There are a lot of groups involved in decision making, but one combination of them appears to win in the majority of cases, although falling apart on some issues, so it cannot be called a permanent majority.	4
Between (4) and (5).	1
(5) There are a lot of groups involved in decision making, and no combination of them appears to win regularly, so that each decision represents a temporary coalition, which falls apart after the issue is decided.	18
(6) Other	3
(7) Couldn't decide because none of the above fit their perception.	4
	34

Over half selected the Temporary Coalition (5) as the model most descriptive of decision making in the city. This model and the Occasional Coalition (4) account for twenty-three of thirty-four responses, and for twenty-three of the thirty who were able to make a choice. None reported a Stable Dominant Group model (1), which some might term "elite". Only one chose the Stable Dominant Constellation (2), and two selected something just beyond that. In short, among these observers, decisional processes in the city were not seen as structured or as dominated by a few. Rather, they claim to gaze upon a scene where political alignments are subject to change from issue to issue with no combination dominating.

However, such agreement might be merely a clever verbal shield to disguise another reality. That is, in a democracy it is valuable to deny the real power that one has.[7] But such an explanation requires evidence that a small group actually has similar interests. That is, if such men are indeed powerful in achieving their common goals, it must at least be shown that they share those goals. Yet members of this knowledgeable set were drawn from diverse segments of the local society. They were bank presidents, commercial entrepreneurs, officers of trade unions, editors, partners in major law firms, recognized ethnic spokesmen, and officials in city government. The diversity of representation does not necessarily guarantee diverse interests, of course; but as later chapters will show, some are bitter critics of the decisional process and its results, while some are its avid supporters. Some heatedly oppose other members of the set on issues of great moment, and unite later with former opponents on equally crucial matters. Despite this diversity of institution and position among these observers, table 2 reveals substantial agreement in their perceptions.

This common outlook is demonstrated even more clearly in table 3. Though they come from a variety of ethnic groups characteristic of the city, and they differ in their locations in private or governmental life, these observers saw much the same decisional scene about them. If their different characteristics were to be the basis for different perceptions, their views should have differed more than this table indicates. I believe that the reactions reflect an approximately accurate judgment of what takes place and provide a rough framework for subsequent testing by analysis of numerous decisions. To deny the validity of this survey out of hand is to imply that these qualified observers have been seized by a collective madness or that they are conspiring liars. At least let us test the validity of this outlook.

TABLE 3

Frequency Distribution of Perceptions of Decisional Process,
Based on Ethnicity and Location of Observer (in percentage)

	Temporary Coalition	Occasional Coalition	Stable Dominant Constel- lation Dissentious	Stable Dominant Constel- lation Consensual[a]	Stable Dominant Group	N
Ethnicity						
Irish	71	14	0	14	0 = 100%	7
Black	67	33	0	0	0	3
Spanish	0	50	0	50	0	2
Jewish	100	0	0	0	0	2
Italian	100	0	0	0	0	2
Other[b]	64	9	9	18	0	11
Life Sphere						
Private	54	15	8	23	0	13
Public	78	14	0	7	0	14
Gov't. Level						
Legislative	78	11	0	11	0	9
Executive- Adminis- trative	80	20	0	0	0	5

[a] Combines this category with those indicating intermediate with dissentious model.
[b] Includes English, German, Greek, and French.

Indirect Tests of Leader Cohesion

The above finding is uncongenial to those who believe that all communities are run by cabals who monopolize resources and decision making. Such commentators claim that in San Francisco it is the model of a Stable Dominant Group that is the reality. Some test of this claim is in order, starting with closer analysis of the observers surveyed. At a minimum, acceptance of this model requires proof that the "dominant" group is very active on many issues. If that requirement is not met, this group can hardly be truly successful across many issues, as befits the model.

The observers surveyed in 1968 were highly active community actors, many seeming, by their command of finance, political powers, or publicity, to fit aspects of the Stable Dominant Group model. Yet, when asked to identify one man or group whose support was essential to get things done in the city, almost without exception they denied that such a powerful entity existed; the few who did not agree varied in their choices. Interviewed again in 1971 and 1972, a sample of the same observers again insisted that no such group or person existed.

Indirect evidence of the lack of any group dominance over many issues of community life is seen in how active this set of observers was. They were provided a checklist of twenty-four issues,[8] both narrow and large, permitting comparative analysis of their activity. Each was asked for those with which he had been "involved." The last term was put broadly to invite maximum response; follow-up questions delved into the exact form and extent of involvement on each issue checked.

Table 4 reveals that the high degree of overlap in issue involvement characteristic of the Stable Dominant Group model is little in evidence. Of the thirty-four member set, six either could not find a single issue involving them or cited their organization's policy of non-involvement in local affairs. In at least two of these six cases, there was independent evidence that the observers actually were involved in local issues, but only on occasional matters affecting their companies. Fifteen selected no more than one issue, while ten cited five or more. Only one of the last was a member of the San Francisco Board of Supervisors, who by the nature of their work must be "involved" with multiple issues. Other supervisors restricted themselves to many fewer issues.

The ten who expressed involvement with five or more issues distributed their interest among issues as shown in the right column of table 4. It would be too much to expect all observers to declare involvement with all twenty-four issues; they might constitute an "elite" in that case, but it would be an exhausted one. Nevertheless, we should reasonably expect that many of the most active would concentrate on a substantial number of common issues if the Stable Dominant Group model actually existed. But table 4 shows that on only two issues—Negro relationships and city elections—did as many as seven of these ten indicate involvement. Transportation involved six observers, and another four issues involved five persons each.

Analysis of these issues of multiple involvement gave no evidence that the observers were acting in concert, as the Stable Dominant Group model requires. For example, the city election issue involved

TABLE 4

Involvement of San Francisco Observers in Selected Issues

Issue	N Observers	N Multi-issue Concerns (10)
Election to city offices	21	7
Negro relationships	11	7
Transportation	8	6
Urban renewal and slum clearance	7	5
Chinese-American relationships	6	5
Local conservation	6	4
Tax structure	6	5
Local roads	5	4
Port facilities	5	5
Building permits	4	4
Cultural activities	4	4
New business	4	4
Poverty program	4	3
Zoning	4	4
Education	3	3
Police and fire protection	3	2
United Fund	3	3
Health and welfare	2	1
Hospitals and medical facilities	2	2
Low-income housing	2	1
Juvenile delinquency	2	2
Mexican-American relationships	1	0
Recreation	1	1
Unemployment	0	0
Other	3	
None	3	

Summary of Frequency

N of Issues Selected	Frequency
0	6
1	15
2	2
3	0
4	1
5 or more	10
	34

persons who publicly *opposed* one another over candidates. As we shall see, little has been done to meet the demands of black San Franciscans; the concerted effort here is one of inaction, not un-important in community life. This is one indicator of the degree to which demands of the disadvantaged were a "non-issue," ignored by those with some power.[9]

As many as five or six observers claimed involvement in other issues. Improving transportation and seaport facilities, clearing blighted areas for convention and athletic facilities, structuring taxes —all contribute to the economic health of any city, and should evoke widespread involvement among active participants in city affairs. But only one-half of those observers with multi-issue concerns indi-cated their involvement in such vital matters.[10]

Concerning other issues, observers of the city generally report a kaleidoscopic decisional process. Their own involvement is limited because it is highly dispersed; most pay attention to but few issues. Even those active in more issues than usual do not share their in-volvement very extensively with others. Thus, their general percep-tion of a local context, characterized as a Temporary Coalition, is borne out by their own segmented involvement with others. This is a political process that Madison long ago foresaw for the new republic. In the variety of interests across the nation, he predicted that de-cisions would be the result of "temporary coalitions of shifting ma-jorities." Almost two centuries later and a continent away, within this city beside the bay, that phrase describes what knowledgeable observers now see about them, regardless of their base or place in the community.

Other qualities of this process emerge from the accounts of these observers. They gave particular emphasis to an awareness of change working in the city. In 1968, with a new mayor, Joseph Alioto, there was a clear sense that the Temporary Coalition context already existed; events in the next five years amplified that theme. Of the eighteen in table 2 who claimed that this model was indeed charac-teristic, twelve also commented on how a decade earlier the decisional system had been more constricted. In addition, of the four who chose the somewhat less open Occasional Coalition model, three also claimed that the community was moving into a more diffuse system, more like that in the Temporary Coalition model. Moreover, one each of those leaders selecting models (2), (3), and (4) in table 2 also described the opening up of decisional control.

Key features of this flux were the shifting nature of older power groups and the appearance of new ones. A small-business-oriented Downtown Association, known for its lack of, and resistance to, innovation in community policy, was regarded as having lost influence to a Chamber of Commerce that was more aggressive in its search for civic projects.[11] Another aspect of the flux was political. Old-line Democratic politicians were suddenly replaced by products of the Stevensonian and California Democratic Club revolution of the 1950s. A pattern of appointment followed by election to the board of supervisors was broken, with more supervisors securing office initially through election. The new mayor, Alioto, undertook to energize that constrained office. San Franciscans who were once tightly controlled or silent began to speak out, expressing their definitions of public policy, including the notion that the definitions of the business community were ill-conceived. More important, these newcomers to city politics organized almost overnight, whether in an ethnic enclave, a residential neighborhood, or a single-issue, city-wide, mass membership. The "feds" were suddenly on the scene, too. Sometimes this was a dramatic and community-wide intervention, like the court-ordered desegregation of the city's school system in 1971. Sometimes it was less noticed and more specific, like the provision of some jobs in poverty programs or of some school funds for children of the poor. All these components of the shifting scene will be treated in later chapters.

DIRECT LEGISLATION IN THE DECISIONAL CONTEXT

When the political picture in San Francisco began to change in the late 1960s, the power of some groups such as business and labor was retained, although erosion was everywhere claimed. One distinctive source of data in the decisional processes in San Francisco—the ballot proposition—enables us to look directly at the purported power and its erosion.

In keeping with the Progressive heritage, a large number of ballot propositions appear in San Francisco elections, designed to authorize programs and funds not available in the tight cage of the city charter. The detailed nature of the charter, now grossly swollen by such changes, is important in provoking a continual referendum on minor as well as substantive matters. Issues routinely handled in urban administration elsewhere must here be put to the voters. While that requirement has existed since the origin of the present charter in 1932,

the demands on the political system—transmitted through this channel
—may fluctuate with time. If so, the fluctuation may be a sign of a
new power context in the community.

In San Francisco, groups and individuals endorsing or opposing
each ballot issue can have their names and arguments entered into
a pamphlet sent to each voter. Such names, analyzed over time and
by issue, are indicators of group power, and test the accuracy of
local beliefs that "business runs the town," "when business and labor
get together they are unbeatable," and "new groups are beginning
to have their say." Of course, these data test directly only one manifest form of the use of power. But, measured by the size of the resources dispensed or checked in these actions or by the number of
persons they affect, direct legislation involves a significant distribution
of resources, which must be successfully backed or blocked if any
small group "has power."

This instrument of popular sovereignty thus may illuminate community processes. The relative ease of securing signatures to place
a proposition on the ballot, or of pressuring the board of supervisors
to do so, should make this a sensitive barometer of new electoral
moods. If, because of demands on urban resources, a more closed
system were giving way to one more open and shifting, it should be
manifest from the referendum record in two ways. First, a larger
number of bond and amendment issues would appear on the ballot.
Particularly would this be true for charter amendments, which characteristically seek to favor special groups by altering either the city's
basic governing procedure or its distribution of benefits. These amendments require a mere majority for passage. Bond issues, however, are
different in substance and volume; under the state constitution, they
require two-thirds support for passage. These outlays tend to be
restricted to a few costly municipal functions. Because of these restrictions, the incidence of bond issues should not fluctuate as much
as the incidence of amendments, although one would expect a few
more with the recent increase in demands on the city treasury.

A second indicator likely to be found in the referendum, if a more
open decisional context has emerged, would be the acceptance of
fewer of either charter amendments or bond issues than in the past.
Bond issues have characteristically appeared as the end product of
institutional forces that must use the ballot to raise funds, and these
forces have over time developed successful strategies for manipulating
that political environment. This is particularly true when those out-

lays of funds have built-in constituencies, such as municipal employees who can mobilize support at the polls. The rallying around at levy time by administrators, teachers, and PTAs is characteristic of school referenda throughout the nation. But when new actors appear on the local scene with new definitions of policy objectives and priorities, the fundament of consensus may be broken. So, fewer bond issues should pass the electorate.

Why the victory rate of charter amendments should also decline is less evident until one examines the nature of coalitions. The key factor here is that it is hard to mobilize successful coalitions but easy to veto them unless the dissident is accommodated. In a small coalition, therefore, each participant has a larger share of power than in a broader coalition. Hence, when more groups enter more claims upon the polity, each one has proportionately less power to affect electoral outcomes. Accordingly, under conditions of lesser individual group power, demands may be rejected more often.

Table 5 summarizes data on these theses concerning an increase in the defeat of ballot measures when the power context is loosened. Two equal periods of seven years each bracket the mid-1960s, when observers insist that the context changed. Indeed, the data strongly support the propositions advanced above, although the number of bonds offered declines slightly instead of increasing. But otherwise, table 5 demonstrates that the frequency of amendments increased sharply, that the rate of their success dropped, and that the rate of success of bond issues dropped dramatically. Had a closed decisional system continued to operate in San Francisco, there would have been no sign of increasing group claims on the political system reflected in these charter amendments, and the rate of success would have continued as it had been when a few managed such affairs. Instead,

TABLE 5
Voter Response to Referenda in San Francisco, 1958–1971

Type of Referendum	1958–1964	1965–1971	Total
Bonds			
Offered	24	23	47
Passed (%)	83	39	62
Charter Amendments			
Offered	66	99	165
Passed (%)	70	53	60

claims on the charter increased by 50 percent, while the rate of success fell sharply for both kinds of issues. Even without a consideration of the specifics of these issues, all of this is suggestive of a new environment for processing decisions in the political system.

Shifts in Group Success

These indications of a shift in power do not tell us, however, who won and lost in that event. All observers agree that in earlier years a business group had dominated all city affairs, including City Hall. Also, labor has had a reputation for political strength for many decades. But those knowledgeable individuals interviewed for this study claim that these conditions no longer obtain, although the deterioration is not severe. If so, analysis of the records of these groups in support of ballot issues should permit a direct perspective on such an alteration. Accordingly, the record of success of group recommendations was calculated for the period 1958 to 1971. A "business success" occurred if one or more business groups, such as the Chamber of Commerce, the Downtown Association, and others, endorsed a ballot issue that passed or opposed one that failed; a similar method was employed for labor councils and international unions. The results appear in table 6 across three segments of recent years.

The evidence about a changing power context for major groups is contradictory. On bond issues, where voters can authorize costly outlays for civic programs, both groups have moved from a very high to a middling average of success. Business success was down

TABLE 6
Success of Recommendations by Business and Labor in
Direct Legislation, 1958–1971 (in percentage)

	Business	Labor
1958–1962		
Bonds	87	69
Charter amendments	53	54
1963–1967		
Bonds	80	78
Charter amendments	81	36
1968–1971		
Bonds	50	41
Charter amendments	92	64

from almost nine issues in ten to one in two, while labor's dropped from two issues in three to two in five. Here is suggestive evidence again of old power patterns in flux. However, quite the opposite is true for charter amendments, those persistent efforts to change basic government to the advantage of city workers or private groups. Here, the success of both major groups has increased, steeply in the case of business, almost precisely the mirror image of its success on bond issues. Labor fell off badly in the mid-1960s, but thereafter made successful recommendations on about two in three issues. These alterations took place when both groups took stands on about the same number of bond issues, although business was active on many more charter amendments.[12]

The weakening influence of business and labor in San Francisco over the authorization of further bonded indebtedness may well have been part of a nationwide tide of opposition of this kind. Inflation, the Vietnam War, the politicization of school issues, racial strife— all played some part after the mid-1960s in weakening support for schoolbonds and tax levies all across the nation. It may well be that in the San Francisco data we are witnessing just such popular recalcitrance. But whatever its causes, these bond issue results do little to suggest that a small group dominates the city's affairs in an important arena.

A clearer picture of that popular mood and its impact on significant local groups emerges from a more detailed analysis of the kinds of bond issues won or lost and those who supported them. Table 7 enables us to determine for the most recent years not only group power but popular preferences. It shows that voters had some consistent moods, regardless of which city leaders and groups backed or opposed them. San Franciscans refused outlays for park and recreational uses, municipal buildings (including schools), and programs for their worst slums in Hunter's Point. They would support water pollution control and acquisition of the port, but not improvement of street lighting and fire protection. In short, San Franciscans were not of a mind to finance better urban services and protection for their most disadvantaged citizens, the segment that would benefit most from improvement in rundown schools, bad lighting, poor fire safeguards, crowded courtrooms, and skimpy recreation.

This popular judgment was carried out despite the contrary will of a popular mayor and the chief administrative officer (CAO), and of purportedly powerful business and labor councils, liberal groups,

TABLE 7

Group Endorsements of Bonds Lost and Won, 1968–1971

	Urged a "Yes" Vote								
	Mayor	C of C	Labor	Downtown Ass'n.	Liberals	Celebrities	City Workers	LWV	CAO
1968									
Bonds Lost									
Recreation-Park	x	...	x	x	...	x	...	...	x
Cliff House Purchase	x	...	x	...	...	...	...	x	x
Bonds Won									
Market Street Development	x	x	x	x	...	x	...	...	x
Water Pollution Aid	x	x	x	x	...	x	...	x	x
Hunter's Point Recreation	x	...	x	x	x	x	...	...	...
Transfer of Port	x	x	x	...	...	x	...	...	x
Control of Port	x	x	x	...	...	x	...	...	x
1969									
Bonds Lost									
Recreation-Park	x	x	x	...	...	x	...	...	x
Hunter's Point Development	x	...	x	...	x	x	...	x	x
Capital Improvement	x	x	x	...	...	...	x	...	x
1970									
Bonds Lost									
School Buildings	...	...	x	x	x	x	...	x	...
Street Lighting	...	x	x	x	x	x	...	...	...
Fire Protection	x	x	x	x	...	...	x	...	...
Hunter's Point Development	x	...	x	...	...	...	...	...	...
Bonds Won									
Water Pollution Aid	x	x	x	x	...	...	x	...	x
1971									
Bonds Lost									
School Buildings	x	x	x	...	x	x	...	x	x
Hall of Justice Building	x	...	x	...	...	...	...	...	...
Bonds Won									
Port Improvement	x	...	x	x	...	...	x	...	x
Fire Protection	x	x	x	...	...	...	x	...	x

and local celebrities. Some of these were about equally on the winning and losing sides (mayor, CAO, business, celebrities); labor lost more often than not; while liberals and the League of Women Voters (LWV) won only one in five. What about those ostensibly unbeatable combinations, as many San Franciscans believe them to be? Such alliances would be the mayor, the Chamber of Commerce, and the labor council; mayor and chamber; labor and chamber; or chamber and "Downtowners." The record shows that the "unbeatable" could be beaten, for these won only six out of ten such efforts; the mayor and labor together won even less, eight of seventeen. Little of this fits the picture of a small band in some board room or hotel suite exerting unbeatable control over a span of major city decisions.

Rather, such data better fit the decisional model which, according to the report of knowledgeable observers, had come to prevail by the late 1960s—the shifting of temporary coalitions with issue and election. We can determine that quality by calculating the rate of success of many groups active in these contests over issues. A hyperactive and looser decisional context would require groups in these elections to participate in only a few permanent endorsement coalitions (e.g., business + labor + mayor). Yet these "powerhouse" lineups were only middling successful, as noted above, and they occurred only on a few major bond issues. When we turn to the records of the success of individual groups in recent years, as in table 8, we see differences in success and in frequency of entering the fray at all. Some, like the mayor and labor, entered often and spread their recommendations widely. Others, like merchants, city workers, and good-government specialists, husbanded them carefully. Yet there is only a modest correlation between the number of recommendations and success. Thus the Municipal Conference (commercial interests), the Municipal Improvement League (city workers), and the League of Women Voters, who put their stamp on about the same number of issues, varied widely in their rates of success—91 percent, 55 percent, and 30 percent respectively. Moreover, success varied with the year for about every group in table 8.

OLD AND NEW MODELS OF POWER

All of this bears the mark of an ad hoc politics, the kind which knowledgeable individuals insisted had come into being. Few if any groups could mobilize the electorate consistently across the years

TABLE 8
Success of Recommendations by Mayor and Urban Groups
on Referenda, 1963–1971

	1968		1969		1970		1971		Total	
Recommender	N	% Won	N	% Won	N	% Won	N	% Won	N	% Won
Municipal Conference[a]	1	100	4	100	2	100	4	75	11	91
Civil Service Ass'n.	5	80	1	0	4	75	5	80	15	73
Chamber of Commerce	9	100	4	25	7	57	4	75	24	71
Downtown Ass'n.	6	83	e	e	7	43	2	100	15	67
Labor Council	20	80	11	27	13	46	16	62	60	58
Citizen committees[b]	5	20	4	50	7	100	7	43	23	56
Mayor Alioto	14	79	12	25	14	43	18	67	58	55
Municipal Improvement League[c]	1	100	4	25	e	e	6	67	11	55
Liberals[d]	2	100	2	0	1	100	1	0	6	33
League of Women Voters	3	67	4	25	1	0	2	0	10	30

[a] Organization of apartment house and building owners and managers, retailers, realtors, and the Downtown Ass'n.
[b] Ad hoc groups, usually not active across two elections.
[c] Organization of eighteen city employee groups.
[d] Either groups like NAACP or recognized liberal names.
[e] No recommendation.

in support of major decisions on resources. Such was the report, and the previous tables are consistent with that perception, rough-hewn though those measures may be. History left its mark by creating a major forum for decision making, where big issues were passed to the electorate. But where there had once been popular acquiescence on bond issues—an undeniably large allocation of resources, which characteristically reflects established power relationships—after the mid-1960s the consent was withdrawn.

What has emerged instead is a politics of acute sensitivity to the demands of both great realty investment and small neighborhood groups (to be illustrated later in chapters on governance and the politics of highrises). But it is a curious openness, not one befitting any notion of a closed decisional system where only business or labor is effective. Big money interests have always been active and usually successful on the urban scene. When large investments poured into highrise construction and related developments during the 1960s (a move paralleled in many other urban centers), their voice was undeniably heard in this little land. To have expected otherwise would have been unrealistic. Indeed, as we shall see, there has been almost overwhelming *popular* support for that set of decisions, as measured by elections.

The other kind of openness, to neighborhood groups, does not fit the closed model. Associations—both temporary and permanent— named for hills and valleys, ethnic and occupational groups, age and sex distinctions, sprang up during the last decade like the city's fog late on a summer afternoon. Their representatives, often backed by vocal constituents, have become familiar figures before councils, commissions, the mayor, and the media. There has appeared an almost sudden politicization, so diverse and fragmented that observers unanimously insist that a "new politics" has appeared here.

The causes are diverse, and they lie partly with newly sensitive ethnic concerns, partly with new values about the redistribution of municipal services, and partly with threats to income, safety, and deference. But there is a major cause for which the others are but more visible signs—decisions that are made outside the community and that impinge on it from governmental and private centers elsewhere.

Thus, the explosions of civil rights in the South after 1960 were heard by this bay across the continent, and as a result local ethnic politics has been shaken up in entirely new ways. When national corporations across the nation were seized with the desire during this decade to build national headquarters in San Francisco, the politics of profit here took on a new dynamism—and the city's landscape and economy altered drastically as a consequence. The state of the national economy had reverberations here, as always; but it may well have reached down to influence voters on bond issues, regardless of the preferences of local political, business, and labor leaders, in a sharp shift from the early to the late 1960s. Earlier, the national economy had been growing with minimal price inflation, but later, real incomes sank before rising prices as part of the war-based inflation. As a result, income redistribution measures for education, health, and welfare were more acceptable to San Francisco voters in the early years of the decade than in later years.

The central fact of decision making in the city is that there is now no single "power structure" working its way on an unsuspecting or apathetic public. Rather, groups of all kinds and interests are enmeshed in a highly complex politics; with the biblical Joel, I found that there are "multitudes, multitudes in the valley of decision." Here, as with any community or society, whether power and authority are fragmented or unified, there is inequality in the distribution of socially significant values; not all groups are equal here or anywhere. Accordingly, those who enjoy a preferred position will preserve and reinforce it by all available means, whatever the challenges they face in any era. But, as we have seen above and will witness later, the favored do not always win, and so in San Francisco they must know some constraints. Some of these arise outside of the community, some are imposed by historical decisions, but all come together in the local arena. The nature of that arena has changed, and for reasons which I do not believe are special for San Francisco.

As a carrier of demands into the political system, then, there is little of the local "community power" which resembles a "structure." Rather, there are signs, only sketched to this point, that in this diverse community there are many involved in decision making, different combinations of group interests are at work, many of these are opposed, and so the political environment reveals less of structure than of turbulence. To understand this amorphous reality, however, we must expand the context for viewing such decision making. One looks better for the essence of power in the realities of group conflict and accommodation than in Shelley's "awful shadow of some unseen Power [that] floats, tho' unseen, among us." For that purpose then, I examine next the city's electoral process, itself a major carrier of demands into the political system, where we can see more clearly the reality of a multigroup politics and its shaping by historical and external forces.

CHAPTER 4

Elections and Decision Making

Public opinion has been wryly defined as "those opinions held by private persons which governments find it prudent to heed." [1] The simplicity of the definition masks a complex set of linkages between many publics and the political system, between public demands and the reactions of political authorities. These linkages vary greatly in the volume and kind of demands, in the channels used to transmit demands, in the prudence and responsiveness of political authorities, and, in the end, in how the society reacts to authoritative action. Many citizens would agree with Henry James that it is all a "buzzing, booming confusion."

The purpose of this chapter is to determine the manner and quality of San Francisco's party activity, which serves as a carrier of demands into the political system. Party activity is important because it has served traditionally as a channel for *mass* input to public decision making, while "power structures" have provided access to a selected minority. The latter we reviewed in the previous chapter. There, as in this chapter, we will see that the voters are not without influence, making it prudent for political authorities to heed them.

We turn first to a brief sketch of the historical constraints and the state's culture which set the context for the city's political process. Then we will examine how the electoral process operates here, given these constraints. Throughout, the emphasis is on the characteristics of decision making when elections are the mode and citizens engage in them.

HISTORICAL CONSTRAINTS ON LOCAL POLITICS

Because San Francisco is subordinated to a state constitution, shares political values common to the larger nation, and knows a special history, its political process is not autonomous. The interaction between city and state has been extensive, with the former dominant for much of their history. Although it could be more independent in the earlier days of booms in gold, silver, and wheat, forces outside the city have increasingly been felt. Not the least of these has been the development since 1900 of a state political culture, that "system of empirical beliefs, expressive symbols, and values which defines the situation in which political action takes place." [2] The central political phenomenon in the history of Californians is their suspicion of political parties. This attitude was a reaction against dominance in the nineteenth century by the Southern Pacific Railroad, which led in the Progressive Era to laws that have shaped the state's political course ever since. Both party-in-the-government and party-in-the-electorate were affected. That is, party as an agency to govern and to mobilize candidates and voters was totally restructured in reaction against the blatant corruption of earlier parties.

The Era of Corruption and Color

It would be easy to linger on that corruption, for if one is far enough removed in time, it seems ingenious, not devilish, and its leader is seen "not as an ex-tyrant, but as an 'old-timer,' a 'colorful' character." [3] It is as if Shakespeare's aphorism were reversed for these bosses of another year—"The good that men do lives after them, the evil is oft interred with their bones." It may be amusing to read of San Francisco reformers who, to defend themselves against the boss, placed polls high atop a thirty-foot ladder, which could be shaken if the climbing voter asked for the wrong ballot. But to have lived under this political system was far from amusing if one were out of favor or lacked sufficient resources to secure that favor. The wellspring of all the corruption in this state was the Southern Pacific Railroad, which owned utilities, land, and politicians in breath-taking amounts, with towns merely one set of chattels. It was a fair imitation of feudalism, all things considered.[4]

San Francisco was not immune. Long the largest city in California, it reflected even if it did not generate whatever transpired within the state political culture. Alexander Callow has summarized the city's political environment of that era:

San Francisco already contained the forces that would complicate the city's growth and render it accessible to the control of a city boss. A spirit of violence and excitement, generated in the old days of the gold rush, was perpetuated by the Vigilance Committee of 1856 and, through the decades of the 1870's and 1880's, by the sand-lot riots, the Workingmen's Party, and the anti-monopoly crusades. Increasing numbers of Chinese and Catholic-Irish fanned the fire of racial, religious, and labor hatreds. The potential of great wealth and great corporations grew rapidly and sought to dominate both economic and political life. But municipal government did not keep pace. A city charter, weakened by a host of amendments, made the office of mayor an ornamental figurehead. Civil responsibility was divided into so many parts that any centralized authority was impossible. The city grew in giant convulsions, leaving a wide gap between the ever-expanding economic organizations and the lagging agencies of government. The man who could step into this breach and act as a middleman between the economic and political institutions could have the title City Boss. It required a man who had a capacity for organization and a character not overburdened by a scrupulous regard for ethics.[5]

In another case of the times producing the man, San Francisco was ruled in the 1880s by Christopher A. Buckley. He was unlike the run of city bosses of the era only in being totally blind from his heavy drinking.[6] Buckley viewed himself as a broker of competing self-interests. Thus, he could and did work with the local Republican party to mutual advantage. Once he swung the key votes in the legislature which permitted Leland Stanford and George Hearst to become the Republican and Democratic U.S. senators. Control of the party's county central committee led to control of the party, which led to control of the primaries, which led to control of the board of supervisors and the legislators. His power was based on organized clubs, money for voters, violence, and patronage—about par on the national scene for city politics in those days.

Typical corruption attended each of these points for transmuting political power. The ballot boxes were stuffed, with the votes returned from each polling place limited "only by the modesty of the election officials," in the phrase of Abe Ruef, whose judgment on such matters should be accepted.* Supervisors thus elected could legislate the interest of the Blind Boss and his business allies. State representatives from San Francisco were a biddable bloc in legislating and in electing

---

* On one occasion, the crews of two visiting French warships voted, another sign of the influence of France on the culture of San Francisco.

United States senators. All of this brought "Buckley and his lambs" considerable fortunes, as every city job was for sale; the buyers threw public privilege to private interests, who in turn rewarded Buckley. Even to be a teacher in the schools required a fee of $200, while the schools themselves deteriorated rapidly as money appropriated for repairs disappeared.[7] But then, as Buckley put it frankly, "The game of politics is not a branch of the Sunday school business," echoing the words of ward boss George Washington Plunkitt on the opposite coast that "Politics ain't beanbags."

Of course, highly publicized scandals of the usual sort for those days finally brought Buckley down under strong reformer pressure. At this reversal he observed, "When I saw what was within the scope of a reformer's vision, it was with sadness and humiliation that I realized the narrow limits of my own imagination." For the means used to unseat him, including guarded ladders to polling places, were not too different from his own techniques.

Despite anecdotes and the outrage of reformers, the Buckley episode typified decision making in that era at both state and local levels.[8] Decisions were made by a few, who mutually exchanged their blocs of resources—club followers, money, balloting, skills, knowledge of formal rules, and even violence. As Lincoln Steffens found, the relationship of politician and businessman was symbiotic, although their relationship to the community was parasitic. In exchange for votes, the party performed tasks for citizens, such as social and economic assistance, relief from legal demands, outlets for ethnic identification. Nor was such effort restricted to the poor; a San Francisco saloon boss noted that "it was his duty to be in close touch with all the strata of the social system." [9] However, average citizens exercised little independent influence in these operations, unless they were stirred by threats dramatized by reformers—for example, Irish fears of competition from Chinese workers. But aside from such occasional heavings, urban decision making before 1910 here and elsewhere was a game of very high payoffs among very few players.

Progressive Reaction and Republican Dominance

It was against such local and state corruption that reformist passions coalesced in the Progressive movement and centered on the political party, which had for so long controlled access to the political system. Knock out this underpinning, Progressives proclaimed, and boss control, which meant corporation control, would be abolished in one stroke.

San Francisco played a leading role in these events, which can only be sketched here.[10] Workers' revulsion against bossism led to formation of the Union Labor party in the city in 1901, but Ruef promptly captured it to lead on to corruption surpassing even that of Boss Buckley.[11] Ruef's arrangements with the Southern Pacific Railroad were laid bare by a young attorney, Hiram Johnson, who then rode to Progressive leadership by winning the governor's office in 1910 on the simple promise to sever the political and economic power of the Southern Pacific. There followed a secular version of driving the money lenders from the temple in the form of laws that restructured parties, elections, and balloting; reorganized administration; and reformed educational and labor policies. All this not only severed the Southern Pacific's ties to the Republican party and state government, but it also introduced new standards of morality and practice which shaped for decades the fashion by which elections transmitted private demands into the political system. Moreover, it contributed to the dominance of the Republicans for almost a half-century, despite the New Deal challenge.[12]

Because of its large working class, San Francisco's role in the evolution of this political culture was significant.[13] The Workingmen's party prior to 1900 reflected a first show of strength, which grew as union membership jumped during the period 1900–1910 from 20,000 to 50,000. Populism never attracted the support of workers, but Progressivism did enlist them strongly because of its labor reform laws. In San Francisco a complex, divided labor movement provided the opportunity for one set of leaders to rally workers to the new standard. The presence of labor in a movement that was elsewhere middle class was explained by the weight of San Francisco in the state population and of the workers in that city.[14]

The long Republican hegemony did not finally break until the late 1950s. Labor and San Francisco[15] joined the nation in voting Democratic for president and Congress during the New Deal, yet that party never carried both houses of the legislature, and only one governorship, during that era. But during the 1950s Republican fortunes declined sharply, and in 1958 the Democrats carried both houses and all state offices except secretary of state. There had emerged a California Democratic Club movement, which provided an organizational base for two-party competition, augmented by changes in electoral laws, new issues, and a changing population.[16] Probably the major stimulus of this change came from the abolition in 1954 of cross-filing,* a Progressive inheritance, which had benefited Republicans so well for so long.

San Francisco in the State Culture

As a result of such events, California now exhibits a complex political culture of sharp distinctions. There is not just one political culture, but what Lee has called "two arenas and two worlds." [17] There is first a statewide arena of party activity which is highly competitive, prone to turnovers in contests for the offices of president, governor, and U.S. senator. There is also an arena of congressional and assembly districts; because of the gerrymandering which produces a set of one-party, noncompetitive districts, this arena is immune from the political tides that roll across state and nation. Imposed on this division is another compounded by geography, which has created at least two regions of party voting. Just north of Los Angeles is an invisible border separating what seem to be two nationalities, the subcultures of Los Angeles and San Francisco.† Far more relevant is the differing persistent voting pattern of the conservative south and the liberal north on candidates and issues.[18]

These elements of the state culture are reflected in San Francisco. In many presidential elections after 1856, the city vote was the state vote because of the weight of its population; between 1860 and 1900 it was less Republican than the nation. In this century, it has not only followed national trends, it has accentuated them; Coolidge received 88 percent of the city's vote in 1924, and Johnson 75 percent in 1964.

---

* Candidates were listed without party affiliation, and voters could vote in either party primary. Winning both primaries meant the candidate had no contest in the fall election. Progressives thought this would abolish the influence of party leaders in nominations by permitting only voters to make such decisions. However, from 1914 to 1957, citizen choice became constricted by this device. About one-half of all state contests had cross-filing, of which about one-half were successful. Add another one-tenth where there was no opposition, and we see that about one in three seats in this era offered citizens no choice. See Robert J. Pitchell, "The Electoral System and Voting Behavior: The Case of California's Cross-Filing," *Western Political Quarterly,* 12 (1959), 459–484.

† The patronizing attitude of San Franciscans is well reflected in the comment of the late Lucius Beebe, "Isn't it nice that those people who like Los Angeles live in Los Angeles."

Also, in major state contests the city's vote paralleled the state vote during the New Deal and later. But during the 1930s Democratic registration in San Francisco doubled, the city's vote during and after the war years established a slight Democratic edge, and after 1958 the edge grew much larger, regularly ten percentage points more than the statewide vote. More than ever, it has become the core of the other political culture of California. But because the weight of voters in the state has tilted heavily to the more Republican south, San Francisco veers consistently from the state norm.[19]

At the local level, San Francisco reflects some of the Progressive ideals, particularly in congressional and state legislative seats. The "irrational" pull of party voting, against which those earlier reformers railed, is blurred in these contests. Prior to 1958, cross-filing had been commonplace, muffling party competition while encouraging candidate competition; between 1920 and 1950, when no more than one in five contests took place for such seats, the Progressive dream had thrived.[20] Even after cross-filing was eliminated, party competition for many legislative seats did not thrive in the city. Thus, Democratic dominance in state assembly districts has regularly produced Democratic winners. But candidates for other seats, such as Congress and the state senate, demonstrate less pull of the party upon voters.

Note that the two congressional seats which split the city have regularly been filled by a Democrat in one and a Republican in the other. Similarly, the two state senate seats in the city have been regularly filled with a Democrat and a Republican. The social composition of the two congressional districts differs somewhat, with the Democrat Philip Burton representing more the worker and black-brown neighborhoods, and Republican William Mailliard more the white-collar areas toward the ocean and across the Golden Gate in heavily affluent Marin County. But these are not districts sharply distinguished by party registration. Although Republican Mailliard had a district with a distinct Democratic edge in registration (Humphrey received 52 percent there in 1968), he regularly carried it during the 1960s by about 75 percent, even though state Republican candidates were losing badly beside him. He did face a major threat in 1970 and 1972, where his margin fell to 53 and 55 percent. His record in Congress reflects no extremism. In the many measures used to gauge a member's support of his party or interest groups, Mailliard characteristically ranged around the midpoint of such scales, except for his strong support of President Nixon. On the critical issues of recent years involving federal action, he has backed some and denied others.

In all this account of Mailliard's district there is much of the Progressive ideal that candidates should be supported not for their party label but for their stands on current issues. A district with a Democratic majority that regularly supports such a Republican, and a representative in Congress who generally votes with the majority of his party only about half the time, with the bipartisan majority about 80 percent, and with the conservative coalition about 50 percent—all of this would have gladdened the hearts of the earlier reformers. That would be true far more with Mailliard than with San Francisco's other congressman, Philip Burton. His district is much more weighted with those farther down the life-opportunity scale,* and he is a regular bulwark of liberal blocs in Washington and in state and local politics. Is the independence of Mailliard voters a reflection of the Progressive ideal still at work among those citizens—professional, middle class or higher, better educated—whose ancestors were the bulwark of Progressive leaders? They were "these fortunate sons of the upper middle class" in the eyes of their historian George Mowry, and Mailliard enunciated a trustee—almost noblesse oblige—concept of his representative role, which also echoed those early reformers. Or does the district's behavior reflect a growing independence from blind party support, which accelerated in a mobile society of the 1960s? That breaking of old bonds appears nationally most often among just that kind of better educated, affluent citizen who fills the flats, valleys, and hills of Burton's district. Clearly, less of it is seen in the Burton district—and nationally—among citizens with less advantages. We raise the query without providing an answer, for this is one of many aspects of the city requiring further study.

But partisanship is still a factor at the state level. The increased Democratic registration and vote in San Francisco after World War II influenced statewide contests, as California moved from a normally Republican to a two-party state. As will be shown, however, this did not mean that a conscious and active party structure accompanied this shift. For San Franciscans have all the pleasure of political party life without the benefit of parties.

The strongest influence stemming from historical and external

---

* Two black ghettos, Hunter's Point and the Fillmore, were placed in Mailliard's district by the legislature, an action the state supreme court upheld in late 1973. He shortly thereafter retired, replaced by John Burton, Philip's brother.

forces working on San Francisco is to be found in the Progressive insistence on abolishing parties in order to achieve nonpartisan local elections. This requirement, combined with other party constraints, sought to focus voters' decisions not on party but on the quality of governance and governors, unmediated by any intervening influence. The intensity of the battle to establish nonpartisanship is hard to understand today. Nevertheless, here is another evidence of the city as a time machine. The last hurrah has long since died away across this forgotten battlefield of public policy, but the victors' banners still hang today in most city halls of this country.[21] As a result, as Eugene Lee has noted, "the state provides probably as 'pure' an example as possible of the effect of the absence of formalized party structure." [22] Every local candidate for elective office in county, city, and school or special district is elected without a party label. That is, without the radar of party identification, voters are expected to find those candidates who reflect their local interests.

There is a special bias to this nonpartisanship, as Eugene Lee, for the 1950s, and Willis Hawley, for the 1960s, have demonstrated. Formal, organized party activity is absent at the local level, but nonpartisanship tends strongly to benefit certain groups who possess particular political advantages, such as education, knowledge of local affairs, finances, organizational activity and expertise. These advantages are much more associated with persons who tend to register Republican. As a result, more nonpartisan candidates of Republican registration get elected to local office than there are Republicans in the communities they represent. In a few special communities, this disproportion works to the advantage of Democrats, of course, but it is mainly Republicans who prosper under nonpartisanship. That this advantage provides some benefit to the GOP as a party and to its values is indisputable in light of these analyses. This has enabled Republican registrants to dominate local government despite a statewide Democratic edge in registration. While the CDC movement of the 1950s broke Republican dominance at the state level, it did little to affect local control by Republicans.[23]

These are the historical and external circumstances which have constrained party activity in San Francisco. What parties can be is a function of what the state and past permit them to be. But, in this context, where neither party is expected to do much locally, do the functions of party disappear? There are the familiar—because manifest —party functions of nominating candidates, getting out the vote, expressing stands on issues, and, if the candidate is elected, governing with the authority given by voters. There are less familiar functions, those that are latent in party operations in the larger political system: consensus building; recruitment of political authorities; distribution of resources; political socialization; and maintenance of the political system's legitimacy. Do these disappear with nonpartisanship? Are these transmuted into ways distinctive to this reform? Does the behavior of political actors change? Do the links between public and political authority alter in some significant way? These questions lead into the mosaic of San Francisco party politics.

Local Parties in a Nonpartisan Context

The formal requirements of local party organization and operation in California are few. The county central committee is forbidden by law to work in party primaries or endorse candidates, but it must conduct the campaigns of those candidates in whose selection it had no voice. Although it may develop a precinct organization, little of this is done, so into this vacuum step extra-party groups, including candidate organizations. As the 1950s closed, Lee found a widely moribund local organization. In only 9 percent of 192 cities surveyed were there reports of any visible party activity in local elections. The chairmen in only eleven of the forty-four counties reporting had noted such activity, and then even for only one party; only about one-half the party leaders were reported to be active; and there was more activity in the bigger cities and among Republicans.[24] Basic to all this, however, is the absence of major sources of power, an absence directly attributable to the reform of a half-century earlier. James Wilson's review of these defective instruments explains it well:

In [American] cities where parties are strong, that strength results from the existence of an effective precinct organization, the ability to determine who shall be the party's nominees, and control of the patronage resources of the government. In California, all three of these sources of strength are lacking. There is no precinct organization within the regular party, no way to deliver nominations to endorsed candidates at the local level, no way even to make endorsements at the state level, and parties are excluded from city and county affairs. Only from the state and national governments may the parties receive patronage. In California, the merit system is effective at the state as well as the local level, and only a few desirable jobs, most of them judicial appointments, are available to state officers.[25]

Local parties are also constrained by nonpartisanship laws from providing organizational vehicles for the expression of public will for the most numerous elections—those for office in the city and in the school and special districts. As a result, voters pay little attention to these contests, preferring to vote for higher, partisan offices. Analysts have found monotonic decrease in turnouts with a decrease in the size of the governing unit, from state down to special district.[26] But underneath this cloak of nonpartisanship some degree of partisanship operates. Compared with most cities, Berkeley and Pomona had parties in the 1950s that were more visible and active in local affairs. More frequent than such overt partisanship, however—and most typical—was the presence of various quasi-public groups which endorsed candidates, mobilized the electorate, raised finances, and otherwise carried out party functions.

Californians conduct party functions under the name of nonpartisanship because a Banquo's ghost of former corruption inhibits them. After all, local party organs are *not* forbidden to take an active part in local nonpartisan politics. Also, San Francisco could amend its charter any time to provide for partisan elections, and the Democratic majority could thereby expand its number of local offices. Neither of these events takes place, nor is likely to, and the reasons are clear from interviews for this study. Observers unanimously agree that such obtrusive partisan action would face a hostile local majority, for whom nonpartisanship ranks somewhere in the scale of life values between godliness and cleanliness. Observers insist that no one can understand local politics without taking into account this popular opposition to partisan organizations operating in contests for city office. The knowledgeable individuals in San Francisco, and many rank and file citizens as well, have a wide knowledge of the partisan identification of major candidates and office holders. But for a local party group to proclaim support for its men is heretical, rather like the Convention Bureau announcing that Los Angeles is a much fairer city than San Francisco.

If we accept this local ethos as a real constraint, why does it exist here and elsewhere in California? Some might think that the influx of new San Franciscans that was noted in chapter 2 had introduced notions prevailing back home about local partisanship and thus had contributed to the change in the local view. But most home cities of these immigrants were also nonpartisan as a result of the Progressive victories decades ago. In all these cases we see the heritage of historical decisions that have become institutionalized in the lives of persons, providing them with a major outlook on the proper nature of local politics.

Exploration of the meaning of nonpartisanship in the city's life requires, then, a deeper analysis. As Charles Adrian has noted, the concept can mask quite different modes of political behavior—including full party operation.[27] Closer inspection will also reveal the fashion in which elections serve to provide a channel for demands into the political system. Finally, such analysis will also provide a testing ground for the presence of the coalition principle which city observers cite as the main process for community decision making.

Because of statewide forces in the 1950s, San Francisco turned away from a local party system that was noncompetitive, nonpartisan, and oriented to local business. Instead, there emerged in the 1960s competition for office, visibility of individuals' party labels (especially Democratic), and responsiveness to a broader range of ethnic and economic interests. Yet, there still remained some of the older pattern; nomination, presentation of issues, and mobilization of voters in contests for sixty-five elective offices still were based not on party, but on the individual.[28] Nevertheless, there was an increased local politicization, flowing from the statewide CDC movement discussed earlier, which was manifested in the degree of partisanship in mayor and supervisor contests.

It had been a longstanding practice to elect a Republican to the office of mayor, although his party was never stressed. Another custom had been for the mayor to appoint new supervisors from his party. Outgoing incumbents would politely resign a few months before the next election, thus permitting the appointee to have the status of incumbent when facing the voters. The results were a board and a mayor who were usually Republican because of such self-regeneration, and supervisors, known informally as the representative of certain business or labor interests, who were of no particular quality.

Whatever defects this practice might have had, they were minimized by two factors. The municipal charter, by its exquisite delimitation of authority (to be treated in the next chapter), gave little chance for elected officials to go astray—indeed, to do much of anything. Corruption becomes possible only when, in the words of the legendary Plunkitt of Tammany Hall, "I saw my chance and took it." But first there must be the chance. A second factor which caused little questioning of this perpetuated government was that for much of the charter's history there was little stress put on the tasks of governing. The conditions of city life, public expectations of City Hall, group mobilization to translate wants into policy demands, the thrust of resources from the outside to deal with local problems—all of these were to expand in the late 1950s. One consequence of these events was an alteration in the conditions surrounding the election of mayor and supervisors. Also, the charter, by its resistance to those events, rechanneled the desire for change into a new political context.

Beginning in 1963 with the election of Democrat John Shelley as mayor, the new context surfaced. Shelley began appointing Democrats to the board of supervisors when vacancies arose, as well as to many other slots in the commissions and boards that festoon city government. Though Shelley was later abandoned by local Democrats fearing his defeat in 1967, he and his appointments are regarded by friends and enemies in both parties as the key factor in the changing partisanship in the city. These new men with city-wide exposure now gained the immense advantage of incumbency.[29] Now there was Democratic publicity for administrative decision and there were Democratic names in many offices. Republican leaders interviewed for this book complained of new qualities in these appointees, such as toughness in political infighting, unlike the "gentlemanly" element known before; responsiveness to issues and groups new on the scene; and, above all, the distasteful partisanship that now marked political life. The Republicans' real problem, however, was that their nonpartisan cover had been blown.

Democratic and Republican Factions

The transition generated an intense intraparty factionalism, especially among Democrats, and these elements must be seen as a background to the new party life. Thus, the local partisan organization of Democrats provided by state law was cornered by one faction, but in reality the distinctive quality of the Democracy was its fragmentation into personal cliques. Before World War II, the Democratic county central committee under the leadership of William Malone had real power. But factional differences were irrepressible over the years, so that by the 1950s there were three factions, two of the old-line Irish and one of the new CDC. Two of the three had to combine to make decisions, and usually it was the Irish against the new liberals. But in a few years the CDC grew to capture county committee posts in the primaries; in the late 1950s, twenty-five CDC groups flourished. In this formative period, a trade union official and congressman, John Shelley, brought together an effective, grass-roots organization based in the unions and with the CDC as allies. But this evaporated in Shelley's four-year term as mayor in the disappointment of even his strongest supporters at his alleged ineffectiveness. State Senator J. Eugene McAteer emerged as the next strong man, supported by moderate and conservative Democrats, as well as by businessmen. But his sudden death in 1967 ended all that.

On the San Francisco political scene were several other factions that sought control. Thus, the CDC movement developed the leadership of Congressman Philip Burton. The epitome of the new-style liberal Democrat—issue oriented (but with a traditional block organization), utilizing new survey analysis techniques—he appealed especially to the emerging black and brown ethnic groups. Burton's screening of liberal candidates for approval in order to impose some party discipline was resented by many Democrats, particularly in labor, which reflected different ethnic interests and issue concerns. Even Burton liberals increasingly found their own bases of power and in time moved from his camp. Nevertheless, he got his brother elected to the state assembly,* and he did control the party's county central committee, although few observers regarded the latter important because of its legal limitations.[30]

The election of Joseph Alioto as mayor in 1967 changed what had been almost full control by Burton over the Democratic party. Alioto reassembled the McAteer coalition of Democratic factions and Republican business support to defeat both a Republican and Burton's candidate. By the 1970s Mayor Alioto was regarded as the most powerful and prestigious city Democrat, although he had been able to transfer relatively little of this influence to the support of party candidates. In Alioto's successful reelection in 1971, against a liberal Democratic supervisor and the Republican he had beaten in 1967, he demonstrated even greater financial and group support.

Another element among local Democrats is found in two young state legislators, each with his own group basis in San Francisco and with expanding contacts across the state. George Moscone, an energetic state senator with growing influence in Sacramento as chairman of the party caucus in the senate, had risen under Burton but moved on his own later. By 1974 he and Alioto were energetic, though unsuccessful,

---

* And, in 1974, to Congress.

gubernatorial candidates. A growing ethnic component of the party were the city's blacks, with Assemblyman Willie Brown in the Burton camp and Supervisor Terry Francois friendly with Burton but more detached. By 1972, Brown, active in Sacramento legislative councils and nationally in the new black political cadre, was being openly mentioned as the city's next mayor. Then there were Democrats who were anti-Burton liberals—for example, assemblymen Leo McCarthy and John Foran—and conservatives who supported Alioto because they opposed the congressman; here would be some businessmen and the party's major financial supporters, Benjamin Swig and Cyril Magnin.

The party's organization, then, is many things. The formal apparatus of the county committee is an empty corridor of power along which struggle factions and strong personalities. There is no power gained by "winning" its control, as it has no resources to dispense. It oversees no precinct organization that could generate support for favored candidates, as there is no precinct organization to speak of, particularly now that the CDC has shrunk from twenty-five to a handful of clubs. The county committee has no patronage, for what little exists comes through local congressmen. Indeed, such is the political ethos of San Francisco that candidates and elected officials do not want to be obligated to a major institution like a strong party.

The party looks more like some current notions of "post-bureaucratic organization," a combination of factions whose membership—if not direction—changes with time and with the impact of strong personalities. Some cohesion may occasionally be imposed on all this by a Malone, a Shelley, a Burton, or an Alioto. But in the absence of any enduring partisan structure, this cohesion disperses under the forces of personal ambitions, group priorities, and new issues. This party is only as strong as the elected officials to whom it is linked, and when these have differing ambitions or policy imposed by the groups they represent, they cannot be a source for continued party cohesion and strength.

In these years of Democratic resurgence and squabbling, the Republicans were like the eucalyptus tree, continually losing leaves of supporters and campaigns but remaining alive. They have only about one in three of the registered voters, many fewer campaign workers than the numbers who battled under the banner of CDC, limited organization, and, in general, little effect on the donnybrook of the other party. While this judgment was widely expressed by Republican leaders surveyed for this study, none seemed upset about this moribund condition. The registration advantage of Democrats is a product of the migrants to the city; the young white-collar workers with a mildly liberal tinge and the increasing blacks joined the old-line liberal element in the labor unions. But the GOP had lived with that Democratic edge before the advent of the CDC and yet had thrived. The party structure mirrors that of the Democrats, essentially ineffective in the last fifteen years, and both reflect the state's political culture. The GOP has also known factionalism. A local internal struggle after World War II ousted an older and inactive set of leaders and ushered in young men who built precinct organizations of great effectiveness. But that too faded away as energies were diverted elsewhere by career claims and as the Democrats mobilized for their new dominance. By the end of the 1960s, though, another cycle of bright young Republican businessmen and professionals was appearing.

Yet at that date the local GOP was inactive, except for an effectively united fund-raising committee. Even that became split over right-left conflicts over endorsements, so that many candidates began to raise their own money. A few men of considerable wealth were recognized as "the powers," although it is not clear what power they had. Having sold the city on nonpartisan municipal politics and having seen it administered rather much their own way for a number of decades, they faded before the onset of the issue-oriented CDC, which sought to favor other groups in society. Many GOP "powers" no longer live in the city, and they restrict their concerns to the world of finance and commerce in a few square blocks. Not all are conservatives by any means; one financial supporter estimates that most of the party's present leaders are liberals of the Rockefeller variety.[31]

In the early 1970s only a few leading Republicans could see some lifting of the clouds of Democrats that had lowered over them for the past decade. Only three of eleven supervisors were then Republican, although none reflected Rockefeller liberalism. As was noted earlier, a popular state senator, Milton Marks, remained strong through this whole era, and Congressman William Maillaird had held firmly to his post since 1952. Moderate conservatives, both men had overcome the local Democratic edge by their acts. But none of the four Democratic assembly seats looked assailable, Mayor Alioto soundly thrashed his GOP opponent in 1971, and Maillaird retired in 1974. There is little in this scene to suggest that any basic alteration of party preferences is under way among San Franciscans.

Electoral Functions in a Partyless System

If we stand back from these personalities and factions to ask how local parties operate as carriers into the political system, the conclusion must be that the historical force of the Progressives still acts to sever party and government. In the four traditional functions which parties are said to perform for the political system—nomination, issue presentation, voter mobilization, and governance—the parties of San Francisco are consistent in the emptiness of their efforts.

Party nomination for local office is forbidden by law, of course, but even informal screening has failed in both parties. Such efforts by Burton and the CDC generated counterpressures against this control, while Republican attempts to dispense funds only to approved candidates also ran aground on similar individualism. Access to finances acts as a nominating agent in San Francisco and elsewhere. Obviously those who have less of it are more easily discouraged from running, while those who have it can effect entry into the political system by their own candidacy or by supporting—if not choosing—special spokesmen among political authorities. There were tales of supervisors in the 1940s and 1950s who were the "men" of business and labor, but obviously this did not stop the rise of the CDC—it may even have helped spawn it—and the defeat of kept officials. In the 1960s, Democrats turned up on the wrong side of votes that were important to the alleged backers of their campaigns for election. Businessmen who contributed to Mayor Alioto's campaign found him calling early and often for business to bear more of the city's tax burden. It is clear that here, as elsewhere in life, men do not live by bread alone.

The screening function of money is complex. Candidates without it may substitute manpower; the numerous CDC supporters who confronted superior money power found in their numbers, energy, and élan the substitutes for such money. Further, money does not issue from a single source with singular objectives. The money world of San Francisco provides some range of policy objectives and hence different notions of desirable candidates. The money that backed the nomination and campaign efforts of the liberal supervisor Diane Feinstein in 1969 is unlike that behind the conservative supervisor John Barbagelata, but both won. In short, if money is a screening device for nominations, the mesh is not all that small, and once through, candidates do not always retain their tags.

Party can serve another function for society by providing forums and spokesmen for alternative definitions and solutions of policy and problems. Elsewhere, groups seek such party advocacy in exchange for electoral support, but in San Francisco parties do not take such stands —the individual candidates do—since the mechanism to produce a local party platform is missing. Because individual candidates may speak or not, the function of presenting issues is thereby diffused, for what they say may be unclear (a device that some use to avoid controversies), or party members may take opposing stands. Decades of the absence of a link between party and public issues are reflected in the lack of competition in the city. The community has come not to expect candidates, particularly for the board of supervisors, to talk sense—or at all—about major current issues. Nor can party perform this function that helps to transfer group demands into public policy through the political system. In this, San Francisco shares with most American cities, where nonpartisanship prevails, a breakdown between party and government.

The mobilization of voters normally requires the party to seek support, across the boundary of society and state, from those groups whose demands signal social stress. In San Francisco that function is the most fully performed of the four here discussed, but it is not the party that performs it. Instead, it is carried out by the candidate's personal organization, often without regard to any other party element. Even quasi-party devices like candidate slates have been rare here in recent history. Rather, it is the individual candidate who performs the familiar actions of "getting out the vote," with some special twists.

But the atomization of party noted elsewhere exists here also. It is rare for candidates who share similar views to share campaign labor and money, so duplication of effort is the norm. Symbolic of this confusion is the appearance of the walls of houses and their fences during campaigns (and for months afterward). A rash of posters kaleidoscopically shows everyone's appeal at once, a message too mixed to attract anyone's attention, for the medium blocks the message. Also, fearful of any loss, every candidate usually appears at the innumerable endorsement meetings of business, ethnic, and neighborhood groups —although the effect of such endorsement in the election outcome is never examined. Unorganized as a whole, divided if not divisive in its impact, wasteful of limited resources, such mobilization efforts result in no one being quite clear why anyone won or lost. One may know where he won but he cannot know who voted for him or why.

Not knowing even this basic signal from the constituency, the elected are hard put to define to whom they are responsible. Uncertain about that relationship so fundamental in a democracy, they are ill-equipped to perform the fourth party function, that of governing, that is, acting as a *group* responsible for the use of power and responsive to supporters' wishes about public policy. That obstacle is compounded by another factor to be treated in later chapters—the division of power in the local charter which inhibits consistent party responsibility across the separate authority of mayor, administration, and supervisors. Thus, institutional limitations are joined to atomized party structure and confusing electoral signals to deny the possibility of party responsibility.

PARTY ACTIVITY, RESPONSIVENESS, AND RESPONSIBILITY

Let us note briefly the effects of all this on responsiveness and responsibility in two products of this system, the contests for seats in Congress and on the board of supervisors.

The Case of Congressmen

Within the same city boundaries there have been for years two congressmen of different parties.[32] These have been William Mailliard since 1948 for the GOP and Jack Shelley for the Democrats until his election to mayor in 1963, after which Burton took his place. We met Mailliard and Burton earlier, but their places in party conflict should now be seen. Each has developed his own organization, sources of funds, and stands on issues. But they are also part of a national party system, in which each party carries somewhat different policy orientations reflecting their constituency differences; those differences also exist in these two districts in the city. Mailliard has represented adjoining Marin County* and the western white-collar half of San Francisco; Burton speaks for the eastern half, heavy with working-

* Marin County is a wealthy, liberal Republican, antiwar enclave, which has resisted Ronald Reagan's conservative impact on the party. "It's the kind of place where people wearing $80 sweaters go shopping barefoot," observes Michael Barone et al., *The Almanac of American Politics—1972* (New York: Gambit, 1972), pp. 52–53, which is also the source for the data that follow.

class and ghetto residents. The Republican's district was 58 percent white-collar, and Burton's 56 percent blue-collar. Both districts had the same proportion of foreign stock, but Burton's had four times the blacks and over three times the Asians that Mailliard's had, until the legislature in 1973 moved black—and Democratic—ghettos into the Republican's district.

Those status differences of about 15 percentage points were imposed on districts where the 1972 Democratic registration difference was about the same—68 percent in Burton's and 54 percent in Mailliard's. The results were to reinforce Burton's Democraticness and diminish Mailliard's Republicanism, as their congressional roll call votes during the 1960s demonstrate in table 9. When a Democratic president sat in the White House, Burton strongly supported presidential programs generally, domestic and foreign policies specifically, as well as his own party's and bipartisan programs. When a Republican sat in the White House, however, Burton's support fell off sharply for all programs that were initiated there, while he still stood with his own party on most votes.

Mailliard, on the other hand, was a man under cross-pressures. His district looked Republican in status terms, but its registration was Democratic and it voted for liberal Democrats in other contests. So he had reason to fend off his national party's more conservative center and to support it less than Burton supported his party's liberal center. The Republican did support more presidential programs coming from Nixon than from Johnson, but the switch was not as abrupt as Burton's; in foreign policy the two were not too unlike. The cross-pressure effect in table 9 is best seen in Mailliard's less than half-hearted support of the conservative coalition (actually below his party's norm) and of his own party's voting stands. Even this effort to find a middle way out was not enough to keep his district support form falling off, from 73 percent in 1968 to 53 percent in 1970—although it recovered to almost 55 percent in 1972. His continuing support of the Vietnam War accounted for much of this, given San Francisco's reputation as a major antiwar center in the nation. But he could also support about one-third of both the Great Society legislation of 1965 and later programs that Burton supported.[33]

Local and national constituency influences are thus not always the same.[34] For Burton they are reinforcing and hence make him a strong liberal, but for Mailliard they conflict at numerous points and make him a moderate. But in both cases, it should be noted, the congressmen

TABLE 9
San Francisco Congressmen's Policy and Party Support Records,
1965–1969

Roll Call Measure	Democrat Burton		Republican Mailliard	
	Sup.	*Opp.*	*Sup.*	*Opp.*
Overall Presidential Support or Opposition (%)				
89th Congress	84	8	51	32
90th Congress	81	13	63	27
Year 1969	47	36	67	20*
Domestic Policy Support or Opposition (%)				
89th Congress	83	9	46	37
90th Congress	81	13	57	32
Year 1969	45	38	63	23*
Foreign Policy Support or Opposition (%)				
89th Congress	88	2	72	14
90th Congress	83	13	93	3
Year 1969	60	20	100	0
Larger Federal Role Policies (N = 23)				
89th Congress	22	1	10	11
Conservative Coalition Support or Opposition (%)				
89th Congress	0	92	43	41
90th Congress	1	94	45	41
Year 1969	13	78	36	33
Party Unity (Support or Opposition Own Party, %)				
89th Congress	89	3	49	34
90th Congress	92	2	45	36
Year 1969	78	13	48	30*
Bipartisan Score (Support or Opposition Bills Supported by Majorities in Both Parties, %)				
89th Congress	75	20	77	5
90th Congress	71	21	80	6
Year 1969	60	25	80	2*

SOURCE: *Congressional Quarterly Almanac*, 1966, 1969.
* Not eligible for all votes this session.

are not fully autonomous. Burtons hears but a single voice when district and national party speak, but Mailliard hears two voices. Isolating the national influence on Burton's actions would be difficult, for the interests of the two levels are so similar. But the national influence in

Mailliard's case is more clearly visible, as his record suggests efforts to satisfy both. This can work until one issue—in this case a war—becomes highly visible and is opposed by the district but which the representative must support in order to stand with his national party. The result could only be that large amounts of his local support must fall off. For Burton, the requirements of responsiveness and responsibility are easy to meet because local and national influences run parallel, although they are hard to separate. For Mailliard, these two requirements are difficult matters because the two influences, although easy to sort out, sometimes run counter. When reapportionment in 1973 moved large blocs of poor neighborhoods into his district, he decided to leave Congress and was replaced by liberal Democrat John Burton.

The Case of Supervisors

Whatever may be the effect of different city bases on the congressmen, a different context exists when supervisors run at large. Here winners emerge from the same boundaries but are supported by diverse social strata, which raises a question: To which signals do the elected feel responsive? Any election raises this question, but note as an example the supervisor elections of 1965 in table 10, which ranks the five winners in the thirteen major districts sketched in figure 3 of chapter 2.

Two patterns exist there: one was ranked either equally (Peter Tamaras, William Blake, and Roger Boas) or differently (Joseph Tinney and Jack Morrison) among all districts. Each set raises different problems of maintaining responsibility to those districts. For those districts ranking a candidate equally, it is fair to conclude that no one district could lay any special claim on him. Put in another way, if all districts, with their differing compositions and hence different policy preferences, support him, how can he be responsive and responsible to *all* of them?[35]

Tamaras and Morrison raise different problems. Morrison ran well and Tamaras poorly in the Western Addition with its black ghetto, and they reversed standings in the more affluent districts of the Richmond and the Sunset. We might therefore conclude that different social sectors of the city respond to the candidate differently and that this difference can be translated responsibly into voting differences by their representatives. However, that easy conclusion is marred by two other observations. The relative standing of the two was equal among other districts, which were neither poor nor rich. Tamaras could look

TABLE 10

Rank Order of Supervisors Elected in 1965 According to
Votes Cast in Thirteen Districts

	Tamaras	*Tinney*	*Blake*	*Morrison*	*Boas*
Outer Richmond	1	2	3	5	4
Richmond	1	4	2.5	5	2.5
Marina	2	1	3	5	4
Russian Hill–North Beach	1	3	2	4	5
Western Addition	4	5	2	1	3
Buena Vista	2	5	1	3.5	3.5
Mission	2	1	3	4	5
Potrero–Bernal	1	2.5	4	2.5	5
Bayshore	1	4	3	2	5
Outer Mission	1	2	3	4	5
West of Twin Peaks	2	1	4	3	5
Sunset	1	2	3	4	5
Downtown–South of Market	1	4	2.5	2.5	5
Total city	1	2	3	4	5

SOURCE: Calculated from "The Political Anatomy of the City: An Election Study," *San Francisco Business*, July/August, 1966, M6-7.

at his votes and conclude that, because he was first choice almost regardless of these district differences, there was no special claim on him from any one district or social segment. Boas could conclude much the same from his consistently low standing in the same districts. Interpreted in this light, while differing life styles evoke different demands upon the political system, these could be interpreted pretty much as a representative wishes. That is particularly true when as a close observer has noted, "The two front runners opposed nothing and took no strong stands." [36] Even if those elected could detect constituency differences which should affect their behavior, this is far from responding to demands of the *total* population, because so few participate in these elections. In 1965 the winning supervisors obtained the votes of 49–60 percent of those registered; but these represented only 18–23 percent of San Franciscans over twenty-one years of age, and only 14–17 percent of the total population.[37]

The whole picture demonstrates the salient characteristics of the local arena of California politics: limited interparty competition for office, limited alternatives for voters, and as the most likely result, low voter interest. Interest varies by status here as elsewhere, for those

disadvantaged by the existing distribution of resources are least interested in electoral channels. With a diffuse system one gets diffuse
candidates. It is hard to see any "mandate" to govern when the two
front runners in 1965 were a Republican and a Democrat and the
ethnic representation of the winners, in order, was Greek, Irish, Irish,
English, and Jewish, with the losing runner-up an Irishman. Because of
historical and outside influences imposed on the city, party qua party
said nothing about local issues—of which there were many—while
candidates said only a little more. And all of this transpired in a campaign where each man pursued his own course in securing his nomination (by petition), in mobilizing voters, and in presenting issues. Little
wonder that the vote differentials among the winners in most districts
was quite small.[38] In short, beneath the façade of nonpartisanship in
local politics in San Francisco is an atomized electoral function basically unrelated to party activity, despite the existence of individual
partisans. Moreover, this city's citizens prefer this structureless context, to judge from the failure of recent referenda seeking to alter at-
large elections to the board. In November 1973, only about 35 percent
voted to replace it with a district election system.* At the same time,
however, 53 percent agreed to substitute a runoff election in the contest for mayor for the plurality system in existence for forty years.

THE 1967 MENDELSOHN CAMPAIGN
AND PARTY FUNCTIONS

Even if party does not perform these major functions, they do not go
untended. Because at least two—nomination and voter mobilization
—are crucial to his survival, the candidate must perform them in any
political system. "Here," one veteran political reporter said, "party is
the tail of the candidate and not the other way around." In effect,
electoral politics reflects another aspect of the city's coalitional
dynamic, noted throughout this book. For here the candidate's basic
strategy is to form a coalition among the party and nonparty groups,
thereby providing the best of a limited set of electoral channels for
local demands. This is illustrated by the campaign of Robert Mendelsohn for supervisor in 1967.

---

* The level of a precinct's opposition and its status were closely associated, except
among blacks. Among the poorest blacks (Hunter's Point), the reform carried only
two precincts; Alioto's supporters here were used to opposing it. However, among
Portrero Hill blacks, it carried eight precincts and got 40–50% in ten others.

Background Conditions

As a political science product of the University of California at Berkeley, Mendelsohn sought a bridge from academia to politics in a private foundation studying San Francisco's problems. His report on the city's Redevelopment Agency led to his joining it for community relations work, which put him in close contact with ethnic problems. Several years later he joined the staff of State Senator J. Eugene McAteer, representing him in the city while he was in Sacramento, building knowledge of both political worlds. After three years of this political education, he was ready in the spring of 1967 to organize McAteer's coalition for mayor, then regarded as a certain victory. Mendelsohn's task was to extend the senator's conservative Irish base into the liberal community with which the younger man had worked in CDC, "good government," and ethnic groups. This massive coalition, if formed, would have been a base for even higher office, given McAteer's moderate record, personality, group support, and so forth. In May 1967 the senator had a fatal heart attack, and the coalition flew asunder. Part of it reshaped behind Joseph Alioto, a relative unknown in city politics, despite a brilliant legal career and service on the school board. But part of it also supported Mendelsohn for supervisor, after he had spent a few days considering his chances. He assembled much of this coalition and ran his own campaign, the details of which tell much about the partyless milieu of San Francisco.

Mendelsohn benefited, in a sad way, from the death of McAteer, and in a fortuitous way from the fact that the board of supervisors was in political trouble. For what it considered good and sufficient reasons, the board had recommended that the legislature act to increase assessments. This not only was a gratuitous recommendation, but like most unsolicited advice, it brought down local wrath. One incumbent supervisor was under strong fire from the *Examiner* for his liberalism and from others for his alliance with Burton. Another was having health problems and was often absent. A third's support from old-line politicians was criticized by the CDC. These vulnerable incumbents were suddenly confronted with a few strong, attractive candidates among the mob of forty-four who needed to secure only ten signatures on a petition and to post $30 to be nominated. Mendelsohn, considering these factors over the weekend after McAteer's death and consulting other supporters of the senator, decided to run.

The Making of a Coalition

In the campaign, the key to Mendelsohn's success was the assembling of support from as many nonparty groups as possible. New to the voters, he could not rely on incumbency or even on a distinctive ethnicity with many voters. While the Burton faction did not closely support him, neither did it oppose him; Mendelsohn did obtain the congressman's personal support, however, because of Mendelsohn's ties with the CDC. Of the then nine CDC groups, he was endorsed by six, but he also went to Republican meetings, playing the nonpartisan theme. Further, he sought "good government" sponsors, relying on his earlier foundation work. He also sought ethnic endorsement, making sure that his organization was as ethnically representative as possible.[39]

Then there were the group endorsements. In San Francisco there are a host of nonpolitical groups which, as a regular practice, endorse local candidates. Neighborhood improvers, businessmen, various ethnic boosters, (including the grand-slam Irish-Israeli-Italian Society) conservationists, civil rights protectors—all proliferate in the diverse interests of an urban society. In the mid-1960s homosexuals began reviewing candidates for endorsement, seeking their views on civil rights. Many groups are politicized, working on endorsements, local referenda, or legislative hearings. While group endorsement is as characteristic of San Francisco electioneering as eating blintzes in New York or handing out name cards in rural Mississippi, politicos disagree about what difference it makes. It is questionable how much influence the endorsement has when group members are divided over it. Yet, in a milieu where small differences produce a total result in the election—you either win or lose—it is the rare candidate who ignores the practice. At the very least, as liberal Democrat Mendelsohn thought when attending Republican club meetings, it might get a few votes for his very presumption.

Beginning in August, candidates would appear at these meetings for a few minutes chance to declare their virtues. Some endorsements were arranged beforehand, but it was not wise to stay away from even these, as his opponents' advocates in the club could sway the membership. The picture of numerous, hypercharged politicos gathered in an anteroom waiting their turn to speak for three minutes, nervous and smoking, controlled politeness heavier in the air than the smoke—it is all rather reminiscent of college freshmen waiting on the night of fraternity bids.

Mendelsohn's primary objective was simple—to assemble more of these endorsements than anybody else. In this he had the advantage of having taken McAteer around or of representing him to many of these groups in earlier elections. He was not entirely successful, however. He lost the endorsement of the Lafayette Club (conservative but pro-McAteer) because he did not attend the full meeting, thinking the earlier executive committee endorsement would swing it. He lost the Columbus Civic Club (French and Italian interests) when his friends there did not work for the endorsement of the meeting because they thought it certain for Mendelsohn. As a counter, he worked especially hard—and successfully—to corner the Italian-American Federation. Young Democrats were unhappy with his stand on a referendum dealing with the Vietnam War; he ended up with individual but not organizational endorsement from them. Endorsement by the Mexican-American Political Association's executive committee was diluted at the full meeting when he shared it with another candidate.

Yet his files also show many groups that did provide the talismanic endorsement: McAteer's conservative business and Irish supporters; Italians and blacks; "good government" reformers and old-line Democrats who liked the government as it was; the CDC; Jewish societies; neighborhood improvement clubs that usually oppose any change, and the prestigious Civil League of Improvement Clubs and Associations which since 1906 has backed some major changes, including the Golden Gate Bridge; veterans and ministers; and labor, of course. In this listing is visible the mosaic of group life in San Francisco, a virtual reification of much, but not all, of its social structure. The range ran across a wide political gamut between limits of the radical right and left. Republicans and Democrats were represented, some of whom were actually formal members of the party structure. No major ethnic group was omitted, including its factions. Labor and business contributed support, often financial. Conservatives and liberals on human rights were there, along with standpatters and reformers on social policy. That range of support erased Mendelsohn's fears of his Jewishness and his long name, and contributed positive resources of publicity, money, and issues.

The Presentation of Issues

The presentation of issues is a need arising out of the imperatives of a democratic system. If some men are to represent others, they come to be judged in part by their stands on critical issues. Where partisan identification does not exist to provide the represented with some cue to the representative's stand, other cues are sought. In a party void, that can come from others who think alike on salient matters, and in San Francisco such groups abound. But again it is questionable how fully they serve as selection devices for the represented, because many candidates tailor their remarks to the audience before them. This may be democratic control in the form of anticipated reactions, shaped by the candidate's knowledge of group demands, which become policy directives after election. But the variety of issues in any campaign, some ongoing, some ephemeral, gives a candidate considerable option in choosing what to transmit to groups from the list of his views on policy.

Notice how Mendelsohn performed the function of presenting issues. Central to his issue orientation was his tie with the late Senator McAteer; he always insisted that publicity stories and introductions should refer to him as the senator's "former assistant." This central theme was expanded to adopt McAteer's viewpoints, both those known before his death and those he might have held. Mendelsohn and Joseph Alioto, the successful candidate for mayor, worked intimately but separately. While the younger man was Alioto's campaign chairman (primarily honorific), each ran his own campaign on different themes. This was partly because of the different campaign conditions imposed by the varying degree of competition. Alioto was one of three major candidates while Mendelsohn was one of forty-four. The latter could afford less to lose even one group—except those beyond the pale of left and right; in the mosaic of groups, each group constituted for Mendelsohn more of a marginal loss. The overlap of groups represented by these forty-four meant that Mendelsohn had to work harder against more numerous opponents seeking the same group.

Another reason for different strategies lay in the different powers available in the office sought. The mayor has powers that are primarily implicit, few that are strong or clear. He can talk about some issues but not others, get publicity on some but not on others—if they relate to his tenuous power as mayor-to-be. Alioto could talk about reducing "crime in the streets," for the mayor would have some powers over the police department. However, the issue was a highly charged one in the nation's racial crisis, as the phrase was a code to some for "control of blacks." But Alioto used the code, an implicitly tough signal to the whites, while also telling black audiences that *they* were by far the most serious victims of "crime on the streets" and so needed more protection. On the other hand, Mendelsohn steered away from the phrase, partly because supervisors have little formal authority over the police but also because it would alienate the white liberal element he needed. Alioto was not likely to get that group anyhow, since it was attracted in this campaign to a liberal candidate for mayor, Jack Morrison, an old Mendelsohn friend and supporter. Alioto could talk of drawing up a citizen's commission on crime (which he later did, producing some highly critical reports), but Mendelsohn would not have that power as supervisor.

What Mendelsohn did present were carefully chosen issues of both substance and style. Substantive issues were designed in part for their novelty and also because many had no conservative or liberal orientation. Thus, what *kind* of business tax do we need? How *do* you control the flood of rats released by the new subway construction? How *do* we prevent any further deterioration of the bay? But there were also issues of style, matters of how the political authorities should relate to the wants and demands of the public. Thus, Mendelsohn claimed that officials should go out more often to the people to hear their views—let's decentralize City Hall into neighborhood subunits. We need more citizen concern in the problems of the city so that "interests" do not surreptitiously steal everything in sight. And always he was "the former assistant to the late Senator McAteer."

All of this insistence on taking stands on issues (many supporters wanted him to run merely on his having been the senator's assistant) was fitted together in a two–three minute spiel for use at clubs and luncheons and in press stories(they were unusually frequent). He also helped himself by such novelty issues as urging mini-buses for downtown traffic, or by ten-second TV spots concentrated on one station in the last week. His finances were not too difficult; an early fundraising dinner provided one-half of his funds, word of this success was circulated by the press, and others quickly came in to back a likely winner. Much of this went for TV, billboards, and thousands of housefront posters.

On election day, November 7, 1967, he received 102,000 votes, fourth highest in a field of five winners but highest of all who were not incumbents.

Responsiveness, Responsibility, and Coalitional Politics

The most significant aspect of this case study is the coalitional basis of partyless politics in San Francisco. In that same context candidates are compelled to construct quasi-independent campaign instruments and issues. There are limitations on their independence in this coalition building. Certain viewpoints and groups cannot be enlisted, or candidates prefer not to have their kisses—for example, the radical right and left were limitations on even the broad range sought by Mendelsohn. And the problem of finances always limits independents, as does the clash of opposing interests in a hot debate that inhibits the choosing of sides. The very office sought, by its institutional restraints, proscribes what may be honestly promised. When it is said, therefore, that candidates have independent organizations, this applies only to independence from a political party's formal hold.

Nevertheless, candidates for local office are still enmeshed in the total political system's process or group decision making. As Gene Geisler has noted about a similar campaign here,

the campaign or the candidate [are not] outside or independent of the local *political structure* where important decisions are made and of which the party organizations may be separate components of local political structure, using the term . . . to include all elements of the social system which intentionally influence, over time, the allocation of scarce values. In this view, party structure is only a small part of that process and not necessarily always an important part. . . . Decisions of overwhelming importance to his election or reelection—such as resolutions to contribute and support his campaign by friends, newspapers, unions and other financial and interest groups—are generally made in the larger political structure; few serious candidates can successfully function independently from this larger decision-making process.[40]

With such constraints on "independence," some individuals, or their reference groups, have a potential for democratic control, just as they would if effective parties existed in the city. This sweaty pursuit of endorsements from groups big and small, from newspapers, financial supporters and voters at large, is a control mechanism familiar where highly organized parties eixst. That is, both systems involve a pledge for mutual exchange of things of value—a trade-off of votes for promises to protect or enhance some group's income, safety, or deference. Even the "ethnic" candidates, running on the geniality of their Irish names, are implicitly pledging something—primarily deference—to Irish followers. But because no group is currently powerful enough to elect anyone, candidates must reach for more group support and hence seek coalitions.

This, then, is one side of the mutual exchange occurring in elections, which treats responsiveness to the group demands made on candidates. The other side of this exchange is responsibility, the degree to which the promises are kept. To insure it is the task of a few who watch closely, i.e. those more organized in the city's group life, particularly business and labor. But the task is complicated and tiring, even for constant guardians. After an election, new issues arise on which no exchange had been made at campaign time. When Robert Kennedy was assassinated in Los Angeles in June 1968, Mendelsohn dramatically sought a gun control law. But that had not been an issue in his campaign, hence was not the subject of his responsiveness and responsibility to the voters. In a later election, irate gun-owners or pleased gun-haters might work their wills, but that was three years away, and memories and passions fade. To whom is he now responsible in this case?*

A further complication exists in the indefiniteness of the responsiveness cue given by a candidate. If Mendelsohn equivocated on the crime issue for the reasons given earlier, to what action is he being held responsible when it is necessary later to vote on substantive crime control issues? Does he vote against all such issues because of that liberal and ethnic base of support that is suspicious of the police? Or does he support the mayor because that is his responsibility under the charter? Does he "go fishing" when a crucial vote is before the supervisors? These queries illustrate that where candidates take no clear campaign stands, any later judgments about responsibility to their publics are impossible.

Another complication in judging responsibility applies in a party, as well as a partyless, context. What is one to think when the candidate supports many issues, as Mendelsohn did, but when the time of accounting comes around it is found that he achieved some and failed on some, and that on others the results are not yet in? What kind of batting average is necessary to achieve the status of "responsible"? The query is further clouded by the fact that there is no uniform standard for relating hits to times at bat. In the world of politics, one man's hit lowers another man's pitching average, and there are different fans in the stands booing both batter and pitcher. This is a problem not only for the representative but for the represented, who finds his agent now with him and now against him, across an array of issues.

These complications are raised to make two points. First, the coali-

* In 1971 he was reelected, second in votes; a 1974 attempt at state office failed.

tional imperative in partyless politics makes it hard for the candidate
to be either responsive or responsible, even with the best of motives
to be both. The queries raised above are not idle ones, but those he
must live with in campaign and office, and this contributes to the
ambiguity of his task.

The second point is that this nonpartisan politics may well account
for the poor citizen interest in local elections. What is true for the
candidate is true for the voter about the above queries—they create
considerable ambiguity. When this ambiguity is added to the voter's
costs of finding sufficient information to determine responsiveness and
responsibility (the costs are greater when there is no party as a reference group) the incentive to vote is further depressed. When all of this
transpires in the knowledge and emotional map of most Americans,
in which politics is not merely peripheral but sometimes totally off that
map, it is understandable why, as one summary of voting in the Bay
Area concluded, "The voters stay away from the polls in droves." [41]
It also explains why the incumbent has an advantage. Part of this may
stem from positive feedback to voters about his actions since the last
election. But it is equally likely that the "incumbent" label helps to
relieve ambiguity felt by the voter—"Well, at least he knows the job,
and I haven't heard anything bad about him, so I guess he's O.K."

It is not certain that a different local politics with a full party apparatus would ensure greater responsiveness and responsibility. Little
if any research has been addressed to the comparative inquiry of
whether the party or the partyless political system better serves these
two ends. Given the one-party nature of most cities, we could not expect to find many in which two parties compel each other to be more
sensitive to voters for fear of losing elections. Within one-party urban
systems, there exist patterns of control which run from monolithic
(Chicago) to oligarchic (Baltimore) to multi-factional (New York)
to a chaos reminiscent of Hobbes' state of nature, or "war of all against
all." That variety infers patterns of institutional sensitivity which preclude any quick judgment that party life means more responsiveness
and responsibility to demands.

Although this may be a lament for the irretrievable, the party milieu
did perform these functions—nomination, mobilization of voters, presentation of issues, and responsibility for governing—with much less
ambiguity. Parties may have done the job dishonestly and irresponsi-
bly in the eyes of those not benefiting from these lapses. But at least
one knew what group had nominated the rascals, stuffed the ballot

box, stood for the wrong things, and filled their pockets while in office. It is not all that certain that all of these ethical lapses disappear with nonpartisanship. So, asks the voter, why should he contribute—he might make things worse.

The irony, of course, is that Progressivism sought nonpartisanship in order to expand, not contract, citizen participation in political decisions.[42] Yet not only has there been contraction, but participation also operates differentially by class. That is, nonpartisanship produces electoral inputs that are not merely more limited but more enjoyed by those higher on the scale of life opportunities. The historical pressure has contributed to a middle-class urban politics by removing the force of party, with its greater, selfish interest to recruit the poor, than actually develops under nonpartisanship.

In the only contemporary analysis which offers a carefully reasoned argument for strengthening party life at the local level, Hawley has demonstrated how nonpartisanship advantages Democrats more than Republicans in the Bay Area and how it also favors certain kinds of issues against other kinds. He concludes that

party reform offers much to the "have-lesses." . . . We have allowed our parties to atrophy to the point that they are more symbol than substance. Symbols such as these are useful to the stability of established political systems; they are less instrumental to those who favor change.

Certainly, restructuring of our political institutions is no panacea. But the abandonment of the search for a more effective party system seems ill-conceived if one is interested in developing a political system that will engage and resolve a broader range of social conflict.[43]

MANIFEST AND LATENT FUNCTIONS
IN A PARTYLESS CONTEXT

This questioning of the way in which partyless politics affects responsiveness, responsibility, and participation should not ignore the fact that party-like functions are performed. Nominations do take place, issues do appear, voter mobilization is stressed, and, after the last hurrah, governance proceeds. Because these transpire within a larger political context than the party alone, as Geisler points out, the Progressives' passion to reform politics by abolishing party was naïve. The functions are performed, under different auspices to be sure, but nevertheless performed. Corruption may have died out, compared with pre-Progressive days, but that is an uncertain inference about cause and effect. While corruption may take different forms today, its old form is not precluded, as will be seen later in police and assessor scandals in San Francisco and lobbying scandals in Sacramento. After all, independently of party reform, values may have changed about this kind of corruption since the Progressive era. To determine whether nonpartisanship was cause or effect in that change needs empirical study instead of frequent assertion.

While the political system can endure without the parties' *manifest* functions affecting nominations, votes, issues, and government, it may be well to note here the consequences of partyless politics for their *latent* functions. Society must provide outlets for new ideas about the distribution of resources, but the divisiveness that accompanies this function requires alternative methods of holding society together. In democratic nations this function of building consensus has been assisted by parties. Driven by the democratic legitimacy of majority vote, parties must bring segments together to obtain that majority, a process necessitating some compromise. Failure here would bring to power a minority party, often with its innovations.[44] This means imposing on national and state party members a common orientation to public policy—a central characteristic of those who identify with a party.[45] That orientation serves to build a consensus, and the two—or more—parties serve to create division. In San Francisco, division is fostered and consensus is ignored through the city's partylessness.

Parties may not always serve to focus the resources and values of the community on common goals. But without them, such focus may be provided by a dominant interest—most often business—or not at all. If a single, nonparty interest provides the focus, there is an obvious bias about whose issues and interests are served, for which the community pays a special cost. Thus, the frustration and bitterness of those excluded may erupt in ways that threaten the income, safety, and deference of the dominant interests—in gangs, criminality, political corruption, mob action, and so forth. It may even take legitimate forms, as in the rejection of any political authority's largesse—for example, the defeat of bond issues for services more helpful to the disadvantaged. Such "crime" as there is in this reaction (in one sense some crime is a political response to a political monopoly) may be functional for its beneficiaries; it is one—maybe the only—way of adding to their safety, income, and deference.[46] Someone in the community must "pay" for these illicit benefits, however, a cost factor to be weighed by those whose interests are reflected in prevailing political institutions.

The absence of any focusing political mechanism, such as party or a dominant interest, also entails costs. One aspect not yet made explicit is that the coalition which springs up in the absence of party involves an inordinate expenditure of resources because of the duplication of effort. In partyless life it is hard to form coalitions but easier to run in splendid, pure, ideological isolation. Mendelsohn's effort to reach out so broadly was not the norm for every candidate; instead, candidates usually sought fewer of the relatively satisfied who were concerned more with maintaining, rather than changing, conditions. Even then, Mendelsohn did not reach for support from the radical right or left, who after all represent those most interested in drastic change.

Another latent function that parties may serve, but cannot in the partyless context, is the recruitment of political leaders. On this measure, Lee found by the end of the 1950s that nonpartisanship provided " 'about average' ability and integrity of elected public officials." [47] The question is not like that in consensus building, which is: Is the job done at all under partyless politics? Instead the question is: How well it is done? After all, nominees for public office come forward under any political system, whether monarchy or direct democracy.

However, determining the quality of leadership is not easy. There is a high degree of honesty among San Francisco officials, and even those observers most inclined to criticize inadequacies in government nevertheless agreed on its honesty. But if another measure of the quality of leadership is its adaptability to new demands on the political system, another judgment may be had. As we shall see, the mass of city employees, the bureaucracy of urban life, feel no responsibility to such new demands. In a government dominated by clerks, the first organizational imperative is the maintenance of procedure; that is not only a legal and professional responsibility, it also best protects one's progress through the system. But new claims on government create stress because by their very nature they challenge maintenance of those policies and procedures.

Lack of sensitivity in a bureaucracy has many causes, of course, but it is not improved when bureaucrats know no party system to hold them accountable for accommodating to new political demands. Obviously, American society has decided for many decades now that such sensitivity will *not* be required. Party has been separated from city employment, and within the bureaucracy there have developed job safeguards that make firing even the most inept civil servant the eleventh task of Hercules.[48] Further, even in American cities with a more vigorous and disciplined party life than San Francisco knows, much of administrative work also goes untouched by party controls. Thus the criticism of local officials for resistance to new demands is not distinctive to the partyless context but more characteristic of bureaucracy everywhere. Yet the city's nonpartisan elections remove even the possibility of a party acting through elected officials to impose a responsive program, in unified fashion, on the bureaucracy. When only a coalition exists to elect one man and it dissolves during his term because he cannot please all its components, this system cannot touch bureaucracy nor can voters hold responsible those groups that put him in. All of it dissipates like San Francisco's summer fog in the morning sun, and the remaining streamers are just as hard to pin down.

In all this, party life in San Francisco reflects its ties to historical forces in the state's political culture. A history of past decisions still affects how the political process is conducted, who participates in it, and what its products are. That historical force contributes to the difficulty of citizens in using that political process to enforce responsiveness and responsibility on political authorities. Filled with issues of limited relevance, with little meaning in its furious activity, the electoral process of partyless politics does little to stir the interest of San Franciscans in their leaders and government.

The studied ambiguity of these manifest functions are matched by that surrounding the latent functions of party activity. There is much variation, stemming from material and symbolic differences in group life, in how well these latent functions are handled. Judgments of effectiveness vary with the group that judges. This is particularly true when we ask how adequately the political system performs functions other than building consensus and selecting leaders. Thus, how well does it distribute scarce resouces? The president of a major bank has one answer, the leader of ghetto blacks or Chicanos yet another. How well does it socialize citizens to appropriate beliefs and actions in the political system? These two spokesmen view in different ways the political action of demonstrations, boycotts, and violence. Or, how well does the political system ultimately contribute to its own legitimacy? Banker and black are given to describing as "immoral" what others judge to be proper.

Such different perceptions of how well the political system performs are inadequate without an exploration of how San Francisco's governing institutions receive demands and convert private preference into public policy. To that task we now turn.

PART III

THE MOBILE OF GOVERNANCE

OATH OF THE YOUNG MEN OF ATHENS

We will revere and obey the city's laws and do our best to incite a like respect and reverence in those above us who are prone to annul or set them at naught; we will strive unceasingly to quicken the public's sense of civic duty. Thus in all these ways we will transmit this city not only not less but greater, better and more beautiful than it was transmitted to us.

CHAPTER 5

The Historical Imprint
on the Present Governance

The political system is more than governing organs, for it involves links to other social systems. Yet for a truly political perspective, formal government provides the key to an understanding of the political system. It is this system which is the object of political demands for relief from stress existing in the social and physical environment. It is this system which converts some inputs into public policy by the interaction of political authorities. And it is these outputs which determine the system's sensitivity to societal crisis and its ultimate ability to persist. A central element in this system is the formal government, and it is this which we examine in the following chapters as part of the larger decisional context of San Francisco. The guiding theme is that over time different values have shaped the designs and actions of governance. In each period there was a distinct mixture of three major values: the insuring of honesty, competency, and adaptability in government. "Honesty" involved the blocking of efforts by individuals to enrich themselves in a manner the community disapproved. "Competency" charged governing officials to act both equitably and efficiently in dispensing benefits to the community. Finally, "adaptability," the most complex, sought to provide institutions capable of responding to special urban demands for new benefits based on new ideas.

These three elements are conceived here as constraining values within which the political system must operate. Governing arrangements to ensure these values arise from community demands generated by frustration, anger, or revulsion against existing governance. In another perspective, each value is the cause of a crisis which is transmitted through the political system to cause new arrangements to be written into the basic contracts between authorities and community. At any one time, conflict over one value dominates, as the others are either secondary or only latent. The three are not always reinforcing, indeed, may be contradictory.

These considerations are developed below where the history of the city is seen as reflecting shifting priorities among these values of honesty, competency, and adaptability. This chapter demonstrates the course of the first two over time and the force of their historical development on the current political system. The next chapter explores the contemporary crisis of governance—the ability of that system to adapt to new group demands.

In portraying any government, it is well to emphasize that the evidence offered of its nature is shaped in part by what one sees. Of course there is documentary evidence, a formal constitution or charter, often of unconscionable length. Then there is also a much larger set of charter implementations (ordinances, court decisions, administrative regulations), as well as similar instruments provided by state and federal law. However, evidence of governance may also be found in the characteristic interactions of the political authorities. Both the documentary and the interactional evidence are partial, although interlinked, pieces of the full picture. There must be documents to set the larger grants and boundaries of governmental authority. But what men may do is not what they will do, so an understanding of the formal grants of government requires illumination of grantees' behavior. Several significant case studies later serve that purpose. But behavioral evidence is also incomplete, because what one sees as "characteristic" behavior is the result of one's vantage point in the political system and of one's values concerning what is seen. Particularly in the large cities, there are few if any who can view all of what transpires and hence who can precisely define the "normal" interactional system. The whole is not known by even the "insiders" —veteran officeholders, newspapermen, lobbyists—whose account of "reality" is often contradictory.

Consequently, these chapters employ both documentary and behavioral evidence of governance but with the clear warning that only basic patterns are developed. The patterns of past governments in San Francisco are incomplete because the data are only documentary, albeit buttressed by an occasional event unusual enough to make the newspapers. In the recent period, while there are more data, the problem of perceiving everything must be kept in mind. Yet this caution should be laid alongside the findings in chapter 3 that there is wide agreement among the city's observers concerning the main qualities of contemporary governance. Not the least of these qualities is the press of history on the current scene in a particularly dramatic fashion.

THE GROUP VALUE BASIS OF LOCAL GOVERNANCE

Only in the banalities of civics books are institutions of government unrelated to the values of the groups that are governed, for in reality those institutions either inhibit or enhance group values. Local government in the United States has gone through successive waves of attachment to particular institutions, and in each there is reflected some predominant value. Elements of these still inhere in community decision making, so a brief historical review is in order.

The Republic began with an attachment to concepts of British local governance, with the executive primarily ceremonial and the councilmen dominant; only some of these were elected, for only one-third of the then few cities used elections.[1] There was little evidence of popular control, since suffrage was limited and the common councilmen selected aldermen from their membership. After the Revolution, control over state constitutions and charters passed to state legislatures, which assumed that they had full power, including that over city governments; this domination lasted throughout the nineteenth century. That control was augmented by the development of a characteristically American practice of government drawn from Jacksonian philosophy.[2] Central to this was the importance of the common man and his ability to govern himself. From this came the expansion of the ballot by elimination of such restrictions as ownership of property. From this popular sovereignty it followed that officials should be elected rather than appointed, since elections guaranteed a more effective check on the use of political power imposed on the common man. As a consequence, there developed in local government the long ballot, domination by a large council, and the subordination of a weak mayor.

But over the nineteenth century the development of local parties and strong bosses took popular sovereignty in directions inimical to the values and interests of some groups while benefiting others.[3]

Protest, stemming mostly from middle-class businessmen abetted by intellectuals, stimulated political reform movements across the country around the turn of the century. The central charge was that the promises of Jacksonianism had been perverted into benefits for corrupt business and political leaders. Implicit in this struggle, and often made quite overt, was an ethnic-religious controversy. The "corrupt" boss represented the ethnic groups emergent at the time, often Irish and German, while the protesting reformers were more often "old stock"; that the former were often Roman Catholic and the latter Protestant heavily reinforced the ethnic rivalry. What was "corruption" to the established white, Protestant, middle class were the "benefits" an ethnic boss extended to his followers as he redistributed city resources to those without them. The former group, themselves recipients of benefits from a much earlier allocation of values, viewed the redistribution not merely as a threat to their power—which it was—but as immoral, a judgment that merely tended to heighten the normal group conflict.

Each of the two contenders, then, supported alternative forms of relating the citizenry to political power. The ethnic boss had a basis of power in the major resource of his supporters' numbers, who required extensive and decentralized organization and wide representation.[4] Selection to office was not merely a matter of securing the votes —ethnic leaders could almost always guarantee that. Rather, loyalty to the organization and its ethnic base was the prime criterion for selection to greater responsibilities and rewards. On the other hand, honesty and efficiency were criteria of only feeble importance. If the result meant that some individuals and groups benefited especially, and if opponents preferred to call this "graft," that set of violated norms was meaningless in the defense of one's own group.[5] For the ethnic boss, therefore, local institutions were preferred which were more sensitive to the resource of loyal numbers—thus the preference for the long ballot, the large council, easy enfranchisement, fragmented administrative services, and the absence of corrupt-practices acts.

The major resource of the old-stock, ethnic leaders, however, most often was in money, so they gave primacy to the values of efficiency and economy in a government that would least restrict that resource base. Of course, they could not restrict suffrage, but they could restrict its targets—thus their support of the short ballot and of city services removed from direct electoral control. Their reform proposals also stressed strong-mayor or city-manager plans as well as integrated administration, with each bureau responsible ultimately to department heads and through them to a single executive. This faith in efficiency and distrust in parties changed local government drastically as the result of a reform movement which agitated the American scene for many decades and with considerable success.

In the over half a century since the climax of that movement, the scope of problems and the number of groups generating demands on local government have altered immensely. A consequent change has taken place in the way in which urban decisions are made, particularly in the biggest cities. Many of the elements of that change as it has taken place in San Francisco will concern us in the chapters that follow. The thrust of that analysis will be to answer for San Francisco whether there is truth in the proposition advanced by Charles Adrian and Charles Press that "the municipality has not ceased to be a decision-making center, but it no longer makes its decisions alone, and the decisions that emerge are increasingly based on the policy goals of professional administrators rather than of amateur grass-roots leaders." [6]

City government has had other purposes than providing a framework for popular sovereignty or ethnic conflict. Oliver Williams and Adrian have suggested that urban Americans have four views of the functions of local government, all of which intersect in San Francisco.[7] It may be "an instrument of community growth," which contributes thereby to "progress." So in San Francisco this boosterism is reflected in those with an economic share in urban affairs—merchants, editors, Chambers of Commerce, and some bureaucrats. Others see another purpose, "the provider of life's amenities," and for them the highest goal is comfort, protection, and the use of public money to facilitate the good life. In San Francisco this is implicit in the outlook of supporters of culture, conservation, and natural beauty.

Others view city government as a "caretaker," doing the absolute minimum—which also means the least in costs and hence taxes. Other functions should remain in the private realm, otherwise heavy financial burdens would fall on marginal incomes or on neighborhoods that already have adequate services. In San Francisco this is the outlook of fixed-income retirees and taxpayer groups, particularly middle-income homeowners. Finally, some see local government as an "arbiter of conflicting interests," charged to resolve conflict over the allocation of scarce resources. Government, in this view, is to maintain rules that guarantee all interests access to the arena and that make local government an umpire. In San Francisco, as elsewhere, this view is often expounded. But the reality suggests that its proponents often complain of a neutral arbitration when it decides against them. Of course, these images overlap in any one place, except possibly the very smallest towns. But normally there are spokesmen for each perspective, and very often the conflict over a substantive policy is at root a conflict over these purposes.

So, in San Francisco, values regarding government must be judged in terms of the contributions of the past. During the past, shifting priorities concerning those values and alterations in group dominance interacted to change particular institutions. Throughout this history, though, community efforts to achieve honesty, competency, and adaptability were motivating forces overriding particular issues and events. This historical influence is the concern of the remainder of this chapter.

CONTRIBUTIONS OF THE PAST TO PRESENT GOVERNANCE

Early Government, Legitimate and Otherwise

While San Francisco is governed today by a charter adopted in 1932, it bears the marks of earlier efforts.[8] The catalyst of the gold strike started a long period of adapting local government to a new urban form and making it competent. The city's first government after incorporation in 1850 consisted of a council of sixteen elected by wards, and numerous executives elected at large, all serving for one year. The 1850 act clearly made the council the central organ, under little restraint except the requirement of annual elections. As long as a councilman could satisfy his ward, little else in the charter could hold him. For eighty years there ensued a struggle to make this agency a competent, honest, and flexible instrument of local democracy. The failure to do so was responsible for many of the limitations on the council in the present charter. In keeping with the then prevailing conditions—with local government doing more than government at the state or federal levels—there was an array of powers granted to legislate and license, to regulate and fine, to protect and prevent. These powers, reaching over the barriers of intervening charters, were the ancestors of many still operating in the city today.* If this first government lacked constraints, it did not lack problems. The first mayors told the council of the need to

---

* An exception is the now lost power "to regulate the weight, quality, and price of bread" (Act of Incorporation, 1850, Article 3), an interference with free enterprise which has roots in colonial New England.

build more wharves, to establish wells and cisterns on public squares and fire reserves in reservoirs on the Bay, to erect market places, to remove garbage from the street, to organize a police force, to light the city at night by street lamps, to decrease the amount spent on the sick and destitute, $80,000 having been extended in nine months, and to recognize the importance of the permanent grad[ing] of streets.[9]

Ironically, most of these are still the goals of modern mayors, except that they seek *more* for the "sick and destitute." However, contemporary efforts in the city to improve the port, create major trading centers, provide better slum garbage removal, improve police resources to fight "crime in the streets"—all echo today the needs of twelve decades ago.

But in those early days the fumbling efforts at new government did little to deal with those problems, for there was a recurring search for an effective structure. The 1850 charter was replaced in 1851 and 1853, and the state legislature in 1856 mandated a new one, which lasted through the romanticized and corrupt years of the city's history until another charter in 1879. Obvious dissatisfaction with that one and its attendant corruption led to four reform efforts over the next two decades, with success in 1898; that charter lasted until the adoption of the present charter in 1932. The details of these struggles to find a document that was honest, competent, and adaptable are not important here. What is significant is the manner in which they reflect the nature of the developing community and how the failure of each contributed to the next.

San Francisco came almost fully born into our history, without the benefits of experience and with its economy and population exploding in a social vacuum. These qualities were pinpointed by the San Francisco *Daily Herald* of that day. "The hamlet has sprung into a city—five hundred inhabitants have swelled to thirty thousand; the solitary coaster in the harbor has given place to a fleet of five hundred sails; the muddy, sandy beach has yielded to a network of wharves, and all this change in three years." [10] Streets were bogs, where garbage lay stinking and uncollected, and rats rippled everywhere. Many transients, including the feared Australian convict criminals ("Sydney Ducks"), moved in and out with little attachment to San Francisco or its laws. In this social maelstrom the understaffed, underpaid, and less than competent officials were simply swamped. Moreover, civic corruption emerged in associations formed openly to sell members' votes to the highest bidder, and in groups of men marching about the city on election day voting "early and often." Such inefficiency and corruption persisted in the police and in the courts, despite loud complaints by newspapers.

There were several collective efforts to meet such problems, and not all were legal. A half-century before the initiative, referendum, and recall, San Franciscans developed another means of direct intervention in bad governance, and thereby gave the word *vigilante* to the American language.[11] Through the haze of much romantic writing, we can make out certain common features of this and later vigilantism. First, it was precipitated by fears for life and property, initiated by prominent citizens, and justified on the grounds of the breakdown of legitimate authority. The public was frightened by an outburst of violent crime for which the transients were blamed. But if law protection was bad, law enforcement was worse—for example, from 1849 to 1856 there were about a thousand murders but only seven executions. During thirteen months alone, of 184 persons who had been arrested, at the end of this period only 7 were in jail; however, 61 were acquitted, 21 escaped, 40 skipped bail, 7 were discharged, 6 died, and 2 were pardoned.[12] For many this was evidence of the corruptness of courts and police; at the very least, the jails seemed somewhat insecure.

A second point of this amateur governance is that far from being a furtive, hooded mob, the vigilantes and their lynchings were well publicized; indeed, information on culprits was solicited through newspaper advertisements.[13] While all this had popular approval as well as upper-class leadership, it was also denounced by men of equally high standing as a violation of constitutional safeguards. The latter were right, of course, for history has condemned the action in the bad connotation the modern era puts on the word *vigilante*.

The actions of the vigilantes during two outbursts of the 1850s need not concern us in detail, except to note that they dealt directly with a problem in which established government had failed. Police were simply shoved aside as the city's respectable citizens formed teams to arrest, hear, and execute, with the result that scores died on the end of a rope with no pretense at a trial. Outside authorities were helpless; the state militia would not obey the governor's request to stop the activity, and his subsequent request to President Franklin Pierce for use of the regular military was denied. However, after ten weeks in 1856, the committee did disband,* in the belief that the regular police could then handle affairs. They left behind the ominous threat of rebirth, and a reminder. When a political system becomes insensitive enough to demands for basic competency, citizens may restructure that system on an ad hoc basis.

Vigilantism was not the norm, of course, in these early efforts to create effective governance. Parallel to this illegal course, citizens were seeking a basic charter for government—recall that there were four of these between 1850 and 1856. In provisions of these and subsequent documents, the problems of establishing an honest, competent, and adaptable government are visible. Again, details are not important, but the highlights will demonstrate that achieving these three values took a long time.

Through these four charters, increasing attention was paid to limiting dishonesty by specifying official powers and duties and by electing more officials. Mayors, councilmen (supervisors after 1856), police, controllers, and other administrators found in successive charters that less discretion was given to them in the exercise of power. Financial matters became more detailed and hedged by requirements; limitations on taxes and expenditures became stringent and numerous, and a controller was created in 1853 to authorize and account for all spending. From an elective mayor and council totaling seventeen men, in six years there were thirty legislative and administrative offices which voters filled, including the harbor master and directors of neighborhood schools.[14] All of this, joined to the vigilantism, highlights the fact that honesty was the prime value for these citizens, with competency in the matter of law and order close behind.

Thereafter, from 1856 to 1879, the city struggled through successive crises generated by the Civil War,† economic booms in mining and agriculture, the struggle to develop a local social structure, and a rampant corruption in government aided and abetted by business giants. The threat of renewed vigilantism (former members acted as an informal political party to screen police officials and

---

* The city took a holiday to witness the ceremony of disbandment, including a procession of over 5,000 vigilantes, companies of artillery, and the police themselves.
† The city's first riot came when the news of Lincoln's assassination caused a mob to wreck Southern sympathizer newspaper offices.

their operations) kept violent crime under control, but funds for other services either were skimpy or drained away into civic corruption. Many charter changes seemed to assume that all corruption lay with the availability of money to officials, thereby ignoring the great source of corruption in the power to grant permits to do business in the city. Nevertheless, limitations on urban finances were installed. Tax cuts did little more than reduce services; school enrollment, gas for streetlights, and street repairs became victims of this attempt to deal with honesty at the expense of competence.

Whether under a home rule charter or a legislative charter, dishonesty and incompetence simply got out of hand, while the only adaptability to be found was that of the formal structures to the corruptive influences of party and business. As scholars have pointed out, under bosses Buckley and Ruef the municipal authority to grant franchises and set rates for public utilities became a source of gold well removed from the Sierra.[15] Boss control of the party permitted control of the election of a majority of the councilmen and hence control of their formal actions. Bribes to the boss went back to councilmen for favorable franchises and rates. Such transactions were hard to prove in court, of course, so that graft became not only widespread but almost invulnerable to attack. In short, formal government requirements seemed allied with, if not a cause of, the prevalent corruption and inadequate services.

Municipal Reform and the Ruef Scandals

Consequently, in San Francisco and elsewhere across urban America, an extended campaign got under way to root out the evil by changing the formal requirements—in short, municipal reform. In 1880, 1882, 1887, and 1896 local efforts to adopt new ideas about government were mounted, but they failed. These efforts were local signs of a national battle whose passions are hard to grasp now, although they still burn strongly in this and other cities. But in those years many middle-class Americans saw the promise of democracy frustrated in public and private by those whose greed blinded them to the common good. The "urban crisis" of that day was the lack of honesty and competency, the repair of which meant abandoning old urban forms for new ones along the lines of the modern corporation, with clear assignment of responsibility and power.[16]

There appeared in San Francisco many of the reform movement's proposals: centralization of administrative power; coordination of departments by abolishing independent boards and placing them under the mayor; restriction of the council to legislative activities only; substitution of civil service for the spoils system; election of fewer offices, the better to fix responsibility. When members of the Good Government Club of San Francisco in 1895 urged such changes, they saw their principles as self-evident truths: "It conduces to efficiency. It saves money. It makes public life more attractive to the honorable and capable, and offers fewer opportunities to the corrupt and incapable. It destroys Bossism at a blow for it removes the patronage which is the life of the Boss. It purifies elections. Its theory is thoroughly democratic." [17] Yet despite references to experience in other cities, they gave little evidence that these changes had elsewhere reduced corruption and inefficiency or created a government more responsive to popular will. But they were not seeking evidence—hard facts are ill adapted to moral crusades.

When San Franciscans finally ratified a new charter in 1898, it was clear that the reformers had won. The document included combinations of reform for honesty and competence: initiative and referendum (pioneered here); a board of supervisors barred from administration, their budgets checked by a mayor's veto; a mayor appointing fewer officers; fewer elective officials; departmental reorganization; city contracts to be let only to the lowest bidder; the beginnings of a municipal budget and a civil service system. While not adopting all the national movement's provisions, there is an innocence about these barriers against misuse of power, this detailing of the biblical injunction "Put not your trust in princes." For this new government became the springboard for the biggest political scandal in the city's history—Boss Abe Ruef. In an era when "the shame of the cities" was the prevalent liaison between politicians and businessmen for corrupt purposes, the San Francisco story is noteworthy only for the extraordinary volume of testimony published about Ruef's operations, so ably analyzed by Walton Bean.[18] There followed almost four hundred indictments, but while Ruef went to jail, only a few officials and no businessmen went, because of acquittals or reversals.

The series of events were gaudy and involved, but it is sufficient here merely to note that the relationship between this corruption and local governance was much the same as in prereform days under Boss Buckley. Franchise and rates had to be authorized by some political authority, and whoever it was, Ruef had appointed him as a result of having captured control of the dominant party and having elected the mayor. Bribes greased the way around reform obstacles, patronage continued to provide the strength in government and party operations, and businessmen worked with the prevailing system. The later exposé stimulated the Progressive movement in the state—its main leader, Hiram Johnson, prosecuted Ruef—and subsequent state law constrained such massive corruption.

One conclusion to be drawn from this set of charter reforms is that the effort to ensure honesty, and to some degree competency, was not effective until the intervention of an external force into the community made it possible. The systematic looting of the city by the union of party leaders with businessmen and others did not stop just because of locally based charter reform. Ruef had made a mockery of those earnest concerns by actually beginning as part of the reform movement and later distorting its victory of 1898.

While great gains were made in the search for municipal honesty, it still left to local authorities the continuing quest for both competency and adaptability. It was the failure of the 1898 charter to accomplish the latter, not its failure with dishonesty, that led in 1932 to a new form of government. Yet there lingered even at that later date a community recollection of rampant corruption which would shape thinking about the new charter.

THE PRESENT CHARTER

The Beginning

As early as 1916, the state's Real Estate Board held conferences on reform, leading to creation of the local Bureau of Governmental Research, which for the next fifteen years generated discussion of reform. Through the 1920s there were civic conferences, with business most visible and vocal, demanding special reforms which were to appear later. One observer of the 1932 reform found its roots in the increasing discontent among business and professional groups.[19] They claimed that city government lacked the competence to provide amenities because of insufficient centralization in the executive office. Note that this group's particular demand runs through all talk of reform from the nineteenth century to today, despite the fact that Buckley and Ruef had provided full executive centralization. Another source of discontent was the fact that, by 1929, 425 sections of the 1898 charter remained intact, but another 105 had been amended and 89 added. "It resembles an old sheet-iron stove patched with pieces of tomato can fastened on with haywire," charged the San Francisco *Examiner* in 1930 when calling for reform.[20] The complaint was of the increasing inappropriateness of the charter for a city adjusting to social and political change. Adaptability was thus becoming a more pressing need than ever before, although the need for honesty and competency abided.

After some dispute over the method of reform,[21] the board of supervisors voted in 1930 for a fifteen-member charter revision committee; business, labor, city workers, and ethnic groups all provided representatives. The key issue was the executive's power and his relationship to the voters. There were two groups with different views on these matters.

One, consisting chiefly of downtown business interests, favored appointments generally, and sponsored the city manager plan until it was defeated by the board and thereafter endeavored as next best thing to have as many officers as possible appointed by the chief administrative officer. The other, consisting of those endorsed by the labor unions and by city employees and other groups independent of the larger property interests and of the Charter Revision Committee, favored elections generally, or when election was impossible, appointment by the elected mayor rather than by the appointed chief administrative officer.

. . . The test seems to have been this: if the office involved determination of matters of policy to a large extent . . . or was one of the highest trust . . . it was to be elective; if it involved policy forming and quasi-judicial functions to a somewhat lesser degree, it was to be appointed by the mayor, that it might be but one step removed from the people; but if it comprehended purely administrative affairs, it should be under the chief administrative officer.[22]

The results will be seen later in more detail, but a brief summary may be noted here. The mayor did receive more authority than before, primarily appointive and budgetary (the competency thrust); he can veto, subject to a two-thirds override by the supervisors. Diluting his authority is a chief administrative officer (CAO), a cross between the strong-mayor and city-manager forms (the honesty thrust). The CAO is appointed by the mayor, but can be removed only by two-thirds of the supervisors or by recall; this gives him the potential for long tenure (competency), which has become a reality. City-manager aspects are seen in the grouping of some administrative departments under the CAO (competency), but others, such as fire and police, are controlled by commissions appointed by the mayor (honesty).

A controller was provided with sweeping powers over all public agencies, and, for the first time, an executive budget system was adopted, with expenditure and revenue estimates assembled by the controller and funneled through mayor and supervisors.

The supervisors were reduced in number from eighteen to eleven, but they were more drastically reduced in authority. Specifically, they are prohibited from interfering in the administrative functions of the executive branches; typically, the power that Ruef had used so profitably—the right to pass on permits—was taken away (honesty). The ballot was shortened even further to cover fewer supervisors and administrative officers (competency).

Many elements of San Francisco were drawn into the referendum on the finished product. This was articulated through the sharply divided Hearst newspapers, which opposed the *Chronicle* and the *News*. Hearst's *Examiner* spoke for many who feared a nonelected CAO with real administrative power while the elected mayor had none. "The mayor will preside at luncheons, and shake hands at dinners, and flit from whither to where looking pleasant—and that will be that. The business of the city will be up to the Mysterious Stranger." [23]

Some Catholics opposed a nonelected board of education* and CAO; as a general rule, the Church has supported direct election wherever possible because of its fear of covert cliques that would exercise power over citizens—many San Franciscans are Catholic. However, the Archbishop did not act on the 1932 referendum, because his parishioners were divided; some had been on the charter committee, and many prominent laymen supported the reform.

The San Francisco Labor Council also opposed the charter reform because of the lack of popular control of the CAO. They saw the hidden hand of business reaching for more direct access to government than was available to citizens. Other opposition came from the Teamsters' Union and city employees. The latter particularly objected to making political participation in the appointment of public officials the cause for city workers' suspension or dismissal; they were well known for such politicking. Changes in pension matters were opposed by the Catholic Federation of Teachers, police and firemen, including the chiefs. Undoubtedly, higher-ranking figures in City Hall could only view with suspicion this rearrangement of the basic structure that they had come to know and love. In short, if all of these spokesmen

---

* Not until the issue of busing for desegration inflamed the city did the board become elective, by voter action in 1971.

had had their way, the new charter would have been pecked to death.

But in the end the revision carried by 56 percent (59,084 to 45,741), including ten of the twelve election districts. It lost or narrowly won only in the working-class Mission districts, and swept the middle-class and wealthier areas. Despite a challenge in the court,[24] it became effective on January 8, 1932.

Structure and Purpose

The city finally came to grips with Buckley and Ruef and the problem of honesty in this document and later amendments. But that value may have also hindered the search for competence, and it certainly made adaptability less attainable. Despite some provisions for centralization (hence competence), in the view of observers then and now the 1932 charter was primarily designed to block corruption from a too-powerful council. The key to the change lies not in the creation of a chief administrative officer, but in the ban against interference by the supervisors with any administration. Urban administration is much concerned with licensing, that governmental discretion to grant public privilege to private individuals. Whether someone is seeking to have a ticket fixed, a garage added, or a street closed for a skyscraper, the private demand on the political system is the same—for the authorization of privilege. Prior to 1932 the board of supervisors had been notoriously involved in that authority. By removing all such discretion from the board and placing it elsewere—in commissions, CAO, controller—the 1932 charter sought to protect the present against the evils of the past.

While there had been controversy about centralizing the executive, there was little support for its extreme form, the city manager system. Instead, executive power was dispersed throughout the structure of government. Some notion of this diffusion can be seen graphically in figure 7. What the city has is a mixture of traditional governments with strong mayor-council and city-manager systems, plus citizen agencies, and with city and county functions combined. These types of urban governance create a mélange of relationships between constituents and decision making.[25] But in such a context, it was argued, it would be difficult for any one segment to aggregate power tyrannically or corruptly. We shall later see whether that has been the result.

The strong-mayor aspect is seen in a chief executive with a major role in budgeting and appointment, if not removal. The city manager notion is embodied in a CAO and a controller who have centralized

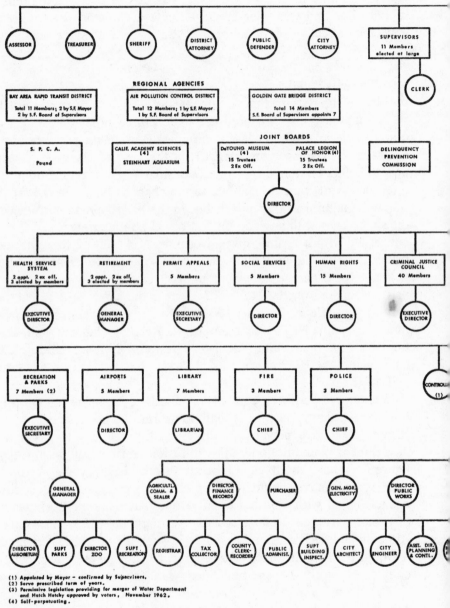

Fig. 7. San Francisco consolidated City and County government.

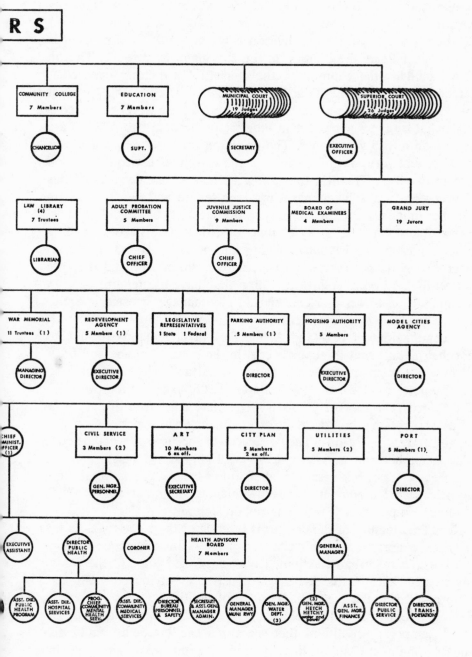

COMMUNITY COLLEGE
7 Members

EDUCATION
7 Members

MUNICIPAL COURT
19 Judges

SUPERIOR COURT
20 Judges

CHANCELLOR

SUPT.

SECRETARY

EXECUTIVE OFFICER

LAW LIBRARY (4)
7 Trustees

ADULT PROBATION COMMITTEE
5 Members

JUVENILE JUSTICE COMMISSION
9 Members

BOARD OF MEDICAL EXAMINERS
4 Members

GRAND JURY
19 Jurors

LIBRARIAN

CHIEF OFFICER

CHIEF OFFICER

WAR MEMORIAL
11 Trustees (1)

REDEVELOPMENT AGENCY
5 Members (1)

LEGISLATIVE REPRESENTATIVES
1 State   1 Federal

PARKING AUTHORITY
5 Members (1)

HOUSING AUTHORITY
5 Members

MODEL CITIES AGENCY

MANAGING DIRECTOR

EXECUTIVE DIRECTOR

DIRECTOR

EXECUTIVE DIRECTOR

DIRECTOR

CHIEF ADMINIST. OFFICER (1)

CIVIL SERVICE
3 Members (2)

ART
10 Members
6 ex off.

CITY PLAN
5 Members
2 ex off.

UTILITIES
5 Members (2)

PORT
5 Members (1)

GEN. MGR. PERSONNEL

EXECUTIVE SECRETARY

DIRECTOR

DIRECTOR

EXECUTIVE ASSISTANT

DIRECTOR PUBLIC HEALTH

CORONER

HEALTH ADVISORY BOARD
7 Members

GENERAL MANAGER

ASST. DIR. PUBLIC HEALTH PROGRAM

ASST. DIR. HOSPITAL SERVICES

PROG. CHIEF COMMUNITY MENTAL HEALTH SERV.

ASST. DIR. COMMUNITY MEDICAL SERVICES

DIRECTOR BUREAU PERSONNEL & SAFETY

SECRETARY & ASST. GEN. MANAGER ADMIN.

GENERAL MANAGER MUNI RWY

GEN. MGR. WATER DEPT. (3)

GEN. MGR. HETCH HETCHY water and power (3)

ASST. GEN. MGR. FINANCE

DIRECTOR PUBLIC SERVICE

DIRECTOR TRANSPORTATION

administrative responsibility. The CAO oversees numerous city departments, while the controller, appointed like the CAO, is the chief fiscal officer. This functional division between CAO and controller is enough to indicate the dilution of the city manager concept. That in turn highlights the triumph of the concern for honesty over competence and adaptability. Further dilution is visible in the fact that the police and fire officials are appointed not by the CAO or the controller but by the mayor. Yet in other respects these two officials are more than any city manager. The provision for their removal means in effect that if supported by four of the eleven supervisors they can remain in office. This has been the case in the four decades of this charter, for these officials have had long tenure and hence wide experience in management of the city. More secure than elected officials, responsible for a wide array of functions, they have become a force in local governance beyond anything known to a city manager elsewhere. They do not serve at the pleasure of the mayor and they are not reachable by the ballot; in reality, they have life tenure.

Imposed on this mayor-council and city-manager mosaic is a citizen-agency form of government—figure 7 reveals some twenty boards and commissions of this kind. While the mayor appoints them (but not their department directors except in the cases of police and fire), he may not remove them and has no formal authority over their executive power; indeed, the 1932 charter was designed to remove those powers from the mayor. These agencies were conceived in the image of a corporation's board of directors, to devise broad policy which administrators carry out. They reflect a vague urge for competence plus adaptability in major services. Invariably stocked with eminent representatives of business and labor, it has been suggested that these agencies seem "a remnant of the old vigilantes committee of 100 which continues in popularity as a 'blue ribbon' committee." [26]

One final feature of the charter is the role of the electorate. As the previous chapter noted, this city shares the California mode of nonpartisanship for urban elections. I have suggested some of the consequences of this practice for the responsiveness of local governance. Also noted was the fact that the lack of political parties removes a potential control over the behavior of officials between elections. Instead, temporary coalitions that support a candidate can easily dissolve by the next election, thereby rendering impossible any program continuity or citizen responsibility. While the charter seems to emphasize the frequency of electoral control of power, it also reflects business-oriented checks on having *too* much of that popular control. For example, municipal elections are removed from partisan general election dates—and their attendant larger turnouts. Supervisors' elections are at large, precluding too-narrow interests from an institutional base; the last chapter noted the diffusion of responsiveness inherent in at-large elections. Too, the voters cannot elect or remove certain powerful officials, and even the mayor and all eleven supervisors never come up together for accounting. In short, the 1932 charter reflects the compromise between majority rule and minority right which radiates from our national Constitution and ideology.

Despite these limitations on the voters, their weight does appear through two channels, in election to office and in public issues put on the ballot. There are twenty-five elected at large, including the eleven supervisors (with staggered terms) plus administrators; in addition, until 1971 members of the board of education were first appointed by the mayor and then confirmed in an election. Forty judicial posts are also elected.[27] Turnout is very high in these municipal elections, whether held at or off general elections; in the November elections of 1971 and 1972, the turnout was 76 and 74 percent.[28] This is in keeping with the high voting rates found in the West.

Popular participation in law making through the ballot is such a characteristic feature of the city's governance and politics that the reasons for it are often lost. These lie in the content of the charter itself and the role of city employees. That document was large to begin with and has expanded greatly in the intervening forty years, so that it once again looks like the "patched iron stove" of its forerunner. The vast detail it represents is not statutory in nature but constitutional, which means that changing any of its portions, no matter how small, is not a legislative matter but requires voter decision. So if the supervisors wish to legislate on a municipal action that elsewhere would normally be in their jurisdiction, in San Francisco they must put the matter on the ballot.

Too, citizens may change the charter by placing initiative and referendum issues on the ballot for resolution by the voters. Some of those citizens are city workers, who find the charter a vast "cupboard of goodies," in the words of one longtime City Hall figure. To add to their store, then, workers need only mobilize support for the issue by putting it on the ballot; given the fact that there are over 20,000 such city employees and that about 300,000 voters turn out in a typical election, the workers and their families constitute a formidable agent of charter change. While they have been successful about half the time in recent years (see table 8 in chapter 3), close observers claim that their record is better on purely personnel matters; they are very successful on salary changes, moderately so on vacation matters, and weak on retirement changes. Ironically, then, denial to the board of supervisors of the power to legislate on many matters that are elsewhere councilmanic in nature (designed to keep corrupt businessmen away) has led to the practice, early begun with this charter, of permitting labor a greater chance at another set of resources.

The document's grossly swollen body may seem disorderly and confused to the uninitiated, but those who know it benefit from it and, as we shall see, resist firmly any efforts at sweeping change. The electorate, then, by their own efforts have made the charter adaptable, but only to those with sufficient numbers, expertise, and mobilization skills to make the structure perform sensitively. The electorate at large is not always so manipulable, of course, for as we saw in chapter 3, major groups and figures can lose on issues they support at the polls.

VICE, VENALITY, AND GOVERNANCE

In this chapter and the next, the three values of honesty, competence and adaptability are related to patterns of governance. We begin with determining how honest this government is, both in its treatment of commercial vice (an aspect of every urban scene) and in the venal conduct of its officials. How local government handles the whore and the gambler, and whether its officials steal from the public, are fair—but not the only—measures of a political system's ethic.

The Popular Vices

San Francisco has always had, if not enjoyed, a reputation for commercial vice, from the early days of the Barbary Coast, which served sailors from around the world. Like its fog, prostitution was a familiar feature of the city's past, both mixing freely with all people and generating a rich romanticism. But a study of "the madams of San Francisco" [29] makes it clear that their notoriety fit a life style which, like many of the city's landmarks, has faded as quietly as the fog. Much is made of Maiden Lane off Union Square, once a street of prostitutes, and accounts are still heard of the glittering brothels and flamboyant madams. But Maiden Lane now is filled only with boutiques, and the last of the great madams has long been retired. Another commercial vice, narcotics, has always been a part of the city scene, from earlier Chinatown's opium to Haight-Ashbury's heroin in the 1960s. Gambling, once widespread, today can be widely found only in Chinatown's pao gai or fan tan, or in almost any bar in town with its dice cups.

In any community, widespread popular vice exists only through the venality or incompetence of the police force. In this city's history, whether the police chief was elected or appointed, control of vice by either method has not been effective. Charles Raudebaugh recounted extensive police venality with a payoff system, in the first decade of the 1932 charter.[30] This was forced into public view when an official in the Internal Revenue Service casually told a service club of a San Francisco madam's attempt to deduct police payoffs as a business expense. The resulting publicity led to an investigation and the dismissal of some patrolmen and officers—but no jailing. In all of this, little influence of the new charter can be seen, because it faced a well-established fusion of police and private interests, whose structure and ethos were the products of many decades of mutual benefit.

For a few years after the charter was adopted, the police department continued to be organized by precincts, with the precinct captain literally lord of his district. The Downtown and Mission (working class) districts were particularly profitable because of their collections from prostitutes. The centralizing reorganization of 1937, it was alleged, simply led to the centralization of collections for many years, with the "take" still filtering down to district captains and patrolmen. Accompanying this behavior was a clearly benevolent attitude of the police toward prostitution and gambling. Each side benefited from the other in a symbiosis that looked like civic venality to some. An experienced observer of the process has put it otherwise:

The Police Department, incongruously enough, is one of the last realms of Old San Francisco. . . . Our police are the inheritors of an easy-going, small town tradition. . . . In Old San Francisco, he co-operated good naturedly with his superiors' policy of keeping the more businesslike crimes both small and home operated. . . . A bookie was tolerated, most of the time, so long as he did not aspire to become the owner and operator of all the handbooks in town. When busted, he was busted apologetically, usually as a gesture to placate The Better Element. In the bootleg days, as old timers tell it, the same criteria applied. Illegal booze could be sold quite freely—so long as the market was kept open and nobody got too big or muscular about it. So also with them fillies dee joy, whether free lancing or as inmates of a fancy house. So also with the backroom dice game, pai gow, the lotteries, and all the other little grifts and grafts. The prime directive was, "No rough stuff allowed." The citizen's right to be secure in his person loomed very large in the considerations of both the people and their police. This benign operation was, strictly speaking, neither good law nor textbook civics. But it worked fine, provoking just enough complaints from The Better Element to keep the newspapers lively.[31]

Into this protective society intruded outside forces, with the usual restrictions on local affairs. For house-based prostitution dramatically declined during and after World War II; more than 130 places had closed down by 1950. This decline stemmed not from any upsurge of civic morality, but from the intervention of Sacramento and Washington. First there was the state attorney general's report on prostitution, which started the cleanup in the late 1930s, and then the military suppressed brothels to protect troops during the war. As a result, where once there had been scores of houses that were not homes (so numerous in some places that private homes had notices on their doors for identification), call girls and walking trade are now more evident.

Prosecution of the street trade is by all reports honest, occasionally enthusiastic, but far from effective.[32] Over the last third of a century, the annual number of arrests for prostitution peaked at 5,600 at the outbreak of World War II, dropped dramatically to a modern low of 330 in 1960, but in the ensuing decade rose sharply to over 3,200 by 1969. This latest increase distinguishes San Francisco from the record elsewhere; arrests in Boston were only one-quarter, and in Washington one-tenth, of those in San Francisco during 1967. But the prosecution effort seems wasted, as only about 15 percent of those arrested have been jailed, usually for only a few months. As elsewhere, law enforcement does not deter the trade, for the occasional conviction is regarded as the cost of doing business—although no longer written off in tax records. Ironically, according to the San Francisco Committee on Crime report in 1971, "the whole process resembles a game" which "offers the public the *appearance* of 'controlling' prostitution" but in reality results in institutionalizing that vice more tightly in the control of pimps. But the point more salient for our interest is that this business flourished both before and after the 1932 charter and thereafter was subject to sharp fluctuations in enforcement. The structure of government, then, does not predetermine the quality of honesty.

Similarly, although large-scale gambling has also disappeared, here again outside forces have been at work. Everywhere in the nation, the big gambling clubs were hit hard by the Depression, while in San Francisco state prosecutors made it difficult for gamblers to maintain overt, large establishments. In nearby Reno, big gambling thrived in the aftermath of World War II, brought closer to San Francisco by faster roads and planes. Lotteries also faded, although they once operated even in police headquarters; Chinatown gambling had once created a special police squad for that area; by mid-1974 a federal crime task force was rumored at work on the problem.

There remained a jumble of contradictory state and local laws and a pattern of enforcement that "has been largely along racial lines." [33] The contradictions are numerous. Under state laws, stud poker is illegal (a "banking or percentage game"), while draw poker is legal (a matter of skill); those who know both games find the distinction amusing. Under city law, no public games of chance are permitted, except that dice may be "thrown for merchandise within a place of business where such merchandise is ordinarily sold." This means that white professionals can roll dice for drinks and meals in business district restaurants, but that blacks shooting craps in a Western Addition garage are law breakers. "The difference," the Crime Commission laconically noted, "is one of cultural values, carved into the law to protect a cultural pastime of the majority."

That judgment is supported by the record of prosecutions. While gambling arrests are few (1 percent of all arrests in 1969), 86 percent are of minorities, overwhelmingly black. There is no record of arrests for bingo (hardly an affair of skill), or for high-stakes, private poker, and rarely for workers' football pools. But neither is there evidence that large-scale gambling exists—much less thrives—in the culture of modern San Francisco. For those who need it, a round trip by bus to Tahoe costs less than $10—with $8 refunded, along with a drink, once the patron is there.

Yet if administration of the charter is not effective in dealing with vice, still it is honest. Those knowledgeable about the city consistently aver that endemic police corruption has disappeared. An occasional patrolman is found to be "on the take" and is dismissed, but the old days are gone when the brass-buttoned cop winked at the madam or gambler as he strolled by. Some regret that passing, just as they regret any change in San Francisco. But it is far from clear that altering the internal structure of the police or their relationship to the mayor and supervisors was instrumental in removing corruption. Regardless of governing forms, such venality was the hallmark of law enforcement in big cities for much of this century, as it was in San Francisco. Similarly, on the national scene in recent decades police corruption of this kind seems to have sharply declined, despite occasional publicized evidence to the contrary. This national change is attributable to a number of factors, including voters who are more concerned and active about removing venality, and the increasing awareness and application of professional standards by the police. That structural changes did play a large part in this seems unlikely, given the fact that a corrupt, as well as an honest, police force can exist under similar structures of government.

Civic Corruption

There are other forms of civic dishonesty which the 1932 charter attacked, but here the picture is much less clear. The focus is on special favors offered to business, the civic vice that, unlike prostitution and gambling, serves only a few. The immense real estate construction after 1955 in the business district required building permits. This authority is vested ultimately in the Board of Permit Appeals, which receives appeals from decisions of local licensing agencies. It decides whether an appellant's "interests or property or that the general public interest will be adversely affected," even if that decision can create conflicts with other public policies, such as zoning ordinances. Courts have upheld the breadth of its powers, including the reexamination of the case from the beginning. Clearly, equity considerations loom large here, to the disgruntlement of lawyers, who claim that the board acts neither judicially nor judiciously. That attitude may reflect the board's indifference to lawyers; lawyers have recently been a minority on the board, and there is little use of lawyers by appellants. Those interviewed for this study estimated that less than 10 percent of the cases involved lawyers, and those were mostly for big corporations.[34] As a result the board has some reputation as a "poor man's court." As one observer reflected, its members "share a common stance of staring over the bureaucrats' shoulders, and therefore serve a useful purpose—providing the citizen a chance to protest decisions where the legal answer is not necessarily the equitable one."

But how well the board's five members serve as gatekeepers to governmental benefits is a matter of some dispute. No evidence of venality has come to light, although there are rumors that they exercise discretion improperly by supporting the appeals of friends and opposing those of opponents. Some charge that firms seeking major realty improvements hire attorneys who have friends on the board. But the close-knit network of government officials and hangers-on in the city contributes to this dispute. There exists an "old boys club" of politicians and administrators who went first to St. Ignatius High School, next to the University of San Francisco (all Roman Catholic), and then into government or related enterprises like law firms.

One of the qualities of such informal groupings is that they form mutual protective agencies against critics and, indeed, may be able to conceal relevant evidence of misdeeds. There is no full analysis of the extent to which this board makes decisions favorable to major realty interests. But in mid-1973 one study unearthed "conflict of interest" violations of the city's charter. The chairman, also president and director of a savings and loan company, was reported to have given favorable board consideration—and influenced other board members that way—to persons his company had provided with thirteen loans. These had raised eleven appeals to the board against rulings of other city agencies that would have required expensive additions to business properties of the borrowers. This occurred in this limited number out of over seven hundred loans made by the chairman's company, it should be noted. He denied any such knowledge of the background of those appellants before his board, but later stated that he knew five. Subsequently, the chairman required future appellants to state their connections with any board members, but fiercely denied any wrongdoing.*

While failure to declare an interest in actions pending before such agencies raises serious questions of conflict with charter provisions (Section 8.105), that this is full evidence of civic corruption is less certain. This board has a reputation of upholding a large proportion of challenges to the city's bureaucracy, of which these eleven occasions may be but a small sample. What no one takes time to consider is the extent to which the totality of such an agency's actions benefits major groups, such as realty interests; or the extent to which there are ties of kin, association, or interest between those who dispense and those who seek privilege. This is part of the absence of study of the

---

* For details of the charges, see San Francisco *Bay Guardian,* May 24–June 6, 1973, pp. 5–6, and newspaper dailies for reactions. Of the eleven appeals, the chairman supported the borrowers in nine cases but failed to in the other two. For the *Bay Guardian* both to support *and* deny meant that the president's company benefited.

city noted earlier; those operating in any alleged relationship are not noted for publicizing it.

But a recent episode suggests that widespread corruption could be kept hidden for some time because of the interlocking, small-town nature of private-public relationships in San Francisco. In 1966 there was a statewide revelation of scandals among some county assessors, who were giving favorable assessments to friends and supporters. San Francisco's assessor, Russell Wolden, had been reelected successively for twenty-seven years after replacing his father, who had also held the office for decades. Here as elsewhere after the state scandal broke, a taxpayer suit sought to claim taxes lost when Wolden had allegedly assessed property improperly. This led to Wolden's conviction for improper assessment and for bribery involving campaign funds. In the process, prominent businessmen in the city were implicated for receiving favorable assessments and providing Wolden with campaign funds. Wolden went to jail, and about $9 million in taxes, lost through improper assessments, have been sought through legal action. Almost without regard to political party, Wolden was helped by leading San Franciscans who claimed that their campaign assistance was not a trade-off for his assessment benefits, because they had no knowledge of his improper valuations of their property. That members of both parties received his assistance seems fitting in a political system of exaggerated nonpartisanship.

But it is important to bear in mind two characteristics of this incident. The first, as reflected in interviews for this book (including interviews with some who benefited from Wolden's generosity), is that judgments of the incident were ambivalent. They agree that the whole affair was bad; nevertheless the city government was remarkably honest compared with that of earlier days; and Wolden's actions were undertaken more in an effort to be accepted by leading San Franciscan than to make a fortune. A major point, though, is that Wolden received relatively little financial reward for his assistance. Measured against other cities where officials have been caught in malfeasance, and certainly compared with the immense illegal benefits of Boss Ruef, Wolden's dishonesty set a low standard.

A second point about the affair is more important. This scandal broke only as a result of *outside* forces generating the concern of taxpayers within the city. Had the story not broken across the state, there is no indication that Wolden's actions would have been detected even at this writing. As with local prostitution and gambling, outside intervention accomplished what the acclaimed charter's search for honesty could not. The assessor is chosen by election, which the 1931 charter convention had insisted upon by a vote of 14 to 1. But electoral control failed in the Wolden case, for his incumbency demonstrates indifferent citizens' use of the ballot.

This suggests again that corruption is not demonstrably related to specific structures of government, for those in this city provide little report of possible covert ties between public power and private gain. Such ties are legitimate in the main, but they can become corrupted by avarice or vanity almost without detection. In the intimacy between public officials and private interests, corruption may arise from a desire not only for money but for status. The days of flat bribery of a city official may well be gone, like so much of San Francisco's overly romanticized past. Instead, more subtle venality may operate—less known, less detectable, and less dramatic when revealed, than in Ruef's era. Arnold Rogow and Harold Lasswell note that any functional definition of bribery "allows for the possibility that the inducement given or sought makes use of other values, such as power (e.g., a higher office or a voice in party councils), respect (e.g., favorable publicity), well-being (e.g., luxurious entertainment), affection (e.g., acceptance in a family circle), enlightenment (e.g., inside dope), skill (e.g., access to advanced training), and rectitude (e.g., moral support from a cynical group)."[35] In short, man does not corrupt by bread alone.

Given this broader context for subtle corruption, even greater problems arise in building defenses against it. The mechanisms for uncovering this sweet poison in community life are not that well developed. Innumerable audit controls can be built into the fiscal process, of course. But how does one review the administrative judgment that there should be issued a certain permit, which then stimulates immense realty profit, when board members and realtors' lawyers are old schoolmates or social friends? There are prior problems that hinder development of such controls. Thus, there is no agreed-on standard of all the lines between public and private benefit. A diverse society provides multiple definitions of such lines, although the law reflects agreement on some aspects. Behind this problem, however, is the historical insistence that private interests be served by public authority, that the two sectors should be fused, that this is "the American way."

Another prior problem is inescapable, in that the exercise of public authority always involves some use of discretion. If that exercise finds that there is no public inconvenience if a permit to construct a high-rise apartment is issued, it is difficult in law, if not in reason, to accept another party's claim that alternative values have been denied, such as maintaining a beautiful skyline. However, losers in such cases are prone to suspect corruption. The resolution of such problems of discretion would be easy, indeed, if one could find an unexpected $90,000 bank account in an official's background, as was the case with a policeman in the 1930s probe.

But it is more likely that discretion by administrative agencies in the city is honestly exercised. That was the overwhelming judgment of those interviewed for this study; it was confirmed even by city hall reporters, elsewhere repositories of the grimy, covert side of urban life, but who here spoke of the general honesty of government.[36] After all, officials need not be bribed to believe that men should be able to profit from building skyscrapers and filling in the bay. Certainly the charter does not prohibit profit making as a criterion of officials' judgments. The difficulty is that such judgments can on the surface be legitimately derived while concealing venality; on this problem, charters have little to say. An active press may investigate suspected collusion, and outside public agencies may unearth unsuspected crimes. But the pursuit of honesty in San Francisco government—whether by centralizing power for a Ruef, or compartmentalizing it for a Wolden, under different charters—is not demonstrably related to structural forms. The same forms in the 1932 charter exist with both endemic police graft and police honesty, or brothels and call girls. In retrospect, the city's present knowledgeables, when pressed, conclude that it is actually the quality of public officials that makes for honest or for graft-ridden government. And there is little knowledge, here or elsewhere, concerning how political systems, or their social environments, can regularly produce this quality of honesty in governance.

Crisis and Adaptability in Governance

We have noted that at least three major values—honesty, competency, and adaptability—have shaped the origin and performance of urban governance here and elsewhere, and that different eras have insisted on different priorities for these three values. There has developed much criticism of San Francisco's government on the ground that, like other cities, it is unable to confront the set of problems that in the 1960s came to be termed "the urban crisis." In San Francisco the particular charge is that government has become so fractionated—first because the charter intended that it should, and later because groups have vested interests in its remaining so—that it is not capable of adapting to the new urban stresses and their attendant demands. Inertia, it is argued, reinforces interests that are blind or indifferent to new needs and demands.

San Francisco observers and participants, who rarely have an overview of their government, evaluate its totality from the portion that reflects each one's interest. Businessmen see in the board of supervisors a threat to the tax structure, because the board seeks to respond to new policy demands by searching for new revenue. City workers cherish the detailed protections of job and income inbedded in the charter and its commissions. Those, like the League of Women Voters, who emphasize rationality and efficiency in organization, are aghast at an elected mayor of limited power, but are mollified by the existence of a chief administrative officer (CAO), who is, however, virtually untouchable by the electorate. Opponents of school

131

busing denounce an appointed board of education and urge that it be
elected (which was finally achieved), while the proponents declare
to the contrary. Newly arriving ethnic groups cry out against a merit
system whose examinations they see as irrelevant at best and discriminatory at worst. But those responsible for such tests, including
some ethnic members well fixed in municipal service, defend them
as models of efficiency and professionalism.

The city's political authorities also have differential judgments
about the charter. The mayor decries his lack of authority over most
administrative activity, which hinders him and his counterpart everywhere in big cities from meeting the developing problems of urban
life. Supervisors complain of a charter that explicitly prohibits them
from even inquiring into the implementation of ordinances they have
passed. Professional administrators despair of a system in which even
minor changes in personnel or duties require amendments to the
charter and hence all the expense and uncertainties of a public referendum. The CAO and the controller have little to complain about
in the charter, as many of those interviewed reiterated; because the
charter's provisions give them a long tenure, they attain an expertise
in charter interpretation and hence a power over small and major
public policies possessed by no one else. But they, too, complain
about the charter's restrictive budget and civil service. Finally, there
are the city workers, usually regarded as being able to obtain anything
they want. But they must face an uncertain electorate for increased
benefits, matters that elsewhere are settled administratively or legis-
latively. However, their electoral record has been very convincing
with increasing years, so charter limitations may be more apparent
than real.

We are concerned with this fragmentation because of its consequences for the decision making, governance, and group interests in
San Francisco. Central to the intermittent criticism of the charter
since 1932 has been the question of its efficacy. Critics charge that
fragmentation renders the city helpless to meet a growing "urban
crisis." The defense has been that the charter has been very effective,
which means effective for those groups advantaged by its provisions. In short, defenders insist that the definition of effectiveness
arises out of group values—who is benefited by this particular instrument of government. For those benefited, the charter reinforces the
security that comes from a responsive government. It is not put quite
this blatantly, of course. Rather, defenders appeal to Jacksonian sus-

picions of centralized power and insistence on dividing it, while imposing electoral controls over the result.

This chapter explores the links between the questions Who governs? and Who benefits? One assumption of this analyses is that the search for adaptability—like that for honesty and competency—does not involve universal standards for measuring the results. Rather, the question is never *whether* government is adaptive but *for whom* is it adaptive. In this decisional environment, particular groups find the governing system honest, competent, and adaptive, while others do not. Whether one analyzes systemic processes, episodic policy conflicts, or major reform efforts, the "mobilization of bias" operates within a context of coalitional politics. To demonstrate these connections among system qualities and group interests, this chapter focuses on the budgetary process, a typical conflict over parking, and a recent charter reform effort.

THE DYNAMICS OF FRAGMENTATION:
THE BUDGETARY PROCESS

The dynamics of system and group interaction are illustrated in San Francisco's budgetary process.[1] Because there is no single agency authorized to make the budget an instrument of public policy, it provides little oversight of the city's problems, resources, and policies. Characteristically, budget requests come from department heads, some of whom are responsible to the mayor, some to the CAO, and some to independent agencies. Department requests are therefore dominated by the particularistic concerns of their host agencies. Further, on its completion the department budget is sent to the CAO, whose prime imperative is to "provide essential services at the lowest cost." But when he meets with the staff of each department, the CAO most often does not cut the budget, either because he strongly supports a project or because the department head strongly favors a special project and the CAO wishes to maintain administrative harmony. It is always possible, however, for the mayor's office later to cut new and expensive budget additions. At any rate, this varied collection of special pleadings termed a "budget" is compiled by the controller.

The mayor, who receives this document, has a staff for fiscal assistance, but they are too few, mostly civil servants not always reflecting his viewpoint. Even if the mayor wished to impose policy objectives on the budget, he is restrained in at least one major respect. Much of the budget—both revenue and expenditure—is mandatory as a result of state and federal policy formulas or of charter requirements concerning salaries. In short, both historical and external factors combine to sharply reduce the initiative, the resources, and the policy agenda of local government. After a series of conferences by the mayor with department heads, where the main interest is in what is cut or kept rather than any policy consequences, the modified but still unintegrated budget is handed to the supervisors. However, until the early 1970s when several budget analysts were hired, that council has had no staff for analysis in the few weeks allotted for the digestion of hundreds of pages of particular requests.

In this fashion, the city's budgetary process makes the round of the seasons in manner and times detailed in the charter, though with little provision for a coordinating authority that could mesh needs and demands with available resources. Few if any officials know how much revenue will be available, so that tax estimates and budget requests remain separated until the composite goes to the supervisors. This condition is like that in the federal government before the creation of the Office of the Budget in 1921.

Yet there are new stirrings in this field. An awareness of the concept of a "program budget" has worked its way into this system as a result of proddings from business and the federal government. A program budget makes explicit those implicit values embedded in budget requests; once they are made visible and are endorsed, less room is available for compromises familiar in the old negotiation process. By comparison, in "line-item budgets" each item is a point for negotiation, which administrators use to advance their total interests.

There is steady progress being made within the bureaucracy to adopt the program budget as a result of a quiet effort funded by the Federal Regional Council. The Chamber of Commerce in early 1973 had requested that $300,000 of new revenue-sharing funds be allocated for such a program budget, but Mayor Alioto rejected the request. But by mid-1973, Alioto had changed his mind, rather as had Mayor John Lindsay in New York on the same issue. Federal funds had become available to institute the new analytic process, and federal and private parties had insisted on its utility for maintaining an executive's power.

At a minimum, such techniques might increase his knowledge of the money flow. One of the clearest examples of this "competency gap" in San Francisco's government is its inability to track incoming federal funds for its own budgetary purposes. The enormous growth of these incoming funds, as a later chapter will show, has had great consequences for the local exercise of authority. By the early 1970s, the city had to rely on officials from San Jose's government for technical assistance. A number of cities around the country are ahead of it in this vital area of intergovernmental capacity. Oakland across the bay possessed a full tracking record of federal funds well before San Francisco did.

But by mid-1973 the mayor's staff was beginning to develop new tools for data collection and analysis of their money flow. The "feds" had provided a $50,000 grant for the study of better budgetary techniques. If adopted, the 1973 recommendations would enable the mayor to (1) issue annually program-by-program statements on budget allocations; (2) set up a municipal clearinghouse to coordinate application for and receipt of monies from other governments; (3) devise new program budgeting techniques; and (4) coordinate these innovations with other governments. By such methods the mayor could provide reports each year on objectives, priorities among these objectives, and implementive programs for evaluation by supervisors and the public. In short, the process would enable someone in this maze of public finance to define where local government was going and with what speed. Several years are required to put this into operation, and again it will be federal funds that will make it possible, if the supervisors authorize the program.

This future of the vital budgetary process must be compared with the past and its system of free enterprise among agencies.[2] Experienced administrators in the city know that their own budget success has depended on their credibility with significant other officials. That credibility, in turn, required them to be visited regularly. By this means, the mayor's staff, the clerk of the board of supervisors, the controller, and others are informed of current projects and future plans. The controller is visited because he handles all interdepartmental transfers of funds and so can expedite such matters if he chooses. The clerk of the board is visited because he is the only nonmember present at the executive sessions of the supervisors' finance committee; consequently, he must be relied on to explain these departmental budgets when questions arise. But rarely are the members of the supervisors' finance committee visited, both because they are too busy and because they would resent such informal pressures. Other budgetary strategies are possible, such as soliciting outside support from affected interest groups; labeling as "replacements" as many expenditures as possible, for such items are not usually questioned; and keeping as small as possible the amount of undisguised new expenditures, for amounts are usually unquestioned in succeeding years unless there are "substantial deviations from allowance ordinarily approved." [3]

Behind these tactics lie major consequences for government and its adaptability. Most basically, such a budgetary process strengthens the separation of governmental domains. By promoting interagency battles over redistribution of resources, the process simultaneously militates against any centralized oversight of diverse programs. Rather, each agency constructs over time its own scenario, complete with supporting esthetic theory, emotional appeals, intricate choreography and stage movements, and a cast of characters. While these differ among the agencies, each scenario is primarily designed to present the best possible claim on the pool of city resources. Annually, each agency repeats its scenario with the same characters, maneuvers, and rationale. This Oberammergau production has a regularity heightened by the charter's calendar requirements for each budgetary stage. But for those who must sit as annual audiences, like the CAO, the mayor, and the supervisors' finance committee, it is all rather like having season tickets to a repertory company with an unvarying program. For others, however, who would like to know the cost of maintaining Golden Gate Park or the city's famous but expensive cable cars, it is more like a theater of the absurd.

Because in recent decades the men of long tenure receiving these demands have been honest, there has been little corruption in this city. But if one seeks to judge by another value—the adaptability of government to emerging critical problems—then the budgetary process supports several other conclusions. At best it provides only limited information on the overall direction of the total policy course and hence little intelligence on how this value of adaptability is being satisfied. Second, because it is designed as a zero-sum game, where one group's gain is another's loss, the budgetary process compels all participants to focus only on parochial goals and nowhere enhances or rewards concern for broader goals. Third, and consequently, the process necessarily serves groups—such as departments or their clientele—rather than the community, thus illustrating the orientation of local governance to groups powerful enough to make the charter work for them. Fourth, without major program directives, responsible to different constituencies that provide conflicting mandates, and deprived by the charter of instruments to provide such oversight, elected officials in San Francisco spend much time mediating conflicts among such powerful public and private groups. With that preoccupation, if there are other goals—such as fostering community growth or providing life's amenities—they are merely byproducts of this mediation of conflict. Yet, as a study of over eighty cities in the Bay Area has recently demonstrated, "Where major priority is given by policy makers to the mediation of group claims at the possible expense of achieving efficient or practical solutions for community problems, the system may fail to adapt itself to a changing environment." [4] That tendency, as we have seen, is reinforced by the inclination of political parties in the city to do little to overcome the concern of these officials with narrower group interests. And always there is the charter behind which to hide when officials are asked to do more.

THE DYNAMICS OF NON-DECISION-MAKING: THE WASHINGTON SQUARE GARAGE

When we turn from the budgetary process, central to the activity of all local government, to policy-making activity of different kinds, there develops a pattern best characterized as "non-decision-making." As I reported of leaders' perceptions in chapter 3, decisions are possible only through coalitions of affected groups. But the coalitions are not simple to form, and their life is brief. The result is that many demands for governmental action go unheeded. Meanwhile, governance proceeds in accustomed ways based on past decisions. In that context, the normal process of local governing rests in the hands of the bureaucracy of city agencies. The news media may headline the elections, speeches, or laws of mayor and supervisors. But it is much more characteristic for a decision in local government to be made by a clerk filling out a form implementing an old ordinance based on an obscure section of a charter made forty years ago.

These are minute acts which attract little attention, but they form the stalactites of governing decisions.[5] Exercises of administrative discretion, they proceed from precedent and a narrow view of their impact on the community. That small decisions have major social consequences has long been known. One such decision may have made this nation; it is said that Lord Cornwallis lacked expected support at Yorktown because a clerk in London had handled a troop transfer too casually. These myriad decisions mostly reflect a past as they move along tracks laid down in earlier days. But overall this kind of decision making shows little awareness for or concern with the upthrust of new social forces and their demands. These have the limited effect that seasons had on the Ice Age; indeed, the speed of this governance is not unlike glacial drift. When demands for innovation appear on the scene, generated by stress in some group, one consequence of this pattern of official decision making most often prevails, that of veto-inspired nondecision.

An intensive study by the League of Women Voters of one such event will be illustrative.[6] Respondents in the city agreed that the general pattern it illustrates is correct, even though they differ over the League's judgment as to the right or wrong of this affair. The stress that generated the particular incident was the increasing problem of the lack of parking on city streets. This provoked a demand for a 535-car parking garage to be paid for by a $5 million subsidy extended over thirty-five years. In the event, the effort was defeated, but in the failure much may be learned of the characteristic nondecision-making in the city's government.

A period of six years and eight months extended between the introduction of the first proposal until its final defeat, so only the briefest chronology is possible here. In early 1960, the board of supervisors authorized an engineering study of the feasibility of building a garage under the Washington Square Park in the business district. However, a letter from the Department of Public Works to the Parking Authority reported that its preliminary study showed that the garage was not warranted. The issue lay dormant for almost five years, until December 1964, when a supervisor requested that a board committee consider the proposal and that the Parking Authority attend committee hearings on the matter, a request referred to the board's transportation committee. In early 1965, requests for hearings were adopted, but no action transpired. Almost a year was to pass before the board acted to endorse a study of the proposed garage sites.

The resolution was referred back to several committees over the intervening months while reports were being received from administrative agencies and interest groups; among the latter, the Telegraph Hill Dwellers Association was particularly aroused against its construction. The first agencies heard from were the Parking Authority and the Recreation and Park Commission, advising on questions of parking needs and financial feasibility. The Real Estate Department also entered feasibility estimates, and in early May 1966, both the authority and the commission proposed joint working agreements to lease property and construct the facility at Washington Square. The supervisors waited over the next months until other agencies were heard from—City Planning, Public Works, the Municipal Railway, the controller, and Redevelopment. Both Public Works and the Art Commission disapproved, and the controller indicated that greater than expected costs were involved.

With all reports in by mid-September 1966, a supervisor committee voted 3 to 2 to approve construction, despite heavy opposition from a majority of city agencies and many incensed neighborhood groups. The San Francisco *Chronicle* joined the chorus with "The Story Behind the Pressure for That Garage."[7] It pointed to city studies and the recommendations against the garage's financial feasibility and to the need for a subsidy to build and operate the garage; some of these funds were purportedly going to the garage promoters, including attorneys and consultants. Despite this opposition, the supervisors approved the initiation of the action by a vote of 6 to 5. Mayor John Shelley opposed it, but four of five supervisors he had appointed supported it. Not surprisingly, in mid-October 1966, the mayor vetoed the proposal, an action endorsed by the *Chronicle*. The measure was then returned at the end of October to the supervisors for a veto override, but only six of the eight votes needed were cast.

Without detailing the roles and views of participants in this action, it is enough to note that fifteen city departments, agencies, or commissions took part; these included three committees of the board of supervisors, the mayor, the controller, the city engineer, the city attorney, and numerous commissions. Flocking around the official action were four city newspapers, four major interest groups, and more than a score of individuals and companies with direct interests in conflict over the matter. The closeness of the contest is reflected in the opposing balance of interest groups, such as the Telegraph Hill Dwellers against the North Beach Merchants, and the narrow votes in the supervisors' actions.

So many governmental agencies were involved because of charter requirements. The mayor and supervisor are obvious participants, but note also the charter responsibilities that brought the following agencies into the decision-making process:

1. *Recreation and Park Commission:* complete and exclusive control, management, and direction over Washington Square site.

2. *Department of Public Works:* under the CAO; responsible for

examinations, plans, and estimates required by the supervisors for public improvements.

3. *Parking Authority:* operates under a state statute; established by supervisor resolution to provide additional off-street parking facilities.

4. *City Planning Commission:* advises supervisors and other local agencies on the physical improvement and development of city and county.

5. *Art Commission:* advises supervisors; approves works of art and designs for structures built on city and county land; its approval required before the erection of any such building.

6. *Public Utilities Commission:* in charge of all public utilities, which in San Francisco includes public transportation; this proposal involved municipal subsidy for a shuttle bus costing $2 million.

7. *Redevelopment Agency:* operates with federal money under state law to buy and clear, sell or lease housing; new construction to conform to master plan as approved by the supervisors.

8. *Controller:* chief fiscal officer of city and county; reviews all financial legislation.

9. *City Engineer:* under the CAO; provides parking and traffic surveys.

These diverse authorities played different roles in the Washington Square Garage decision. The proposal was vetoed by the Art Commission, which has no clear jurisdiction over garages but does have it over what goes into parks. Several, like the controller and the Public Utilities Commission, reported that it would cost more than anticipated. Others, like the Recreation and Park Commission and the Parking Authority, endorsed it "in principle." Yet others, like the City Planning Commission, while finding it not incompatible with the master plan, had suggestions about modifying its scale and details.

The mayor vetoed the proposal, but that was his only strength, as he had little authority for coordinating and administering departments. The supervisors were split as a result of the diverse influences operating on these part-time officials. Contractors, unions, neighborhood merchants, restaurateurs, consultants (some of whom were prominent political campaign managers and fund raisers), and architects' associations circled the supervisors like Indians around an embattled wagon train. While the main demand of supporters was for more parking space for merchants' customers, the League of Women

Voters study found it "hard to consider Washington Square Garage related to a disinterested desire to provide parking spaces." Instead, it was argued, "for business interests and influential citizen proponents, the provision of this 'service' by the city represents 'the new property.' The new property is a sophisticated modern concept. It is not money carried in satchels, the classic graft payoff. It is instead property interest found in franchises, leases, permission to do business by 'city-endorsed' and credit-rated license." [8] These "new property" interests will be heard more of in succeeding chapters.

The details of this hurly-burly of the city's political system should not mask major aspects of local governance under the present charter. First, the fractionation of public agencies generates a babble of authoritative statements which makes it hard for the average citizen to accept or clearly judge *anyone*'s authority. For the public at large, the impression is that there is no central focus in the political system, or else no one knows what he is doing. Second, for specific protagonists this multifaceted system provides multiple-access channels, so that their demands may be heard and they may enlist authoritative support. Third, effective innovation in policy is possible only with a substantial coalition of both governmental and private forces. Fourth, the mayor provides little in the way of centralized control over administrative agencies, not because of personal weakness or lack of will, but because the charter has granted quasi-independence to these agencies. An energetic mayor may accomplish much more within these constraints, of course, but the limits are severe.[9]

Finally, it should be noted, as the league did, that "basic questions about the Washington Square decision did not come up [namely] (a) Is a parking facility needed in North Beach? (b) Where, if needed, should it be located?" [10] These queries highlighted the point that fractionated power, plus a government that emphasizes resolution of conflict rather than coordination of goals, makes it difficult to discover basic problems and their alternative solutions, much less to mobilize support for any solution. Little of the advice provided or solicited went to the larger questions concerning the comprehensive parking needs in the entire city, now and in the future, the integrated programs to be devised for meeting this emerging problem, the order in which these programs should be initiated, and the attendant resource requirements.

Many other questions are provoked by this case, but for our purposes it illustrates the inability of officials to see the larger picture because of a preoccupation with narrower conflicts of interest which the charter fastens on them. Particularism generates parochialism, and in this foreshortened perspective, reasons not to change are always more numerous and powerful than the reasons to change. The result has been a characteristic politics of inaction in the city's governance. That this result is not casual was demonstrated when serious effort was made to devise a new charter in the late 1960s.

THE LENS OF CHARTER REFORM

Complaints against these conditions of governance began soon after 1932, but five charter reform committees failed in the next thirty-five years. However, the 1960s, as we have seen, imposed on San Francisco new demands, which were generated by new configurations of wants in the population, economy, and party life. Complaints accelerated, despite continuing support of the charter by advantaged groups, until 1968–1969, when a sixth reform attempt was made, using immense resources. In many meetings over many hours, the energy and intellect of a significant proportion of the influential people in the city were brought to bear on what most regarded as a crucial problem of inadequate government. But the proposal eventually secured the support of only 37 percent of the electorate. In these events there is much to learn about the city's political system, the modern urban crisis, and its attendant dialogue between those with few and those with many resources. In a real sense, then, this charter reform effort provides a lens for an examination of the basic nature of decision making in San Francisco.

Preparations

There was no question late in the 1960s that the charter had been the object of much discontent. For decades city candidates had thundered against its shortcomings, but as the chief clerk of the board of supervisors, Robert Dolan, observed, this demonstrated only that it is a safe issue on which one could thunder with impunity.[11] In 1966 the Chamber of Commerce noted that of a sample of city officials three in four had found the charter a hindrance to effective government, while four in five thought it inadequate to the future needs of effective government. Indicative of what was to happen, though, they were divided on the method of revision; 55 percent opposed the supervisors doing it, 70 percent opposed a committee elected as in 1932, and 55 percent supported a massive charter study with professional and local experts.[12]

Early interviews for this book found a similar discontent joined with pessimism about its change, as table 11 demonstrates. Of the twenty-four respondents with opinions on the subject, fifteen supported a strengthened mayor and board of supervisors and a centralized administrative structure to be offered in one package, while

TABLE 11

City Leaders' Preferences and Predictions on Charter Reform
before Revision Campaign, 1968

	N	%
Preferences		
Major reform package	15	62
Piece-meal reforms	3	13
No change, good as is, minor change	5	21
Undecided	1	4
	24	100
Predictions		
Major reform fail	6	25
Major reform pass	3	13
Outcome uncertain	15	62
	24	100
Opponents will be		
City workers	12	50
Bureaucrats	3	13
Unions	1	4
Newspapers	1	4
Taxpayers	1	4
Don't know	6	25
	24	100
Supporters will be		
League of Women Voters	3	13
Chamber of Commerce	3	13
Newspapers	1	4
Minorities	1	4
Don't know	16	67
	24	100

another three supported some of this package. But if three out of four knowledgeable and influential city leaders supported reform of some kind, only one in eight thought the total package would pass, one in four were certain it would fail, and over 60 percent viewed the outcome as uncertain. They overwhelmingly attributed the likely defeat to the power of those working at City Hall—employees, bureaucrats, or trade unions. Significantly, two-thirds could point to no specific group support for change in this period before revision was fully under way. On the other side, the few defenders of the charter agreed that it was working well; at best, weeding out redundant or obsolescent sections was the most this group would support.

In this milieu of general disgruntlement and pessimism, the city moved to amend or revise its charter when the board of supervisors in 1968 established a twenty-one-member Citizens Charter Revision Committee (CCRC) to undertake a three-year study. Although the resolution came from Supervisor Terry Francois, the Chamber of Commerce may have suggested breaking up the study into three years. The strategy was that, by not entangling city workers' fears of changes in personnel and working conditions with the need for change in powers, the latter might be approved by the voters. Consequently, the first year was to be dedicated to the powers, the second year to personnel problems, and the third year to final details. Eleven members of the CCRC were selected by the supervisors, with one appointment for each, and ten by the mayor. The resolution was approved during the last days of Mayor John Shelley's administration, but an agreement was worked out to permit the incoming mayor, Joseph Alioto, to pick his ten allotted members.

There were early grumblings in the business world that the CCRC was labor dominated, but the more accurate version, according to others, was that it represented numerous facets of the community as perceived by the mayor. Indeed, the mayor appeared at the CCRC's first meeting to recommend as chairman and vice-chairman two of his appointees, who had been key organizer and campaign aide in his 1967 campaign. Some objected to this domination and called for separate elections, but Alioto's choices were elected anyhow. Some of his other appointees had been campaign aides, including Harry Bridges, famed longshoremen's leader, who had swung his men's vote to Alioto.

Yet a fuller judgment of the CCRC's representativeness is that it reflected, if not precisely at least roughly, major elements among the city's influential groups, although not always the top leaders. Labor was well represented by four men, representation from the professions leaned heavily to lawyers, but the ethnic spread was much greater. Thus, there were three Irish, three Italians, two Jews, and one Spanish-speaking member. Business was represented, although less than it wished, in a Chamber of Commerce official. Professional women were represented, as was the League of Women Voters, although a member was appointed only after last-minute lobbying by the League, which until then had been ignored. The supervisors' choices were often a close campaign worker or a law partner, while the mayor's were most often bright young men on their way up in the politics or economic life of the city. In short, the CCRC represented the usual San Francisco mix to be found any time a civic group is organized, with some people as group spokesmen, some as guardians against change, and some as recipients of rewards for past work.

CCRC Recommendations

With funds and professional staff in place by mid-June 1968, the CCRC embarked on a year's work of revision. For four months information came from witnesses at public meetings, questionnaire responses by 160 city officials, and staff papers, all of which briefed the committee on government operations, problems, and reform alternatives. At the end of these few months, a set of general principles was devised by the CCRC and relayed to the staff for charter changes that would embody them. Subsequent staff recommendations made up the agenda of later public hearings, which preceded the hammering out of the CCRC's final recommendations by mid-June 1969.[13]

The essence of these 138 pages, plus two appendixes, is simple to describe. First, the charter was found to be full of defects: "too long and hard to understand . . . has lagged behind the times . . . robs the city of effective fiscal control . . . fragments responsibility and authority [and] blocks the citizen out of city government." An explicit theme touched on by each complaint was that the city was living under principles of government which, although important and effective forty years earlier, were insufficient for the problems and needs of later generations.

Second, remedies were urged, namely, greater grants of authority to supervisors and mayor, centralization of administration in the mayor's office, and the corollary elimination of independent agents under the existing charter. Six basic recommendations embodied these remedies. First, the charter was to be made simple, clear, and adaptable to changing times, with details left for ordinance or executive regulation. Second, the board of supervisors was to be reequipped as a major organ of policy making, with simplified and publicized procedures for law making, budget control, and analysis, thereby strengthening its check on the executive. Third, the executive office was to be massively reorganized to obtain that ideal long sought in the city's governing—"effective, efficient, economical, and responsive city management." Specifically, this means such changes as a new Office of Finance combined with an Office of Planning as staff support for the mayor, with the CAO directly responsible to, and removable by, the mayor. The CAO in turn would be a city manager over eight new agencies, which would combine numerous present commissions.

A fourth major recommendation continued and extended safeguards against graft by creating offices with independent authority over finances, permit and license appeals, and human rights, as well as an ombudsman for information and complaints. Fifth, an overhaul of the city's budget and fiscal procedures would make the budget a source of information about the city's activities and costs and not simply an accounting system. Finally, devices for opening the government to citizen participation were included, such as the ombudsman, public hearings on budget proposals, the publicizing of administrative regulations prior to adoption, and so forth.

Dramatic as this final recommendation seemed, it came about only after other changes were fiercely resisted, particularly by the independent governmental authorities. Thus, the Planning Commission was finally made independent of executive and supervisors in order to protect long-range planning considerations. Boards and commissions which the staff had proposed to be only advisory were changed by the CCRC to have real policy-making authority, although administration was turned over to department heads. When it was suggested that the presently independent museums be incorporated into a cultural and recreational resources agency, strong protests from prestigious museum directors led to a change in the appointment of trustees. Further, fears that insufficient protections had been provided against abuse of the mayor's new strength led to adding even more.

The CCRC report concluded that these specific reforms would lead to highly desirable public ends: a government more responsive to citizen needs, more efficient and economical in operation, and more protected against abuse because of new checks and balances. In sum, these proposals and the justifications for them are much like those frequently urged in this city's history and elsewhere in urban America.

The Opposition to Reform within the CCRC

But it was clear even while the CCRC was being formed that not all groups viewed these reforms with unalloyed joy. The CCRC's own report implied that outside criticism of staff proposals had had an effect on final recommendations. Inside the CCRC itself, several members interviewed for this book reported that the conflict was minimal, relative to the long list of proposals considered. But there was considerable conflict over whether the first year's decisions on reorganizing the government could take place independently of the second year's decisions on personnel matters. The powers and independence of the CAO, particularly his relationship to the Civil Service Commission (to be considered the next year), and the role of the ombudsman with city employees were closely contested. Thus, would the CAO do the bargaining for the city employee contracts? The recommendation that supervisors investigate the administration of their ordinances was fiercely opposed by city employee spokesmen, and even some supervisors questioned its wisdom (new responsibilities are not always welcome).

While there seems to have been no consistent coalition on all issues before the CCRC, on some matters there was reported a business and labor coalition. Committee members reported that these two voted together on recommendations that threatened the existing status and income of city employees. Indeed, from the CCRC's first deliberations, labor representatives questioned the tripartite method of revision; it would be impossible to consider the reorganization of governmental powers until it was clear how city employees would be treated in the next year's personnel evaluation. This opposition crystallized when the CCRC report contained a dissenting opinion against putting the reform on the November ballot. Labor and Chamber of Commerce representatives joined a banker in various dissents. Labor found the 1932 charter to be a workable document, needing only some purging of outdated language; more specifically, though, employee protections concerned them at some length. While most of the CCRC disagreed with specific rejoinders, the dissent was a public indication that labor and business in San Francisco did not endorse the reform. However, not all labor spokesmen dissented; the only city employee on the CCRC and an attorney frequently representing city employees did vote to submit the whole package to the electorate.

The Opposition to Reform from Outside the CCRC

The next requirement was the approval of the supervisors, and here, too, the labor-business opposition spoke out. A Chamber of Commerce spokesman echoed objections that some propositions were not ready for the voters in November 1969. The secretary of the San Francisco Labor Council repeated his fears that city employees would lose bargaining powers. Much blunter than the chamber and admitting that he had not read the report, he engaged in an abusive shouting match with a CCRC officer and refused a supervisor's request to put his views in writing. But there was also support before the supervisors, from Harry Bridges of the ILWU, the Civil Service Association (largest group of city employees), the League of Women Voters, and some neighborhood clubs. But ominous was the lack of any comment by the Real Estate Board and the Downtown Association. Former mayor George Christopher attacked the document for destroying checks and balances and thus opening the way to graft, particularly when the CAO and the controller would be subservient to the mayor. Other proposals provoked further opposition, but the labor-business opposition was clear to city officials with sensitive antennae. After rancorous hearings before a supervisors' committee, the full board met before a packed house, with an agenda loaded with amendments on employee benefits, and an evening of debates and some changes. At the end the final vote was 9 to 2 to place the package on the ballot.

Three days later the executive committee of the Chamber of Commerce refused to endorse the reform, the kick-off of a campaign of coalitional opposition. Some neighborhood clubs supported putting it on the ballot, even though they knew they were going to vote against it. These were early negative signs out of the community, indicating to the CCRC that their chances were dim. This continued in the opposition of the San Francisco *Chronicle,* although the *Examiner* supported the reform, a shift from its position of forty years earlier. But even here, editorial support was weakened by stories describing the growing opposition.

The voters' referenda pamphlet for November 1969 provided explicit clues to these divisions. There was an impressive list of supporters, eighty-eight groups and individuals. In government they ranged from the mayor to CCRC members, state legislators, local judges—almost all Democrats. Reinforcing this Democratic cast were several local Democratic organizations and their officers, as well as numerous Democratic appointees to city commissions. Labor leaders were there for the ILWU, the Civil Service Association, and two small unions. Officials represented all major religious denominations and ethnic associations. The Barristers Club, the League of Women Voters, the Society of Professional Engineers, and other large and small community organization spokesmen appeared there, too. Prominent were the names of city celebrities popularly associated with influence and winning causes.

On the other side, the list of names was smaller. But it included separate statements by the senior and junior chambers of commerce, the Labor Council, the District Merchants Associations, the Municipal Conference (realty and retail interests), citizens' committees, and private individuals. In addition, there was a significant departure from practice in the public opposition of a major city official Robert Dolan, clerk of the board of supervisors, as well as the *Chronicle*.

Despite the longer supporting list of prestigious names and organizations, in the weeks before the election there were few of these who would privately claim that the measure could pass. The man leading the list, Mayor Alioto, was very quiet about the whole matter. Some CCRC members believed that by and large he had kept his hands off their operations, being much less a grey eminence than was supposed. Even though numerous members were his appointees, contact between the CCRC and the mayor's office was limited and cool during the formation of the proposals. It seems clear that he saw little to gain in supporting what was becoming an obvious loser when he needed his limited resources for much more likely programs. As it was, there was a more than faint tinge of party conflict over the issue (labor was on the wrong side for this to surface); and stirring up that particular dogma in a political culture that reveres nonpartisanship is never wise.

An ad hoc CCRC campaign committee had some hope of success

when it began.[14] One hope was the Chamber of Commerce, crucial for its support with campaign money, influential names, and wide use of the media. Another hope was labor support, although it alone would have been insufficient, even though their many campaign workers could usually mobilize voters. When, however, both the chamber and big labor, plus one newspaper, declared their opposition, CCRC members did not need the negative feedback from neighborhood clubs to know that chances were dim. With only two months to campaign, supported by inadequate funds, and faced with this opposition, it should be no surprise that the measure was defeated in November 1969 by 63 percent of the voters.

In the following months the CCRC limped along uncertainly under the second phase of its reform—personnel matters. But the arguments continued. CCRC officers resigned, as did the LWV representative when the mayor appointed new members whom she regarded as opposed to reform. No second report was issued, and finally the CCRC was officially, if not mercifully, relieved of its task.

COALITIONS, POWER ENTRY, AND
THE MEANING OF CRISIS

Who Sought What in Reform

What all this illuminates about government in San Francisco is easy to forget in the cut and thrust of political conflict. Yet when we view these events in light of the history of the city's charters, some basic generalizations emerge. The making of charter decisions is another way to govern by coalitions, as fierce opposition by a major group to an issue that vitally affects its interests is usually sufficient to block change. In the latest effort at charter reform, as with its predecessors, the failure of the CCRC stemmed from its inability to negotiate support of either or both of the two major economic elements in the city, labor and business.

Although not all labor unions were opposed, they were regarded by many as exercising their veto here. There was no direct evidence that the first year's reforms would adversely affect the interests of city employees; the support of the Civil Service Association is a clear sign this was not the case. But among the three major city-employee unions, a power fight was under way over securing and using collective bargaining. By opposing the first part of this reform, some unions could bargain their support in return for concessions in the second part, which dealt with personnel matters. This may at least be inferred from the admission of the Labor Council's secretary to the supervisors that he had not read the first year's recommendations for reform.

The veto of the Chamber of Commerce was more complex. While their CCRC man had dissented from the final report, chamber opposition was not that certain when the supervisors considered it. Its main objection was to permitting removal of the CAO by the mayor, and, incidentally, placing him under the power of the voters. This electoral control had not existed for forty years and earlier chambers had sought to prevent it. But there were reports of an eleventh-hour compromise the day before the supervisors voted to place the measure on the ballot. This would have made the CAO removable by either mayor or supervisors for cause (i.e., some particularly reprehensible conduct), or by joint action of mayor and supervisors for other causes, such as nonfeasance. However, the same reports allege that chamber staff members convinced their executive committee that the compromise was unacceptable and that the CAO should be made even more immune from democratic review, that is, "insulated from politics." [15] Whatever the reality, the aggressive chamber, long a critic of the disorganized administration under the present charter, failed to support the CCRC's proposal, which sought just such integration.

Businessmen with somewhat less resources, banded together in neighborhood merchant associations, furnished further opposition. Their concern was that changes in the Board of Permit Appeals and the Parking Authority would restrict their present influence with those agencies in local commerce. Similar grounds seem to underlie opposition of other business groups, such as apartment house associations, building owners and managers associations, retail dry goods associations, the real estate board, and the Junior Chamber of Commerce —all organized into the Municipal Conference.

These components of the business world of San Francisco approach the acquisition of profits in different ways, but their remarkable unity of opposition suggests a unanimity of interests that is somewhat less than accidental. Notice that the combination of a strengthened mayor and planning department, a board of supervisors that could investigate the actions or inactions of administrators, and the elimination of independent commissions threatened the economic development that had dominated the city for the past fifteen years. The concern may have been that of a small merchant in North Beach to secure more parking space to attract more tourists, or of representatives of major realty corporations and their satellites. But all could see in some part of this reorganization an obstacle to their common concern for economic expansion.

In their view the function of local government is to promote long-range community growth, and to that end a city administrator was needed who was immune from the shifting winds of elections. Elections are devices whose main resource in the form of votes is not available to businessmen, and where white-collar, clerical, blue-collar, and jobless citizens can outweigh them. In the kind of insulated positions which business sought, the day-to-day contact of small, private, dedicated groups can be more effective in influencing outcomes. The focus of the Chamber of Commerce on this one issue of an independent CAO suggests something more than support of a principle of "good government" and its attendant values of efficiency, economy, and rationality. Those values certainly played some part in the chamber's perception of the prerequisites of local government. But if those were their highest values, they could just as easily have been satisfied by the CCRC proposals that spoke directly to them. The crucial difference between the two proposals was that the CCRC made the CAO vulnerable to the mayor and electoral winds, and the consequent reorientation in that office would insulate him from informal contacts, which the chamber preferred.

It is not known what role was played by the bureaucrats, whose powers would at worst be reduced or at best be made insecure by the CCRC changes. Many if not all of these men have built allies in other agencies and with the clientele whose interests they regulate or at least affect. It is clear from the CCRC reversal of its first decision to shift the appointing powers of museum trustees that many such commission members are important people with significant contacts for maintaining their positions. In interviews for this book, one former supervisor commented, "How those commissioners love those positions! It gives them such great ego support. They have no great economic value, but the prestige they bring identifies them as important people when they deal in business." Possessed of resources of position and status to mobilize against abolition of these positions, there are indications that commissioners did so. However, among those officially listed as sponsoring the change were at least 8 serving commission members. But against these 8, as reference to the organizational chart of the city in figure 7 will show, at least 133 who could have endorsed it did not do so.[16]

Finally, there was little in the way of political party organization to mobilize support for this or any other coalition. As we have seen, parties in the city are mere wisps of what they are elsewhere, because of the impact of historical and external forces. San Francisco's party leader, Mayor Alioto, provided some support in organizing endorsers of the referendum; but as was noted, he did not actively campaign for it. Members of the CCRC find it difficult to remember any speech he made in their support, his postelection regrets were admirably restrained, he thereafter cited the need for compromise if any reform were to take place, and in general he assisted in the demise of the discredited CCRC.

In this demonstration of the centrality of coalitional decision making in San Francisco in the charter reform effort of 1968–1969, a curious feature emerges. The obverse proposition of coalitional decisions is the considerable power in the hands of a significant minority, particularly when the referendum is employed. Among these, the role of the city employees is pivotal. This group often offers support on issues it cares little about in order to garner support for those it does care about. The 21,000 city employees possess the resource of numbers, for use not merely in the referendum but also in election of officials. Knowing what may happen in subsequent elections, few supervisors dare to oppose pay increases or improvements in working conditions, no matter how much these would increase the financial burden. This becomes particularly effective when, as of late, the board of supervisors is filled with young politicians ambitious for higher office.

In the larger decisional context, we can also see that each group employs its best resource. Business maintains constant contact with political authorities across a broad array of policies, reflected in the highly resourceful and active Chamber of Commerce; a decade or more earlier, the Downtowners were the key business group. Unions rely on the city's reputation for good labor relations, which means having officials located in the governing structure who are sympathetic to their interests. Besides, unions also have the resource of votes, on issues and candidates, which in traditional fashion can "reward friends and punish enemies." Newspapers use the resource of publicity, the constant, daily exposure of the citizens to information and impressions in stories and columns. The *Examiner* has the fuller coverage of the local government,[17] but through constant contact both newspapers seek to create impressions in the public mind concerning issues and officials.[18]

Then, too, there are a number of emergent ethnic groups, to be considered later, who increasingly provide a new force among the veto groups. Manipulating the press (this may be the easiest city in the country in which to attract a press conference), increasingly using demonstrations and confrontation politics, constantly making claims on the white conscience, and slowly developing a new cadre of leaders, the blacks, the Asians, and the Spanish-speaking are in different stages of emerging power. Few in the city give little thought to what this emergence means for decision making in the city in the next decades. It is certain, however, that these minorities will increasingly gain a share in the coalitions and veto groups that shape decisions here.

Who Has Entry and Voice in Coalitions

Besides the coalitional principle, a second proposition to be drawn from the defeat of charter reform is the degree to which the city has a multiple-access government, which is particularly fitting to the multifaceted community described in chapter 2. The cross-sectional nature of the CCRC membership was not accidental, for it symbolized decisions by the mayor and the supervisors about what interests are deemed representable. In that collective judgment is a sense of a heterogeneous society where many groups with their many claims to public resources must be heard. The Chamber of Commerce might have regarded the CCRC membership too loaded with labor or Democrats, but even under a Republican mayor there would have been labor representation and some Democrats.

Others could well claim, however, that there was inadequate representation of the least advantaged citizens, of that large and unnumbered segment below the blue-collar level. Yet, the CCRC report was not unaware of that segment. In its preamble it stated that a major objective of local government is "to assure equality of opportunity to every resident," it urged an independent Human Rights Commission, and it contained ethnic members. And yet, it is hard so see how such members with their advantaged background could perceive and accurately interpret the interests of a disadvantaged segment whom they hardly knew. This is to suggest that even the variety of access available on the CCRC still reflects only an upper-middle-class bias, which others have noted in institutions proclaimed for their variety of representation. As Schattschneider wryly noted, "The pluralist chorus sings with an upper-class accent." Even the brief account above of this contest over reform demonstrates the implicit "mobilization of bias." [19] No wonder that there was hostility toward devices that would have directly widened access for new players in this game —the ombudsman and community councils.

One further inference may be drawn from this attempted reform, besides those of innovation requiring coalitions, of the power of veto groups, and of the multiple but still limited access to government. This is that the "stress" which generates inputs into the political system is politically defined. This is not to say that some in a community are not under stress, as they define it personally or for members in their group. But the larger community may not accept such personal or group definitions. It is not merely that the political system does not provide responses to all demands on it. Rather, the point is that the political authorities in that system must *first* perceive that stress exists. Without acceptance of that perception, any wants arising from one group's stress will not be recognized by other groups as demands that must be met.

This quality of urban governance will be met later in this book, but at this point note its application to the reform effort. Many knowledgeable people in influential positions in private and public places insisted that a crisis existed in the city's inability to deal with modern stresses. One stress was attributed to a charter deemed inappropriate to modern conditions. These statements in San Francisco, as elsewhere, are filled with symbols of crisis psychology. There is appeal to abstract and concrete values of rationality and economy in the reforms urged. The present charter and its resultant government are pictured as frameworks creaking under unbearable stress because of new conditions with their new problems pressing for resolution.

In this reform movement, as in all earlier ones, cries of stress filled the air long before reform succeeded. The crisis was one of honesty and competency before the 1898 and 1932 charters, although the latter was accompanied by demands for a more efficient and centralized administration. The 1968–1969 effort dealt little with these crises, since none was thought to exist, and more with the adaptability of existing frameworks in meeting new needs. The call was for government to be more centralized and coordinated so that community resources could be more effectively mobilized and employed to meet the new stresses.

Yet, both political authorities and private citizens of influence fell into dispute over the seriousness of the proclaimed stress. What the League of Women Voters defined as a "crisis," brought on by inaction or sloppy administration, the public and private defenders of existing government could not perceive. The CCRC defined a "crisis" of disorganization, which required reforms such as a strengthened mayor and supervisors with powers to investigate. But these were viewed by others as leading in turn to "crises" of dangerous centralization with a potential for corruption, or of destruction of the gains of a merit system. An ombudsman and a community council were for some actors two crucial devices for bringing ignored citizens into the political system, thus giving them a sense of participation in their own governance and thereby overcoming the "crisis" of credibility in government. But others saw these two as a standing invitation to another "crisis," through harassment of honest administrators and diverting them from competent courses.

In short, many may agree in general that a "crisis" exists without really believing it or without accepting the particular implementation designed to relieve it. The Chamber of Commerce had long supported overhaul of this government, and its spokesmen were strong against dangers to come unless remedies were provided. But that crisis was not so great as to prevent its opposition to the entire reform package when reform would interfere with its more important economic interests. Nor did every member of the League of Women Voters support the reform without persuasion.

This notion that definition of stress is a political act raises an important theoretical question, however. Given the efforts of many groups to gain acceptance of their definitions of stress, so as to secure from the political system some adjustment to their demands, under what conditions *does* the political system accept the stress definition and when does it *not?* An answer requires more than a recounting of "who wins and who loses" across an array of policy conflicts. We need a statement of why some group definitions of stress go unmet while others are easily facilitated.

We have seen some indications of that answer in the focus of these two chapters on the manner in which the framework of government has been created and has operated. This account informs us of several major components of the city's decisional context. First, for the introduction of major innovations as adjustments to stress, broad coalitional support is necessary. Second, multiple, although still limited, access to crannies in the governance structure creates a public and private veto system which provides an institutionalized bias against change in the distribution of resources. And third, without a generally acceptable definition of stress, group power provides the standard by which that judgment is made, whether the stress concerns honesty or competency or adaptability. This also makes difficult any major adjustment that threatens existing values.

What we have seen to this point, then, is that (a) developments in the society and economy of San Francisco have created new demands on the community's resources; (b) two major carriers of these demands into the political system have been an amorphous "power structure" and electoral system, which operate under a coalitional principle that exerts little responsibility upon political authorities and reflects diffuse if limited community demands; (c) the formal government has received and acted on some of these demands over time, but its fragmentation of power and authority protects and augments selected private and public interests by emphasizing the veto strength of each interest.

This broadly sketched decisional context requires exploration of major policy conflicts to give it full meaning. We turn in the next part to the politics of highrises, mainly a struggle over income, because it involves an issue of enormous scope in the resources and personnel affected. A subsequent part turns to another kind of politics, ostensibly that of ethnic groups, but also a struggle over deference. Throughout, the conceptualization of group and citizen behavior drawn from this and earlier chapters will be employed as guides to how the city's internal decisions are products in part of historical and external forces.

PART IV

THE POLITICS OF INCOME

> When will the efficiency engineers and the poets
>   get together on a program?
> Will that be a cold day? will that be a special hour?
> Will somebody be cucoo then?
> And if so, who?
>
> CARL SANDBURG
> *The People, Yes*

CHAPTER 7

The Political Economy and Highrises

ASSUMPTIONS OF COMMUNITY ECONOMICS

It is well first to understand the guiding assumptions in these chapters on the role of economic decisions and of the politics of profit in San Francisco. In chapter 2 it was noted that cities have always been places of special transactions and new opportunities, which distinguishes their social form from that of the farm or the nomad tribe. These transactions have always been partly economic, for the city appears as a trading place in all history and cultures. The distinctive functions of the merchant are not merely abstractions of a sociological model, for from Mesopotamia to the modern metropolis, he may be seen in records stretching all the way from clay to computer tapes. His role may have had low status in Periclean Athens or Victorian London; but it was highly valued in the Hanseatic League and is now in contemporary America. Nobility, clergy, military, intellectuals—one or more of these may have dominated the culture of values and skills from place to place and time to time. But in each place and time, the economic function has existed, and those most skilled in it have known some power in the community.[1]

This pertinacious and pervasive quality has existed because ownership of land, labor, and capital, and the skill to combine these—no mean resources anywhere—affect every segment of the community. While such decisions may be originally private in nature—such as the corporate decision to construct a skyscraper, or a union decision to demand higher wages—their public consequences cannot be denied. The decision to build or to strike also creates opportunities and obstacles, not only for immediate participants, but, in a rippling effect, for more remote citizens also. Nor is the line between economic opportunity and obstacle clear-cut, because each opportunity for one group creates an obstacle for another. Building a factory will mean that even before it opens it will create construction jobs, material contracts, transportation needs; at a micro level, it means that nearby merchants will sell more sandwiches and beer for hungry workers. But the decision also has adverse effects—on property values of nearby homes, on traffic flow during rush hours, on municipal services, on air pollution, and so on.

In a nation with some responsiveness to public opinion, the bad consequences of such ostensibly private acts have brought the political system onto the scene with varying force. That variation reflects in part the notions of different eras concerning its desirable relationship to the economy. In colonial Boston and gold-rush San Francisco, political authorities regulated the price of bread, so vital was it to the common weal; in our time, both power and will are lacking for such municipal action.[2] This variation in the role of the political system can also exist within the same period, because communities differ in what they prefer the political system to do, considerations that were raised in chapter 1.[3]

There has also been variation in the degree of collaboration and antagonism between local political and economic authorities. For much of our history, however, the relationship has been more a partnership than a vendetta. The "company town"—and its rural equivalent, the "plantation town"—may not fully symbolize this relationship, but they are closer to the continuing historical reality than communities that fully regulate business. Indeed, it is impossible to illustrate the latter historically. After all, when the local economy lacked diversification, as in a coal town or a farm county seat, there simply was no alternative power base from which to challenge the dominant economic interest. Whatever evils such domination might bring were rarely checked by local governance; outside government had to be mobilized to counter (but not always end) the domination of railroads in the plains states less than a century ago, of coal companies in Appalachia over thirty-five years ago, or of white plantation discrimination against black workers in the 1960s.[4] Local political systems could not be handmaidens of local economic reform when officials of the two institutions shared the same values and benefits in the status quo.[5]

But the persistence of a community's economic transactions gives us no clear guide as to *how* those decisions will affect the community. Given a varied history of a diverse people with contrasting preferences in the political economy, we cannot expect a uniform blueprint of public policy. Such policies have changed with time; we may no longer expect a city council anywhere to price bread, but almost everywhere we expect it to provide zoning restrictions on the use of land so as to shape the price of land. Even that policy differs with group values; high-income suburbs are more restrictive of nonresidential land use than communities with lower land values and greater tax needs. Such policy will also differ with community size and heterogeneity; a wider range of life styles generates a wider range of policy demands to which the political system must respond.[6]

CORPORATE POWER IN COMMUNITY POLITICS

These assumptions concerning the politics of capital allocation must be joined by an understanding of the role of corporate involvement in municipal politics across the nation, before we turn to San Francisco. Until the early 1960s, the American corporation had gone through two stages in that involvement.[7] There had been, in the nineteenth and twentieth centuries, a phase of corporate dominance of local politics, in which the "company town" was both the symbol and the reality of a rampant capitalism. There was a rationale as well as a philosophy to justify this, a theory of economic manifest destiny that linked corporate power and democracy, which would move the nation upward and onward toward a better life. But against this early concept of the corporate state there emerged questions about its morality and power. Partly this was the notion that bigness had limits in political and social life, that a man should not "owe his soul to the company store." [8]

A second stage occurred after World War II when some corporations began to withdraw from direct participation in local affairs, whether from some sense of noblesse oblige or a practical calculation of the resulting benefits. After all, local decisions had insufficient impact on resident corporation branches to justify the concern of headquarters. Corporate leaders were "corporate birds of passage," to use Norton Long's term, too transient to give much time to the cut-and-thrust of local disputes. Rather, their participation was limited to the noncontroversial, all-community causes where the effort was more ceremonial than not. In sum, in this phase such figures became "more the representatives of a foreign power than the rightful chiefs of the local tribe." [9]

This withdrawal phase seemed to alter somewhat during the 1960s, however. By 1968 a survey of over a thousand firms found growth in both their political concerns and their governmental inputs.[10] Almost all reported that they reviewed legislative issues at all three levels of government. Half of the big firms, but only about a third of the smaller firms, paid "continuous" attention to federal policy. The small—unlike the large—firm characteristically paid more attention to municipal affairs—for example, in contacting local officials. However, the vast bulk of messages from business expressed opposition to proposed local policies and offered alternatives. Another survey found that businessmen believed their firms were far less engaged in politics than the earlier study had found. But it noted also that they felt a need for such involvement because past activity had not been effective in blocking legal restrictions.[11]

This third phase of local corporate politics seems to have left a disparate pattern, shaped possibly by the size of the locality. David Rogers and Melvin Zimet find evidence of increasing dominance of small towns by resident corporations, especially if their headquarters are there. In big cities, too, corporation involvement in certain issues emerges. Particularly with municipal amenities seriously deteriorating in the "urban crisis," major business firms have attempted some leadership of other civic elements.[12] Yet this is far from the monopoly of dominance known in the "company town" of past and present.

What emerged by 1970 was a variegated pattern of corporate involvement, which is categorized in table 12. While only summary characterizations, they are important in two respects. Such categories suggest both a complex, not a simple, model of corporate power in community affairs and the need for comparative analysis instead of case studies.[13] Such analysis might well examine the degree to which firms possess and utilize basic resources. Edwin Epstein has characterized these resources as "organization, riches, access [to decisional forums], patronage [dependency of other groups] . . . surrogateship [a deputy for government in carrying out a public function of contribution to the commonweal] . . . influence . . . over mass media, the backlog of political success accumulated by corporations over the years, and the high status and reputation of business and of business managers in American society." [14]

While these resources serve as critical variables in comparative

TABLE 12

Characteristics of Corporate Involvement in City Politics
by Place and Business

More Involvement	Less Involvement
Type of Business	
Family	Absentee-owned
Local markets	Regional or national markets
Extractive or distributive	Manufacturing
Interbusiness Relations	
Centralization of influence	Fragmentation
Cohesion of interests	Factionalism
City Characteristics	
Small- or medium-sized	Large
Limited industrialization	Highly industrialized
Economically undiversified	Diversified
Minimal heterogeneity of population	High degree of heterogeneity
Limited unionization of blue-collar workers	Extensive unionization
One-party predominance	Two or more vigorous parties
Nonpartisan politics	Partisan politics
Limited differentiation of polity from family and economic interests	High degree of differentiation
Limited organization of interests countervailing those of business	High degree countervailing organization
South, Southwest, or Midwest	East or Northeast

SOURCE: David Rogers and Melvin Zimet, "The Corporation and the Community: Perspectives and Recent Developments," in Ivar Berg, ed., *The Business of America* (New York: Harcourt, Brace & World, 1968), p. 56.

analysis, they also emphasize the impressive potential for influence of such groups. Yet a thorough analysis must also consider the operating constraints that prevent corporate power from possessing a one-to-one relationship with political power. Not all political resources can be brought to bear by the corporation; other groups possess potentially countervailing resources; the general public provides broad notions of limits of power not to be transgressed without political repercussions; intercorporate conflicts operate as checks, and even within the firm there may be limited concepts of needs that political action can satisfy.[15]

Whatever these limitations, however, corporations during the 1960s were increasingly and systematically using some resources for political mobilization. This is seen in the 79 percent of the firms noted in an earlier survey who increased their participation in local public affairs. For example, more than half offered their employees "bipartisan" courses in political education; even more gave money, loaned staff and provided space for community activities, and encouraged employees to serve on local governing boards. By 1964, such major corporations as IBM, Xerox, and Sears, Roebuck gave large sums to President Johnson's campaign,[16] although they were disenchanted later. A more systematic mobilization of major national corporations transpired during the 1960s to coordinate a common concern for conservative values. Such a "peak association," to use Robert Brady's earlier term,[17] generates an interest in and develops a curriculum for individual corporations which seek to be politicized,[18] or it stimulates community intervention groups and methods. They became wrapped in an allegedly nonpartisan banner of "public affairs" activity, symbolically powerful for identification of "community interest" with their own; but they also backed this with significant resources of great potentiality. Hence, as observers have concluded, "discussions of whether or not large corporations have any place in politics are somewhat academic. They are in politics, somewhat hesitantly and perhaps fumbling at first, but they are there. . . . They are in politics at the community level and that is where the major political battle lines appear to be forming." [19]

In that case, then, it is well to recall Andrew Hacker's comment that "when General Electric, American Telephone and Telegraph, and Standard Oil of New Jersey enter the pluralist arena we have elephants dancing among the chickens." [20] That, at any rate, is one model of what transpires when large business firms become interested in local decisions. But it may seem to be an inadequate model when the countervailing constraints against business are recalled. That, in turn, suggests a second model, in which business consistently succeeds to the degree that it can convince other powerful groups to act in concert. Here, the chickens are faced less with elephants than with a wolf pack.

These two models will be explored as we turn from this national background to more immediate inquiries into the power and the actors in the political economy of San Francisco. External forces are operating here, too, but it would take another book to trace their influences on decision making, in view of the altering community and national pressures on economic transactions. Whereas chapter 2 sketched these past pressures, the aim in this chapter is to view them in the current political economy as a background for the politics of profit involved in highrise construction.

THE CONCENTRATION OF ECONOMIC POWER

Every American city is an oligopoly, not a commune, in its economic resources. Where one company may dominate we may speak of monopoly,[21] but the usual context is a concentration of economic resources among a few persons. In what follows, the concern is not with the value of oligopoly but with whether such an economic structure can agree on its goals and can achieve its purposes. As a ground-clearing task, then, it is necessary to lay out the nature of the oligopoly in San Francisco.

As was indicated earlier, this is a city of large corporations and unions, and more of the former are arriving. Here in the early 1970s were the headquarters of the world's largest bank (Bank of America), and of the eleventh, twelfth, and twenty-third in the nation (Wells Fargo, Crocker, Bank of California). Here too were the centers of the nation's largest privately owned public utility (Pacific Gas and Electric), the largest railroad (Southern Pacific), and almost a hundred other national corporations. Most of these corporate headquarters are located, indeed jammed, within a downtown district that contains 3.4 percent of the developed land in the city, 9 percent of the residents (but 50 percent of the business-day population), and 64 percent of the highrises.[22]

This concentration is not merely physical, but financial as well. In 1970–71, the nine largest landowners controlled 7.3 percent of San Francisco's acreage but about one-third of the choice acreage. Of these nine, Southern Pacific had the most (335 acres), while the PG&E utility held the least, only 25 acres. Not surprisingly, the top ten property tax payers—including five big landowners—paid a large share of local property taxes, over 16 percent in 1970–71.[23] Again, because San Francisco is not a commune, one expects to find such concentrations.

Nor do corporations stand in an alienated isolation. Rather, their directors intermingle on one another's boards and in such organizations as the Chamber of Commerce. In figure 8, these linkages are portrayed graphically for major banking., construction, insurance, transportation, and utility firms located in the business district. The source of this figure notes in addition the interlinkages of this set with many more large local firms not represented on the board of the Chamber of Commerce. Bank of America, for example, interlocks with the following: Standard Oil and Getty Oil, land companies, Kaiser industries (steel, cement, and aluminum), large farm produce firms, private utilities, insurance companies, department stores, newspapers, and so forth.[24] That range is not surprising, for banks must invest their funds, and diversification is a hedge against market uncertainties. The interactions of figure 8 change with time in their detail but not in their pattern.

The communication media are another interlinked element of this corporate system. No national media are headquartered here, however, although the San Francisco *Examiner* was the first, and one-time "jewel," in the Hearst empire. Neither it nor the *Chronicle* is regarded by professional analysts as distinguished, but their columnists may represent the best single collection in the nation. Herb Caen achieves most recognition outside the city, and there are other excellent columnists on local politics and government (Guy Wright and Dick Nolan), the absurdity of public figures (Art Hoppe), reflections on life in general (Charles McCabe), travel (Stanton Delaplane), sports (Wells Twombly), and television (Terrence O'Flaherty).

Like newspapers elsewhere, these have their own interests to promote. Some interests are political, for they support national political candidates in their news columns as well as editorial pages.[25] Other interests are closer to home, like maintenance of their market. During the 1960s, the antiestablishment press, particularly the *Bay Guardian*, began condemning the *Chronicle* and *Examiner* as monopolies in San Francisco and the Bay Area, which fired staff members who had new ideas, harassed critics, and in general were reactionary.[26] The Federal Trade Commission failed to substantiate the monopoly charges, however, but did evoke confessions that critics had been investigated. Undoubtedly, press men are fired here, as well as elsewhere, for noncompliance with the publisher's requirements. But the charge of "reactionary" must be viewed from the critic's perspective, which has been increasingly "radical." Thus the *Chronicle* was an early supporter of Southern civil rights protests and an early critic of the FBI and the Vietnam War.

Another interest has been in highrises, although columnists have often opposed the editorial support of this development. Owners and controllers of these papers and television-radio stations (in some cases the same) have ties to highrise development groups. Some tele-

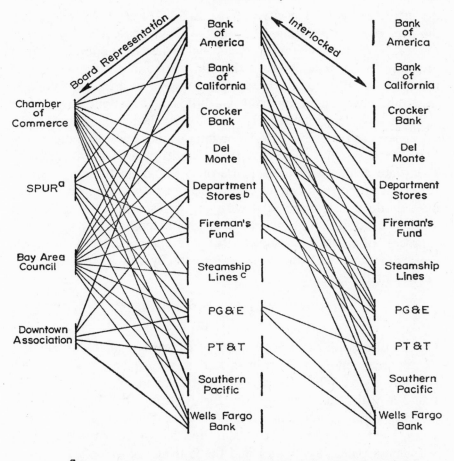

^aSPUR - San Francisco Planning and Urban Renewal Association

^bEmporium-Capwell complex of 28 stores

^cNatomas, Pacific Far East, and American President lines

Fig. 8. Overlapping corporate representation in San Francisco, 1970–1971. Source: Constructed from data in Bruce B. Brugmann, *The Ultimate Highrise: San Francisco's Mad Rush Toward the Sky* (San Francisco: San Francisco Bay Guardian, 1971), pp. 85–86.

vision stations' use of "public service" announcements to support Chamber of Commerce views in favor of highrises—but not opposing views—indicates a more than casual interest. Indeed, the stations' stake in highrises may be quite direct. None of the television stations mentioned an agreement during the mid-1960s that led to the construction of a transmitter nearly 1,000 feet high on 900-foot Mt. Sutro in the center of the city.[27] (The Eiffel Tower is 984 feet high, the Empire State Building 1,250 feet without its 222-foot television tower). Not until it was well up, and only when the nonestablishment press broke the story in late 1971, did television cover the story of the structure. By then the construction was so well locked into contracts and government approval that little could be done.

From such descriptions as these, some would be quick to describe the context as typically "elite." The interlocking lines of figure 8 project a direct sense of an in-group pursuing its own goals which, critics claim, are achieved at the expense of those not in the magic circle. But these propositions about exclusiveness and cohesion over special interests do not describe fully what transpires within the total decisional context of San Francisco. Chapter 3 noted how city figures saw a process of transient coalitions. We will explore later whether the desires of those with more resources actually run against the preferences of the community.

PERCEPTIONS OF ECONOMIC INTEREST:
THE BIG AND THE LITTLE RICH

One problem with any simple thesis of elitism is that the distribution of resources among top business leaders varies sharply, along with their life styles. When Hunter surveyed them in the early 1960s, he found a distinction between "the Big Rich and the Little Rich" in San Francisco and other cities. Among other things, this distinguished amounts of personal wealth and its source; the former possessed more inherited money and the latter more earned. Both were "working rich," however, having increased their fortunes in their life times. The Big Rich were based more in banking, shipping, manufacturing, and engineering, with a newspaper owner and a real estate developer thrown in for seasoning. The Little Rich were merchants and processors of consumer goods, realtors, and professionals. Status distinctions operated among these wealthy San Franciscans, even in such matters as who was tapped first for leadership in community fund raising. But their private lives were usually circumspect; their homes in the suburbs were "very much like hundreds, if not thousands upon thousands, of their neighbors," although they might have more than one; and few, especially among the Big Rich, liked to display their enormous wealth.[28]

In the late 1960s, banking executives and Chamber of Commerce directors volunteered much the same distinction to the author. They

perceived first "the Establishment"—officers of the largest corporations, utilities, and banks, who are also chamber-oriented. But their
potential political power is rarely exerted at the city levels by such
devices as talking with supervisors or mayors. Second, there exists
another group of lesser wealth having different business roots. These
are "business politicians," personally exercising their muscle with
local officials on matters often directly affecting their pocketbooks.
All observers regard hotel owner Benjamin Swig as having had great
influence during the last two decades with Democratic presidents and
City Hall leaders to whose campaigns he contributed. Department
store magnate Cyril Magnin is in much this same league, with national contacts and local influence (he arranged the wedding for
President Lyndon Johnson's daughter).

It is important to grasp what distinguishes these business-oriented
Big and Little Rich, who seem alike to the outsider, for it tells us
much about the differential influence of those who amass capital. It
is not that one is materialist and the other not, for both expect profits.
But the Big Rich seek them over a longer period of time while the
Little Rich want short-run rewards—many years as against a few
years. Also, the former, oblivious to local political figures and power
configurations, may use the Little Rich for their few local political
purposes. The latter, however, know and utilize the realities of local
politics—what kin or friend is placed in the positions of government,
what factions will not combine because of past injuries, who is influential with or an athema to labor or neighborhood groups, and so forth.

What do the Little Rich obtain from this operation? Some of
them benefit by favorable zoning changes or other direct aid to
their businesses. Others benefited from the decisions of tax assessor
Wolden, described in the last chapter. But some like the deference
that is possible in local politics, such as that surrounding national
politicians who swing into town to talk and dine with them in well-
publicized settings. The Big Rich are not averse to these political contacts, of course, but they enjoy them, like everything else, quietly in
their homes at Hillsborough or exclusive club retreats like Bohemian
Grove. In this nexus of social, political, and economic shared interests as well as frequent face-to-face contact, the Little Rich busy
themselves about town, seeking favors in exchange for campaign contributions, camaraderie, and deference. Little if any of this is dis-
honest, it must be made clear, and much of it is accompanied by a
boosterism aimed at improving the city's economy and culture.

THE NEW CAPITAL AND LABOR

New Money in an Old Money Town

While both groups shared an interest in the profits of highrise development, as we shall see, the Big Rich provided the leadership in making the city a major financial center. San Francisco had emphasized shipping as a main economic transaction from the gold rush days, but this, as well as industry, went into decline after World War I, leaving mostly distribution and service activities. In the judgment of a leading banking executive interviewed for this study, "by World War II, San Francisco was a dying city like Portland today." The shift to a financial center is attributed to the post-World War II success of the Bank of America (originally Bank of Italy), now the largest bank in the world. It has always had its center in San Francisco, where its founder, A. P. Giannini, underwrote much of the interior valley farm expansion,[29] and successfully pioneered retail, or branch, banking. This and other banks provided credits of a size to participate in large companies' request for development funds and to enter the national and world finance markets.[30]

This postwar capital aggregation took place just when the nation's population was tilting westward, with an attendant business growth, and when trade with the Pacific basin opened up. These conditions provided enormous opportunities to expand, both domestically to capitalize business development and internationally to finance burgeoning trade with the Pacific. Thus, trade with Japan went up 150 percent during the 1960s, and in the early 1970s dominated both import and export activity through this port. In addition, the banks in California developed an enormous consumer-service function. They were the first to introduce retail credit, data processing, installment loans, and ready reserve accounts, to bank by mail, compute income taxes, and—on the lighter side—to provide scenic checks.[31]

All of these services contributed to the capital focused in the city's banking power. The total potential of this power cannot be fully estimated, but its outlines are visible in the weight of the city's banking in that of the Bay Area, the state, and the nation. Among the fifteen banks headquartered here in mid-1970, there were $41.4 billion in assets—97 percent of all assets in the nine-county Bay Area, 66 percent of those in the state, and 6.2 percent of those in the nation. However, those fifteen banks represent only a small fraction of all banks—37 percent in the area, 14 percent in the state, and 0.1 percent in the nation.[32] More simply, these data tell of enormous

TABLE 13

Employment by Industry in San Francisco, 1960–1970

	1970 Total (000)	1960–1970 Increase (percent)
Services	122.6	28.4
Wholesale and retail trade	111.7	−0.3
Government	90.4	26.4
Finance, insurance, and real estate	69.0	31.9
Transportation, communication, and utilities	61.4	11.6
Manufacturing	58.1	−15.7
Contract construction	21.8	10.1
Agriculture, forestry, fisheries, and mining	1.3	44.4

SOURCE: "A Study of Growth and Economic Stature of the Nine Bay Area Counties," Economic Research Division, Security Pacific National Bank, 1971, p. 58.

concentration. Only one out of each thousand banks in the country sits in San Francisco, but together they control one out of every $16 of the nation's banking assets. Moreover, as figure 8 indicates, these assets are not idle. Rather, they move to finance large corporations, utilities, transportation companies, and construction.

There are other signs of this financial growth visible in the kinds of workers entering the job market during the 1960s. Table 13 shows that the largest proportional growth in employment occurred in exactly the financial domain which the preceding figures on bank assets would require. Of the almost 109,000 workers in the entire Bay Area in 1969 in this category, 84.5 percent worked in San Francisco or Oakland; of these, 35.8 percent were in insurance and 30.9 percent in banking.[33] Growth in the largest category—services—reflects work supportive of the needs of an increasingly white-collar community.

New Labor Power in an Old Labor Town

Yet another component of the city's political economy is organized labor. As was noted, San Francisco enjoys a reputation as a "good labor town," a condition which several generations of rough-edged workers had to earn literally with blood. In the last quarter of the nineteenth century, a Workingmen's party with origins in anti-Chinese fears had much strength here.* In the early 1900s, a Labor Union party seized control of the government, only to produce the

---

* Like a modern Cato's *Delenda est Carthago!* that party's leader, Denis Kearney, concluded each speech with, "And whatever happens, the Chinese must go!"

corrupt regime of Boss Ruef.[34] But in the economic realm, labor-management conflict has been as bloody here as elsewhere. A mid-1916 bombing of a parade of business and military preparedness supporters, resulting in ten killed and forty wounded, precipitated the arrest and conviction (under vigilante-like conditions) and life imprisonment of two social agitators, Warren Billings and Thomas Mooney; business leaders described Mooney as a "labor leader," though he was not. The issue contributed to breaking the 1919 maritime strike, and notions of the innocence or guilt of these men were as fixed as such ideas about Sacco and Vanzetti a decade later on the East Coast.[35]

In particular, waterfront troubles have afflicted the city from the earliest days, mostly because of the basically exploitive nature of working relationships which existed for so long in maritime shipping. There have been waterfront strikes since at least 1886, but the bloody climax was reached in July 1934, with a running fight between police and workers in the streets of the city, killing two and injuring sixty-four, including thirty-one who were shot. Then, as before but never again, the state joined local government as a supportive agent of the shippers. One analyst summed up an investigation of those events: "The record in that strike is abundant with unlawful arrests, unlawful searches and seizures, excessive bail, unfair trials, convictions without proper evidence and in some cases without even 'a day in court,' the denial of counsel, deportation of workers, and other violations of the fundamental rights of American citizens." [36] The violence precipitated a general strike, which was joined by almost every union in San Francisco and Oakland. But after four days its failure was evident, and the strategy was never tried again, here or elsewhere. Yet a battle lost became a war won when a change in outside forces produced a change in local decision making. That is, President Franklin Roosevelt obtained successful arbitration of the conflict, which led to a closed shop through the hiring hall, the longshoremen's major demand. In those naive days, when employers and unions viewed their interests as totally incompatible, employers thought this federal intervention had brought revolution an immense step closer.[37]

The years since 1934 have been good to organized labor, in the city as in the nation. Membership lists swelled, but then declined in the postwar cycle. The federal intervention of 1934 expanded to provide maximum and minimum guarantees, services, and benefits.

In response, trade unions became predominantly Democratic, affluent, and increasingly tied to business.[38] By the late 1960s in San Francisco, labor was institutionally in its middle age, thriving, even powerful, but there was a noticeable loss of energy. There were 4 departmental councils, 9 trade councils, and 122 local unions affiliated with the San Francisco Labor Council. But this organizational base was eroding, as table 13 demonstrates. Employment in manufacturing, a likely union membership pool, dropped heavily during the 1960s, while that in services, government, and finance—less likely membership sources—was up sharply.

But during that decade, organized labor came to have an influence in local government it had not known since the days of the Union Labor party. We noted in chapter 4 that former labor leader John F. Shelley, congressman in the 1950s, became mayor in the mid-1960s. Labor was thereafter instrumental in the shift to Joseph Alioto when its leaders thought Shelley might lose to a Republican in 1967; they would not support for mayor their longtime friend, Supervisor Jack Morrison, because he seemed a loser. There were explicit signs of implicit trade-offs between the mayor's office and the unions, particularly the Building and Construction Trades Council and the longshoremen. In his 1967 and 1971 elections, Alioto received the benefit of labor's campaign workers and fund raising; the funds were drawn widely from members, as few labor officials' names appeared among Alioto's donors for 1967.[39] In return, unions received help in major strikes in the form of mediation by the mayor, sympathetic police in cases of picketing, and zealous efforts to attract construction projects with their attendant jobs.[40]

There were appointments from labor's ranks, giving them access and visibility, as well as an education, in urban problems. Not all of this was attributable to Alioto, however, for labor had had its men in before. One study a year before Alioto's election reported that 22 of 104 appointments by Shelley in the previous three years had been from the ranks of labor. But that improved with Alioto, as may be seen in just three city agencies with power in building construction— Board of Permit Appeals, City Planning Commission, Redevelopment Agency—each with five members. In late 1966 there was only one union man on each, but by late 1971 there were several on each. That is, a clear labor majority existed on the first two while two sat on the third and on the new Port Commission.[41] The longshoremen were represented on all but the Bureau of Permit Appeals; ILWU president Harry Bridges himself served on the Port Commission, an ironic memory of the 1934 bloodshed over shippers' power. Equally direct representation is seen in an Elevator Constructers Union leader who serves on the City Planning Commission, which recommends the feasibility and design of highrise construction. Many other labor officers sit on other agencies of government, of course, but these three show a basic change between two administrations, even when both were pro-labor.

While this is a "good labor town," there still remain differences between labor and management. As everywhere, they differ on taxation, both on its incidence and its kind. Businessmen think labor too strong in Alioto's administration, and particularly contest city employee efforts at higher salaries and benefits. However, labor leaders think business should encourage the development of more new industries, where unions are traditionally strong, rather than financial institutions, where they are weak. But this opposition is moderated by differences among businessmen themselves. Those in industry and building construction work well with unions, which are close to their operations. On the other hand, some leaders in finance and merchandising, who need not face labor directly in their offices and aisles, share a suspicion of organized labor that is reminiscent of earlier decades.

But there are yet others who see labor and management inextricably mixed because of a common quest for income. They have struck a *modus vivendi,* to the mind of many interviewed for this study. As one critic put it:

The City has been organized for so long that labor and management are very comfortable with each other. . . . The leaders on both sides have dealt with each other for years, and it's inevitable that many of them have become very friendly. [There is] something of a feudal system . . . a fragmented kind of tribal government. In matters affecting labor, business allows labor to call the tune; on matters affecting business, labor returns the favor and lets business call the tune. . . . The unions are an arm of the downtown establishment, playing pretty much of an establishment game. They stand by while business dictates the course of San Francisco and, as long as they get theirs, they don't rock the boat.[42]

To the degree that this is true it reflects the coalitional dynamic of decision making in San Francisco. In "the ecology of local games," clearly not every decision is of this kind. The succession of power in an institution like a trade union or a bank, the routinized acceptance of a new voter registration or seasonal fertilizing of rhododendrons in Golden Gate Park, the professional wisdom of a lawyer requesting a trial delay until he can get a sympathetic judge—these all embody private decisions with little effect beyond one's private subsystem. It is when the institutional resources of the economy and the government are transacted on a large scale that the coalitional dynamic comes into play. Illustrative of that factor in the quasi-public lives of such institutions was the dramatic emergence of highrise construction after 1965. As a result, the skyline of the city was transformed enormously and quickly. The large scope of these transactions and their necessary involvement with the political system and private fortunes provide insight into a highly visible politics of income. Surrounding such politics is a dialogue, often heated, about the benefits and costs of the results, which can only be sketched before we turn to the decisional process.

THE DIALOGUE OVER COMMUNITY COSTS

Although San Francisco has known realty growth before, during the 1960s the landscape suddenly sprouted high towers. Thus, where five stood in 1954, another twenty-eight skyscrapers were to spring up in the ensuing fifteen years in a few score blocks. This was clearly a highly valuable enterprise and was becoming more valuable; in seven years, over two-thirds of a billion dollars were thrown into the city in such construction. Like many metropolises elsewhere, the Bay Area was growing out and up during the 1960s, and most of it could be seen on the San Francisco skyline by any visitor. And that altered view, among other things, created a controversy higher than the tallest tower.[43]

For those supporting this growth, the issues were few, simple, and clear. These highrises meant jobs for construction and service workers —increasingly minority members—in the initial stage, and white-collar jobs thereafter for offices in these commercial cliffs. They provided desperately needed tax monies, these supporters argued, for like almost every modern city, San Francisco was short of revenue. Political leaders who sought and supported such construction gained prestige for "bringing business to town." And corporate leaders increasingly expressed a need for such facilities to satisfy their desire to move into the Bay Area, and especially to San Francisco. If one read only the viewpoints of such supporters as the Chamber of Commerce or Mayor Alioto, this was an unalloyed treasure thrust onto the scene, against which any critic would have to be a nit picker, or maybe worse—opposed to progress. Yet three central issues emerged —whether these buildings were economic, safe, and aesthetic.

It must not be thought that these three values were new here, for many features of the city now regarded as essential to its special quality were in their times hotly debated along these lines. The development of Golden Gate Park late in the last century was seen by some as a waste of money in an attempt to grow grass and trees where only the skirmishing sand then poured. The Ferry Building and Coit Tower were seen as artistic blights at first. Even the one symbol most linked with San Francisco—the Golden Gate Bridge—was damned and feared as unbuildable, dangerous, and an inexcusable barrier to "the view." Elaboration of these issues of profit, safety, and beauty is not possible here, but a sketch will indicate the different visions of urban society that underlay them.

One issue is over profit, namely, whether highrises return more in dollar value to the community than their costs. This is no mere summing of debits and credits to arrive at a verifiable and precise total, because it is not all that clear what constitutes a "cost" or how it can be measured. On one side, critics claim that highrises have a larger balance sheet than is publicized. Specifically, their list of charges has included the following:

(1) Far from "subsidizing" the municipal budget, as claimed by real estate interests, the downtown highrise district in 1970 actually contributed $5 million *less* than it cost.

(2) Property tax payments from the downtown, instead of providing relief for homeowners through assessments on expensive new highrises, actually *declined* by 16 percent as a proportion of the city total over the decade of the skyscraper boom.

(3) Head-spinning growth in downtown land values "rippled out" to all San Francisco neighborhoods, causing assessment increases as high as 380 percent and leading, in many cases, to destruction of a neighborhood's original character.

(4) Changing patterns of land use and other highrise-related phenomena drove 100,000 middle-income San Franciscans to the suburbs and mauled the city's delicate demographic balance.

(5) Highrises not only failed to provide new white-color jobs for San Franciscans, but caused the loss of 14,000 blue-collar jobs.

(6) Highrises were the prime villains in tripling the city's welfare costs over the decade.

(7) Transportation facilities to service skyscrapers cost taxpayers a staggering $5 billion over a ten-year period.

(8) Police costs for protecting the downtown highrise district averaged at least ten times the cost for protecting the rest of the city.

(9) Highrises caused vast amounts of air and water pollution, which will cost the city close to $1 billion to clean up.[44]

The rebuttal to the economic criticism, led by Chamber of Commerce studies, provided equally specific data to claim that (1) opponents' definition of the business district concealed the presence of many low-income citizens, who everywhere require inordinately large shares of municipal services; (2) highrises were necessary for the new kind of employment in handling information in modern business; (3) curbing the height of these buildings would drive employment demands outside the city to more congenial sites, thereby losing construction and other jobs for local citizens; (4) highrises did pay their way in the revenue they returned, which exceeded the costs of servicing them; (5) tax revenues will not decline; (6) by making for greater downtown density, there will be greater use of public transit, thereby diminishing use of the private auto, leading in turn to less traffic congestion and air pollution, and so forth.[45] The defense argued that with commuters expected to pour into downtown San Francisco in the future, the only question was not how to stop them but how to accommodate them—in which case, the highrise was appropriate. Critics, however, argued that such construction caused —and was not the result of—this growth.

In this debate over economic costs, there was no such thing as an "objective" study. Critics, using social research as part of a campaign to block "Manhattanization," had all their evidence aligned with their purposes. Supporters made much the same use of social science, but in defense of a contrary purpose. The one truth is that no satisfactory evidence existed here or elsewhere concerning the actual economic costs of highrises—for example, what municipal burdens are entailed, how tax sources and revenues are impacted, who loses and gains employment, and so forth. In that debate among the deaf, arguments pass one another like ships sliding past the Golden Gate. In broader perspective, misuse of social analysis is greatest when the research question is new, the group division is sharp, and the material or symbolic resources involved are substantial. All three conditions have prevailed in the highrise controversy, and have thereby made for uncertain knowledge. So the city has marched ahead with no clear idea of the economic costs and benefits of its highrises.

If the question of monetary cost lacks hard answers, the second cost factor is both more intangible and more real. This is the future cost of these buildings in lives and money in a major earthquake or fire. This is intangible because authorities cannot predict *when* that will take place. But it is real because they are unanimous in the belief that it *will* occur. Indeed, most predict that the consequences will be disastrous, most likely exceeding those of the famous earthquake and fire of 1906. Against that certitude, highrise opponents foresee even more serious danger stemming from having these buildings located on quake-prone sites.

The physical problem at hand is simple. The city sits on a geological time bomb; earthquakes have cataclysmic power (in 1906 equivalent to 12.5 million tons of TNT); no one knows when and where they will strike; but one is possibly overdue in San Francisco.[46] Between the complete certainty of their power and the complete uncertainty of their time in coming lies the dubious knowledge of their effects on modern highrises. A "moderate" quake ten miles outside the city in 1957 (5.3 on the Richter scale, only 500 tons of TNT) caused considerable interior damage and broken windows in an allegedly "safe" building in the business district—with fourteen stories, a steel frame, and structural supports 125 feet deep. A quake in 1969 in Caracas, Venezuela (with a substructure like that of San Francisco), collapsed five of these steel and glass boxes, which were built to more demanding codes than San Francisco's. Even worse, eighty-nine buildings,[47] constructed here before the code, stand over artificial fill and other shaky substrata, most subject to the highest intensity temblors when the big quake comes. But of greatest significance, the most severe quake zone is also the heart of the highrise zone.[48] Against these dangers San Franciscans are currently protected only by an ordinance against parapets, which has never been enforced.

There is another danger in these highrises, whether on solid ground or not.[49] Their height transcends their fire protection. The most modern, and often the highest, of these soaring towers are essentially boxes which are enclosed (air conditioning is more effective when windows will not open); filled with new and flammable plastics; inaccessible to fire fighters by their height and the absence of access channels; poorly fireproofed; and penetrated by conduits of shafts, stairwells, and air ducts which spread the fire's heat, smoke, and gas very quickly throughout a building. But requirements that would make these buildings less flammable or more easy for firemen to enter and attack flames have been lacking in the city's codes. Strong

—but unsuccessful—demands by the Fire Department sought code changes that would require automatic sprinklers, openable windows, foolproof elevators, more space between floors, fire-blocked ceilings, and so on. That is, most new buildings have been built without what seems like the minimum standards of contemporary life for fire protection.

In November 1970 the fifty-two-story Bank of America building had a sudden fire on an upper floor. Firemen rushing to the scene had ladders reaching up only eight stories, so they had to move to the one entrance channel available—the elevators. Later there were confused stories of elevators being stuck on wrong floors and of cliff dwellers seeking to get down stairwells obviously too small to handle large crowds. However, that fire was extinguished rather quickly, despite the fears of highrise critics. But the potential danger remains, although it is difficult to see how significant changes can now be made to the numerous buildings recently built without safeguards. One can imagine what the scene might be if an earthquake were to precipitate fires in even one of these—much less several—with the street piled with debris of glass and exterior panels fallen from on high, with water pressure uncertain from a water system yet untested by a temblor approaching that of 1906, with hundreds fighting to get down the few stairways, and with elevators out of service, and so on. Highrise opponents do frighten themselves with such macabre scenarios, while supporters claim that existing safeguards make these merely false tales told to scare an unknowledgeable public.

Part of this insouciance reflects the lack of certainty in estimating the danger. The truth is that no one really knows how bad the damage and loss of life will be. The important variables cannot be quantified until the quake hits—for example, its intensity and the time of day, the transmission quality of the substrata, the impact on underground water reservoirs for fighting fires, the distance of the quake's epicenter from these buildings, and their construction materials. These uncertainties constitute an enormous gamble in which the city is engaged; some gamble high and others low on the costs, but none can make anything like a definitive estimate. Both sides exploit emotions, of course—highrise opponents, the subsurface fears of citizens about these quakes, and supporters, the popular desire that all will be well. But no one wishes to be in one of these stilted towers when the first rumble of a great temblor suddenly fills the air over this one-time sandy cove and mud flat.

There is a third cost in this dialogue, the aesthetic and environmental impact of highrise construction. Perhaps in no other city in America do citizens so seriously discuss these implications. This stems from their traditional pride in the special effect on the senses to be found in the meeting of land, water, and sky. This is involved in the special mystique of San Francisco—part historical, part romantic, and part a sensitivity to environmental beauty—an aesthetic of place.[50]

But this aesthetic becomes an issue when there is a threat, whether it is one of blocking "the view," polluting the bay or filling it in, or destroying historical buildings or parks—all in the name of "progress." These are most often united emotionally in a sense that here, at the land's end of the nation, a stand must be made against changes. These decay the spirit and the emotional web of the city as it once was, so warm to memory, where, as Herb Caen wrote, "There was a heady feeling that you belonged to the best Club anywhere." [51] Like most romantic visions, this one charges the spirit by narrowing the view. In those "better days" the city was indeed opulent (but also filled with poor immigrants), glamorous (but infiltrated by civic and individual vice), and expansive (but not for the Irish in shanties or the Chinese in underground warrens).

Whatever its origins, this aesthetic of place surfaced as a political force in the late 1950s and blocked in mid-air a freeway circling the Embarcadero and another connecting with the Golden Gate Bridge. It received impetus in the early 1960s when it generated a state law to protect against further land fills in a bay whose waters were already reduced by one-third after a century of use. Only the outside force of the state could block this encroachment, as the fragmented local governments around the bay were either unwilling or unable to act. The base for the movement inside San Francisco has been the neighborhood association, seen earlier as a major element in city elections.[52] Named for a section, hill, valley, street, or park, they have an intense concern about taxes, "the view," traffic congestion, housing values, and so forth. Joining with larger conservation and ecology groups like the Sierra Club, this coalition institutionalized the fears that highrises threatened the aesthetic of place, which many regarded as vital to a special life.

Against these criticisms, highrise advocates were not silent. Rather than making for more traffic congestion, Chamber of Commerce reports noted, highrises would create population density, which would lower use of the auto through the use of public transit. "Save the view" was not a city-wide problem, supporters asserted, but the cry of only a few people—and wealthy cliff dwellers at that—who wished to protect a view against a trade-off for jobs. A union observer was quoted to the effect that "Some of those guys wouldn't know a worker if he bit them. . . . Eight-hundred guys sitting in our hiring hall waiting for work . . . a lot of them black . . . and the conservationists are screaming about the U.S. Steel project blocking the view. View? How many working people have a view? That project means jobs—and that's what counts." [53] In a similar vein, one black leader was reputed to have said that he would favor filling over the entire bay if it meant jobs for minorities.

The major rebuttal was wrapped up in one phrase: "Are you against progress?" Highrise supporters privately mutter that their opponents will never be satisfied, because they want to return to the "good old days" and cannot. San Francisco has always adapted to each era's dominant land use and attendant land economics, they have argued, so that maintenance of the status quo is unrealistic and unhistorical. Others simply cannot understand the opponents' basic premise that realty development may be bad for the city. These supporters have totally accepted the national wisdom that equates change with improvement, more with better, and higher with best. For them to believe otherwise is unthinkable. For others, a highrise means no more than a job, and all the talk on either side is so much blather. It is in this context that we turn to the actual conflict over the issue of highrises.

CHAPTER 8

Visions, Decisions, and Highrises: Four Studies

EMBATTLED VISIONS OF THE CITY

The emerging political economy and its attendant conflict provide an important arena for illumination of the decisional process in San Francisco. We will find here a junction of the themes of coalition and external impact applied to decisions of large scope, probably the largest since the city was rebuilt after 1906. But it is well first to grasp a basic understanding of what the process and the issues are. The root of the matter is that each side carries a different dream of the city in its head. Both speak well of its hills and streets, its views and ambience, but each side is talking about a different conception of the good urban life.* For highrise supporters, it is quite clear that goodness is associated with profit in its classic sense. Whether the developers come from Kansas City or have a local base, those in the city who reinforce them—banks, realtors, city officials, news media—expect themselves or the community to make money on this transaction in the best American tradition. Of course, they also believe that the landscape will look better for highrises, but they are not in it primarily to beautify a beautiful city.

There is a second part to these highrise supporters' conception of urban form. Interviewed for this study, they explicitly asserted a no-

* Maybe the first local political clash over this difference came in 1847 over the matter of the first town survey, at a time when only thirty houses were standing. See Geoffrey P. Mawn, "Framework for Destiny: San Francisco, 1847," *California Historical Quarterly*, 51 (1972), 165–178.

tion of natural urban change, in which urban shapes, uses, and qualities are transformed through time as an inevitable—hence right—process, almost a natural law. With this perspective they stand in the past, present and future. This is how it has been, now is, and will be, they are saying, for the American tradition is that nothing physical lasts forever. In this they reverberate to another old theme, that change is good, that everything works out for the best. This is the basic optimism, joined with pragmatism, which provides the characteristic brio of American history and the despair of foreign observers, who regard this as naïveté. Yes, say the supporters, maybe so, but we know we are riding the tides of the past into a better future, for that is the way it has always been.

Implicit in highrise supporters' vision of the city is a third aspect, a perception of the economy as a seamless web. As will be seen shortly, a rapid transit line was supported because of its contribution to the concept of a regional economy. Facilitating the access of commuters to San Francisco offices would induce more national companies to build and hence bring more workers to live around the bay. Bankers see themselves and the city as a pivot to an immense Pacific trade, with the emergence of Japan, and possibly China, as world economic powers.* The Big and the Little Rich both move within a national economy, with contacts in other cities, including Washington. Such are the overt signs of highrise advocates' sense of the connectivity of national economic life, in which San Francisco plays a part but is not the whole.

Against this, the vision of the city held by the opponents emerges in a curious mirror image. Profit is not all there is to life, they insist, and an urban life so rooted ignores the spiritual qualities of existence without which men are machines or animals, blind to the garden of the city. It is not that men cannot, it is that they should not, live with bread alone. In short, this is the romantic version of man's existence.

In part, it is seen in the romanticizing of the city's past, which was really disorderly, violent, competitive, and exploitive. In this romantic vision, the Barbary Coast, Chinese opium-smokers, bordello queens, acquisitive railroad and land barons, vigilantes, corrupt bosses —all become etched with mezzotint, in a picture of a life that had to be better than the present. Moreover, their dream of the city is of a

---

* In 1971, after President Nixon opened relations with The People's Republic of China, the first imports directly from the mainland in two decades appeared in Chinatown—dried fish.

smaller town, where neighborhoods prevail in safe isolation from challenging life styles, distances are walked or ridden in comfort and safety, the few elite families are well known, and imposed upon all is a common set of values about life. But the present is a time when neighborhood barriers are no longer assured, when out of fear or discomfort no one walks far or often, and when the old families die out or leave town, to be replaced by the nouveau riches. The fundament of common values is broken apart, symbolized by the sudden upthrust of the high towers of Manhattan. They block old corridors of sight and travel, attract more displaced Eastern commuters, and threaten not merely lives in an earthquake but the very universe of values once so familiar and comfortable.

There is another facet of the vision of the opponents of highrises that is like that of the proponents—a sense of connectivity with life outside the city. For some it is the connection of man to a natural ecology that is endangered by these changes in urban form. For others, it is another vision of the connection with the economy of the area, in which business firms should be more dispersed around the bay, thereby avoiding rapid transit and corporate concentration inside San Francisco. Most of all, there is the sense that the battle here is companion to others around the nation, fought against a rampant materialism that destroys spirit and feeling. This is the embattled vision now, as events increasingly dissipate it. It can claim the occasional victory, but as is indicated by the new cluster of skyscrapers, the war is being lost. Both the wins and losses form the substance of the politics of income in this chapter, as we turn to the particulars to illuminate these visions of urban life.

This book has dealt with each phase of power in the city by moving from general descriptions to a case study designed to illuminate the human nuances of decisional processes. In this chapter, four such studies will be needed, since one study alone cannot illustrate the richness of the patterns of decisions about the largest resources with impact on the political system and the community. The first two cases were victories for the construction forces—in building a regional transit system and in erecting the most distinctive skyscraper on the city's skyline. The second two cases were defeats, one for highrise and one for lowrise forces. One was the failure to secure authorization for the highest building yet proposed, and the second was the failure of highrise opponents to secure six-story limits on all future construction. In general these cases cover events from the late 1960s onwards. But each has its roots well beyond these years in economic forces and urban visions.

THE BUILDING OF BART

The seventy-five miles of the Bay Area Rapid Transit (BART) system were designed to link San Francisco as a work site to surrounding counties as residence sites. In development over two decades, BART has had leadership from the large corporate firms and trade unions discussed in the previous chapter. Corporate leadership, in particular, was vital: it moved the original idea through various stages of authorization by state and local political systems; it suggested and implemented BART's financing; it publicized the concept through a major referendum campaign; and, near BART's completion, it trumpeted to the business world the desirability of location in San Francisco.[1] In the event, it is clear that this leadership expected BART to implement the urban vision of a regional economy focused in the city. As such, BART is a link to the highrises, in many respects preceding and contributing to such buildings.

Conversion from Private Preference to Public Policy

World War II made explicit the regional linkages of the Bay Area, with shipbuilding, embarkation, and population movements around and across the bay to further the war effort.[2] In 1947 a military study actually recommended transbay, underwater transit. But official action dates back to a 1949 state law that created a Bay Area transit district, although it had little authority. A 1951 amendment created a commission, representing nine Bay Area counties, charged with creating a rapid transit plan and providing estimates of its cost. Two years later, the commission reported a need for mass transit and more comprehensive planning. The legislature accepted these and also agreed to fund it jointly with the nine counties; a commission hired consultants in late 1953 to provide that fuller plan. After two extensions of time by the legislature, the consultants reported in early 1956, calling for a fixed-rail transit system costing as much as $717 million, depending on the alternative chosen. For a year, the Bay Area commission debated those alternatives, finally recommending to the state a regional transit district, BART, which then became law in mid-1957. Five of the original nine counties were put into the program at this stage.

Further delays ensued, however, for BART consultants' final plans were not submitted until mid-1961. This called for a five-county system requiring ten years in time and just over $1 billion in costs, the bulk to be raised by general obligation bonds. For a year the five counties debated participation, and two more dropped out, those just north and south of San Francisco. But in July 1962, three county boards of supervisors—including San Francisco—did approve the plan, moving the decision to their voters. A special campaign committee operated a campaign in these counties, well financed and with little obvious opposition. A later San Francisco Chamber of Commerce report noted, "It was a grassroots campaign aimed at giving the electorate something to vote against. The demon at hand was the automobile, and the evil it was perpetuating on the Bay Area was traffic congestion." [3] But the vote was quite close, and had the legislature a year earlier not reduced the majority needed for passage from 66.6 to 60 percent, it would have failed. Among the three counties it secured a combined total of 61.2 percent: 68 percent in San Francisco, 60 percent in Alameda (Oakland and Berkeley), and 55 percent in Contra Costa (commuter suburbs). Thus was the authorization stage of BART completed in 1962, eleven years after the first multicounty commission had been created to study its possibility. A subsequent half-year of blocking tactics through litigation failed.

The next problems were those of financing and construction. Between 1962 and 1965, BART basked in a honeymoon of popular support and a general notion that it was well financed. That period was also taken up with detailing the construction requirements of engineering and aesthetic design, and the evaluation of these by prospective builders. But when the bids for the first track mileage and stations in Oakland arrived during the Christmas season in 1965, BART found that its lowest bidder was $13 million over the estimated $47 million. Rather than eat into their reserve funds or reduce the system to fit such bids, BART directors asked for new bids on smaller sections, and thereafter obtained a $49 million bid. But it was clear that BART was in trouble financially; projections of $150 million deficit for the whole system were heard, and inflation was taking a deeper bite than was anticipated, partly from the widening Vietnam War. Financial woes did not come to an end, however, until after several years of fruitless negotiation with the state legislature, which denied BART more bonding capacity or a portion of auto taxes. The concept that was approved, however, appeared in 1968 and was passed in 1969. This was a temporary one-half cent additional sales tax in the three BART counties.

The aesthetic aspects of the system, such as train design and station appearance and location, brought further trouble, particularly from the San Francisco *Chronicle*. Prominent architects resigned from BART, charging they were compelled to report to engineers who rejected their recommendations for technical not aesthetic reasons. This departure was filled by the dean of the environmental design school at the University of California, Berkeley, who thereafter reported only to BART directors. Racial antagonisms also entered the picture when Berkeley citizens insisted that the elevated transit line through their city would effectively create a barrier between the black, less affluent "flats" and the white, more affluent "hills." In the event, Berkeley demanded and got the line put underground, although the city was required to pay for the added cost.

Meanwhile, transit design, construction, and testing moved along, albeit slowly. As late as mid-1967, ground-breaking in San Francisco for Market Street's underground portion of the transit took place with characteristic publicity. For at least another five years, this main artery was to upset San Franciscans and visitors with never-ending noise, rubble, and ugliness. In mid-1970 the prototype cars arrived to be tested for another year or more.[4] Problems developed in replacing underground cable, whose sheathing some rodents found particularly tasty. With all this, deadlines for boarding the first passengers kept receding. But in the autumn of 1972, the first section opened for use, south from Oakland, followed by a flurry of engineering problems, including a minor wreck; the second section opened north of Oakland in January 1973, and the rest during the ensuing year, except for the underwater, transbay section to San Francisco, which was delayed because of safety factors until late summer of 1974.

The Role of Business in BART's Conversion

This account immensely condenses the events and issues of two decades, so it must not be thought that BART lacked controversy. A comparative analysis of San Francisco with other cities on the transportation issue[5] shows clearly that it was highly contentious in this city. Generally in such an issue, public and private leaders have to be reconciled. This meant for San Francisco an understanding of the influence of neighborhood groups and the home-rule tradition, as well as home-rule concerns in the suburbs. BART might have the power to make decisions, but central cities and counties could veto them; witness the successive reduction of the participating counties from nine to five to three. There were key issues to divide private groups and political systems. Particularly salient for San Francisco, compared with other cities, were such issues as the impact of BART on neighborhood integrity, race relations, preservation of the heritage of place, aesthetics, conservation, taxes, and the health of the central business district. On the other hand, limited salience was found for low-income housing, unlike Boston. Too, the question of public ownership was controversial in Baltimore and Houston, but not in San Francisco. Other contentions arose over operational costs, service, fares and jurisdictions, although they were very low in Los Angeles.[6]

One finding is important for our purposes, however, and that is the pivotal role of business leadership in originating, implementing, and supporting the concept of BART. Note business participation at key points in this brief chronology. The Bay Area Council, representing major area businesses, was an early supporter. The original commission in 1951 was chaired for a decade thereafter by a Bank of America executive and former president of the San Francisco Chamber of Commerce. The latter always supported BART in its later troubles.[7] According to the chamber's own account, early business supporters "included manufacturers of transit hardware and software as well as institutions that could provide financial, engineering and other services [as well as] merchants and property owners who would benefit through proprietary interest from construction of the line." The final plans in 1961 incorporated engineering recommendations from the Bechtel Corporation, a major national construction firm located in the city. The campaign which led to the three-county vote for BART in 1962 was financed by the Blyth-Zellerbach committee, whose members the chamber bluntly describes as "San Francisco's most powerful business leaders whose purpose is to act in concert on projects deemed good for the City." This committee's members included heads of the Crown-Zellerbach paper company and the Bechtel Company, and executives of Pacific Gas and Electric Company (which powered BART), Bank of America, and Standard Oil.[8] The fund raising for the campaign was directed by a retired chief executive of the Bank of America, and the head of Kaiser Industries in Oakland was also active in that campaign. The local Chamber of Commerce sponsored the Market Street groundbreaking ceremony in 1967 and originated the successful suggestion of an increased sales tax in BART counties when its finances were in trouble.

Explanation of this collaboration by the business community cannot be satisfied by attributing it only to direct benefits made from selling materials to BART. A fuller understanding comes with the realization that for some time San Francisco business leaders, joined by others around the bay, had wanted to develop the downtown area. To do that, it was necessary to provide a mass transit system that could carry commuters in great enough numbers to fill the buildings, and do so without adding insuperably to traffic congestion. We have seen in the last chapter how the Chamber of Commerce sought to explain why highrise and mass transit would do just that. However, whether a rapid transit system can actually build a stronger downtown is debatable. It has done so in New York, Chicago, Philadelphia, Boston, and certainly in San Francisco. But downtown Cleveland still is in decline even with such a system, while cities without it expand their downtowns, such as Los Angeles, Atlanta, Houston, and Dallas.[9] Nor are businessmen elsewhere as influential in this matter as in San Francisco, but when they do work well with city officials their power is enhanced at the level of state decision making.[10]

Yet a recent national analysis concludes that

the key supporters of *major* (that is, rapid) transit improvements are almost never the operators, the users, or even the direct beneficiaries of construction expansion programs. . . . They are the CBD [central business district] business community and the central city government. Their objectives are not transportation improvements; they seek what might be called spinoff effects, namely strengthening the downtown, discouraging further decentralization of middle-class residences, rebuilding the tax base.[11]

The argument here is not that pecuniary influences do not play upon businessmen. After all, banks that did not support a program designed to generate over $1 billion in general obligation bonds should not be in the business. Rather, it is to say that San Francisco's business world had accepted the premise of the planners. That is, to develop highrises and the attendant cluster of business activity, it was necessary to plan how to move into the city the several hundred thousand workers needed without flooding the town with cars.

For this, a transit system was ideal. In function it would do for San Francisco what the subway did for Manhattan, where highrise construction and transit became necessarily linked.[12] In the process, the automobile was made the scapegoat for this vision of urban form. Yet as critics of highrises and of BART asked, was that the only vision? "The question that the daily newspapers never allowed to be asked [in the 1962 referendum on BART] was: What would happen if the

Bay Area followed a plan of decentralization, calling for people to live and work in the same community rather than commuting to San Francisco?" [13]

But it was not business alone that brought off this economic coup. Organized labor consistently and fully supported it for the obvious construction jobs it created and the transit workers it would employ thereafter. The city's local officials among the BART directors have never faltered. The board of supervisors never exercised its function under state law to refuse to sign the agreement, as it did in the famous "freeway revolt" against the Embarcadero system in 1959.

But more significantly, the voters of San Francisco supported it directly and indirectly at the polls. They gave BART the largest percentage in the three-county election in 1962, although in 1966 a majority refused a multimillion-dollar subsidy to their own outmoded municipal transit. They also voted funds to build an additional BART station in the heart of the business district and to rebuild Market Street. In short, these citizens did something more than vote against automobiles and for mass transit. That they did clearly, in their Embarcadero victory, in preventing any freeway link to the Golden Gate Bridge, and in backing Mayor Alioto's opposition to double-decking the Golden Gate Bridge. But even more, San Franciscans, in accepting the jobs and income that BART meant, also accepted the vision of their city of the highrise advocates—"Manhattanization," that is, high and close buildings used by commuting workers. As we will see, at every electoral opportunity they have backed BART, not merely in authorizing the act of union but in providing their own taxes.

With this provision of transit support, the city will change, as it always has, of course. For BART was the key to the subsequent construction. It made possible the attraction to the city of businesses whose workers could commute with greater ease from the East Bay. Failure to provide links to commuter suburbs in counties to the north and south may well be serious constraints on the future success of BART in making the vision of a regional economy come true. Chamber of Commerce publicity made it clear that BART meant highrises and more commuters, but those costs were to be outweighed by benefits to local citizens, who would be part of a new economy of the region centered upon San Franciscans. In election pamphlets of that 1962 election and subsequent referendum campaigns, business has beat out this message. It was an effective combination of appeals: to direct, personal, economic gains—more jobs, more revenue sources; to

Americans' traditional susceptibility to economic expansion schemes; and to San Franciscans' pride of place, which would be boosted by centering the city in the regional economy.

Critics of this and other highrise programs have complained that the people were misled. Certainly, not all the grandiose promises will be realized; BART started in fiscal and commuter trouble and will most likely remain so. But inspection of the publicity materials reveals that voters were given a full blast of appeals to material and emotional sides of the question, while inspection of their votes, shown later, reveals that they repeatedly bought the entire package. It just might be that they sorted out the conflicting promises and fears in such campaigns and decided on quite rational bases of self-interest, discounting the excesses always attending such promotional campaigns. The losers claim the voters were misled, but in San Francisco a wide range of citizens voted for the issue of BART and since then have benefited, from jobs at least.

THE TOPLESS TOWER OF THE TRANSAMERICA PYRAMID

Without a full analysis of the public authorization of all the highrises which the city witnessed in the 1960s, it is not possible to select one that is "typical." But it is known that each building involves at some stage an action by the local political system, which can block or spur the construction. In San Francisco, those actions are the issuance of a building permit and approval by the Planning Commission. This section describes this public linkage to private allocation in the affair of a pyramidal highrise, headquarters for the Transamerica Corporation. This Transamerica pyramid thus typifies some aspects of the involvement of government; but in another respect, it was more than typical, since the board of supervisors was also required to act. But, as with Marlowe's Ilium, it was to be a force outside the city walls that "burnt the topless tower."

The Coalition Context

The Transamerica Corporation is one of the few hometown businesses that turned to highrise headquarters during the 1960s. A typical conglomerate, with assets over $3.5 billion and operations around the world, it had begun in San Francisco; until the pyramid was finished, it worked out of a four-story building. When planning began for a new center, Transamerica's officers believed that a new building would require a tripling of their own floor space needs if it were to be economically feasible. The distinguished architect William Periera designed a narrow-based, 1,000-foot pyramid—a rare design in modern buildings. Its form was urged as one that permitted less obstructed views and more light and air into the street below than did the prevalent slab design. There was no question, whether one listened to its supporters or opponents, but that it was a dramatic concept. By late December 1968, Transamerica's directors approved this design.

The pyramid broke upon public awareness with carefully staged public relations.[14] But before that, business and government figures received a preview. As Transamerica's public relations director noted, "The Mayor and his chief administrative officer [Thomas Mellon] were the first city officials invited in to take a look, and to advise us as to the proper steps for approval." The city planning director, among other officials, also got a peek in the month between board approval and public announcement. In late January 1969 there was a Hollywood type of press conference, complete with the sudden unveiling of a five-foot model before the assembled press; the joining of this event later that day to the annual Chamber of Commerce banquet was also carefully planned. Invitations to the press conference had gone to key city officials, officers of neighborhood groups, and leaders of the Chinese and Italian communities in which the pyramid was situated; not all attended, however. A special luncheon for publishers and owners of radio and television stations in the city also filled a busy day for Transamerica executives; both the *Chronicle* and the *Examiner* later provided supportive editorials.

In short, this day initiated the first stage in highrise authorization —mobilizing a coalition from among the political groups that fill the city scene. Thereafter, Transamerica officials acted much like candidates for city office in their efforts to obtain community support; they earnestly appeared before any group they could assemble. As the public relations official noted in an account which glosses over much of the group opposition, "It soon became apparent that many individual battles would have to be won, that a complex community relations job was needed in order to win approval for the project." City officials were dined, singly or in clusters, to hear the Transamerica spokesmen on the beauty and commercial virtues of the pyramid. Among the groups so approached were city department heads, including engineers and traffic specialists; labor leaders; and neighborhood groups (some of whom spurned this approach), while individual briefings were reported for supervisors and reporters.

This stage of coalition mobilization—standard strategy in city decision making here and elsewhere when large resources are at stake —was designed to generate inputs into the political system for the next stage of authorization. This was punctuated by problems, many of which were displayed earlier in the Washington Square decision. For example, the chosen location brought in the Planning Commission, for it had discretion over any structure erected in a designated "transition zone," even if it met all zoning requirements. Complicating the matter was the 1,000-foot height, almost twice that of the Washington Monument. This feature alienated not only "save the view" groups but the city planning director, who saw it as exorbitant in that neighborhood, overlooking Chinatown and North Beach. Even more complicated, the Transamerica pyramid, unlike most other highrises, had to cover a narrow city street; straddling or bridging it was not structurally feasible. That meant that Transamerica had to buy a portion of a city street, which by city charter only the board of supervisors could approve if the Planning Commission first recommended its closure.

For a year Transamerica presented its case to city agencies, both informally and in public sessions. The course of events need not be detailed, but put briefly, all agencies gave their approval, albeit with some contingencies. One event was a public relations skirmish with outraged community groups. There was also some unfavorable publicity in the national media generated by hostile architects, who pointed out a severely altered skyline so different from what millions of visitors had known and loved. The shape and height of Transamerica's pyramid was a constant source of public and private debate. Skyline maps dramatically drawn by opponents showed that "view corridors" would be blocked if it went up; supporters enthused about its aesthetic lines and its world distinction; and both sides engaged in a guerrilla publicity war. The last included the infiltration of opponents' meetings by Transamerica, hiring hippies to demonstrate as "artists *for* the pyramid," and sending pretty secretaries to serve tea and Chinese cookies to demonstrators.

But the payoff was in action by political authorities, and here the result was success tempered with small concessions. The height was reduced, and after several reviews, the supervisors approved the street closing and sale to Transamerica. A supervisors' committee that first

heard the request approved it 2 to 1, after four hours of hearings before large crowds and television cameras—and a surprise visit from
Mayor Alioto to testify in favor of the Pyramid. Before the full board,
the vote to close the street was 10 to 1 in favor, again with public
clamor. Thereafter, Transamerica officers and the architect, feeling
they had conceded too much, redesigned the height, the top, and other
features of the pyramid. But these changes were enough to require
Planning Commission approval again, so the whole process was re-
negotiated. Finally, in December 1969, a site permit was issued, and
Transamerica broke ground without public notice, almost furtively.
That permit was challenged, of course, before the Board of Permit
Appeals, but to no avail. In early 1972, the 48-story pyramid was
topped with the traditional evergreen tree, and later that year it was
ready for its first occupants. By then the Transamerica pyramid was
advertised in national business journals as "a San Francisco tradition
since 1972," a mixing of the opposed views of The City.

Public and Private Trade-Offs

These events portray a clear victory for highrise forces, despite
the building's novel form and unusual height, which had enraged opponents. This account also shares several features with the BART case.
Clearly both displayed corporate and union power, consent, and
enthusiasm. The Chamber of Commerce endorsed the building by
using its auspices to unveil it, for the pyramid would provide extra
office space to attract outside businesses. Construction unions saw job
opportunities in the tower, as in every highrise. Both BART and the
Transamerica Tower were part of businessmen's vision of the urban
function of this city; the building would be but a few blocks from a
downtown station. Most important for our analysis, however, is the
fact that both cases demonstrate the support of political authorities
when basic decisions have to be made about main allocations of private capital. BART took longer, of course, because more political systems were involved and the basic problem was more complex, requiring more planning and implementation. But at every decisional point
in these procedures where one can trace some kind of public-to-private
transmission channel, most political authorities supported these private
decisions.

Not completely, of course, for in both cases concessions were part
of the necessary trade-offs between public decision and private preference. BART could yield on questions of which counties would join,

what financing could be arranged, whether lines would be above or below ground, and where stations would be located. The Transamerica pyramid's extraordinary height was lowered in the negotiations; only those closest to the corporate decision can know whether that 1,000 feet was simply an opening ploy in the bargaining. Transamerica officials, as hometown boys, could not have been ignorant of the fervor of questions of heights and protection of the view which were emerging on the local scene. Also, some safety features and urban services were provided because of demands by city officials. But the heart of the matter is seen in the power the supervisors had to simply stop the building entirely by refusing to close off and sell that street section. That was their ultimate weapon (not available to them in all cases, incidentally) for securing concessions to some of the public outcry against the Transamerica building. But in the end, they were not of a mind to prevent it, just as they did not disapprove of BART participation in the early 1960s.

While highrise opponents could look upon this as a victory for corporate and union forces, it must not be seen as a decision which municipal officials were browbeaten into making. Rather, in decisions concerning both BART and the Transamerica pyramid, as in many other highrise decisions, they shared this urban vision of San Francisco as a new regional and national administrative center, in which highrises were essential and beneficial components. Their critics saw such officials as somehow either venal or victims. But recall what Samuel Johnson once noted: "The writer of news never fails to tell how the enemy murdered children and ravished virgins." City officials in this decisional context were neither. If one needs an analogy, more appropriate is that of the Sabine women and their subsequent satisfaction.

UNITED STATES STEEL: THE TOPPLING OF A TOWER

Accounts of successful new construction do not provide the total context of highrise politics, however. Some proposed buildings are not erected, although to judge from recent events, they must be few. There is much to learn about highrise decisions from these failures. Such an opportunity arose in the late 1960s when a major national corporation, United States Steel (USS) failed to negotiate the tower it sought. This failure, even though USS had the full support of San Francisco businesses and unions, was one of the few victories for a new coalition of environmental groups emerging late in this decade. Finally, the account informs us yet again of the connectivity of the city to other levels of government, for at a crucial point it was the failure of an external force to support USS that made the difference. Intergovernmental agreement, the existence of which created BART and the lack of which blocked USS, is another aspect of the decisional context, as crucial as the local coalition.

The City Acquires Its Port

San Francisco never owned the port that made it so famous, except in its earliest years. Mismanagement caused the state to take it over in 1863, and there it remained for over a century of growth and profit. But toward the end of that era, the city's port trade dropped off, as the state had done little to improve the facilities. Los Angeles ports, located in areas with new legislative power created by larger population and apportionment, did little to help this competitor. Oakland also began to out-perform its neighbor by innovations in quick-loading devices. By the 1960s, the port of San Francisco was an inefficient revenue drain on the state's resources. Its piers, built during a half century, once thronging with carriers from every port in the world, were now shabby and unused. Tourists jamming the city now came by plane and car via airport and streets municipally owned. But along the historic Embarcadero, which once rang with the frequent cries of "Men needed along the shore!" only the cries of wheeling gulls were heard now above the empty sheds.

All this began to change through the efforts of city businessmen and government officials.[15] A campaign to return the port to local control climaxed in a 1968 city referendum in which almost 75 percent of those voting approved the transfer. This cleared the way to meet the objectives of leaders in the campaign—conversion of the port property to provide revenues for maritime uses and to develop it commercially. Such plans, involving a longer account than required here, were to be shaped by the costs which the city paid the state for title to the port. These consisted of $53 million in bonded indebtedness, two gubernatorial appointees among the seven port commissioners, legislative clearance of future expenditures over $250 million and a promise to spend $100 million on shipping improvements (half within a decade and half within twenty-five years). Most significant, though, were the constraints on leasing the port's private property for commercial uses.

Even before the local control referendum, the state-appointed Port

Commission had been thinking about developing its lands. After the transfer it tended to insist on independence from city agencies, although its budget was subject to review by the board of supervisors. Yet the board, in placing the transfer issue on the 1968 ballot (by 10 to 1), had divested itself of any authority to review the port's commercial operations. The commission saw its main task as commercial competition with other ports; because it could operate without local tax support, it should be autonomous. Its influence was enhanced by its allies. Cyril Magnin and recent Alioto appointee Harry Bridges proclaimed a concept of port development with which the Chamber of Commerce and the unions enthusiastically agreed. Central to this support was a vision of land along the great sweep of the port's piers being converted to commercial development. That enthusiasm was well reflected in Mayor Alioto's statement that the northern waterfront was "one of the hottest pieces of real estate that anyone could get." [16]

Alternatives for such development went back to 1959, when Commission chairman Magnin revealed architects' concept of an "Embarcadero City" on the north shore. It would contain offices, hotels, and recreation facilities to help pay for new port facilities farther south, below the Bay Bridge. Other consultants in 1966 provided the port commissioners with an appraisal of the port's economic future. They accepted the earlier thesis of commercial development north of the bridge—although with fewer and smaller buildings—which would support shipping facilities to the south. In 1968 the Bolles Plan initiated the first acted-upon port planning, again featuring commercial development of the northern waterfront. Submitted to a joint meeting of the Planning and Port commissions a few weeks after the referendum transferring the port to the city, this plan set height limits of 64 or 84 feet, depending on location. By mid-1969 the Planning Commission had accepted the 84-foot limit, and by October 1969 it had approved implementing amendments from its Planning Department—except for holding open such a decision in the Ferry Building area at the foot of Market Street. Later recommendations from the department said that to the north it would be 65 feet, close around it 84 feet (with exceptions up to 125 feet), and to the south of it 84 feet (with exceptions of 175 feet).

The United States Steel Proposal

While these limits were being worked through city agencies, the Port Commission sought to attract customers to what was being

planned. At the end of 1969, it had evoked interest in bids from as
far away as Italy, Hawaii, and the East Coast. In December 1969,
architects told the Planning Commission that the United States Steel
Corporation was interested—although USS gave no direct commitment
then or thereafter—in a project to be built over the water south of the
Ferry Building. This multifunctional structure would handle ship
passengers and would include two commercial buildings, a twenty-five-
story hotel and a forty-story office building. While nothing was said
about height, these structures were in excess by several times the
limits under discussion by city agencies.*

While the opposition was immediate, it was to die away and then
flare up sharply later with the intervention of a coalition of conservation groups. The first criticism was from the Planning Department, that
the corporation had ignored this agency's role. Conservation groups
like the Telegraph Hill Dwellers and San Francisco Beautiful also
weighed in with their opposition. But the San Francisco Planning and
Urban Renewal Association (SPUR), known for its concern for
aesthetic and rational planning, came to the support of USS.[17]

Meanwhile, as 1970 opened, city agencies went ahead with consideration of height limits in the port area. By late March, the
Planning Commission had acted on height limits, much as its Planning
Department had requested. But greater exceptions were also added,
up to 400 feet in one area along the shore, which proved highly contentious when it came before the board of supervisors. Its own committee was split over the exceptions of 125 and 400 feet and made no
recommendation to the full board when reporting in mid-1970. Meanwhile, the Port Commission had already approved the USS plans a
month earlier.

The supervisors proved to be the crucial forum for the decision on
the USS proposal. The controversy deepened at its first hearings in
mid-1970, for the port director declared that not only was 125 feet
not acceptable, but 400 feet would not do, either. Rather, permission
for *550 feet* was requested, along with an increase in the size of the
area in which it would apply. That height, about that of the Washington Monument, would top by a few feet the towers of the nearby Bay
Bridge. Many believe that the supervisors would have accepted 550

---

* A rough rule of thumb is that one story equals about ten feet in such commercial
development.

feet at that point, so intense was the commercial and union pressure for developing the port. But supervisors could not accept an increase in the Planning Commission recommendations of 400 feet without referral back to that agency, which was therefore voted 8 to 2. The commission's Planning Department stuck to its 175-foot limit, but the commission itself rejected this, by a 4 to 2 vote accepting the full 550-foot limit as requested. The issue was now returned to the supervisors, where it seemed certain of support.

That it was not approved can be attributed in part to the protest over highrises and to the intervention of an agency from the outside. The opposition to the 550-foot request, while vocal, was limited. One sympathetic account of the opposition reported internal disagreement about leadership and strategies.[18] Partly it was a case of too many chiefs, since the opposition to the USS project included many affluent San Franciscans with some power in the community. Herb Caen kicked off the campaign in his column in early September, thus mobilizing many persons who were unhappy with the obvious rush to build this tower and who were looking for some way to resist. Allies were found among supervisors; young architects picketed the firm responsible for the project's design and height; the northern chapter of their professional organization condemned it on aesthetic grounds; and SPUR reconsidered its support, demanding that the Port Commission economically justify its position on the project.

By early October an ad hoc committee had been formed to study the economic aspects of the port, and anti-USS supervisors were calling for more delay to consider such a report. Accounts differ on motivations thereafter, but the supervisors voted 6 to 4 in mid-November for three months' delay in the decision, with the port director in support and the anti-USS supervisors opposed. There followed more verbal scuffling in the local press while lines hardened. Even USS entered the fray directly. To this point, the corporation had employed local realty leaders, as well as the Chamber of Commerce, to carry its case. But in an October statement urging community support, it claimed that until the zoning decision had been made, it would not start planning, because of the large costs. When the issue came again before the supervisors in mid-February 1971, after some skirmishing they voted 6 to 4 to accept the 84-foot limit with exceptions up to 175 feet. In the event, limits not only of 550 feet but of 400 feet had been beaten down.

The Role of External Authorities

The key event that produced this result was not the cut-and-thrust of local group politics, however. Rather, it was the intervention of state and regional agencies, which decided in a parallel matter that the Port Commission lacked authority to engage in *any* commercial building. The state actor was the attorney general, and the regional group was the Bay Conservation and Development Commission (BCDC). BCDC had been created by state law in 1965 to develop a "Bay Plan" for the legislature, which it did successfuly in 1969. That plan gave BCDC limited jurisdiction over developments as far as one hundred feet out from the bay shore, primarily in fill and overwater developments. Filling can be done for a "water-oriented" commercial project only if it is on private property and mostly on land. That is, no commercial development is allowed if it is on public property and mostly over water. Moreover, by the plan, fill projects are approved only if they produce clear-cut public benefits, and even then only if for "water-oriented" uses and when no alternative "upland location is available."

BCDC had been asked to review applications from both United States Steel and a Ferry Port Plaza, which had been urged as acceptable on two grounds. They were in line with the "water-oriented" requirements, and although they would involve a net loss of water area at their sites, this would be balanced off by opening up an "equivalent" water area elsewhere along the Embarcadero through the removal of old piers. Because no such rule of equivalency existed in the Bay Plan, BCDC turned to the state's attorney general for advice on the plaza project. In the three-month delay of the supervisors between November and February, the attorney general struck down the "equivalent" concept and emphasized that water-oriented purposes must be met by construction only on *private* land—little of which was found in the plaza project. Similarly, then, the USS project was equally deficient on several grounds; it relied on equivalence, it would be built on public property, and little of the project was water-oriented.

So it was that when the supervisors met in February 1971, both the state and BCDC had preempted their authority to act on the tall tower that USS desired. Yet the supervisors were still under pressure to proceed as if BCDC had not acted. For the Port Commission was suing BCDC for its rejection, and many USS supporters, thinking they would win the suit, wished local authorization for the higher limits so as to be ready. But the combination of popular outcries, intervening governments, and pressure from anti-USS supervisors carried the day.

In this account, further aspects of the coalitional dynamics of San Francisco's decision making can be seen. Business, labor, and municipal authorities were in agreement on commercial development of the port, on the utility of highrise projects for this purpose, and on a vision of progress that was limited to material gain for supporters. That the coalition was defeated, however, cannot be attributed to an outraged public opinion. Even the visible opposition—the ad hoc conservation groups—had a hard time agreeing on objectives and methods. If public opinion is supposed to be reflected in the supervisors, that group was certainly not opposed to great heights. Close participants believe the 400-foot limit had a clear majority among supervisors, but the sudden demand for 550 feet upset that acceptance.

Clearly, then, what defeated the coalition was the action of external political authorities. A spokesman for one conservation group was quite frank about it. "It was something of a miracle. . . . It came out of nowhere and saved us for awhile. Because we were just too disorganized, too petty and too poor to really stop those projects. A lot of people are taking credit now for saving the waterfront, but really, it was that technicality. For once, the technicality worked for us." [19]

Visible in this case once again is the effect of outside forces. In the BART case, the regional authority's interests paralleled those of local private and municipal authorities. In the USS case, however, the regional authority, prodded by a state official, opposed the local interests and succeeded. The implication is that there may be other areas of the *local* decisional context that are influenced, if not dominated, by *external* power centers. Local coalition agreement alone is not enough to carry the day when extramural forces are opposed. This aspect of the city's decisions will be fully explored in a later chapter.

Ironically, BCDC was not a complete outsider to the city. Part of a regional movement during the 1960s, BCDC has members from San Francisco on its official governing body, and many suburban members tend to identify closely with the city; its director had once been an executive at SPUR. This kind of organization with its boundary-spanning nature, a new presence in the Bay Area, has an intense upper class, conservationist orientation that is backed by state authority to protect and maintain the ecology and beauty of the bay. It was that perspective which overcame BCDC's empathy for the city and the fierce coalition of pro-USS forces, including an energetic mayor for whom this was a major defeat. It was not the last time that the city was to be opposed by regional organizations, as we shall see, and the result has been to make many civic leaders in San Francisco hostile to external constraints on their vision of a regional economy.

PROPOSITION T: THE VOTERS' VOICE ON HIGHRISES

One point may have been missed in the three studies to this point. Whenever San Francisco's electorate was directly involved, there was popular support for highrises and related developments. This voice was heard in the 1962 vote for the city to join the transit system, when 68 percent approved, highest of the three counties. It was also heard in subsequent referenda to provide special BART stops downtown and to pay for the extra costs. There was no direct vote on the Transamerica pyramid, nor in defeat of United States Steel's tower, but elected representatives—mayor and supervisors—were enthusiastic about the projects. Highrise opponents might claim to speak for the city's people, but it was unclear how well they represented those who lacked a view of the bay or who cared little for the arguments concerning aesthetics or earthquake danger. Nor was it clear whether already complex arguments over the costs and benefits of highrises were perceived, understood, and accepted by the general public.

However, a clear test of the electorate's attitudes was provided in November 1971, nine months after the supervisors voted down the USS project. It was brought on by a dramatic publicist of the conservation viewpoint, a local businessman, Alvin Duskin. His full-page adds in the local press had earlier challenged efforts to develop Alcatraz Island and claims that highrises paid more than they cost the community. What Duskin did now, with the support of groups that had mobilized against Transamerica and United States Steel, was to put the question of height limits directly to the voters in an initiative, designated Proposition T on the ballot. This volatile issue was injected into simultaneous campaigns for reelection by Mayor Alioto and several incumbent supervisors. The usually turbulent campaign ensued, with eleven candidates for mayor and thirty-three for supervisor on the ballot, along with twenty propositions.

The clashing contentions are briefly put. Duskin called for a limit of six stories or 72 feet, whichever was smaller, on all future public or private construction. For six months before the election,* both sides

* The petition had been drawn and names secured for a special election earlier in June 1971. But supervisors, whether from fear of public action or of the $350,000

developed the arguments laid out in the previous chapter.[20] Ad hoc groups arose on both sides, as did more established organizations for conservation, business, and labor. The three major candidates for mayor opposed it in differing degrees, while eight of the eleven incumbent supervisors also opposed it as charter members of a special group. The rhetoric was flamboyant on both sides, with non sequiturs everywhere. Herb Caen never endorsed the Duskin proposal, but he frequently made clear his opposition to highrises and the "pellmell helter-skelter willingness to trade the God-given beauties of San Francisco for a mess of blottage." The ILWU, in firmly opposing the proposition, declared: "Think of San Francisco without the Ferry Building. Without Coit Tower. Without Grace Cathedral. Without the Top of the Mark. They're all taller than six stories. Not every tall building is ugly. Or every short building handsome. Consider L.A." Or, "Think about this: In Utica, N.Y., where there are few tall buildings, property taxes are twice as high as San Francisco. . . . There are few high-rises in Trenton, New Jersey. Just mile after mile of low-rise sameness. . . . And a bankrupt economy. Don't let them Trentonize San Francisco."

Much was heard of the economic contentions. The Chamber of Commerce produced reports opposing the six-story limit, while the *Bay Guardian* published its critical volume, *The Ultimate Highrise*. Duskin saw it as a "have and have not" contest, claiming that highrise forces raised $400,000 on the campaign. His forces pictured the contest as an Armageddon, whose outcome would determine the course of highrises not only in the city but in the nation. The chamber later noted that Proposition T opponents had included "heavy participation from business organizations that were alarmed at the prospect of so drastic a lid on new development." But it found that both sides, while well financed, spent no extraordinary amounts.[21] The chamber did organize meetings to inform city businesses of the consequences, chiefly the estimate by the city controller that the six-story limit would raise property taxes. He averred that downtown property assessments would be lowered because of lowered property values bound to occur once highrises were precluded; this would cause property owners and

---

cost of a special election, asked the city attorney to find a legal basis for waiting until November. He just happened to find the omission of the word "forthwith" on the election call, justifying the board's subsequent action of deferring the balloting until November. Mr. Dooley once observed, "I care not who makes th' laws of a nation if I can get out an injunction."

renters elsewhere in the city to face the increased assessments that
would be necessary to make up the lowered revenues. Labor unions
were indignant at the loss of construction and other jobs if highrises
were limited. The news media also opposed the measure as a barrier
to their vision of the future city as part of a regional and national
complex.

All in all, by election day one could judge that the voters had been
provided a full coverage of the issue and a clear choice of alternative
visions of the city. One was a low-profile concept, part of the conservation and historical visions that unite the opponents of highrises.
Another was the high-profile concept, part of the economic and national vision that linked the city to the future. The voter's choice of
dreams was emphatic, as only 37.8 percent voted for Duskin's proposal
on November 2, 1971—that is, five out of eight San Franciscans failed
to see the six-story limit as part of their vision of the city. No analysis
is available of what particular reasons so moved them, but observers
believe that the tax increase charge loomed large. In the official
booklet that provided each voter with information on the content,
group support, and tax effect of each proposition, there was a clear,
short statement by the controller that the tax rate would climb sharply
under such highrise limits. It may have been that voters simply were
not in an affirmative mood that day; they also rejected two of four
bond measures, including one for schools, and eleven of sixteen charter
amendments, including Duskin's.

San Franciscans had another chance in 1972 to vote on a modified
proposal on limits and refused it also,* so their actions provide a clear
statement. Whatever the passion of conservationists or the reality of
their economic, safety, and aesthetic claims, the urban vision to which
they pointed lacked popular backing. Condemnation of corporate and
union power or of city officials for alleged greediness found little public
credence when the issue was put in simple terms of low versus high

---

* Another Duskin referendum effort in June 1972 sought to impose limits of 160 feet
downtown and 40 feet elsewhere. It failed also, receiving 43.2 percent, better than in
1971, but less in actual votes cast. It received majority support in wealthy liberal
areas (Pacific Heights) and sites of recent highrise controversy (Russian, Telegraph,
and Nob hills). But the *Examiner* reported that it was killed by large majorities against
it in conservative, middle-class, working-class, and minority neighborhoods (June 8,
1972, analysis by Jerry Burns). Blacks in the Hunter's Point precinct voted it down
16 to 78, it lost 70 to 110 in Chinatown, and so forth.

Finally, in the summer of 1973, the supervisors voted to limit building heights on
a staggered scale from the business heart of downtown outward. But the change in
the cityscape had advanced so far that lowrise advocates could take little heart.

buildings. It can be inferred, then, that this ultimate sovereign in the city's decisional context shares an economic motive with highrise supporters. Neither the argument regarding aesthetics nor that of danger dominates their thinking; maybe too many live too far from the highrise area to see or feel threatened or offended by their heights. Highrise opponents' arguments related to economics may not get through as well as the simple statement of the controller that lowered assessments downtown would have to be made up by higher assessments and tax rates elsewhere in town. More generally, then, on repeated occasions when San Francisco voters have been given an opportunity to speak on the matter, they have chosen the urban vision of the coalition of business, labor, and city officials. As long as they are told that the absence of highrise buildings increases their taxes, that vision will continue to dominate.

DIMENSIONS OF HIGHRISE DECISION MAKING

The Mutuality of Coalitions

These four case studies have emphasized different yet allied dimensions of the politics of income. That three of these four describe victories for highrise supporters symptomizes a larger reality, which can be seen in previous data on the dramatic upsurge of these towers. All four reflect the agreement of a coalition of business, labor, city officials, news media—and, when given a chance to express it, a majority of citizens. All cases show responses, not detailed above, to opposing concepts of urban life and form. All imply the merging of public and private resources to achieve economic goals that redound to the benefit of coalition members.

Further, these cases illuminate and verify the general propositions on economic power in the American community noted in the preceding chapter. In this issue, involving decisions about the largest private resource allocation on which government in the city can have an influence, corporations and their agents were clearly active and overt. Their appearance on the San Francisco scene during the 1960s was sudden, visible, and emphatic, with results overwhelmingly in their favor. All seemed to use *local* agencies to cement their income concerns—*local* architects, trade unions, Chamber of Commerce, realty managers, and, to a degree not investigated here, finances. Some played a highly visible and active game, like Transamerica, while others, like United States Steel, maintained an aloof stance as local agents negotiated the politics of highrise.

Yet it does not follow from this hyperactivity that corporations exerted their influence on other public issues. It may be that the corporations of the size noted earlier do indeed become involved in local issues concerning municipal services. But those interviewed for this book, who were part of the top financial and legal circles, described themselves and their cohorts as usually aloof from such matters. It is hard for such institutions to become aroused over the local furor about closing a police station in Golden Gate Park when the day is spent with calls from Tokyo, Sydney, London, and Paris, and the evening in rural suburban retreats. For such local matters, which are routine or narrow but frequent in local affairs, the Little Rich are the active agents of economic power. But, while having a play of their own in these interrelated games, the Little Rich have also openly and eagerly supported the Big Rich in these highrise decisions. Like all other members of that coalition, the marriage of mutual interests has been the underlying dynamic that generated the decision making.

Trade unions in this major issue are another group which acted as comfortable companions to corporate power, but not because of a "sell-out to the bosses," in the old proletarian belief. Rather, there was a clear mutuality of interest here also, for these buildings meant construction jobs and, later, jobs for service workers. We earlier noted the disgust expressed by a union leader toward the so-called snobs on high hills who protested the interruption of their views when men needed those construction jobs. Or the remark of a black leader that the bay could be filled in entirely, as far as he was concerned, if it meant more jobs for minorities. This is most dramatically symbolized in the alliance on the Port Commission of shippers with Harry Bridges, ILWU president, two groups who thirty years before were battering one another economically, if not in reality. Both agents agreed on the need to strengthen the vitality of the port, and if it meant putting up towers that filled in the bay in order to get revenue to build new piers, then so be it. Nor is this a local phenomenon. The mutuality of interests between labor and management noted in this set of decisions reflects their increasing compatibility elsewhere in the nation, as the two seek to function in a mature industrial economy.

Another factor was the role of city officials. Given the amount of money interjected into the local economy, and the power of labor and corporations, it is hardly surprising that these officials were generally supportive of the highrise boom. Authorities were captivated with the thought of the value of such buildings in the solution of other problems the city suffered. Like most officials elsewhere in urban America, they saw an increasing gap between local resources and local problems. In that "urban crisis," converting the downtown area into a highrise center of capital in the West promised jobs and revenues sorely needed.

To some, however, all this looked as if city officials had been, if not corrupted in the legal sense, then overwhelmingly seduced. Thus, the *Bay Guardian*'s studies showed with painstaking detail that the campaign support for elected officials came from a relatively few people, most of whom were highrise supporters.[22] Thus, of the 244 biggest contributors to three or more winning city campaigns from 1965 to 1970, 85 were "connected with land/development/real estate as developers, realtors, financiers, attorneys, banks and savings and loan institutions." My own analysis of these listings shows, too, that such donors, when they support larger numbers of candidates, are more successful than donors who are opponents of highrise buildings. This is particularly significant when in recent elections the correlation between the amount of money and number of votes received seems quite good.* Too, critics find it suspicious that supervisors receive endorsement from highrise supporters.

But whether they received numerous or few endorsements, most supervisors also supported most of the highrise efforts that came to them for action. Thus, of the supervisors voting on these issues from 1966 to 1971, only one voted no more often than yes, and he was defeated in 1967 in the mayor contest. Nor is it surprising or suspicious that those on city commissions dealing with highrise development turn out to be heavily business and professional—33 businessmen, 14 professionals (9 lawyers), 11 labor (3 ILWU), and 3 other;[23] to live in exclusive areas; and to grossly underrepresent racial minorities. Such is the composition of all other city commissions and of such bodies in other cities.[24]

What the critics lack is perspective on other places and times for municipal governments. The infusion of business goals into governing mechanisms and policy structures of cities in the United States is wide-

---

* A little bit of statistics can be misleading. The *Bay Guardian*'s study focuses only on a few at the top of the list of candidates, ignoring numerous others. Using rank order correlation of votes and money received for only those few, one derives coefficients in the 1967 mayoralty race of 1.00 ($N = 3$, which ignores 15 other candidates); in the 1967 supervisorial race, .49 ($N = 6$, which ignores 38 other candidates); and the 1969 supervisorial race, .98 ($N = 10$, which ignores 5 other candidates).

spread and has been so for much of our history. That characteristic results directly from popular acceptance of the values of acquisition (known as "progress" and "growth"), which are writ large in our history; businessmen are merely their most energetic practitioners. The affirmative response of city officials to those values may in some cases arise from corruption or excessive influence, of course, but it also may simply arise from the sharing of mutual values of acquisition.

In that light, however, two other questions may be properly asked. The first is: How well was the city served by the political system's support of highrise construction? That answer must be most indefinite, not only because insufficient time has passed to judge the effects of this support. Rather, much of the ambiguity arises from a lack of adequate standards for judging the effects of this policy. The argument of the economic cost of highrises sketched earlier is hard to substantiate either way because there has not been much hard study of highrise developments elsewhere. Nor is much light provided by claims that highrises will "Manhattanize" the community or that their absence will "Trentonize" the economy. That critique may arouse antagonists' emotions, but it is a poor substitute for planning based on substantive knowledge.

It may be that such knowledge alone is insufficient to move men of power. For, it is claimed, they use knowledge only when it supports their goals, but otherwise are indifferent or hostile to it. Yet the planning function, with its roots in a knowledge of cause and effects, is not a slave to the interests of the powerful. As Guy Benveniste has demonstrated, there is a tie between the expert and the powerful which shows that each exercises reciprocal influence. Or, as Francine Rabinovitz has shown for city planners, there are different roles the expert may perform which can make him more or less effective.[25]

The Visible Hand of the Public

There is a second question about official support of this policy: To what degree are elected representatives out of step with citizens? The representative quality of public decision making is an important, albeit not exclusive, criterion of a policy's value. There was notice earlier that the public and their agents are aligned, but this can be treated more fully with data on the degree of fit between the judgment of the two on highrises. These would be reflections of the citizens' will to tax themselves or to authorize programs necessary to highrises, whether affecting these buildings directly, as in Duskin's 1971 proposi-

TABLE 14

Popular Support for Highrise-related Referenda in San Francisco,
1958–1972

Date	Number and Content of Referendum	Yes (%)
June 1962	A. Airport improvement bonds ($9.8 million)	70.7
November 1962	A. BART authorization	66.9
November 1964	H. Low-rent housing project authorization	55.9
November 1966	A. Airport bonds ($95.5 million)	66.1[a]
	B. Expand municipal transit lines bonds ($96.5 million)	57.9[a]
November 1967	A. Airport bonds ($98 million)	68.6
June 1968	A. Improve Market Street and vicinity of BART	69.7
November 1968	B. Transfer port to city ($60.9 million debts)	73.0
	C. Creation of Port Commission under municipality	74.0
	H. Public housing for low-income, elderly	52.2
November 1969	I. Permit Port Commission to sell bonds at lower rate	62.3
November 1971	B. Harbor improvement bonds ($34 million)	70.4
	T. Six-story height limit	62.1 (No)
June 1972	Height limit, 160 feet downtown, 40 feet elsewhere	56.8 (No)

[a] Failed for lack of a two-thirds affirmative vote.

tion, or more indirectly, as in the creation of an agency or transportation links important in handling commuters drawn downtown.

Table 14 assembles all seemingly related bond proposals or charter amendments for the period 1958–1972, the era of highrise boom in San Francisco. Of the thirteen proposals there, *only two have been defeated over this period,* and of these two, the airport bonds of 1966 were finally passed in 1967. In short, this tells a clear tale of popular support for creating regional air and land transportation; for acquiring the port, permitting it to be incorporated into city government, facilitating its fiscal purposes, and improving its facilities; for building and financing downtown access to BART; and for letting the height limit go beyond six stories. Even on another construction issue which touches on realty and union concerns—low-income housing—citizens of the city have consistently shown support.

This set of data may suggest other inferences, but it cannot support the belief that elected representatives are distorting popular will in this matter. Rather, it shows enthusiastic popular support, especially in light of the two-thirds affirmation then required for all bond encumbrances. That must be compared with a simultaneous statewide fall-off in support for school bonds (from 67 to 35 percent from 1961 to 1968)[26] and the city-wide drop in passing all referenda after 1962, described earlier. That support runs a broad gamut of social strata, from the poor of Hunter's Point and Chinatown to the working class of Mission District on out to the middle class of sunset district, but stops at the gates of wealthy Nob or Telegraph hills.

More directly for our purposes, however, these referenda show the validity of the coalitional concept of the city's decision making. In the private decisional area with most weight in the city's economic realm and with most consequences for its future, the intersection of private and political authorities was not successful *despite* popular opposition but *with* popular support. The exception arose when outside forces intervened. The picture is therefore not one of a cabal covertly corrupting, a Ruef machine, contrary to the citizens' will. Rather it is one of public and private interests openly running parallel to popular acceptance. No more direct indicator of that acceptance can be had than the defeats of the Duskin proposals. Whatever the details of the vision that motivates private, public, and popular action in this area of policy, it does not possess an urban form that retains much of the past, with its low-rise, small-town appearance.

The city exhibits many deceits, the greatest of which is the impression which visitors entertain from viewing Chinatown, Fisherman's Wharf, and the modern Barbary Coast at North Beach. But towering over and near each of these areas are highrises—a black monolith of a bank, a white pyramidal office, and curved-shield apartments. It is here that San Franciscans increasingly live and work, with little attention to those places which attract the couple from Kokomo. Above all, this is a city of contrasts, one quality on which many observers have agreed. So it was at the beginning when millions of dollars passed through crude, slab-board hotels which served the finest cuisine and women to rough-clad miners. So it continues today in the urban dream that bring tourists into town and sends them away fully believing that they "left their heart in San Francisco." But meanwhile, most citizens by the bay put their money, votes, labor, and skills into another urban dream, in which not cable cars but gleaming new towers "reach halfway to the stars." These are the visible signs of a politics of income, in which the shared values of acquisition fuse most social strata into a coalition of mutual interest.

THE PUBLIC FACE OF PRIVATE DECISION MAKING

The merging of private and public decisions, an implicit theme of this section, does not mean that the two are one. Private decision making is concerned with particular groups' benefits, quantifiable costs and gains, and a narrow community constituency. Public policy making deals with the obverse of these—collective benefits, diffuse dimensions of general welfare, and a broader constituency.[27] Nor should we regard this highrise development as special to this city and this time. "One of the most important activities associated with the history of cities in America," an urban historian has noted, "is the promotion of economic enterprise by organized public and private groups within urban communities." [28] Not new either is the opposition to highrises, as businessmen were early critics, for fear of taxes or of losing land-use advantages. By 1893 Chicago had limited the height of such buildings to 130 feet, and New York's zoning law of 1916 was widely copied elsewhere.[29] But the skyscraper could not be stopped, in San Francisco and elsewhere, for zoning still permitted highrise zones or corridors all over the nation in the 1920s. The rise of urban planning did not stop such a union of public and private interests, for the planning function —itself reflective of special values and interests[30]—never has had the political power to make its plans work. One critic has put it bluntly, "Despite the expenditure of millions of dollars over the past fifty years to produce a myriad of master plans for urban development, few cities in the United States have been developed or substantially redeveloped in accordance with a comprehensive plan." [31] The failure lies partly in the kind of fragmented government seen earlier in this book, which lacks the capacity to integrate its authority. But the far greater reason is the lack of broad public support for such integration and for constraining such growth of highrises.

For it has been this general popular support of highrise development which has fused private and public interests over the past century of urban history. That support has been the ultimate barrier to planning, the electoral base of public authorities, and the beneficiary of the trade-offs that economic development brings. In a policy area where most major constituencies in the community can be shown benefits that are tangible, immediate, and measurable—as occurred in San Francisco—coalitions are easy to mobilize.

Public and private groups share mutual interests in this process, but each enters at different stages. The basic decisions about whether and where to build are privately made by constructor and financier. Such prior decisions receive little advice from the community or its government. Also, private policies reflect little concern for effects outside the immediate building, such as long-run municipal burdens, environmental impact, and so on. When such concerns are expressed, they have been of recent issue and all self-confirming. Rather, such externalities are left for those in the public sector to raise, usually too late, after the private decision has been attractively publicized and supportive groups mobilized. In this context, then, as Leonard Ruchelmand and Charles Brownstein recently concluded, such "public decision-making is largely a reaction to decisions already made in the private sector and tends to be supportive of private interests." [32]

That is the process of this politics of profit, whose immediate and visible results are seen in towers high above the cityscape, now hidden in the fog or glaring in the sun. But the future and subtle consequences are not yet known, for with Chaucer, "Hit is not al gold, that glareth."

PART V

THE POLITICS OF DEFERENCE: ETHNIC DIMENSIONS OF DECISION MAKING

If you don't have a sense of personal history, you don't know who you are or where you are going.　JOSEPH ALIOTO

CHAPTER 9

The Arrived Ethnic Groups

INTRODUCTION

The patterns of decision making analyzed in preceding chapters involve groups of high status and issues of great reward. These decisions constitute, as it were, a politics of income among resourceful groups (here "the resourceful"). But another pattern exists in which the participants, sharing low status and influence, also seek rewards. This is the politics of deference among those without resources (here "the resourceless").

These two decisional patterns are separable only for analytic purposes, for in reality they intersect constantly. Sometimes the interests and resources of these actors are aligned, as was noted in the highrise issue. On other occasions, they are opposed or even indifferently unrelated. Even the distinction between "resourceful" and "resourceless" is not completely accurate. As we shall see, the latter groups have found in recent years new kinds of resources which enable them to enter into the decision-making processes in San Francisco. Nor do the resourceful always succeed in their aims, for the resourceless have succeeded against them. Nor must we assume full homogeneity of interests among members within each category. We have already seen occasions when the resourceful have fallen out, and the same happens among the resourceless.

What the distinction does usefully provide, however, is an awareness that there are different rewards available in any city and that they are distributed differently. That is, some urban groups have much and others little of those resources which are influential in achieving group objectives. Much of the analysis up to this point has focused on those with a larger share of such influential resources for the simple reason that these groups are the most active, visible, and successful in the city's politics and have been so for much of its history. Some of these resources are cumulative but not always monopolized by the most successfully acquisitive. Those with the highest income or control over the labor supply do, however, receive high deference—acknowledgment in the media, appointment to prestigious public and private agencies, wide name recognition as a model of success, and so forth.

It is time, however, to look at the others—not as fully or as often active, only recently visible, and only occasionally successful. I will identify these participants and their resources as a prelude to examining their role in the coalitional processes of the city and to analyzing a basically different kind of politics—the securing and maintenance of deference, that is, the recognition and respect for one's importance in the affairs of life.

THE ETHNIC FACTOR

The guiding framework for the following analysis is that the struggle of the resourceful and the resourceless is in large part set within an ethnic context in which, when one group is denied more material rewards, it then will seek the more symbolic ones. Reports of the city's history abound with the importance of ethnicity, and today knowledgeable observers informally cite its continuing importance in an understanding of city affairs. In a city which since its birth has known a distinctive ethnic richness, the ethnic group has played a large role in providing immigrants with a base of values, resources, and identity with which to confront the new world.

The move of immigrants into American politics was but one part of their adaptation to the national culture. A full literature attests to the pain and complexity of that dramatic social history, one also familiar in California and San Francisco.[1] This developmental process from the mid-nineteenth century onward found each group entering society at the bottom of the ladders of opportunity—political, economic, and religious—and thereafter struggling upward generation by generation. That struggle took place among all ethnic groups, whatever their degree of disadvantage or dominance. Fiction and nonfiction have recorded the great costs and rewards of this struggle for individuals caught up in it, whether as group leaders or ordinary citizens.

The forums for this group struggle were diverse—churches, neighborhoods, families, elections, criminal gangs—and the emotional intensity was grim and often destructive. While this conflict also contributed to the enhancement of these groups as well as to society, it was a real, enduring, and inescapable aspect of new groups growing up in America.

Much earlier in this century, some observers saw the process as one of assimilating people of diverse origins, beliefs, and behaviors into a "melting pot," thus creating a highly desirable product that was totally "American." In the latter part of this century, however, scholars began to question the degree of assimilation that actually took place. Traces of distinctive ethnic behavior still exist, despite the passage of several generations.[2] Accommodation, not assimilation, is now the accepted view of this panorama of social adaptation. The essential ingredient of accommodation is a psychological awareness of one's difference from other groups, even while sharing with them many aspects of life. One part of that awareness is the need to achieve recognition from other groups, that need being variously termed "deference" or "respect."

Each ethnic group found a later generation turning with interest to its origins, a process that Joseph Lopreato termed "cultural atavism."[3] That special language, dress, food, patriotism, and even religion which the second generation of immigrants had tried with such embarrassment to slough off in the rush to be "American," the current generation brings back as attributes of group—and ultimately personal—identity. There is no effort to duplicate the past. No Jew would relish a return to the squalor of the New York ghetto during the early 1900s, though it was later romanticized by Harry Golden. Nor do the Irish want to revive the cold-water tenements and the equally cold Yankee dominance of an earlier Boston. Rather, the wish is to distill from that grim experience the essential meaning and value of being "Jewish" or "Irish." These ethnic groups still interact with out-group members in the marketplace, church, city hall, and schoolhouse without surrendering the core consciousness of their origins.

But there are two strains in this contemporary search for ethnic identity. Those who struggled successfully up the ladders of social reward now look back to their origins as a source of strength, seeing it as an ennobling experience despite its obvious privation and ignominy. But those still at the bottom of these ladders draw from their origins a searing sense of outrage. This emboldens them in a new group solidarity to make the upward climb and demand recognition as persons of worth.

When the Jews, the Irish, the Poles, and the Italians look back they see deprivation, discrimination, and dehumanization, but somehow they find it good, for it justifies the distance they have traveled to their present worth and deference. But the blacks and the Spanish-speaking, looking back, see little in the past that is different from what they now know. Herein is the source of their ethnic-based outrage. Nativist elements in the 1840s actually killed Irish Catholics for religious and economic reasons—even blasted down a church door with cannon in one notorious case.[4] But the modern, affluent Irish lawyer knows that cannot happen to him and realizes how far his kind—and he—have come in community respect in the last 125 years. But black and brown Americans see little objective or subjective differences in their life chances between the two eras. More embittering, they feel this to be true even though their kind have been here longer than any of these other non-WASP groups except the Indians—who have reason to be the most bitter.

All these feelings have political consequences. Ethnic clash long formed one of the bases of American politics, from the Scots-Irish backwoods farmer fighting against the English tidewater centers of commerce in colonial and early Republic days,[5] through the urban Old Yankee fighting the Irish immigrant, and the subsequent Irish dominance, in turn, holding off Italians, Slavs, Jews, and others.[6] Today, in most northern cities, it is the blacks—and in a few western and Atlantic coast cities the Spanish-speaking—who are challenging the dominance of the earlier ethnic groups.

Much of this struggle is illustrated in San Francisco's past and present. In the briefest terms, the Spanish took the state from the Indians, the Mexicans took it from the Spanish, the Yankees took it from the Mexicans, and since then every imaginable ethnic group has been seeking part of it.[7] The cultural mélange that makes up this city reflects the history of ethnic succession. When the pieces settled down after the gold rush, economic and political power was vested in a combination of Yankee and German-Jewish leaders, sitting upon large numbers of the Irish, Italian, and Chinese working class. The Workingmen's party, during the last quarter of the nineteenth century, successfully challenged the political power of those leaders, primarily when the Irish turned against the Chinese. Economic power, however, was much slower to come to the Irish as a group. On the other hand, the Italians thrived first as an economic power—in city commerce and valley agriculture—whereas their political power was not as great as that of the Irish until recent times. Meanwhile, the Chinese and the Spanish-speaking stayed (or were kept) out of all efforts to achieve economic and political power except within the narrow confines of their ghettos (see figure 5 for these locations). Such extramural contact as they knew in political arenas was through ethnic ambassadors to City Hall. Other smaller ethnic groups existed, but as factors in the decisional context of the city they were too small or unconcerned to make an impact.

In that context, however, San Francisco's Jewish community has held a special prominence far beyond its size, but always as part of the larger ethnic context. Politically, they have ranged from Abe Ruef in the first decade of the 1900s—aided and abetted in his corruption by Germans, Irish, and Yankees—to the pillar of community politics in the 1970s, Benjamin Swig. Economically, they have financed much growth in and around the Bay Area from the earliest days, although the Italian Gianninis, the Irish Tobins, and the Yankee Crockers played a much larger role. The cultural life of the city has been powerfully stimulated by Jewish support of opera, museums, and theater, although German and Italian contributions have been equally strong. The result has been that Jews in San Francisco have escaped much of the overt anti-Semitism of their brethren elsewhere, and the city has enjoyed a reputation as an unusually good town for Jewish life.[8]

But for a century, two groups were invisible in the city's decisional life—its black and its brown citizens. The reason for the obscurity of the blacks was simply that their numbers were always so few; when World War II began, only about 4,000 lived in San Francisco.[9] The Spanish-speaking invisibility stemmed from a different source—social blindness—for despite their heritage in California, this group lacked position, power, and status after their separation from Mexico. The "Anglo" community did attest to this subculture's "colorful" past and customs, employing Spanish names for the city's streets and sections —and, of course, its own name. But little of their colorfulness was transformed into any influence on the city's political life or economic decisions. Instead, Anglo culture preferred to freeze them—like the Chinese—into ethnic ghettos to be viewed as part of the city's mosaic of life styles that was trumpeted abroad to tourists.

The preceding is a necessarily condensed sketch of the city's ethnic history before the 1950s, when the roles of these groups began to change. Let us now examine the resources and pattern of influence of each of these groups—in this chapter, those who have already arrived at the top of these ladders of opportunity and deference, and in the next chapter, those who are still arriving.

THE IRISH

In San Francisco, as in other cities where they gathered after the nineteenth century migration, the Irish were the ethnic group most amenable to the political milieu. But it was not the only ladder they used for advancement.[10] In construction, the civil service, and the Roman Catholic Church, the Irish found opportunities for employment. If they were not simply hod carriers, neither were they only saloon keepers, teamsters, or janitors. The diversity of careers open to different generations has been a hallmark of the city's Irish—just as diversity has similarly marked the city's history and people. Irishmen designed St. Mary's Cathedral, fostered the growth of the University of California at Berkeley as well as the Jesuit University of San Francisco,[11] dominated the leadership of union locals and the Church,[12] and made their way into the civil service (particularly the police[13] and fire departments) and elective office.

The Irish incorporation into community life in San Francisco was different, however, from the Irish who settled elsewhere.[14] Those arriving on the eastern seaboard surrendered full loyalties to a political machine. So mean was their status relative to old-stock Americans that only the machine could mobilize individual ethnic resources in order to barter for new opportunities for minorities from a contemptuous local system. But in San Francisco, many of the arriving Irish had come across the continent, bringing their own resources of talent, skills, or finances with them. Moreover, all the Irish—from the East or the "ould sod"—found an open system whose rewards were not dominated by *any* group. With position not ascribed, one could have more confidence that individual effort would bring success. Also, the political machine was not the central institution for mobility—individual or group—particularly when so many other minority groups clamored for a portion of the political pie. In San Francisco there has been little of the anti-Catholicism or anti-Irishism that elsewhere led to the creation of mutual protective associations for the Irish and a channeling of that malevolent issue into the political forum. Instead, there were anti-Chinese feelings, in which the Irish were prime leaders at the end of the nineteenth century.

This is not to deny the special affinity of Irish families for local politics. There have been periods dominated by Irish politicians—a Blind Boss Buckley in the 1880s and Governor James Rolph in the 1930s. But aside from Buckley, there was hardly any permanent clustering of Irish around such leaders as occurred in Boston or New York, or any continuing organizational basis for that clustering. Politics was a larger ingredient in the lives of Irish families merely because so many breadwinners worked where high political affairs were conducted—in City Hall. The discussion during many Irish suppers was about "himself's" revelations of politics, observed and gossiped about from his niche in municipal service.

Whatever the distinctive quality of the city's Irish had been, in the early 1970s they were in a kind of retreat. Partly, it was a retreat to the suburbs, as the children of bartenders and policemen, finding success in professions and business, continued the territorial trek their ancestors had known within—and then out of—the city. (See figure 5.) The hard laborers and draymen, who once lived atop "nobby owld, slobby owld Telygraft Hill," produced children who were artisans and city employees and who moved south of Market Street; and their children's children moved to the new developments out toward the ocean or out beyond the city to higher-income suburbs. Those interviewed for this study recount their father's job career: "cab driver, then construction, then some buildings to redo"; "saloon owner, civil service"; "bought one tavern, then another, then began building"; "was an iceman, then a paperman, then finally a civil servant."

In the process, this physical retreat from working-class origins accompanied a retreat from once familiar ethnic ties. Ethnicity itself became diluted. There were still plenty of those whose memories tied them to old Irish hates and loves. St. Patrick's day or a special program for Emmett Hughes can still bring out good crowds to the parades or parks. There are still the Irish groups—Ancient Order of Hibernians, Gaelic Athletic League, the Irish Literary and Historical Society, the Irish Center Club, and the *Irish Herald*. But all agree that old enthusiasms have waned in such matters. First to go were those pre-1900 groups that were little more than overseas bureaus of the revolution— the Irish Freedom League or the Rebel Corps Benevolent Society; their members once worked extra hours for funds for the "resistance" that would unite Ireland and rebuild its economy. But times have changed; the massive outbreak of violence in Northern Ireland after 1970 found little material support among the city's Irish. Other Irish groups lead a precarious existence, supported by an increasingly older folk.

Nor do the Irish any longer dominate the civil service. While still numerous, many Irish city employees are the last trace of the Great Depression, which made such jobs enormously attractive for their security. But now Italians are also well represented in city jobs, as are all the other minorities—except, as will be seen, those who are arriving. The Board of Elections in 1972 was headed by a San Franciscan of Hungarian ancestry, and his assistants traced their heritages to Ireland, China, and Sweden—but not to Africa or Mexico. The chiefs of police reflected this change; the first non-Irishman since 1920 (with one exception) appeared in 1971, and Italians have just emerged as police captains. City Hall observers claim that this dilution of Irish positions has occurred more extensively in other municipal branches than in police and fire agencies.

Finally, the waning of direct Irish influence appears in electoral politics. Machines that served a Boss Buckley so well may have been vitiated by Progressive reform, as noted in chapter 4, but the Irish influence in political leadership did not vanish as easily. Irish mayors from James Phelan in the 1890s to John Shelley in the 1960s have been in a favorite position of influence. An Irish sheriff in the 1920s was said to wield power from that office, just as the Irish Burton brothers wielded it as congressman and state assemblyman in the early 1970s. But all this is changing. It is not that "the last hurrah" is being heard, but that the Irish lilt in the hurrahing is less pronounced these days.

The clearest signs are in the top elective city offices. Irish incumbent mayor Shelley was induced—or forced—to relinquish his second-term bid to an Italian. One commentator saw in the event a sign of Irish electoral influence, for Shelley's "administration, like the exotic plant that blooms but once in a lifetime, marked the blossom and the death." [15] Shelley would have been replaced by another Irishman but for the latter's death; yet the point was the absence of other Irish political leaders to challenge Shelley.

Even more dramatic is the disappearance of this group from the board of supervisors. When the 1960s began, seven Irish sat on the eleven-member board, but a decade later there were none. Some had been defeated at the polls, others accepted mayoral appointments to other city offices, and yet others sought election to higher offices. But in the early 1970s, the absence of the Irish was symptomatic of their diluted influence in other traditional arenas in the city. None of this, however, provoked outbursts of political action to restore "green power." One commentator's analysis, reflecting our findings of change, saw it as a "subcultural menopause," to which the Irish were reacting mildly because "they always enjoyed politics but their collective well-being never depended upon it. Now secure and comfortable, they may find the political behavior of Robert Gonzales and Dianne Feinstein [newly elected supervisors] curious at times, but never threatening." [16]

Not all the political resources of this group have disappeared, even though many are moving away or becoming more conservative. Those interviewed in the Irish community reported that characteristically their fellows today share some attributes with those of several generations earlier but differ in others. They are usually homeowners, concerned with taxes and property values, feeling threatened in house and person by the rise of blacks. They prefer a strong police force for this reason, but also because with so many Irish on it, "support your local police" means support your kith and kin. Candidates supportive of civil rights are not anathema, as long as they also have a strong concern for workers' conditions, for the "little people," or for neighborhood additions like parks or other city services. Irish demands for a candidate's personal qualities are strict, for he must be respectful of authority, a family man, interested in preserving "the American Way" (sometimes blurred with "the Irish Way"), and religiously affiliated (not Catholic necessarily, but if not so blessed then clearly God-fearing). An Irish name is no longer enough to garner the votes of Irish or other groups in city politics. In 1965 two incumbent Irish supervisors were endorsed by an Irish mayor, and both were familiar in the city's affairs. But one, running poorly among black and brown precincts because of his specifically conservative stance, received only 44 percent of the vote. His colleague, endorsed by liberal Irish leaders and more general in his appeal on the issues, received 56 percent and went on to become a popular city assessor.

If the Irish don't automatically vote ethnically, neither is the Irish officeholder shielded against criticism from his own kind. Special trouble awaits the Irishman who lives among his kind and appeals for their help, but once successful, moves to an affluent neighborhood. There is nothing especially Irish in this, of course; it is a recognized part of local politics. But, as an Irish bar owner and party official put it in the course of an interview, "The Irish are always for the underdog. Be needing some help, and they'd be pleased to heaven to throw you a benefit at the A.O.H. hall. But once you're in the big time, they'll watch you like a hawk and let you know every time you let them down. The best technique is to keep in touch personally; they like it and they'll like you."

This, then, is where the city's Irish stand nearly a century after Boss Buckley: their numbers in the city are declining, the successful ones are moving to the suburbs, and they are becoming increasingly conservative on new social issues as their party and church bespeak new liberal trends, disappearing from elective office and civil service as other groups claim those rewards, forgetting once vibrant and passionate ties to their homeland, and in general settling down on the rungs of other ladders than the political one. But all in all, few cast off *all* ties of Irishness, just as few drop the *O'* before their names. Marriage rates among the Irish hold rather well, according to church officials. Vacation flights by young Irish couples to see their hamlet origins in Eire still do very well. The Irish "curse" of drinking still abides. And among many San Franciscans the image of the Irish is still one of open amiability, conviviality, and respect—which would have surprised their ancestors on "Telygraft Hill."

The judgment of Nathan Glazer and Daniel Moynihan about the New York Irish may be too harsh for this city, however. For decades, they argue, "the Irish did not know what to do with power once they got it. . . . They never thought of politics as an instrument of social change—their kind of politics involved the processes of a society that was not changing." [17] But there were differences between these two cities. More Irish with more resources in hand at the outset of their arrival came to San Francisco than to the East Coast; thus, the political ladder was not the only ladder for personal and group advancement. Nor were their numbers as preponderantly large in San Francisco; from the beginning the Irish had to contend with the more numerous Germans and the active Italians, Yankees, and Chinese. The quality of Irish governance in both cities was also very different. If in San Francisco there was blatant corruption with an Irish Buckley, so was there under the leadership from other ethnic groups. Recall that the outright perversion of due process of law embodied in San Francisco's vigilante committees after the gold rush stemmed largely from Yankee leaders of the community. The Irish weight has also been heavy in the quality of city services which the city has known under its honest—albeit divided—government since the 1932 charter.

Yet the judgment that the Irish did not see "politics as an instrument of social change" is ultimately true in San Francisco as it was in New York. Rather than attempting to make real some urban vision, the Irish used power to assist themselves and their kin in improving their life opportunities. So it was too with the Germans and Italians of an earlier San Francisco, and so it appears is the object of blacks and the Spanish-speaking in our time. But in seeking self-interest, the Irish did contribute to the quality of urban services. Early and late, the range of urban services to citizens has grown enormously, and in much of that growth the Irish were prominent because so many of them were in urban government. The social change that the early Irish in the city sought was a better life for themselves, and the later Irish found that better life through government service, whether through political machines or merit systems. Thus, power *did* become an instrument for social change for their own kin and kith—it levered many in this one group well up the ladder of life chances. In time, those who were boosted upward found other rewards open to them and their children in other areas of society. This use of power may not have set off social change toward some vaguely defined better world, but it did help change the Irish over several generations from hod carriers to bank presidents, from the arriving to the arrived. It was no small accomplishment.

THE ITALIANS

Ethnic influence in American life cannot be understood without reference to the context of that influence. That is, circumstances of time, place, opportunity, and events shape the direction and weight of ethnicity. If, as some have argued, Irish influence on American politics was actually a carry-over of reactions against English rule, and Jewish involvement with financing was the result of exclusion from other occupations since the Medieval period, then the role of the Italians was shaped by their different origins in Italy and different opportunities in America. In the case of the Italians in San Francisco, the major items to keep in mind are that, unlike Italians on the East Coast, they were here earlier and they came from a different part of Italy. The result has been, compared with New York, Chicago, or Boston, a greater and earlier prominence of Italians in the city. On this western shore, they knew well the adjuration of Ephesians, "Now, therefore, ye are no more strangers and foreigners."

The Eastern Experience

On the East Coast, the Italians came after the Irish in terms of arrival date, opportunities, and "Americanization." [18] The 1880 census revealed fewer than 45,000 Italians in the nation, a quarter of them in New York City. Then in succeeding decades, millions emigrated to this nation. Four out of five were from southern Italy and reflected its historic poverty of mind and body. Many had known only the narrow world that stretched no farther than the sound of the village church bell.[19] Unlike the northern Italians who were exposed to European culture, most southerners lacked education, money, and technical knowledge.[20] Once in America, they converted city neighborhoods into simulations of former villages, consisting of a family-based life, economic exploitation by their own leaders, and suspicion of outsiders, education, and a Church staffed by strange Irish priests.[21] Existing social institutions provided little outlet for aspirations, even less than the Irish had found. They deemed the Church closed off, because of Irish clergy and Italian anticlericalism.[22] The Irish and the Yankees on the East Coast closed off political party activity to the Italians; therefore, the focus was most often on hard work at menial tasks to save enough to retire to Italy. Some found an outlet in crime, like other immigrant groups before them.[23] This was attractive when augmented by family defensiveness, contempt for government—here and in Italy[24]— and a swelling desire for material goods newly visible in this urban scene.

Some of all this remains in the contemporary Italian-American culture, despite large-scale improvements in their position. Once-closed social institutions now admit some Italians. Their children go to college and become professionals, although still less than those of other groups who have been as long in this country. Political parties, both in organization and candidates, feel the Italian influence in many eastern states and cities. The Church has found renewed interest among them too.[25] But as their ancestors in this country had to bear the stereotype of "guinea," their children have struggled with the popular identification of crime with Italians. During the late 1960s, they fought against these prejudices with a national organization equivalent to the NAACP. Ironically, an earlier generation would have ridiculed this organization as oversensitivity to foreigners, when the only thing that mattered was respect from family and neighborhood. But the new American of Italian origin is seeking a wider application of respect—his concern now is for deference, not from a village but from a nation.

The Western Experience

Yet this account of eastern Italians does not apply as well to western ones. The immigrants to the western United States came from other sections of Italy and at an earlier time; different also was the social context into which they fell and thrived. The result was more varied roles for them and a fuller share of the city's rewards. All of this can be seen by noting the prominence of these northern Italian immigrants in the area's history before 1885, that is, before the massive migration of southern Italians to the eastern United States. That year marked the time when the Italian Chamber of Commerce of the Pacific Coast was founded, an act that suggests a people more interested in staying in their new land than in returning to the old one, a people drawn as much to an institutional life as to a familial life and capable of gaining affluence from more than manual labor.

There are a few traces of Italians in the earliest history of the West before 1850.[26] They appear in the Church's mission movement and as seafarers*—two were thought to be among the group that first stumbled onto San Francisco Bay. But even among the skimpy Anglo population before the forty-niners, the first San Francisco directory of 1847 contains no Italian names. By 1850, however, the gold rush had brought over two hundred Italians all the way around the world from Italy. Thereafter, in succeeding census reports for the twenty-two states west of the Mississippi, Italians were by far the largest of all immigrant groups, and California was the state where most of them settled.[27] However, after the post-1890 massive flood to this continent, the bulk of Italians settled in the East. Even as late as 1960, only 10 percent were located in the Far West.[28] Nonetheless, there was a constant influx of Italians to California.

These were, in the main, northern Italians, not their southern brethren.[29] Local Italian papers in San Francisco of that earlier day featured the names of Ligurians, Genoans, Turinos, Lombardians, Milanese, and Piedmontese, and of news from these northern provinces.

---

* In *Two Years Before the Mast* Richard Dana records an 1834 visit to the bay, where he saw a Genoan bark, "a large clumsy ship, with her top masts stayed forward the high poop-deck, looking like an old woman with a crippled back."

Different not merely in origin, they differed also in turning heavily to agriculture upon their arrival. About half moved directly to farms in the Bay Area, whereas on the East Coast most remained in the urban scene. As late as 1935, a special census showed the continuing dominance of northern versus southern influences—54 versus 36 percent—in the city. The factor that distinguished the West from the East was that, as for so many others, the gold rush created enormous opportunities for Italians. In effect, the city, as the pivot first for mining and later for agricultural booms, was far more open to new immigrants than the relatively closed societies their compatriots found on the eastern shore. Income and opportunities they had known in Italy and in California were like those of two totally different economies. The cobbler, the tailor, the cigar roller, the cabinet maker, and the leather worker in Italy made one-half to one-third the daily wage of even the lowest paid Chinese equivalent in San Francisco.[30] Land in Italy was not available and not productive enough, whereas the "American Italy" offered vast valleys and hillsides of fertile soil needing but careful irrigation to convert a *paesano* into a *ranchero*.

Records as early as the 1850s reveal the economic success of these Italians in mining, the production and preparation of food, land development, and stock raising around the Bay Area. In the city, meanwhile, Italians thrived on other activities. A salt works developer bought three blocks of land in what is now Chinatown; some became contractors, financers of burgeoning small businesses, importers and exporters, wholesalers, restaurateurs, and food processors—all within the first decade after the gold rush began. There are impressive records of the activity and enterprise of these early Italians from the gold fields and south to San Diego.* Their names—Bruschi, Noce, Vignoli—still are dimly traced on ruins of stores in gold towns. But eventually the concentration came to be around San Francisco because of its pivotal role in the state's developing economy. The Italian contribution to the area was accurately captured by an Italian consular official in the mid-1850s in a report to Rome:

The Italian population is one of the best, most active and hard-working in California. Strong, industrious, and accustomed to suffering and toil, our nationals tend to their own affairs without taking part in those regrettable disorders that the heterogeneous people of the state give vent to from time

* One shipped ice from the Sierra to Los Angeles, the first instance of northern California providing the south with water, a central issue of state politics in later decades.

to time [that is, vigilantism]. Generally, whether in San Francisco or in the interior, the Italians thrive and prosper in their businesses, and there is probably not a village in all California in which Italian business is not well represented, just as there is not a mining district where companies of Italian miners are not noted for their good conduct, their fraternal harmony, and for the energy which they bring to their work.[31]

The Italians on the West Coast differed from their compatriots in eastern cities not only in the economic sphere but also in a variety of other dimensions. In the 1850s they developed their own newspaper, *La Voce del Popolo,* which, in a number of mergers, continued until 1966. This was the first of seventeen Italian papers to come; in 1931 there were five published at one time.[32] As early as 1856 protective societies were formed, including one that was a spin-off of the Italian Hospital in 1859 and is still in existence—*Societa-Italiana di Mutua Beneficenza.* Jesuit priests, mostly from Turin, provided a powerful thrust to Italian education. With $150, two priests founded their first California college at Santa Clara, south of San Francisco, in 1851, and three years later, others founded the University of San Francisco, seven of whose first nine presidents were Italians. Their early emphasis on scientific knowledge led one priest to develop the first carbon arc lights on Market Street. Another early Jesuit father was responsible for constructing St. Ignatius Church, later destroyed during the 1906 earthquake. In the arts, Italians also played an early part. An Italian theater was opened in 1850; opera, for which the city had an inordinate fondness then as now, first came in 1851; and by 1857 an Italian opera company had been formed, lasting fourteen seasons.[33]

In this fashion, Italian life just after the gold rush laid the foundation for an influential community around the bay, which thrived through several decades well before the massive East Coast migration. Italians developed solid business enterprises in mining, marble cutting (families of such artisans were imported), and lumbering. But it was to be in the sea and on the land that Italian commercial life was to grow most effectively and extensively. Although Genoans began the fishing commerce, Sicilians, the one exception to the city's northern Italian influx, eventually took over this enterprise. Although the first Sicilians did not arrive until 1882, by 1884 they had founded the Crab Fisherman's Protective Association and thereafter built fish markets on the site which tourists were to make famous a half-century later, Fisherman's Wharf. There the names of Castagnola and Tarantino on modern restaurants mark the continuity with an earlier day when these families sold their daily catches.

Unlike their countrymen on the East Coast, California's Italians settled heavily on the land, and their names loom large in its agriculture from those earliest decades. With beef and dairy cattle, sheep, wheat, fruit, and grapes, and by ingenious irrigation, these mostly northern Italian immigrants found an agricultural wealth and diversity in California denied their fathers in the homeland. Grape growers from the vineyards of Lombardy were tall and fair-haired, far different from the prevalent stereotype of the East Coast Italian. Because of the opportunities found here, men like Andrea Sbarbero from Genoa could become banker, school builder, and founder of a vineyard cooperative (the Italian-Swiss Colony), which came to dominate American wine production. In later years, two Italian immigrants—Mark Fontana and Joseph Di Giorgio—would pioneer in those diversified, vertically integrated, farm conglomerations now labeled "agribusiness." [34] Much earlier, though, smaller farmers found profit in truck gardens around cities. As scavengers,[35] some San Franciscan Italians used the manure they collected for truck gardens inside the city's borders, which thrived into this century.* Italians quickly made the linkage to wholesale produce markets and to packing this produce for export.

The need for credit in these small and large enterprises gave rise to the banking function by Italians in numbers not known in the East. Indeed, the first commercial and savings bank established by Italians was started here. In all Italian settlements in America, small bankers arose, usually merchants who transmitted immigrants' savings back home. These were the kind of men who laid the foundation on which A. P. Giannini was able to build the Bank of Italy, later the Bank of America, now the largest in the world.[36]

The preceding is merely a sketch of a complex phase of American immigration and ethnic life, but it is enough to make a crucial point. The immigrant history of Italians, as well as the others, was greatly different in the West from that in the East. For those in the East, it was an unsettling experience for people uprooted from a native land and transplanted to a hostile and barren soil in a new urban setting. The western immigrant, however, found openness, opportunity, and

---

* The first manure was spread for a truck garden in the vicinity of the present Civic Center. Windmills for irrigating these plots dotted some sections; the area between Ingleside and Mission was once called Windmill Valley.

welcome—much of it in a rural setting. These were "not 'the Uprooted' but the Upraised," Andrew Rolle concludes from his recent reexamination of this experience.

Too much has been made of the "inner struggle" of the immigrant for security and status in an unfriendly New World. For most immigrants who went west, life was not a disappointment, but rather, a challenge, even an adventure. Their reactions to America were enthusiastic and fresh—in short, the opposite of disillusioned. They generally escaped ethnic crowding, slums, ghettoes, and a large measure of prejudice, partly because of the western outlook. Western attitudes were often generous and easy-going, especially in small communities, where immigrants were less concentrated than in a purely urban setting. Studies of other nationalities than the Italians bear out these generalizations.

Despite their initial sufferings, the immigrants found freedom in America's West rather than rigidity, openness rather than closed privilege.[37]

In California and especially in San Francisco the Italians were part of a wave that mixed old stock with other nationalities; they were not invaders of an established, powerful society. Adjustments of group differences were easier because no group dominated every ladder of rewards. Their skills as farmers, merchants, fishermen, or bankers met important needs for other groups and were consequently well rewarded. Their most prevalent skill—as farmers—found an outlet on the land as it could not for the "urban villagers" of the East. In the West, therefore, organized crime was not the outlet used in desperation elsewhere by Italians arriving where their skills were useless.* There were many opportunities to foster the talents of northern Italians—mutual aid societies, educational institutions, newspapers, the arts—made possible by the economic successes of farmers, merchants, and fishermen.

In short, Italians in the West had about three decades to establish themselves before the truly large Italian immigration began. The result was an ethnic adjustment† to the new culture which bears little

---

* The Mafia has had no known record in San Francisco, past or present, to which investigations by Congress in the 1950s, the Justice Department in the 1960s, and myself attest. A magazine that in the late 1960s tried to link Mayor Alioto to the Mafia prompted an energetic libel trial—and a hung jury; but not even his opponents interviewed for this book credited the story. Italian leaders interviewed reflect a clear awareness of the status distinctions made by the region of their ancestors' origins, even though they came a century ago. To them, the Mafiosos are southerners who are "ignorant greaseballs."

† This also included sharing prejudices against the Chinese. In 1880 they formed a forty-member "Swiss-Italian Anti-Chinese Company of Dragoons" in San Francisco to help city officials remove Chinese. See Rolle (n. 26 above), p. 259.

similarity to the eastern experience. In California, Italians early "looked upon the state as their own Italy," [38] an attitude never expressed by immigrants in the East for their city ghettos. With this background, California Italians could easily incorporate the immigrant wave and assist it in accommodating to the new life. It also enabled them to thrive in San Francisco's economy and political system in the twentieth century. In the 1970s, unlike the Irish, the sense of ethnicity was strong, even though affluent Italians were selling their homes on Telegraph Hill for inflated prices and moving out of their traditional colony. Their people were prominent in law, big business, and big agriculture—and they had Mayor Alioto in the political arena.

POLITICS, VOTES, AND ETHNIC PERSISTENCE

Presidential Elections

I have dwelt on the Irish and the Italians as typical of the arrived minority whose basic struggle had been to achieve deference. Germans and Jews have been equally successful, but the former have just about disappeared as a discrete group, and the latter are a very small group. The two largest of the oldest groups, however, have carried political power for a century, and how they did so is our next concern.

In San Francisco, the Irish were a potent central force in the Workingmen's party and Boss Buckley's machine well before 1900; since then they have provided substantial voting power and also candidates for all local offices. Italians have been equally active politically, although their numbers in office have been fewer until the 1960s. Yet, Angelo Rossi presided as a popular mayor of the city from 1931 to 1944 while Fiorello LaGuardia was presiding with more publicity over the eastern gate of the continent.[39] In presidential elections, more Italians than Irish have voted for Republicans since 1940. Table 15 demonstrates this difference in precincts that Board of Elections officials judged over time to have been heavily Italian or Irish and of similar status. This is only a rough measure, of course, for not all in a given precinct were of the ethnicity indicated, and the precinct boundaries are not always the same over the entire period.[40]

Yet, through such a time tunnel one can perceive a rough impression of how Irish and Italian precincts were responding to presidential campaigns. Irish precincts regularly ran well behind the city-wide Republican percentage and—after 1936—behind Italian precincts, except for the Eisenhower landslide in 1956. Republicanism was making inroads in Irish precincts before the surge to Eisenhower, but this

TABLE 15
Irish and Italian Republican Votes for President in San Francisco,
1916, 1928–1964 (percentages)

	Irish	Italian	City
1916	28	60	45
1928	28	22	50—
1932	20	10	33
1936	15	9	25
1940	28	42	40
1944	32	44	39
1948	31	48	49
1952	38	51	54
1956	44	44	52
1960	27	48	42
1964	16	23	29

NOTE: Precinct sources for this table are as follows: Irish: 1916, Assembly District 24, Precinct 35 (24–35); 1928, 24–43; 1932–1940, 24–29; 1944–1948, 24–31; 1952–1960, 23–79, 1964, 23–132. Italian: 1916 and 1928, 33–10; 1932–1940, 20–6; 1944–1960, 20–9; 1964; 10–14.

These precincts were selected (by criteria the author provided) by officials of the Board of Elections; special thanks are due the assistance of Frank Quinn of the board, and Randall Hough for collecting the raw figures.

fell off with the elections of Kennedy and Johnson. The Republican inroads among Italian precincts were far more abrupt and severe with the coming of World War II. While this shift has been attributed to President Roosevelt's criticism of Italy's joining Hitler in the war, the GOP gain in San Francisco may have been less than in New York City.[41] These Republican gains persisted until 1964, although throughout these years not even the more Republican Italian precincts gave a majority of their votes to the GOP, except in 1952. After 1964 the diffusion of other groups into these precincts became so rapid that the ethnic dominance disappeared, and a later analysis of them would be meaningless.

Supervisorial Elections

Local, as well as presidential elections provide perspective on the success of ethnic groups in the political forum. Table 16 groups the winners of supervisorial contests from 1909 to 1971 by Irish and Italian names (my designation). While the Irish were far from the largest ethnic group of any given period, they dominated these key elective offices. But aside from a flash of old power during the 1950s,

TABLE 16
Proportion of Irish and Italian Supervisors Elected, 1909–1971

	Supervisors Elected (in percent)		
Election Years	Irish	Italian	N Seats
1909–11	50	6	32
1913–21	44	2	45
1923–31	26	17	42
1933–41	30	7	27
1943–51	32	11	28
1953–61	59	11	27
1963–71	25	25	28
	38	11	229

they declined over the decades, reaching a new low in the 1970s. Indeed, in the elections of 1969 and 1971, no Irish candidate won a supervisorial seat; but in the 1973 contest, a former police chief returned the Irish to that board. Meanwhile, the Italians demonstrate a mirror image of the Irish—a larger proportion of the population but a smaller share of these seats; but in the 1960s they equaled the Irish in victories, and in the 1969 and 1971 elections won three seats.

A detailed examination of the post-1960 period indicates that this trend extended to other offices. Irish and Italian candidates for all elective local offices, except the judiciary, the state legislature, and Congress, were analyzed for their rate of success. In the two periods 1960–1965 and 1966–1971, the proportion of Irish candidates running for election declined from 29 to 19 percent while the Italian candidates remained at 7 to 8 percent. More significant, however, is the fact that in the first period 60 percent of the Irish candidates won, but in the latter period the figure declined to 49 percent. Meanwhile, the Italian victory rate rose from 11 to 62 percent,[42] while a wide diversity of other ethnic representatives won yet other seats once held by the Irish. After the 1971 supervisorial elections, of the eleven winners three were German, and one each was black, Greek, and Spanish-speaking —but none Irish. The Irish were still doing well, however, in other offices—three of four state assembly seats, one of two congressional seats, and the district attorney—although their long-standing control of the sheriff's office was lost in 1971, as was the state senate seat with the death of Eugene McAteer in 1967. In this pattern is a sense of a ladder of seats, with the Irish withdrawing to the higher rungs of prestigious state and federal office while others clung to less prestigious municipal offices. These shifts are a sign that the ethnic diversity for which San Francisco had long been famed is becoming a reality in its politics.

Strategies in Ethnic Politics

Whether this change is a sign of increasing assimilation is another question. It surely reflects an ethnic pluralism and the potential for intergroup conflict. But the often expressed notion that increased office holding is a consequence of assimilation seems suspect. Brett Hawkins and Robert Lorinskas have challenged this view: "Office holding may not indicate the adoption of American values so much as the realization that votes are a power resource especially useful to those lacking other resources, such as wealth and social standing. At a minimum, office-holding raises the question of who is assimilating what. Is American society assimilating ethnics or are ethnics grabbing off a piece of American society?" [43]

The Irish and the Italians in San Francisco politics provide part of the answer. Living here for over a century, they have played a prominent role in the economic, political, and governmental aspects of urban life. From almost the beginning of the gold rush, they have been successful in business, election to office, appointment to municipal positions, religious activities, and artistic and educational endeavors—and they have thrived. Much if not all of this was the result of not concealing ethnic affiliation, but rather of proudly proclaiming it. Such has been the norm in a city where they faced no dominant majority culture to subordinate their values and limit their opportunities. In this case, then, assimilation as a concept explains little of what has transpired.

Even in the East, where a dominant culture did confront immigrants, ethnicity was hardly suppressed to the point of disappearing. For the Italians in Chicago the context was different from that in San Francisco, given the different origins, arrival time, and opportunities of San Francisco Italians. But even in Chicago, southern Italians maintained group solidarity although it was based primarily on neighborhoods that were villages removed to the New World; to a high degree, villagers left Italy as blocs and settled in America in the same neighborhoods. Both in Chicago and elsewhere in the East, they came to terms with the new culture within the framework of their old culture.[44] The persistence of that culture challenges Oscar Handlin's judgment that the experience was one of alienation.[45] Rather, old norms and group solidarity provided psychic shields against alienation, even though the group was narrowly defined by the extended family or by neighborhood.

The San Francisco experience was not the Chicago or New York experience, despite the persistence of ethnic outlooks. In the East, the ladders to political and economic rewards were generally closed. Newcomers faced first Yankee and then Irish dominance, both strongly resistant to providing substantial rewards to newcomers—and rarely even to accommodating them—for services rendered. But there were different patterns in this accommodation. In Chicago, Italians a half-century after heavy migration began still had little political power, primarily because of their internal divisions.[46] In wards where Italians fought the dominant Irish, they received little from the Chicago machine. But where they supported the machine quietly in exchange for trade-offs, they did better, receiving control of graft operations but no public office.[47]

In San Francisco, where the community was more open to Italian entry for a longer period, few came into public office until the 1930s with the election of Mayor Rossi and admission to city services. Even then, however, it was not until the late 1960s that they cropped up in elective office, three decades behind the eastern Italian-Americans. Why the delay? Modern Italian leaders claim that their ancestors had worked so hard and so well at commerce and farming that they had had little time or interest in seeking alternative ladders of success. Why the recent emergence in politics, then? The role model of Joseph Alioto was most often cited, for his electoral success had attracted other Italians. That included those increasingly disturbed by the challenges of arriving minorities and by the sense of change in the old order which had benefited them and their kind so much.

In these diverse patterns, then, it is difficult to see how the concept of assimilation explains much. A better explanation is that accommodation and mutual benefit, or conflict and minority suppression, are alternative ways in which ethnic groups have strived to succeed. From place to place, different combinations of leaders and opportunities may exist, ethnic conflict may be more or less intense, and the resulting group accommodation may be large or small. In San Francisco, Irish-Italian interaction has been characterized by less conflict and more accommodation, most likely because of the available breadth of opportunities for success and for resolution of conflict. That is, no one group could monopolize all the ladders of rewards, the Catholic Church could mediate ethnic conflict in a population heavily Catholic, there was a common scapegoat for economic insecurities—the Chinese —and unusually large rates of Irish-Italian marriage provided a calming influence at the family level. This particular combination in the San Francisco experience is not put forth as a model of what occurred elsewhere; the thrust of the evidence concerning these successful minorities here is that they did *not* suffer the eastern experience. Rather, in a context that was most accommodative, ethnicity still did not disappear, just as it has not in context much less amenable to newcomers.[48]

In this accommodation, the struggle to achieve recognition has been rather successful for the Irish and the Italians, and was won rather early—if piecemeal—in San Francisco's history. There is not a social institution in San Francisco where members of the two ethnic groups are not prominent. Many have succeeded so well that they can afford to leave old enclaves like the Italian North Beach for richer sites in suburbia. As a group, their battle for deference has shifted to other values. We find a quite different context, however, for those ethnic groups, still struggling for recognition, who came from other continents than Europe and are still arriving—socially and numerically.

CHAPTER 10

The Arriving Ethnic Groups

Not all ethnic groups in San Francisco have been as successful for as long as the Italians and the Irish—or the Germans, Jews, Greeks, and French. There are others who "look back in anger" and around in frustration. Prototypical are the black and the Spanish-speaking, although with some variations a similar account can be had for the Chinese, Native American Indians, Samoans, and Filipinos. These I have termed the "arriving" ethnic groups, not because they are new to the neighborhoods of the city, although many are, but because, in a fashion not known before, they are moving to participate in the urban decisions that bring first deference and then other rewards. These are "the resourceless," as such things are measured in urban politics, who are finding the means to enter community politics and place their demands on the community agenda. Theirs is not a record of success, however, like that known by the arrived minorities, even though some—such as the Latin and Indian groups—have been here much longer.

This side of San Francisco is not seen by the tourist, and its history is not part of the Convention Bureau's releases. The reality has been a historical experience which

consisted largely of systematic exclusion of minorities from full participation in the life of the community, exclusion supported not only by white public opinion but also, in time, by statutory law, court decisions, and the apparatus of local community power, True, some self-segregation was involved, a consequence of minority commitment to cherished religious, cultural, and nationality values. But that should not obscure the fact that in most cases members of minorities had a very narrow range of choice—and the boundaries of that range were established by whites.[1]

NEW STIRRINGS AMONG THE ASIANS

Much of that history, as well as current changes, is illustrated by the Asian, who has been for California what the black was for Mississippi.[2] It is not overdrawn to suggest that sinophobia has been San Francisco's substitute for the anti-Semitism of eastern cities. Too, Japanese-Americans have been favored in California only in the last decade, although their disgraceful imprisonment and the expropriation of their property occurred but three decades ago. The reaction of both Asian peoples to this discrimination was withdrawal into separate ghettos, as well as passivity and amiability in the face of indignity and injury. The first reaction—withdrawal—provides an emotional reinforcement in ties of culture, language, and religion, which was needed to face the contempt outside Chinatown or Japantown. Their reaction of passivity and amiability was a substitute and a shield for more natural reactions of indignation, a price they paid not to provoke the hostile Caucasian. The similarities to the reaction of Southern blacks to discrimination by the whites are substantial.

This protective tradition of not stirring up trouble is well reflected in Chinatown's role in the poverty programs of the mid-1960s even though there was also visible some stirrings of new leadership.[3] The tourist's Chinatown has symptoms of poverty that are many and intense—almost one-half of these Chinese are below the poverty level of income, and suffer from bad housing, unemployment, delinquency, health problems, shocking suicide rates, and so forth. But when the Employment Opportunity Act came to the city in 1964, Chinese leaders were reluctant to include their area as one of the target areas. They viewed acceptance of the program as public notice of the failure of family responsibility. But this attitude was also in keeping with an old pattern of denying their internal problems to the Caucasian world. Nevertheless, younger Chinese strenuously put the case that Chinatown should be included and convinced the city's Employment Opportunity Council.

The resulting program represented what Ralph Kramer terms "traditional stewardship." Almost nothing was done to provide representatives of the poor on the area's governing board; rather, these positions were held by leaders from the Six Companies (discussed later) and other professional, middle-class agents of commercial, church, and service groups. They justified this elitism as necessary "until the disadvantaged overcame language and other cultural handicaps, including reluctance to be labeled as poor." Moreover, unlike other neighborhood boards, this one avoided fighting with City Hall for control of the program, and it did not delay action until planning could emerge from statements of the needs by the unorganized poor. Instead, it immediately adopted program proposals of the EOC that would promptly provide assistance for many needy groups. On the other hand, not until the spring of 1966 was there grass-roots representation, when four poor Chinese were elected to the area board, even though only one spoke English. Moreover, the board accepted any constraint from city or other agencies on its operations, and restricted itself to informational programs—including the sponsoring of essays.

The trade-off for this apathy, serenity, and complaisance was that "the board as a whole had more cohesiveness, continuity, and stability than the boards in any of the other areas." Meetings were without wrangling or rancor, major decisions having been made earlier in private. Patronage did not divide this board as it did others, and the area director avoided the dispute with the central EOC in which other neighborhoods participated with great vigor. But the board lacked roots in the community, since the concept of community links to representative agencies was novel in this subculture. After a brief time under the control of antiestablishment residents, this program —like many other aspects of Chinatown—was taken over by the Six Companies.

The Six Companies have made Chinatown the social, economic, and political entity that it has been and is today.* In structure, it is a governing body for other organizations based on family and district of origin in China. Its two sections, one based on equality of representation and the other on population, can authorize as well as implement policy. Begun as an informal advisory or arbitration council to deal with the factionalism of the early San Francisco settlement, it was the main instrument for defending this group against the virulent anti-Chinese sentiment of the late nineteenth century. Later it settled the notorious tong wars, built local institutions like schools and hospitals, provided jobs for immigrants, and in general, eased

---

* The following analysis is drawn from the recent brilliant analysis of Chinatown's institutions and people by Victor G. and Brett de Bary Nee, *Longtime Californ'* (New York: Pantheon, 1972), chap. 9.

the transition of the newcomers to an unbelievably different culture.

As a consequence, for over eighty years the Six Companies have monopolized all phases of power in that community. They possess a legitimacy drawn from the formal power of representing almost all Chinese until recent years. Their leaders sit also as heads of family and district associations, business organizations, school boards, newspapers (they once boycotted out of existence a pro-Peking newspaper), and political clubs. They possess most of the available capital in this neighborhood, own some land, and have kept trade unions out of their garment shops, which operate in conditions reminiscent of the nineteenth-century sweatshops. Their politics is mostly an ingrown factionalism, with very limited contact with the political world of City Hall until very recently. The lack of contact has a power basis. Because so many of these immigrants either were here illegally or planned to return home, few registered to vote and hence lacked any electoral power to reinforce potential demands on political authorities. When a few Chinese began to emerge in the city's government in the 1960s, they were invariably conservative members of the Six Companies.

But the companies have come on hard times. Factionalism and deadlock in their own structure have always plagued them. These conditions have rendered them incapable of adjusting to emergent demands unless they were obvious and involved danger. Their insistence on using the old language has barred participation by Chinese of later generations, who speak only English. The new Chinese increasingly resent the structure's rigidity to calls for new directions. Too, the Six Companies' characteristic posture to the Caucasian world —obeisant, indirect, eternally polite—angers the newer Chinese, who want what power the ghetto possesses to be used aggressively to secure new programs and resources. Power institutions being what they are, City Hall appoints the less demanding to public positions, those who will not challenge the extensive discrimination against the Chinese. Timidity, shaped by a history of uncertainties of life in a foreign land, is a weak base from which to launch crusades.

But now there are new Chinese on the scene. Many are well educated, live outside the ghetto—and challenge nothing. But the Six Companies also face strong opposition from other young Chinese who insist on injecting new demands into this urban decisional context. One group consists of the college-educated, professional Chinese. Many of these now live outside the ghetto in middle-class neighborhoods, while some are appearing for the first time in institutions of the city.[4] Through their schooling, they have found new knowledge, organizational skills, and values concerning the treatment of community problems.

A second challenge developed in the 1960s with the arrival of many young Chinese from Hong Kong. They came with no language except Chinese, only to find a school system incapable of teaching them English, a labor market providing only menial jobs, and a low regard from even their host kinsmen. Not surprisingly, this group formed gangs, which by the 1970s were threatening the establishment, either through support of Mao Tse-tung or through fostering a "protection" racket with accompanying murders. The left-wing segment is opposed to America's policy in Asia, to American conservatism at home, to the Six Companies, and to mobility into "establishment" groups. Insistent upon "Third World" unity and much more open to Mao Communists than are most Chinese-Americans, they represent the newest strain of opposition to the establishment, one almost unimaginable ten years before. On all sides in Chinatown, then, there is agreement that a social and political reorganization is under way. The establishment still possesses most resources in this changing scene. But the challengers—just by their novelty—are moving the few square blocks of Chinatown toward a reexamination of the old order.

New Japanese are also in evidence. In the decades after World War II, they had prospered both materially and in the respect of Caucasians. By 1970 national polls would show the Japanese to be the most highly favored ethnic minority, and in 1971 one was elected mayor of San Jose. There were some reports of differences between the generations,[5] but little of this has surfaced as it has with the Chinese. Japanese political organizations are also emerging in the city, along with a new cultural center, as signs of an affirmation of ethnic identity, of a new articulation of its interests, and of a new image among whites. The most significant quality of the group, however, is an intense patriotism that generates very little criticism of the political system. Some young Sansei might be part of the college radical culture, but nothing distinctive could be reported about their politics.

So it has been that even among the once most despised and afflicted ethnic group in the city's history—the Asians—new interests, new resources, and new political qualities have been injected into community affairs. But their numbers are still not great enough to represent a major force. Despite a 61 percent increase during the 1960s, by 1970 only 8.2 percent—almost 60,000—of San Franciscans were of Chinese descent; those of Japanese descent were far less, only 1.6 percent, or almost 12,000.[6] In a political system that reacts most quickly to large, mobilized numbers, the Asians find their limited numbers a handicap. But the fact that some of them are thinking about that system and how to mobilize other resources reflects an important new current. They still differ internally on strategies in this contest for deference—humility versus resentment, cultivating one's own garden versus direct confrontation with the yellow and white power centers, and so forth. But even entertaining the notion that one can reach out as a group to demand and secure respect is itself the most important change.

THE SPANISH-SPEAKING MINORITY

There are also new stirrings among the Spanish-speaking San Franciscans, a particularly important development in light of their long slumber in city affairs. The mark of the Spanish culture has lain long on the city, but after the American conquest of California it was subdued. There has been no sign since Gold Rush days that this culture of the Californios was important for decision making in San Francisco. The reason was simple—their numbers were so few. The flood of forty-niners diluted the state's contingent of those of Spanish, Mexican, or Latin American origin. Succeeding waves of Anglo immigrants thinned their proportion out even more, particularly when there was little Mexican immigration until after World War I.*

Through two centuries this ethnic group clustered south of the city's center, around the Mission Dolores; this "Mission District" remained a rural retreat until the coming of horse and electric streetcars. But that physical and cultural isolation was truly broken by the disaster of 1906. Irish and other workers, their homes destroyed by the quake and fire, moved into the district and dominated it for over half a century. In the process, they made it the center of the city's

---

* The Census Bureau's merging of this ethnic group with "whites" has made precision about numbers very chancy. One estimate is that, by 1850, Mexicans constituted about 15 percent of the state's population, 12 percent in 1860, and 4 percent in 1870. See Richard Morefield, "The Mexican Adaptation in American California, 1846–1875," M.A. thesis, University of California, Berkeley, 1955.

working-class and union activity; most union headquarters are still there.

But in the 1960s, through the affluence of some and the immigration of others, a change came in both the ethnic mix and the political strains of this area, with its heart in the Inner Mission (see location in figure 5). The Anglo population, particularly the Irish, moved out, while the Spanish-speaking, particularly the Central Americans, moved in.* In the 1960s there was an increase of less than a thousand in this neighborhood's population, but where there had been two out of three Anglos in 1960, there was only one in three in 1970. Meanwhile, the Spanish population doubled, from 23 to 48 percent, the Pacific cultures rose from 4 to almost 10 percent, and blacks rose from 3 to 5 percent.[7]

Of great importance for an understanding of what transpired, however, is an additional fact about the new Spanish population: it is not Mexican in origin, but heavily Central American, primarily Nicaraguans and Salvadorians—the "Latinos." Among Latinos there is clearly evident a greater sense and practice of politics; those interviewed for this study repeated the label of "volatile." The prevalent belief was that the Mexican-American had been traditionally inert in the political life of California for a number of reasons. Some ascribe this to their peasant origin, which provided little political orientation or encouragement except obedience to the state and church. Others ascribe it to the dominance of the Roman Catholic Church, which had inculcated an attitude of submission to and disinterest in the political system.[8]

Whatever the reasons for political apathy prior to the 1960s, it is clear that a new political energy has since emerged in San Francisco. This ferment is traceable in part to the arrival of the Latinos, with a new vigor and an old resentment of authority. But equally important is the political substance toward which their political energies could be directed. At the center of this were the poverty and Model Cities programs, which offered some, albeit limited, resources, forums, and rewards for those who would participate. However, unlike the manner in which these programs were carried out in black neighborhoods, in the area with the largest Spanish-speaking population the

* This may now be the most polyglot district in the city. Besides the Spanish culture, there are sizable numbers of Irish, Italians, Germans, Russians, Scandinavians, and blacks, with growing numbers of Filipinos and Samoans; most of the city's Native Americans live here also.

presence of significant other minorities necessitated a coalition style.

As with other target areas in the city, the early poverty-program politics of the Mission District was turbulent, bitter, personal, and ethnic. Consensus—or at least a majority support—was almost impossible to achieve among the more than twenty Spanish-speaking nationality groups; compromise, so vital to the coalitional principle, was defeated in a welter of nationality and personality conflicts. The notion of compromising with non-Spanish groups, particularly with blacks,[9] was another divisive factor in Mission politics. But against this, there was resentment of the efforts of the then mayor, John Shelley, to control this federal program, and of a city-wide Economic Opportunity Council later to impose programs and administrative oversight (detailed below). These provided the impetus toward a coalition with other target areas that was successful—in the period 1964–1968—in decentralizing the program and keeping it out of control of the "Anglo power structure."[10] However, the record thereafter was not one of energetic participation by the Spanish-speaking or of their success in influencing the outcome of the program. In the event, the poverty program was characterized through the 1960s by limited participation, a narrow agenda (mostly providing more of existing social services), and little that affected local poverty.

Then and now, the Spanish population has had less employment and education than the city average, as well as more welfare needs.[11] They were underemployed in unions (only three of the biggest ten have proportionate numbers) and civil service (under 3 percent), and the jobs available through community organization or training programs could provide only a daub on this canvas of need. As the decade ended, then, while the poverty program had energized some new leaders, Spanish group politics was a stew of factionalism. Too, many of these leaders had lines of dependency into the mayor's office, as Alioto went about building a strong base in blocs of arriving minorities.

Yet the serving of Spanish interests in San Francisco may still take place through the coalitional process. By the early 1970s, there was a new vigor in community action in the neighborhood, reflected in the growth and excitement of the Mission Coalition Organization (MCO).[12] Begun in 1967 by Ben Martinez, a community organizer in the Saul Alinsky style, the MCO had in five years given Mission residents the feeling, if not the reality, of independent power to affect area problems. By then, it combined over two hundred smaller groups, with much MCO effort decentralized in special programs, e.g., for the care of children and elders, for delinquents and businessmen, for food and recreation, for language and job training, and so on, in a seemingly endless list of activities. In its collective capacity, MCO organizers worked the streets, identifying block problems and recruiting potential leaders. It also provided the lens for focusing large numbers of Mission citizens upon meetings of city agencies when some citizen pressure was desirable.

But this was not simply an effort of the Spanish-speaking; rather, years of effort were required to convince different ethnic groups to work together for commonly defined goals. Indeed, the effort necessary to provide even minimum unity among Mexican-American and Latin American nationality groups was enormous. Language was not a sufficient tie to bind diverse cultures (dialect differences made one group almost unintelligible to another); and differences in status were another barrier to unity. There were also differences concerning social action. Some wished to work outside the traditional structures in the city and to substitute alternative structures to solve old problems. These tended to do less well in attracting outside funding; indeed, HUD vetoed the first MCO Model Cities plan (even when backed by Alioto and the board of supervisors) because it involved too much community control and weakened the mayor's coordinating functions. Others preferred to stay with what was given. For example, professionals and the businessmen in the older and traditional Mexican-American Political Association stressed the use of elections to bring their members into public office. When Model Cities was undercut by the Nixon administration's "new federalism" program of revenue sharing in 1972–1973, the MCO pulled away from the Model Cities emphasis to exert pressures on traditional municipal agencies, seeking to improve the quantity and quality of their services to the Mission District.

It is not surprising that there were strains within an MCO that represented merchants, unions, tenants, homeowners, welfare clients, youth, senior citizens, cultural groups, churches, neighborhood agencies, and ethnic, social, and fraternal groups. It is worth noting the degree to which the MCO pulled this mosaic together at the end of the 1960s to provide the district and its heavy Spanish-speaking contingent with visible, publicized, and—eventually—respected power in urban affairs. However, some observers regarded particular leaders or constituents of the MCO as part of "the Alioto machine" or the pawns of other Anglo politicians, the Chamber of Commerce, the Communists, juvenile gangs, or other objects of fear.

The Mission representative most visible to others in the city was Robert Gonzales, elected supervisor in 1971 (the third highest vote total, up from his eighth-place standing in 1965). In the 1972 Democratic primaries, he ran well, although he lost, against powerful congressional incumbent Philip Burton, opponent of Alioto's power in the party and the city. Some observers thought the election symbolic of the rising power of the MCO; Gonzales was a part of that coalition, while another candidate, a Republican, was a black officer of the Mission Rebels. As Gonzales noted afterwards, "Anglos are not going to represent this district much longer, either in Congress or the state legislature. People in the Mission have a great pride in being from the Mission and a great pride in their ethnic identity. That's going to make a difference." Another observer was less circumspect. "It is not just chance that the incumbent is Irish and that the insurgents are Latino and black and they're moving in." [13]

What all this meant for the residents of the district was less clear. As in the poverty and later the Model Cities programs administered by the MCO and its predecessors, the material resources were insufficient to change the life opportunities of many. The federal poverty program provided this and other districts with a few hundred jobs, but far more went unemployed. It also helped politicize a new cadre, which may be the most important consequence in the long run. Politics within the MCO was a valuable experience in coalitional politics at the district level, a process also important in the city's mechanisms for the resolution of major conflicts, as seen throughout this book. The new cadre will be heard from in the next decade or so, for behind Gonzales are others, some newly appointed by Alioto to city agencies; for example, Dr. David Sanchez was the first Spanish-speaking appointee to the school board in city history.

Hence by 1973 the Mission District exuded an excitement and promise of neighborhood action not found among the arriving minorities in other sections of San Francisco. The dispute and rancor were still there, but there was also the experience of several years of greater interethnic cooperation, fuller benefits of city services, and more frequent daily contacts, which balanced the more publicized factionalism. While city figures might have strong influences within the Mission, they nevertheless needed Mission citizens for their own positions and programs. In this exchange, the Spanish-speaking could cite some gains in life opportunities, although these were spread thinly, and in the emergence of a voice that could, for the first time, break their geographical and cultural isolation. But much more extensive was this group's growing sense of respect, which reached well beyond the few jobs or appointments.

NEGROES BECOME BLACKS

But it has been the blacks in San Francisco who most represent the ferment of the arriving ethnic group. Others are sensitive to their upthrust, often jealous and resentful. Yet by all accounts it has been the blacks who have most stimulated an ethnic renaissance in others, have most affected the current decisional context, and will most likely shape the city's ethnic politics in the decades ahead. It has been this group that has laid open "the Bay Area's surface cosmopolitanism [which] covers a basic racial provincialism that has been increasingly difficult to camouflage." [14] One observer noted a decade ago that, while blacks had been in the state and the Bay Area in large numbers for only two decades, "in direct but also in subtle and indirect ways the growing presence of the Negro is reshaping the ethos of Bay Area culture, leaving an imprint on the gamut of institutions and attitudes. The Bay Area will not be the same again—that much is known." [15]

History, Demography and Power

The California history of those who have successively called themselves "colored," "Negroes," and now "blacks" has not yet been written.[16] But the specialized studies and records of their role in the state prior to World War II provide a picture of experience in a northern rather than a southern state. From 1850 until 1940, they were too few to carry much political weight—about 1 percent in the state's population. Yet the record also shows that state law voided de jure segregated schools in 1880 and discrimination in public accommodations in 1890. Political position was slower to come and less extensive than such legal protection. There was a long gap between the appointment of the first black to public office (notary public) in 1883, to the first state legislator in 1920, to the second in 1934 (later Congressman Augustus F. Hawkins), and to the first judge in 1941. There is a record of this group's strong public advocacy of equality and justice, and of an organizational life that went beyond the advice of Booker T. Washington about self-help.

Through the nineteenth century, San Franciscan blacks were leaders in this political activism.* They founded the first black newspaper in California in 1856, successfully litigated to protect the right to ride local streetcars in 1864, provided the first appointment of a black to public office in California in 1883, and played dominant roles in statewide mutual benefit groups for blacks, such as the Colored Conventions of 1855, 1865, 1873, and 1882, the Equal Rights League of 1874, and the Afro-American Leagues of 1891 and thereafter. But during the twentieth century, leadership of blacks in the state shifted south to Los Angeles, as have many other facets of the city's once dominant political strength. Thus elective office came first to the blacks of Los Angeles—state legislators, city councilmen, and congressmen—and only later to those of San Francisco. Their proportion of the latter's population in 1940 was slight—0.8 percent —which tells much about their limited influence in local decisions.

They could change only with the creation of new resources that would permit entry to such community affairs, and World War II provided the impetus for that change. Bay Area industry, especially shipyards, recruited extensively from the cheap labor of the South, including rural blacks. During these years the magnet of this force created large colonies of blacks around the bay in Richmond, Oakland, and Berkeley, and in San Francisco, where many occupied homes in the Fillmore neighborhood that had recently belonged to now relocated Japanese-Americans. But large numbers also filled the southeast hillside of Hunter's Point, where scores of "temporary" barracks housed workers for the nearby shipyards. As a result, their numbers grew during the period 1941–1945 from 4,846 to 32,001, and by 1950 to 43,502—or 5.6 percent of San Francisco's population. Whereas in 1940 they were only 3.9 percent of the blacks in the state, by 1950 they were 9.4 percent. During the subsequent decades, even more arrived in the Bay Area and San Francisco, creating new neighborhoods in Ingleside and Bayview; Fillmore became the port of entry for the southern black, and Hunter's Point residents remained in their now deteriorating "temporary" barracks. By 1960, blacks in San Francisco totaled almost 75,000—an increase of nearly 60 percent over 1950—which meant that in two decades they had increased from being less than one in a hundred San Franciscans to being one in ten. The migration and natural increase continued during the 1960s

* And some succeeded economically in unexpected places. See E. Berkeley Tompkins, "Black Ahab: William T. Shorey, Whaling Master," *California Historical Quarterly*, 51 (1972), 75–84.

as it had in most American cities. By 1970 there were over 96,000 blacks, up 30 percent from 1960, representing 13.4 percent of the city's people. This was a net increase, because some blacks in Hunter's Point and Bayview were moving into the adjoining white suburbs of Daly City and Pacifica.[17]

This was a special form of those external influences shaping San Francisco, this one contributing to a shift in the city's basic demography, unlike anything since the almost instant changes in the gold rush days. The stresses caused by the black increases have challenged San Francisco's major public and private institutions, its agenda of community issues, and its status and value hierarchies. When the 1960s began, the civil rights context for blacks was not much different from that in other northern cities, as was noted in hearings by the U.S. Commission on Civil Rights[18] and in a much publicized incident over housing discrimination involving baseball star Willie Mays. By the 1970s, there was a heightened consciousness of civil rights concerns and, as will be seen, a heightened awareness of black demands among the city's leaders.

The romanticism and mystique of San Francisco have not blurred black perceptions of what living there means to them. Compared with blacks in fifteen other major cities in 1968, those in San Francisco were among the highest in dissatisfaction with local discrimination. But whites saw it differently. Table 17 presents the rank of this city among others along a number of psychological dimensions for both races. Here are seen whites reflecting the traditional liberalism, if not tolerance, for which San Francisco is famous; only Washington whites had more racial liberalism and neighborhood integration.

But aside from relative satisfaction with the quality of neighborhood services, San Francisco blacks—and usually whites—reflected suspicion and displeasure with their own life opportunities in income and housing and with "police abuse," although they had experienced much less of it than was reported in several other cities.[19] Political remedies to meet such dissatisfactions represented no ordered scheme. San Francisco's blacks, while in median rank in their dissatisfaction with city government, were also high in their belief in the mayor's efforts as well as high in belief in separatism and the use of violence. Further, a 1967 study of black attitudes found that from 65 to 75 percent thought the city and federal governments were moving too slowly or doing too little. About one-half of black San Franciscans criticized the police for "brutality," thought that school integration

TABLE 17

San Francisco's Rank in 1968 among Fifteen Cities
on Citizens' Attitudes and Perceptions

Measure	City's Rank Blacks	City's Rank Whites
Exhibits racial liberalism	a	14[b]
Lives in racially mixed neighborhood	14	14
Is dissatisfied with neighborhood services	3	2
Believes much housing discrimination exists in city	11	7
Is dissatisfied with own income and/or housing	11	4
Believes there is police abuse	13	11
Has experienced police abuse	8	13
Is dissatisfied with city government	8	b
Believes mayor not trying to relieve conditions	4	14
Favors black rule of black institutions	11	b
Is oriented toward use of violence	10	b

SOURCE: Calculated from Howard Schuman and Barry Gruenberg, "The Impact of City on Racial Attitudes," *American Journal of Sociology*, 76 (1970), 213–61.

[a] Source provided no ranking for this group.

[b] A high number means that the sample in the city scored high on the variable.

was too slow, and believed that riots had prompted the city government to help the black community, and Congress to pass civil rights laws.[20] Much of this dissatisfaction and sense of injustice was quite real, but not all of it could be remedied, even had city authorities desired to do so. What was needed was a political sensitizing of authorities to these demands, although the number of blacks in the whole city population was still not large enough to convert it to their ends.[21]

It is true that in a city which, until the mid-1960s, had not known a black public official, by 1970 there were a black supervisor, judge, and assemblyman; black representation on appointed boards and commissions; and black positions in the city services, including police and, finally, fire protection. Nevertheless, there remained dissatisfactions among the blacks. There was the visible cultural separatism manifest in the slums of Hunter's Point and Fillmore, not unlike San Franciscans' treatment of the Chinese and Japanese. Efforts to break out of these physical limits were paralleled by efforts to break economic and status discrimination during this decade, as Negroes become ever insistent when early demands were denied.

In the process Negroes became blacks. This reflected a growing sense that, despite their individual level of achievement here or elsewhere, all black-skinned Americans were frustrated in their search for fuller achievement, because of white institutions and attitudes against which the only effective strategy was a collective psychology of self-reinforcement (Black Is Beautiful) and collective action in political and economic realms (Black Power).[22] Negroes in the past had most often employed avoidance and accommodation to deal with white discrimination, but with only pitiful gains in power and deference. So, it was heard, the blacks must now turn to competition and conflict, accompanied by a cohesion of spirit and resources that would change restrictions and create a new respect. It is the development of this phase of community politics that concerns us next.

Leadership, Strategies, and Black Politics

This transition from Negro to black had its political attributes, only a small part of which appeared in recent elections. In partisan elections, the black vote has been consistently and heavily Democratic in this and other cities—here, considerably larger than the city-wide percentage in every election.[23] But also, as elsewhere, that power has been vitiated by lower registration and turnout.[24] Of course, as their numbers grew, blacks were not ignored by candidates for office; they became one of many ethnic groups to be approached for endorsement on candidates' night. Moreover, they became an important element in the California Democratic Clubs (CDC) movement of the 1950s, as some blacks began to gain local recognition. Black politicians interviewed for this study looked back with pleasure on those yeasty days of Stevensonian democracy in city and state. Then, as young lawyers or other professionals, they moved from the CDC to the NAACP to the black community, mobilizing support for the then legalistic emphasis on removing barriers to equality.

But it was the 1960s which crystallized the involvement of blacks in the city's decisional context, and also set off discordant strains within the black leadership itself. Over that decade, while the proportion of black San Franciscans inched up slowly (from 10 to 13.4 percent), their share of public office, elective and appointive, increased dramatically, and their share of public attention even more. One sign of these changes is seen among influential citizens interviewed in the late 1960s for the first phase of this study. In response to a question about "the most important unresolved problem facing" the city, they overwhelmingly indicated issues reflecting the demands of blacks over the last decade. Table 18 reveals the heavy racial ori-

TABLE 18
San Francisco Leadership's Selection of "Most Important
Unresolved Problem Facing San Francisco"

Directly Related to Minority Group	
Racial problems, general	5
Minorities, multiple problems	2
Black problems, general	2
Minority housing	1
Black problems, specific	1
Need for jobs for minorities	1
Need for jobs for Mexican-Americans	1
Minority discontent-agitation, general	1
Fear of the Negro	1
	15
Indirectly Related to Minority Group	
Employment needs	4
City's economic security	1
Need for new taxes	1
Deterioration of central city	1
Problems of the poor	1
	8
Not Minority Related	
Lack of leadership in business and government	1
Reform in the city government	2
Transportation	1
Too many to pick one—all interrelated	7
	11

entation of the response. Fifteen of the thirty-four respondents specifically employed direct mention of Negroes or blacks or used the term "minority" (which, in response to a probe, made explicit reference to blacks); only one failed to mention blacks in this context and he was Spanish-speaking. Another eight gave answers related to particular problems without racial references, although they, too, after a probe, mentioned blacks directly. Thus two-thirds of this group were keenly sensitive to black efforts to claim deference, justice, or simply help. To achieve that state of mind, however, it was necessary for the black community to respond to the national currents during this decade and to engage in dual strategies of black politics.

During the 1950s, the leadership, a combination of NAACP and black church and labor leaders, agreed on the general goal of equality and on the general strategy of working within city institutions, including the courts, to accomplish that goal. The establishment of a city Human Relations Commission during the late 1950s, and efforts to seek compliance with state and local laws against discrimination (publicized in the 1960 hearings of a federal commission), seemed to provide the tactical instrument for the struggle. Because law itself is not self-enforcing and compliance automatic, some injustices, such as unemployment, are not easily reached by statute.[25] Certainly not enough gains were forthcoming to satisfy expectations raised in the black community by the events that were initiated in Montgomery and spread throughout the South. As a result, there developed in San Francisco during the early 1960s a split among leaders who, while agreeing on the general goal of black equality, differed sharply on other matters, a relationship of "hostile cooperation," in the words of the close analysis by David Wellman.[26]

The 1960s opened with court attacks against school desegregation,* denunciations of discrimination by private and public agencies, dramatically publicized sit-ins, and the usual settings and personae of a social drama that was to become so familiar around the nation. Probably the year 1964 brought the first full impact of this new protest politics. As the year opened, civil rights groups announced a combined attack against the hiring practices of major businesses, in particular, hotels, auto dealerships, and banks. It took only one week of large and unruly demonstrations in front of one major hotel to achieve an agreement with all hotels on hiring; the auto dealers took somewhat longer.

The banks were much more difficult, though, in particular the Bank of America, main target for the campaign spearheaded by the Congress for Racial Equality.[27] From March to September 1964, the Bank of America and CORE engaged in extended conflict, complete with the usual demands, replies, pickets, negotiations—and followed by black gains. The Bank of America mounted a full-scale publicity campaign to explain its operations and proposals and proclaimed complete willingness to work with state FEPC regulations. But it

---

* Not until 1971 did a federal court order compel desegregation of San Francisco's elementary schools. It was instituted that fall amid outcry, boycott, a change of the board from appointive to elective, election of a conservative board, and the removal of the superintendent, all within one year. But desegregation continued.

would not agree to quotas of jobs for minorities, nor would it provide CORE with personnel data. It did set up job training programs and submit minority data on its personnel to the FEPC publication; yet otherwise it met CORE demands. At the end of August, then, when CORE ended its picketing, the Bank of America had changed its personnel practices (hiring its first black executive at mid–year) and had begun hiring more minority members, which FEPC reports showed were very few (13.3 percent minorities, including 2.9 percent black) and very concentrated in entry positions (only about 0.5 percent were minorities in the highest 20 percent of the jobs). However, whatever the publicity put forth by either side, each had not achieved its fullest goals; although CORE did not obtain access to detailed personnel data or an agreement on job quotas, the Bank of America did change its practices. It was generally conceded by city figures that CORE and other such groups had "won" important victories against major employers in the city in a short, sharp campaign.

That judgment is supported by later events. By early 1973, a report to the city's Human Rights Commission showed sharp gains in the minority hiring practices of the nineteen banks in San Francisco. Minority hiring by then averaged 30 percent. The Bank of America was now one of the three largest minority hiring institutions; the bank hiring the least had a rate of 7 percent. Blacks represented about 8 percent of all employees. The Bank of America's 1972 report, "Social Problems and the Bank of America," cited a tripling of minority employment since 1965, now 23.4 percent of all its employees.

The Militant and Moderate Modes

Yet parallel and behind such protest activities was the struggle over leadership of the black community's political development. It surfaced in December 1964, when in a low-turnout election the local NAACP had a major turnover in officers; in the judgment of the press, the election "swept its traditional leaders out of office and handed the power to a reform administration dedicated to more vigorous action." [28] Thereafter, the NAACP's middle-class and professional membership turned from its exclusive tactic of litigation to support of the new politics of protest.[29] But in the leadership a division existed that was even more complex than that in the conflict over action in the courts or the streets.[30] One set of the city's black leadership, termed "militant," differed sharply with another set, the "mod-

TABLE 19

Conceptual Characteristics of Militant and Moderate Black Leaders,
San Francisco 1965

Characteristics	Militants	Moderates
Occupation	Professional: law, education	Leaders of churches, unions
Ties within change-oriented groups	Tight, formal, rules	Loose, informal
Organizational ties to black community	Almost none, cadre-based	Many, intimate, continuing; mass-based
Perception of leader role	Mobilize and articulate broad views of black community	Define issues and solutions for black community on items of daily economic importance
Conception of social change	Flows quickly and fully from concentrating passion and resources in direct confrontation with contemptuous or indifferent, but always oppressive, system	Drips slowly from daily interaction with white leaders who respect black leaders' institutional base and sympathize with their claims
Ideology	Broad, package of issues, highly moralistic	Specific, itemic, pragmatic
Political tactics	Seek redress by demands, then give show of strength by demonstrations, etc., compromise of "deals" unthinkable	Indirectly indicate potentials for show of power and then bargain; compromise a necessity in bargaining with whites
Contacts with white world of politics and government	Shunned and condemned as corruptive and ineffective; "outsiders" see these as objects of overt attack	Frequent and cherished as major conduit for change; "insiders" see these as the subjects of covert assistance
Basic strengths	Moral passion; initiate redress and focus grievances in direct challenge to the powerful; high payoff possibility for members' goals	Institutional bases provide continuing resources; mass support drawn from close contact with black community; knowledge of local levers; persistence in implementation

TABLE 19 (*Continued*)

Characteristics	Militants	Moderates
Basic weaknesses	Individualistic passion inhibits ongoing collective organization of resources; uncertain notion of means' relationship to ends; vague sense of location of local power; weak skills or will for implementation; lack of organizational rooting in masses of blacks	Institutional ties become ends; maintenance of relationships with white power holders weakens drive for black gains (compromise imperative dims passion); gains made are small on piecemeal basis and often not visible to black community

erate," in composition, in relationship to the black community, and in tactics. That division, still prevailing in the 1970s under new names and personalities, is more complex than labels can indicate. Table 19 summarizes this division by different structural, behavioral, and attitudinal dimensions of the two subsets. Such distinctions should not conceal the considerable agreement concerning the injustice that blacks felt and the need for remedies. But it is also clear that in the black neighborhoods of the city there early developed the schism which others have noted in the emergence of black leadership.[31] Missing was the true "Uncle Tom," although that label became a favorite epithet hurled by militant against moderate.

Then and later the militants shared much with the moderates. Both operated with rank-and-file blacks, who showed little interest in such traditional channels into the city's political system as primaries, general elections, petitions, visiting delegations, press statements, and so forth. In that sense, both cadres assumed the task of defining and expressing the black community's needs, demands, and preferences. But from that common function, they diverged in perceptions of what the community wanted. Both gave an aura of emotional indictment to their statements of needs and actions, but they differed on how central the indictment was to subsequent strategies. Both recognized the dangers of co-optation by white decision structures in the city, but they differed on how susceptible to contamination black leaders could be. Both groups appreciated the use of the show of strength, but they differed about its place in the sequence of social action and what fol-

lowed it. Both desired and expected change, but they held different
stop watches on the feasible pace of change. Both demanded that
American institutions keep their promises, but they had different expectations about their being kept. They were apprehensive and sanguine about the future for black people, but both groups strove
mightily to "fight the good fight" together, whatever its outcome.

Yet there was little evidence that the leadership struggle had firm
roots in the black community. As Wellman noted: "Since neither
style has delivered the goods and neither has effectively mobilized the
black community, there are very few indications that either style is
actively accepted by the community. . . . And in the face of a common enemy or hostility from the white community, their differences
are played down and they work together." [32]

Black Politics, 1964–1965

Although much of this was illustrated in the maneuvering over
the 1964 civil rights protests, the issue was joined even more sharply
the ensuing year as the federal antipoverty program began in the city.
Its requirements of resident participation touched pleasingly on the
militant blacks' desires for community involvement and control over
institutions affecting their lives, while its funds for programmatic approaches to unemployment pleased the more moderate blacks.[33] The
first struggle came over that participatory issue. Ambiguous in its origins, hence subject to manifold local interpretations, and quickly opposed by mayors or party groupings across urban America, the
"maximum feasible participation" clause set off in the city a struggle
between the black community and City Hall, in this case the then
mayor, John Shelley. Militants led the fight to obtain majority representation for the poor on the city-wide, policy-making Economic Opportunity Council (EOC) and for the autonomy of four—later five
—neighborhood poverty boards over programs.

While civil rights protests over hiring practices at auto agencies,
hotels, and banks had split the militant and establishment black leaders, they become united by the subsequent struggle to make the antipoverty program black-dominated. That arose because Mayor Shelley
had appointed to the EOC traditional representatives of the city life.
It was to be only an adjunct to his operation of the program, with
limited black participation (five of fifty, all from the moderate
blacks) and no clear authority except to advise. Black militants immediately condemned this as another effort to use their neighborhood

as a "colony" administered from the outside. They sought an EOC with a majority of the poor, a program focus in selected target areas, and emphasis upon community organizing, not social services. The black moderates joined in with militants when Shelley ignored the former's efforts to be the official city agency. His refusal reflected both administrative and political concerns—the need to enforce his authority for responsibility over use of the funds, and his fear of the Burton organization, which, with black allies, had earlier forced him from his congressional seat. But the black coalition, stiffened by the intervening events of the Watts riots in southern California in the summer of 1965, and reinforced by federal officials' insistence that the poor must have a voice, compelled Shelley to concur in their demands.

But once the coalition achieved the desired representation and decentralized administration, it split within another year. Militant blacks wanted to use the program to build an organization for neighborhood governance and for bargaining with outside "power centers." Moderates, however, more oriented to providing traditional social welfare services to community members, insisted that the program provide such assistance. Moderates won that struggle, mainly because of the failure of the black community to be stirred by militant calls to organize and confront "the power structure" as a political bloc. Moderates, with established channels to public and private agencies outside the neighborhoods, utilized that resource in overcoming the militants. Marjorie Myhill, observing this struggle in the Western Addition, judged that " it was not so much a socio-economic struggle as a struggle between different ideologies in the Negro community— between traditional conciliatory attitudes and a new 'black power' ideology." [34] The details of that program fight were tightly summarized in Ralph Kramer's comparative study of the five programs within San Francisco:

All areas, heavily influenced by the leaders in the Western Addition, who saw an opportunity to organize the poor as an ethnic power base in the ghetto, gave priority to an Area Development Program. Each board became deeply involved in the administration of such a program and in the process of awarding close to three hundred jobs, mainly to neighborhood residents. Considerable jealousy and antagonism occurred between board and staff and various minority groups as they fought to control these new resources. Despite the fears and the hopes of opposing groups, the Area Development Program did not become a significant source of political power. It proved exceedingly difficult to organize the poor and to sustain any new infrastructure. Community organization sponsored by the areas resulted in some relatively minor improvements in neighborhood conditions, but there were no significant policy changes in any of the major community agencies except in public housing and in the effort to block redevelopment in the Mission, both of which were only indirectly related to the target area organization.[35]

Yet the effort had brought some political knowledge to the black factions. The "white power structure" *could* be moved, and the more strident and full-bodied the demand the more likely the concession. This was shown in the 1964 demonstrations against discriminatory hiring. Too, Kramer shows that the "structure" withdrew early from participation in the poverty program after Shelley's defeat; however, Alioto was subsequently to be much more effective in asserting his influence in black areas. A further lesson of these early years was that law—particularly federal law—was an external instrument that could be brought to bear on some phases of the struggle. This was seen in CORE's use of the state FEPC. Also, national and regional OEO offices were of crucial importance in ensuring the participation of the poor in the contest with Shelley, who preferred "traditional" governance—that is, professional, white, and linked to existing "power centers" in the city. Instructive, too, was the lesson that news media could be captured because of their preoccupation with the disruptive in community life. From the 1964 civil rights clashes onwards, "confrontation" styles of political resolution brought the media running to interview "leaders," who could then seek to move third parties onto their side against power centers.[36] Group solidarity could thereby be forged, although only when whites totally ignored black concerns.

In all, even small victories secured from white institutions were thought to serve two purposes. They created respect among such whites and the possibility of more. They also bred some black respect with which to feed efforts at further victories and so on until the characteristically low self-esteem might be broken. For these leaders then, their politics was, in Matthew Holden's phrase, "politics as collective psychiatry, as a way of making people feel better about themselves." [37]

But was this the experience of rank-and-file blacks? The diversity of cultural patterns in black neighborhoods complicates any simple statement, but one observation is made by all who have studied them.[38] That is, for most blacks, such politics—or any politics—has little place in their personal and group life. While most agreed that

that life was unsatisfactory, few were attracted to either leadership cadre during the 1960s as a source for the improvement of their life opportunities. The city and federal poverty programs after 1963 did little to change this apathy; indeed, it may well have aggravated it by promising much and delivering little. Such programs did something else to them, as a black writer in Hunter's Point has noted:

In its scheme to get people out of the cycle of poverty, the poverty program trapped people in its own industry. People found they were being paid well for skills they didn't even have to have or that didn't exist anywhere else. There wasn't much chance or incentive to look for a job somewhere else as a community worker or something; the thing to do was protect the jobs they had.[39]

These elements are visible in the connections among programs, among leaders and nonfollowers, and in the links between City Hall and ghetto programs during this decade.[40] By the late 1960s, the new politics of these black areas was closely tied to a tight federal job economy and to the mayor, a game limited in resources, participants, and objectives—but of little concern to residents. First, there was a cooperative network of community organization programs and the city and federal agencies that administered them. Most were single-purpose programs, and many had a separate community organization responsible for full administration.* But there was a widespread feeling in these neighborhoods that such activities had done little to change social and economic conditions. This was felt despite close cooperation between governmental sponsors and local agents, among whom disagreements were few and trade-offs were settled privately, without the tactics of confrontation.

A second outcome of poverty-program politics was the participation of only a few. These new cadres were highly active, full-time, local politicians who, although paid for their own work, still lacked information and expertise. Such programmatic organizations lacked membership beyond these cadres because they had been unable to arouse neighborhood residents. Possibly this was because residents did not acknowledge them to be community leaders, indeed sometimes viewed them with resentment and outright suspicion. Relation-

---

* The most active were the Joint Housing Committee, Labor and Industry Committee, Poverty Commission, Development Corporation, Coordinating Council, Education Committee, S.E.E.D. Board of Directors, Health Committee, Model Cities Commission, and the different citizen advisory committees of the Model Cities Agency.

ships among these activists constituted a third outcome of this local politics, a relationship best characterized by hostility and conflict. Jealous of others' rewards, activist peers echoed the resentment and hostility they received from residents and hence found cooperation with one another difficult. As a fourth consequence, then, these cadres became demoralized—skeptical regarding the benefit of their activity for the community, and with a sense that the community failed to appreciate them. That outcome, in turn, diverted such effort from social goals to personal rewards, from helping the community to helping one's self. Moreover, these conditions—fractionated program involvement, lack of observable results, passivity of residents to activist efforts, and intercadre conflict—mutually stimulated one another.

The resulting black political system was highly fragmented for two reasons. Coordination was not provided by outside agencies, since each of these was intent upon the success of its own individual black cohorts. Nor was coordination provided by a neighborhood power structure, for such cohesion was defeated by the competing ambitions of suspicious black cadres. Furthermore, cohesion among both the external and the internal activists was more difficult to achieve because of the insecurity engendered by the uncertain state of programs and resources, including cadre positions, over the course of time.

Yet these areas were not without some semblance of community leadership.[41] Some leaders occupied the traditional roles found in long-standing community institutions like churches. Others knew only an uncertain status in the federal program game, often moving from position to position in a government agency and in the neighborhood as the nervous cadres of community organizations. Some joint decision making and coordination were still possible, but communication and cooperation often broke down from lack of institutional machinery for such a task or from personal rivalries. In these areas during the 1960s, then, no inner elite controlled neighborhood decision making, despite a common ideology of black power, a black consciousness, and a common belief in a hostile white power structure.

That cities are places for the exchange of opportunities and that urban organizations exist to facilitate exchange and to utilize opportunities are propositions that have been emphasized throughout this book. In this emergent politics of the arriving minority, in a context of new opportunities, such functions of exchange are potential rather than actual. Common leadership can be a powerful instrument for a group's exchange power vis-à-vis other groups; so it has been for the Irish and Italians in San Francisco's history. But it has not yet become such a resource for blacks, despite the new opportunities. One might judge the failure of the development of a common leadership to lie in the inadequacy of the governmental programs. If, despite the passionate rhetoric, these programs could at best be only marginal in their effect on blacks' needs, a united leadership may have been impeded by the stinginess of the programs. For the smaller the pie of new resources, the sharper the conflict over their allocation, and hence the lesser the cohesion and the greater the dissatisfaction of residents. Alternatively, the failure of a common leadership to form might be a result of the newness of blacks to political power here or elsewhere. It takes time to develop skills of compromise, expertise in intergroup manipulation, knowledge of the political system's operational code, and so forth. Roughly fifty years elapsed between the migration of southern blacks to northern cities during World War I and the emergence of black mayors there. Sizable numbers of blacks were new to San Francisco, hence their factionalism was merely a function of an early stage of ethnic political development.

Whatever the reasons, black politics in San Francisco after the early 1960s was internally turbulent, mobilized only a few into a new but divided cadre, and generated rewards inadequate to the needs of a constituency usually indifferent to their efforts. Some leaders were classic "black bourgeoisie," even though they utilized the new rhetoric of black power and indignation.[42] Others urged a separatist approach entirely, as in the first stages of the Black Panther movement or in the Black Muslims. Some were politically "maze-wise," highly sophisticated analysts and manipulators of actors, resources, and interests either in black neighborhoods or in the city. Yet others never learned the levers of the game, and remained very narrow in territory, outlook, and success. Some operated with a passion for publicity while others were rarely visible; some prevailed by force of personality and maze-wisdom, while others used violence or its threat. In short, this was a highly complex politics conducted by agents of great diversity in skill, knowledge, and success.[43]

Black Politics, 1967–1973

Some of these qualities continued in the next five years when a new mayor, Joseph Alioto, came on the scene and made conscious efforts to build a political base in this cockpit of ethnic factionalism. Especially instructive was the evolution of black politics in Hunter's Point.[44] This neighborhood in southeastern San Francisco has for most of its existence been either ignored or dominated by outside forces—or both. Its life style is clearly different from other black neighborhoods because it houses the poorest blacks in the city. Municipal efforts to improve its housing with urban renewal money, which began in 1953, had accomplished nothing by 1960. In the early 1960s, it was the scene of youth gang warfare, battles with urban renewal agencies, and the emergence of community organizations. The political leaders were women, the "Big Five" in local parlance, who joined with a ministerial council to improve local housing.[45] But facilities and services continued to deteriorate under this leadership with its narrow policy focus. A second stage in Hunter's Point began with a riot in September 1966 after a policeman shot a youth fleeing from a stolen car. The riot was minor by the standards of American cities in those years, but it energized a new cadre of leaders—jobless young men.

With these youths there came a new initiative in social action, which focused on jobs and purposively sought supportive links to City Hall. In his 1967 campaign, by his own account, Alioto forged an alliance with "the black trade unionists, the young poverty workers, and the Baptists Ministers Union," as well as with the women activists. They contributed to his large majority in Hunter's Point and the Western Addition. This was done against the active opposition of other and more established blacks—many of them professionals— who unsuccessfully backed both Congressman Burton's mayoralty candidate in 1967 and Supervisor Dianne Feinstein in 1971 against Alioto. Mayor Alioto's response was that if these professionals "choose twice to align themselves against me and lose ignominiously both times, why should I assume there's any leadership left in those people? It's my assumption that the young men and others I've worked with are going to be leaders in the community. But in partnership with the city." [46]

Alioto's trade-offs to the young blacks were jobs and community leadership, and under the auspices of the poverty program that is what they received. From 1964 to the end of 1971, $8.6 million in poverty funds entered Hunter's Point, of which $6 million paid the salaries for 770 jobs. With top positions for themselves and the authority to distribute many more, these poverty workers became the only black leaders in the city with prompt, supportive access to the mayor's office. Alioto's purpose was clear: "We made a studied attempt to corral the younger tough element and channel their energies." [47] The mayor's objectives were several: help cool a tense racial scene by enlisting strong young leaders, provide jobs, and build a political base. The young blacks received more than salaries for their cooperation; some funds became available to deal—albeit only minutely—with day care, Head Start, legal assistance, summer youth programs, credit unions, and so forth. But the prime purposes of the money were community organization and the development of leadership skills. All observers agreed that the program provided the resources, motivations, and forums for these ends.

The next five years of the poverty program at Hunter's Point, however, did little to meet the needs of that community. Even the city's EOC director, Judge Joseph Kennedy, later admitted such failure. What did develop was the earlier noted poverty program game, characterized by personal factionalism and public apathy in a bitter, emotional context for any leadership effort. More than once, according to publicized accounts, violence and intimidation were part of this game, as those with resources to dispense found themselves "jammed," that is, the object of threats of personal violence in order to secure favors for the intimidators. But it is also clear that young leaders were powerful only as long as they supported City Hall. Alioto's reference to such leaders working "in partnership with the city" hints at what is widely believed in the neighborhood: the poverty game is ultimately controlled in City Hall and is only delegated to local agents. The pattern is like that in many American cities in the history of other ethnic groups. Because they were still arriving, they lacked independent power and hence had to accept subordinate leadership roles within their own neighborhoods.

Nor did this change in 1972 when federal assistance to the ghettos shifted from the Office of Economic Opportunity—the poverty program approach—to the Department of Housing and Urban Development—the "model cities" approach. Planning for the latter in Hunter's Point climaxed in August 1971 with a $3.6 million grant from HUD—stimulated by Mayor Alioto—and $1.5 million from other federal agencies; moreover, the area was to receive about $3.4 million in each of the succeeding four years. The money was substantially larger than OEO funds, there was better provision for community development planning, and the increasingly restrictive limita-

tions of OEO were loosened. Too, the area's administrative agency—
the Model Cities Commission—became a city agency, and this gave
it a direct, formal representation at City Hall it had not known before.

But control by the mayor was, if anything, strengthened. Of the
twenty-one Model Cities Commission members, Alioto could appoint
seven; he promptly filled these in 1971 with his young black supporters. Moreover, all commission contracts had now to be signed by him.
When the commission proposed a $750,000 contract for a health
clinic directed by a black professional who was also an old opponent,
Alioto refused to sign the contract and required its renegotiation so
as to remove that man. Other municipal controls had now to operate; as with other city agencies, the local commission had to meet
charter and ordinance requirements, such as civil service. In sum,
the program represented on the one hand an important step toward
coherent neighborhood planning, backed with substantial—but probably still insufficient—funds. On the other hand, the political reality
was that it was far removed from militant black leaders' notions of
community autonomy or from moderate black professionals' preference for their dominance of the extramural links. Quite clearly, the
new approach to ghetto assistance was designed, and in this city was
implemented, to give mayors ultimate responsibility; this avoided political struggles such as they had known in these areas under OEO.

But Hunter's Point is not totally a "colony." In the February 1972
elections for the fourteen positions on its Model Cities Commission,
Alioto's black leaders were defeated by local residents,[48] and a slate
of the black professionals won, amid campaign charges of "strong-
arm" tactics. A surprising development was the election of eight residents under thirty years of age (one was nineteen) with little clear
obligation to City Hall. The commission then represented an uncertain balance among new youth, older professionals, and the mayor's
appointees. Nevertheless, the options still lodged with Alioto over contract sign-offs, and his highly visible use of them to punish political
enemies made it clear that no cadre in Hunter's Point or other black
neighborhoods could be independent of established power "downtown." Both the young and the professional leaders inferred from all
this the necessity to work with such outside forces; radical blacks
were confirmed in their insistence on the futility of seeking such relationships.

Summary

Thus, the past decade has brought differential rewards to this arriving minority. Black professionals have obtained public office and a key role in neighborhood politics. A few young, poor blacks have obtained jobs in the uncertain and antagonistic poverty game, with an accompanying new local status, even though they are still tied to outside white leaders. By early 1972, 21.7 percent of the city's civil service were blacks, well over their 13.4 percent in the total population. But seven of ten of these were in the lowest categories while six of ten whites were in the highest; too, only 6.6 and 0.4 percent were in the powerful police and fire services. But rank-and-file blacks have found few of these rewards; the over 4,300 city jobs have done little to meet the unemployment needs of the black neighborhoods.[49] The federal contribution to these outcomes is considerable, of course (a matter deferred to a concluding chapter).

White leaders employ different strategies in the face of the new black politics. When the black community is aroused and its leadership is unified—as in the civil rights protests of 1964 and in securing majority representation for the poor on the EOC in 1965—private and public white leaders recede from their first opposition and concur with some black goals.[50] But when the black community remains apathetic—as in the efforts of Hunter's Point residents to remove temporary housing after 1953—or its leadership is divided—as with much of the poverty program and likely with the Model Cities program—white leadership prevails. The last, assisted by white efforts at a divide-and-rule strategy, is long familiar in the majority-minority culture conflict over politics and economics in urban America.[51] But the success of this strategy is equally facilitated by divisions among the blacks themselves. These stresses may be rooted in differences in status, or in age, but most often in opportunity.

Ironically, to many non-blacks it seems that a cohesive "black power" has emerged locally, which obtains what it wants merely by threats of confrontation.[52] Yet we have seen that while many blacks are aware of that white perception—indeed, delight in it—it is not one they believe to be true. They see instead apathy and division, a full and angry rhetoric but less full results, a community still dominated from the outside, and a white world still resistant to any change in its attitudes toward them. For such blacks, there is cold comfort in the relative increases in rewards which the black community has extracted from the white world in a little over a decade. These are judged as being still only limited rewards, spread too thinly to change the net life opportunities of blacks. Much in this judgment was echoed elsewhere in earlier years by the Irish about the Yankees and by the Italians about the Irish, when a few of one's countrymen were co-opted onto lower rungs of the opportunity ladders. While there is no guarantee that history will repeat itself, the city's leaders, when asked to predict the contours of the local political scene a decade hence, overwhelmingly pointed to a steadily increasing role for the blacks.

That prognosis seems inescapable, if black political development in other cities is any guide. If so, then the primary contribution of federal programs was to empower new cadres, not to meet the massive needs of the larger black constituency. The moneys required were only marginal, of course, but in practice they acted like political levers, moving far more than their weight. Too, they enabled the mayor to develop a host of programs small in focus and in finances, which acted like levers to move much political support in these neighborhoods. Moreover, federal funds subsequently irradiated San Francisco's other social structures. As one who was reared and politicized through these experiences, Lenneal Henderson observes of these new cadres that "once they left these programs with skills in grantsmanship, advocacy and organization, they dispersed into non-profit corporations, city and county agencies, political campaigns, and universities, positively charging their new environment with the residue of 'community politics,' while allowing a new generation of 'community officials' to succeed them." [53]

All of this is reminiscent of the political empowerment of the Irish, the Italians, and others in earlier years in this and other cities. There, too, a few resources, like party or municipal jobs, injected judiciously into the ethnic culture by the dominant political system moved first cadres, then neighborhoods, and finally whole ethnic groups into a system of larger rewards. Altruism is a stranger in this process. Old leaders extend, and arriving leaders accept, these resources for reasons of personal advancement. What one gives is less materially to the giver's than to the recipient's scheme of things. The deference which the exchange provides to the recipient is greater within his community than outside it. But enough of such exchanges, and outsiders begin to assemble a picture of the arriving ethnic groups having newfound power. That power eventually is the touchstone for recognition and respect in American politics.

In time, the newcomers will have arrived, in the sense that the gap between the perception of their own worth and that which others have of it is narrowed enough to be endurable. That narrowing process has no time scale built into it. It involves the acquisition of other values as well, such as income and safety; and it is accompanied by injustices and indignities, sometimes even outright violence, against the challengers. But it has operated thus through successive waves of new ethnic groups in American politics.

It may be in San Francisco that local factors will refract that process. The Asians and Spanish-speaking may be too few in numbers to lever much out of the political system; but they have obtained more from it in the last decade when their numbers have reached new highs. The blacks may have the numbers, but still may not achieve that deference—as many of them believe —because of the unique way the nation has dealt with them for over three centuries. Blacks little note that in this city Chinese-Americans once knew a literally murderous prejudice, and the Japanese-Americans over thirty years ago had all their property expropriated; yet they have managed to extract deference and more material rewards from the dominant white culture.*

There are great frustrations still ahead for all three arriving groups. Factionalism will continue, even expand, as opportunities widen. Leaders will sometimes disappoint by their lack of capacity or by selling out. Programmatic panaceas will first excite with hope and later flood with despair. Ethnic slurs will continue at informal levels, even though out of public sight and sound. But as with the arriving ethnic groups of the nineteenth century, those of this century can never again be the same for having entered the contest for recognition and reward. Like the Irish and Italians of that earlier time, so with the blacks, browns and yellows of our time—they all join in the black saying, "I ain't what I will be, I ain't what I can be, but thank God, I ain't what I was"—always the motto of the arriving.

---

* An indirect measure of black gains is found in the number of black businessmen. By March 1973 a directory of black businesses, municipal contractors, and community resources required 192 pages. See Douglas Rainey & Associates, *Where It's At!* (San Francisco, 1973).

PART VI

EXTRAMURAL FORCES AND LOCAL AUTONOMY

The federal system is not accurately symbolized by a neat layer cake of three distinct and separate planes. A far more realistic symbol is that of the marble cake. Wherever you slice through it you reveal an inseparable mixture of differently colored ingredients. There is no neat horizontal stratification. Vertical and diagonal lines almost obliterate the horizontal ones, and in some places there are unexpected whirls and an imperceptible merging of colors, so that it is difficult to tell where one ends and the other begins. So it is with federal, state, and local responsibilities in the chaotic marble cake of American government. MORTON GRODZINS

CHAPTER 11

External Influences (I): Washington

In this exploration of power in San Francisco two themes concerning decision making have been displayed. The most evident theme is that decisions are the products of fluid coalitions, with only occasional—and even then vague—participation of citizens. The fluid quality precludes decisional dominance across the board by a single man or group in an "elite" fashion, while the limited citizen participation challenges any simple notion of "democratic" influence in municipal affairs. The overt quality of coalitional politics does not preclude some covert decision making, although that occurs mostly in the negotiating phases. Only a few decisions are totally hidden, but even these can be unearthed if someone chooses to dig—for example, the friendly assessor, or the Board of Permit Appeals.

The second theme of this book has shadowed the first. This is the degree to which decision making in San Francisco is shaped by forces arising outside as well as inside its compact borders. Extramural forces account for how San Francisco—and probably all cities—arose; here, the presence in nearby areas of gold, and then later silver and wheat, made this an entrepôt, producing a new social order almost overnight. Perturbations in these exterior areas—boom or bust in mines and crops—had direct impact along the shores of the bay. Such links with the outside have increased over a century.

Because its consequence for urban affairs here and elsewhere is so vast, it is very important to explicate this theme. Some of this was suggested briefly in chapter 3, referring to the impact of external factors on both the entry to decisional centers and the nature of the agenda. We also saw these external factors in the effect of the state's political culture on local politics; in the migration of corporations and banks after World War II; in the military's influence on prostitution; and in the federal contribution to the politicizing of arriving minorities through poverty programs.

A first step in providing a fuller understanding of these forces is an examination of their scope and causes. These forces are of two kinds, public and private; the distinction, although not always sharp, is useful for analytic purposes. By "public" is meant the role of state and national governments in shaping the inputs and outcomes of local decisions. By "private" is meant the similar effects achieved by other institutions, particularly the economic and professional. The awareness of these forces provides a much larger framework for understanding this and other cities, as it implies that (1) San Francisco shares a common dimension with the rest of urban America, and (2) extramural institutions are major partners in local decision making.[1]

CONTEMPORARY CHANGES IN INTERGOVERNMENTAL RELATIONS

During the 1960s it became evident that whatever the popular notion of American federalism, all levels of government were becoming interlocked across a wide range of public policies. Even the earlier existence of "dual federalism," with each government having distinct but separate authority, may have been more myth than reality.[2] But by 1970, what had developed was a "new federalism," which Michael Reagan defined as "a nationally dominated system of shared power and shared functions." [3] Washington was not only making many local decisions but also greatly influencing many others. Moreover, there had emerged a sense of a national community, accompanied by belief in the federal government as the setter of national goals and standards for public service. In these interactions the states and localities still retained considerable influence, although increasingly their powers came on the implementation side of national policy processes. Too, the growth in use of the grant-in-aid (GIA) diminished potential conflict between political authorities in the process whereby national goals became accepted in state and local policy systems.

Alteration of Funding Patterns by the GIA

The most visible sign of this new federalism is the ballooning of the GIA, those federal grants of money to assist state and local

TABLE 20
Percentage Shares of Domestic Direct Expenditures by
Three Levels of Government

Government	1902	1927	1948	1954	1962	1967	1969
Federal	17	15	23	26	27	34	32
State	10	15	26	24	24	24	25
Local	73	70	51	50	49	42	43

SOURCE: Michael Reagan, *The New Federalism* (New York: Oxford University Press, 1972), p. 46.

programs.[4] The provender for this growth has been the flexible and fecund federal income tax.[5] In ever-increasing proportions, Washington collects the largest revenues to pour into GIAs;* thus, from 1948 to 1972, GIAs rose from $1.8 to $30.3 billion, by 1972 accounting for one of every five dollars available to states and localities. By the end of fiscal year 1974, it will total $45.2 billion. For specific policy programs the federal contribution rose even more sharply over the course of this century. Where Washington had contributed only 0.3 percent of local *school* costs in 1919, a half-century later its share was 7.3 percent, while the federal share for *roads* increased from 7.1 to 29.1 percent. If one adds to these direct GIA aids the indirect costs also provided by Washington, the federal weight is even greater—about one-third for highways, health, and hospitals, one-eighth for schools, and over one-half for public assistance.

Reagan's analysis of the domestic spending by these three governments over this century produces the simple but significant data in table 20. The federal government doubled its relative contributions, the states were up by a factor of 2.5, while all three were increasing their total expenditures by many magnitudes. If we ask how much is contributed at the grant-giving level, Reagan estimates that domestic spending in 1968 was almost equally divided among these three; thus the local share is even less than the 43 percent shown in table 20. An even sharper sense of the federal weight is seen if one first subtracts from state and local expenditures those financed by grants from above and then asks how much each level contributes to domestic spending *from its own sources*; the results in 1969 were

---

* The federal share of all revenue collected annually in the whole nation between 1902 and 1968 rose from 38 to 62 percent, the states' from 11 to 26 percent, while the local share shrank from 51 to 12 percent.

federal 43 percent, state 29 percent, and local 28 percent. Moreover, this federal contribution is on the increase; whereas in 1960 every eighth dollar of state and local revenue was federal, by 1971 it was every fifth dollar.[6] In that complex flow of intergovernmental funds, figure 9 provides a schematic snapshot of the volume, direction, and sources of this new development in federalism, freezing the flow pattern at the end of the Johnson administration's budget.

This shift in intergovernmental finance must be understood as also a major shift in the volume of federal programs, of which these funds are but the most visible sign. The big change occurred during the 1960s. Of the 530 GIA programs by 1970, 80 percent had been enacted after 1960—and 143 in the first two years of the Nixon administration. The federal funds involved ballooned accordingly: $1.7 billion in 1947, $2.3 billion in 1951, $7 billion in 1961—and by 1970, $24 billion and a year later over $30 billion.[7] Even allowing for inflation and population growth, this represents a totally new fiscal picture of federalism within just a quarter-century—indeed, within one decade.

Alteration of Program Responsibilities

There was also a new kind of federalism programmatically. That distinction between earlier and recent federal programs has been most fully explored by James Sundquist and David Davis:

Before 1960 the typical federal assistance program did not involve an expressly stated *national* purpose. It was instituted, rather, as a means of helping state or local governments accomplish *their* objectives. . . .

Policy making for the established functions, in the older model, remained where it resided before the functions were assisted—in the state and local governments. Federal review and control, accordingly, sought primarily the objectives of efficiency and economy to safeguard the federal treasury, and did not extend effectively to the substance of the programs. . . . The federal agencies saw their role as one of technical assistance rather than control [but] they would not substitute their policy judgement for that of the recipient agencies. . . .

In the newer model the federal grant is conceived as a means of enabling the federal government to achieve *its* objectives—national policies defined, although often in very general terms, by the Congress. The program remains a *federal* program; as a matter of administrative convenience, the federal government executes the program through state or local governments rather than through its own field offices, but the motive force is federal, with the states and communities assisting—rather than the other way around. . . .

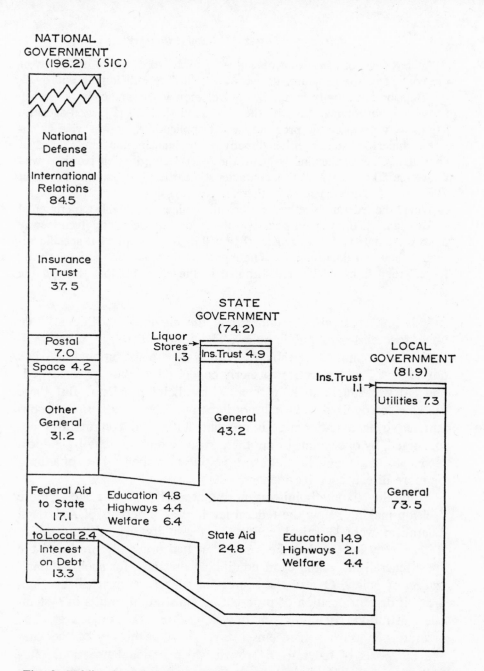

Fig. 9. Public expenditures by type and by level of government and the inter-governmental flow of funds, 1969 (in billions of dollars). Total expenditures (all governments): $308.3 (excludes duplicate transfers). Source: Reprinted from Deil S. Wright, "The States and Intergovernmental Relations," *Publius: The Journal of Federalism,* 1 (Winter 1972), 13.

Achievement of a *national* objective requires close federal control over the content of the program. Projects are therefore individually approved; the state or community is not assured of money automatically through a formula apportionment [as with the older model]. . . , [F]ederal agencies aggressively promote the program, solicit applications, and provide extensive technical assistance, either directly or by financing the employment of consultants. As further inducement, the federal contribution is raised well above the 50 percent that was characteristic earlier; it commonly begins at 100 percent and often remains there. . . .

· Where the federal objectives are broadly defined and highly experimental —for example, the war on poverty—the federal agencies are given leeway as to what state or local agencies they will deal with and what specific activities they will finance. . . . The money is thus put "more precisely on target" than it would be if distributed in the older fashion, through the state.[8]

It is important also to understand the change in public attitude about federalism and public policy. The newer federalism, a nationalization of community problems, knows few constitutional barriers any longer. Problems were formerly conceived as state or local; federal aid was sought to help them with "their" problems. But these are now "recognized as in fact not local at all but as a *national* problem requiring a national solution that states and communities are mandated, by one means or another, to carry out—usually by inducements strong enough to produce a voluntary response but sometimes by more direct, coercive means."[9]

While the Nixon administration sought after 1970 to relocate more decision making below the federal level, close observers of American federalism were skeptical about the feasibility of the approach.[10] Rather, they judged that the forces that had originally produced the "new federalism" would exert continuing pressures for such nationalization of policy. One of the sources of such pressures will be Congress, if decentralization of program administration results in systematic frustration, corruption, or diffusion of program objectives. One or more of those results seems likely, given the history of the GIA and the prism of federalism through which national programs must be transmitted. The desire of governors or mayors to use decentralization methods like revenue sharing to favor groups or localities other than those specified by national law; malfeasance in the use of federal funds; highly publicized failures in state and local administration of national programs—any of these can provide major feedback to

Congress, thus renewing demands for further centralization of national policies.

The second Nixon administration signaled its clear intent to decentralize even further to the states the administration of program objectives and funds from the preceding decade. Several methods were employed: selective nonenforcement of some laws and their disapproved programs—for example, dismantling the Office of Economic Opportunity for fiscal year 1974 and backing away from school desegregation efforts; stringent reduction of funding in other programs—for example, aid to education; and in the fall of 1972, provision of "no-strings" shared revenue, beginning with $30.2 billion over five years.[11] In the process, another effort to reshape American federalism—as well as a constitutional struggle over the president's authority to enforce national law—was under way.

This shift in program responsibility is only the most recent development in an American federalism that has constantly altered. From the earliest days, we have moved from private to public and from individual to collective resources in meeting local policy needs.[12] In schooling, roads, and welfare—areas of the greatest local expenditures —we have witnessed a gradual shift from decisions that were private and individual to those that are now public. Accompanying this shift, not coincidentally, have been other shifts in the sources of money and in policy guidelines—from the community to the state and thence to Washington.

When our only roads were crude trails, maintaining them was the responsibility of the individual homeowner or scattered citizens in hamlet or township; now our roads require immense expenditures, of which the community contributes only about one-fifth, Washington one-third, and the states one-half. Schooling that earlier was a family affair is now also controlled in detail from the state capitol and by outside professional agencies. Since the end of World War I the local share of school funds has dropped from 83 to 52 percent, while the state share has risen from 16 to 41 percent, and the federal share from 0.3 to 7.3 percent. Where welfare was once a private family function—or at best handled by a church or a scrimping local poorhouse—it now involves persons, monies, and actions of great number in many other places than the locality.[13]

This policy centralization is thus not new; indeed, it has roots in the conflict of federalists and antifederalists over adoption of the new constitution almost two centuries ago.[14] But by our time, state and local officials have come increasingly—often eagerly—to support such centralized funds and policy guidelines. In the early 1960s, a survey of "the federal system as seen by state and local officials" found that only 11 percent supported the philosophy and policies of orthodox states' rights. More typically, 43 percent accepted that philosophy but were pragmatic on specific issues; another 33 percent eschewed the philosophy and were pragmatic on issues, while 13 percent supported federal action in both philosophy and issues. In short, even before the impact of the Great Society, three out of four state and local officials daily involved in the matrix of federalism had a pragmatic approach to their responsibilities for local services; this trend was even greater among the chief heads of such services.[15]

COOPERATION AND CONFLICT IN THE NEW FEDERALISM

The shift in American federalism occasioned by the Great Society has not yet shaken down for a full perspective, but it is clear that local officials are in a different decisional context, one in which they face outward as much as inward. A 1969 survey of local executives in over 900 cities provided hard data on what was transpiring.[16] Washington was now viewed as being more helpful in solving local problems than the states (unless reapportionment had taken place). In many cities, particularly the largest, federal liaison offices had been quickly created, resulting in more federal grants; regional federal offices, as well as congressmen, were involved in processing grant applications; while there was some conflict in the federal contacts of local executives, this relationship was most generally viewed as cooperative. However, coordination was most difficult with those federal agencies having an independent power base in smaller communities, as in the poverty and education programs.

The interactions between federal and local governments which accompanied the Great Society suggest much cooperation and accommodation. But this clearly differed with the policy and local context; A. Lee Fritschler and Morley Segal in the study cited above found "joint policymaking, mutual accommodation, innovative conflict, and disintegrative conflict."

Thus, across the nation the Head Start program had a demonstrable effect on local health and educational institutions, which accommodated with surprising speed to this new approach—low profile, nonconfrontation—to aiding children of the poor.[17] Elsewhere, Frances

Piven and Richard Cloward expressed the belief that the federal government itself caused the welfare crisis of the 1960s. Urban renewal, Office of Economic Opportunity programs (including the encouragement of litigation to block local welfare agencies in their arbitrary withholding of client benefits), and eventually successful court challenges—all had the effect of adding many people to local welfare rolls. For example, there emerged from the OEO a thrust to provide welfare clients with more funds and services than they then enjoyed. That was accompanied (with OEO assistance) by formation of the National Welfare Rights Organization (NWRO) as a local pressure group using demonstrations, sit-ins, and litigation to benefit the poor. The intended purpose of increasing welfare rolls was to destroy the existing poor law and so create another with more equity and less rigidity, namely, some form of income maintenance.[18]

But the effort at federal intervention in the local policy world was far from successful. There remain still today any number of ways in which state and local systems can impede and certainly refract interference by the national government. National purposes can be thwarted or altered by delays, by counterpressures transmitted through Congress or party, or by outright refusal to meet legal requirements.[19] The threat of withdrawing fund support from categorical grants would seem to be an enormous resource available to federal officials facing reluctant or obstructive state and local officials. But every scholar of the subject has noted the generic inability of federal officials to use this ultimate weapon. Deil Wright recently observed from his lengthy overview that "basically, categorical grants promote and reward the promise of performance. Accomplishment is clearly expected and accepted. But recalcitrance is tolerated, nonperformance is occasionally ignored, and seldom is flat failure severely sanctioned." [20] Thus, audits of the first years' disposition of large Title I grants under the Elementary and Secondary Act of 1965 found gross misuse that seemed criminal; but not then, and rarely since, have such funds been withheld.[21] The 1964 Civil Rights Act provision for withholding federal funds used to discriminate was rarely employed under the Johnson administration and disappeared under Nixon. Whether it was a Mayor Daley of Chicago under Johnson reversing the efforts of the Department of Health, Education, and Welfare to withhold that city's school funds because of its discrimination, or southern officials successfully appealing to a sympathetic President Nixon against similar fund cutoffs for the same reason, the state and local systems have found multiple access points in the federal system through which to counter national pressures.[22]

Resistance from below can be joined with faintheartedness from above, with a consequent futility of federal effort. In Chicago during the 1960s, civil rights regulations affecting public housing were regularly and blatantly violated. There were the usual discriminatory realtors, and the Housing and Urban Development officials involved adhered to an administrative precept that success depended on local support—that they must serve rather than regulate. The result was, as one analyst noted, that "HUD supported the local constituency whenever it deemed propitious regardless of civil rights laws and Federal Regulations [which] was most of the time." [23] Equally significant in explaining the refractory power of the prism of federalism is the role of local groups for whose benefit the federal law exists. When they are committed and forceful, as in the case of the NWRO and welfare clients, and they operate with an energetic enforcement agent at the national level, as with OEO, then great changes result in local policy. But, less can also be accomplished if, as in the case of public housing in Chicago, the group to be benefited loses interest in the goal of integration, as blacks did toward the end of the 1960s. Even an active federal agency could find little local interest in it as an ally in effecting a change in client services.

So it has been that not all federal weight on the local polity has been successful. At least four major reasons exist for this, which I conceive of as four barriers between the policy as it began and the resulting outcome of that policy's administration. One is the force of huge, private influences, which do far more to shape the basic distribution of values and resources in society than the force of government can counteract. The Coleman Report and its subsequent analyses purported to show the limited degree to which provision of resources by local authorities affected the quality of schooling that students received—independent of the influence of their family and status—or how little schooling affected the chances of occupational success.[24] Similarly, analysis of forty-two federal programs to promote economic and community development found their impact to be only modest, mainly reinforcing slightly existing trends.[25] That is, endemic institutional and economic factors may have far greater influence on conditions than public policy, particularly in an intergovernmental system so complex and unwieldy as to give the policies little leverage to affect such private factors.

A second differentiating force arises from the fact that state and local interests can conflict on a given issue, so that federal programs become diffused or diverted. Thus, the Safe Streets Act of 1968 sought to deal with the problems of crime where they were greatest—in big cities—but because of state pressures on Congress the law gave the states primary power to disburse the funds. During the first year, however, many states gave disproportionately smaller shares to big cities and larger to rural areas, which had less need objectively but more clout politically. As a result, Congress set aside funds for the largest cities to redress this imbalance, after heavy pressure by disgruntled city law enforcement officials, who increasingly viewed the state with suspicion.[26]

A third differentiating force arises from malfeasance; corruption, by definition, displaces the goals of a system with personal rewards. Such charges have plagued ghetto programs through much of their lives. Thus, a mid-1971 HUD study of seventy-four model cities, and the congressional mandate to hire mostly ghetto dwellers, found instead that only 44 percent of the workers met this requirement and that the nonresidents were paid better. However, the requirement was more often met when the black population was larger and the local civil service requirements and municipal executives were weaker.[27]

The fourth factor has particular saliency in San Francisco—the incapacity of the local political system to deliver the federal programs. Governmental structures that fragment authority, as most do formally in this country by separate selection and power for executive and legislature; election procedures that are sensitive to particularity, as in ward-based elections; the brake of the referendum in programs requiring local funding—all of these work against many cities possessing an integrated instrument for achieving national policy goals. Such local segmentation reflects bastions of interest and power within the urban scene which evaluate each national program in their own terms. Their coordination has increasingly become the major task of American mayors in efforts to meet the "urban crisis."

Ultimately, these four barriers that widen the gap between national policy objectives and local implementation are special variants of the fact of the social and political diversity in the American society. That diversity underlies the historical resistance to nationalizing forces sketched earlier. The tension between these centralizing and decentralizing elements of a complex society, operating through a multi-faceted federalism, has been, throughout our history, the generator for national policy conflict. The similarity between Alexander Hamilton's creation of a national bank system and Lyndon Johnson's school desegregation effort may be unnoticed, but the similarity is nevertheless real—the aggregation of national resources to achieve national values which a disaggregated system was frustrating.

In the course of these recent centralizing events, local systems have not been immune from their influence. They are compelled to alter established procedures, to permit once ignored groups a new role in resource allocation, and to consider formerly suppressed values. Despite the resistances to such a national thrust noted earlier, there have been created new elements at the local level involved in "who gets what, when, and how." The existing "mobilization of bias," [28] with its pre-authorization of procedures and pre-allocation of rewards for pre-approved actors, has found a serious challenge confronting it. For example, court orders, in matters of voting or school discrimination, introduce some new values, legitimate some new demands for service, and destroy some old perceptions. By 1970, that device alone, even in the face of a reluctant Nixon administration, had decisively restructured local education in the South and brought an awareness to southern whites that the evil foretold was not forthcoming.[29]

Similarly, poverty programs and Model Cities have provided a new phase to municipal politics. While the former's community action agencies (CAAs) totally failed to provide the coordination in the effort which Congress required, they had other consequences, as Sundquist and Davis document in their full-length analysis:

But the OEO through the CAAs multiplied the political strength of the poor many times over by offering them the jobs, the status, the governmental sanction, and the authority over public programs that the civil rights and comparable movements alone could never provide. . . .

Community action had unquestionably proved effective as a training institution—occasionally for agitators, to be sure, but more significantly for political and civic leaders, administrators and subprofessional workers, and entrepreneurs, all desperately needed by slum communities whose greatest weaknesses had been disorganization and inertia.

As we were told over and over again, in our field interviews, the old ways of community decision making are dead—programs and services designed by experts and accepted by the power structure can no longer be offered unilaterally to the poor, nor decisions by the "establishment" imposed upon them.[30]

There were costs for such new activity, of course. The CAAs were constantly in controversy with local "establishments," finding little acceptance even in cities where the program was relatively peaceful. In many places, such as San Francisco, those of established influence generally withdrew from the program, but this did not prevent the CAAs from having their victories.

The later Model Cities program found more acceptance and participation by traditional power centers; but then, it had been purposefully linked to municipal governance, particularly the mayor, as we noted of Alioto in the last chapter. But the ground broken by the poverty program could not be returned to its old form; as Judson James noted: "In the cities where citizen participation was already widely developed in other programs, especially those of OEO, ignoring the community groups was politically hazardous. Where citizen participation had not developed prior to model cities, the Model Cities program was often open to the control of already established groups with a good opportunity to limit the influence of community participants." [31]

In short, the evidence of these two programs suggests a widespread sense that "things will never be the same again around here." No one can predict the future course of this federal intervention in the local political scene, of course. But all the signs are that, whatever the local configuration of decision making that results—and it will clearly vary with place and issue—some universals will remain. These have been well put by Sundquist and Davis, who concluded that, as always, Washington "must depend upon the competence, and the motivation, of government officials whom it can influence or induce but cannot directly control." And it will most often choose "to rely almost wholly upon systems of mutual adjustment rather than central direction, upon what could be attained through negotiation among equals rather than through the exercise of hierarchical authority." [32]

SAN FRANCISCO AND TRANSFEDERAL FACTIONALISM

The consequences for San Francisco of this federalism shift take a number of forms, the most visible of which is financial. Over the last two decades, amidst increased expenditures and revenues, there has been considerable stability in the proportion of expenditures for different categories of policy—except for the near tripling of welfare costs, which were only 10.7 percent of city costs in 1949–50 but were 27.0 percent by 1969–70. The other budget items declined very little: schools from 22.7 to 21.3 percent; public safety from 15.0 to 10.8 percent; employee health and pension benefits from 10.4 to 9.6 percent; while about a dozen other smaller categories also declined slightly.[33] However, all of these items increased in absolute dollar volumes, as the total budget increased 560 percent over two decades, even though the city's population shrank by about 10 percent.

In this shift, the weight of state and federal subventions became much heavier. Their dollar amount grew from $27.4 million to $177.5 million over these two decades; they rose from 16.9 percent of all city government and school income in 1949–50 to 20.2 percent in 1959–60, and 25.1 percent in 1970–71.[34] Sorting out the federal share of this—much of which passes through the state—is enormously difficult. City reports estimate annual federal subventions of $45–55 million, depending on whether school aid is included. One tabulation for fiscal 1971 shows $44.6 million in nonschool federal GIAs, of which 54 percent aided dependent children and another 31 percent the needy aged—evidence of the federal effort to cope with the swelling relief rolls of this and other cities. These amounts, however, did not include the sizable sums for the poverty program, Model Cities, and aid to education.[35]

It was not until mid-1973 that city officials in San Francisco could assemble even a rough guess of the size of those funds, and when they did it was enormous. City Planning Department officials advised us that after some months of tracking they estimated the total to be about $600 million for fiscal 1972. The San Francisco budget was $800 million, some of which involved federal money but the amount was unknown; their best guess was somewhere between one-third and one-half. Indeed, one of the recent recommendations to the mayor and the board of supervisors by a municipal and federal research team was the creation of a method of regularly inventorying this inflow.*

In short, then, San Francisco reflects patterns noted elsewhere of

---

* These totals were so rough because the department had not finally tabulated federal sources. See San Francisco City Planning Department: "Recommendation for Program Development and Management in San Francisco: A Report to the Mayor," July 1973, and "The Flow of Federal Funds: An Assessment for San Francisco," June 1973. On this cataloging, as on some other urban management tasks, San Francisco was well behind other cities, such as San Jose and Oakland; the latter had assembled this total at least two years earlier.

a growing urban budget with a proportionate shift in welfare costs and growing state and federal assistance. Other governments provide San Francisco with at least one of every four dollars it spends for all functions, up from the one in six dollars of two decades ago. Most of San Francisco's expenditures—and GIAs—went to support the poor, both young and old. A population that is increasingly older, poorer, and more needy—and increasingly smaller—must be served and the demands for more assistance must be met, hence a cost spiral is created.[36] Despite the publicity, only small proportions of federal funds were funneled into the more controversial local functions. In San Francisco for fiscal 1970, the Model Cities program drew about $7.6 million, only 8.5 percent of all federal GIAs for that year.[37]

The picture of this external force of federal finance, then, is not clear, because the total amounts involved are unclear. Direct GIAs constitute less than 8 percent of the local budget, but "pass through" funds from the state inflate the total considerably. Even more significant is the fact that money can have a multiplier effect. It can lever recipient agencies into creating additional funds,[38] adopt new programs which local systems then expand, and provide a channel for new ideas about the redistribution of values and resources. This multiplier effect has been so little studied in intergovernmental relations that we can merely suspect some such effects in San Francisco.

Across the breadth of this federal input into the city, most interactions have been inducive and only a few coercive. The inducive set reflects all those qualities of what Michael Reagan has termed "permissive federalism." When national goals are sought through state and local agencies, the federal emphasis is on negotiation among professionals; in such intergovernmental contacts, sanctions are rarely applied, although implied. This is the dominant tone of the GIA programs for welfare—aid to the young, old, and blind—which constitute such a large part of federal funds. Where such federal permissiveness is successful, the administration of policy becomes highly routinized—the interactions of professionals within an agreed universe of values. In that context, notions of different sovereignties confronting one another are meaningless myths. Much more realistic is the conceptualization of factions cutting across levels of government, acting as transfederal mutual protective associations. Some illustrations of major transfederal factions will be helpful.

In the administration of school aid programs, one finds multilevel governmental factions in a vertical—but not hierarchical—structure, who focus on their own expertise, clients, and federal funds. Specialists on libraries, vocational education, reading, language training, paraprofessional teacher programs—each constellation mobilizes special cohorts of the San Francisco school district, the state school administration, regional offices of the U.S. Office of Education, and USOE divisions in Washington.[39] Penetrating any one of these professional-governmental vertical structures are factions that differ over questions of the effectiveness of policy, the distribution of resources, and the maintenance of status and power. The pattern of inducement that operates is not of one government versus another. Rather, it is of one transfederal faction across a multilevel governmental structure (including its private cohorts of parents, teachers, professors, and so forth) versus another faction, both competing over the redistribution of funds. For most of the 1960s this was often a politics of distribution, as new funds were added in quantum increases, almost enough to satisfy all claimants. But with the retrenchment of the Nixon administration, competition has assumed a different shape around a politics of redistribution. Thereupon the frozen and shrunken pool of resources has had to be reallocated, which upset all the established processes of negotiation that community groups had painfully devised over the last decade.

Among these intergovernmental cohorts, local elected officials came under increasing tension. They, and particularly mayors, faced a growing accountability for the delivery of services financed by "the feds." But they had to deal locally with functional agencies that had growing independence, both in their source of finances—Washington—and in their specialization of skills and expertise. As they found about them ever-hardening pillars of intergovernmental power, mayors sought some leverage for coordinating this policy game. We have noted Mayor Alioto's effort, albeit delayed, to assemble management control mechanisms, which was also stimulated by special federal programs.

Illustrative is the Chief Executive Review and Comment Procedure set up in twenty cities in 1971–72. This is an agreement between the cities and federal agencies on centralizing the processing of federal funds. All local agencies seeking such funds must first pass their application through a local agency for review and comment; Washington will not consider any applications until such clearance has been given. While San Francisco was not in this arrangement by mid-1973, the mayor's staff was urging its adoption, to give him more weapons for participation in this transfederal cohort politics.*

This transfederal factionalism was clearly visible in the poverty and Model Cities programs. These were actually a composite of many specialized programs, each with a bureaucracy reaching from poverty areas of the city through City Hall partisans to regional and Washington offices. Consequently, the local scene was often the battleground for two or more of these vertical structures in dispute in the same program over personnel, funds, and objectives. The previous chapter on the politics of these programs demonstrated the transfederal nature of much of that ethnic conflict. Disputes over representation of the poor, or over program emphasis on community organization versus job training, attracted factions of new versus old black, brown, and yellow San Franciscans. Each faction sought to mobilize allies from among the multiple points of access to the fragmented City Hall, regional, and national OEO offices, and congressmen and senators. Federal decisions in such disputes provided a climax to the dispute, as when OEO insisted that representatives of the poor must be on the city-wide board after Mayor Shelley had stacked it with the "traditional" city spokesmen. That decision affected—if it did not precipitate—another transfederal dispute over the program focus, with frequent appeals to municipal and federal officialdom. The disposition of each of these escalating conflicts not only affected "local" government but also benefited some private groups and disadvantaged others.

The struggle over new directions in welfare programs illustrates this transfederal factionalism equally well. One constellation consisted of a NWRO chapter stimulated by one facet of OEO; social workers, often trained by state colleges or universities and embittered by the arbitrary and frustrating system; congressmen willing to provide national hearings on the futility and waste of existing welfare programs; and public and private agencies (media, foundations, university scholars) publicizing alternatives of income maintenance. An opposing constellation consisted of a local welfare agency of distinctive conservatism,[40] led by officials who resisted confrontation

---

* City Planning Department, "Recommendations for Program Development in San Francisco," July 1973, pp. 30–33.

politics and its philosophy by appealing to orderly procedures and standards of performance (which they dominated); their cohorts in state welfare agencies, who, like their local surrogates, were sensitive to the taxpayers' growing discontent with welfare costs and purported "welfare fraud"; and officials in Congress and the national administration, also responsive to such discontent, insistent that decision making remain with the structure which had made the program what it had become.

Whatever the policy one examines, or the analytical framework, such a federally impacted urban politics is diverse. The resolution of conflict may be viewed as a debate, a game, or a fight, but the contestants are still transfederal.[41] One might further conceptualize such local politics within a systems analysis framework, but the federal government still operates as a major input source to the local system.[42] These interactions might also be conceived as a process of exchange whereby actors seek to satisfy interests by exchanging resources according to some calculus of cost and benefit, all within cultural parameters that regulate the exchange; but the local forum is not the only marketplace for such exchange.[43] In short, any effort to understand conflict and its resolution in urban politics must incorporate the factor of the federal government, which is not just an "alien intruder" joined in combat with other governments. Rather, it is an entity parceled out among other public and private contenders for the stakes of local politics, its chief interaction inducive, its characteristic mode negotiation, and its ultimate power diffused.

While there are occasions when inducement yields to coercion, any transfederal interaction actually mixes both these instruments of influence. Those interactions most obviously inducive still carry an implicit threat of some federal action, although the threat is rarely carried out. Those interactions most visibly coercive will still include efforts at negotiation by the national government so as to avert the clash of governments. Even when Washington is goaded to coercion by one of the transfederal factions, there still transpires a "politesse of federalism," by which the state or local unit is given adequate time for hearing the complaint, delaying its response, and finding some other avenue of conflict resolution.[44] The federal office knows that there are costs for engaging in coercion, and that, even when successful in moving the recalcitrant local system, Washington will pay in some fashion, such as protracted conflict over this issue, shift of dispute to other issues, congressional criticism and budget threats.[45]

PIPING, SCHOOLING, AND TRANSFEDERAL FACTIONALISM

The coercive aspect of transfederal politics in San Francisco in recent years can be illustrated by two disputes, one minor and the other major in the scope of their effects. In the early 1970s, there arose the explicit threat by HUD to enforce the requirement that, in federally financed housing, plastic pipes must be used because of their cheaper cost and easier installation than copper or zinc. This threat mobilized the opposition of the powerful construction unions of San Francisco, despite lengthy federal negotiations in an effort to change their minds. Obviously, the unions foresaw lost wages in such cheaper techniques, which were widely used in other American cities. Accordingly, rather blunt and visible union pressure was put on the board of supervisors, who delivered a resolution refusing to accept such federal funds with that requirement. However, calmer heads in City Hall and the business community regarded this as impractical; "the feds" were insistent that without the requirement all housing funds would stop, a loss the city could not afford. Within twenty-four hours the board reversed its stand.

Of far greater significance was the coercion finally brought to bear on the city's school system in 1971 by a federal court order to desegregate.[46] A decade of negotiation and threats had preceded the act, however, as the notoriously bureaucratized system, with immensely ingrown features and a record of poor schooling, ignored the claims of minority groups seeking desegregation. Litigation was begun, and wended its way through several delays and school promises to improve, which local officials thought would suffice to fend off the threat. This naïveté left them gasping when a federal district court compelled full desegregation of the elementary school system within a half-year.

There followed the familiar sequence of hurried planning, parental protests against busing, school boycotts (which the Chinese made effective for several years by creating private schools), return of the white children to schools, and a sharp diminution in public protest as the change failed to realize white fears. As is often the case, the superintendent responsible for administering the court mandate generated such opposition that the board of education sacrificed him at the end of the first year of desegregation, and his successor made little move to challenge the mandate. One consequence of this federal coercion was that the voters replaced the mayor-appointed board with an elective agency, the better to oppose desegregation. But as is regularly the case elsewhere with boards, whether elected or not, they were powerless to block the mandate. Mayor Alioto also expressed displeasure at the federal intervention, just as has almost every mayor in the nation, but this affected very little except possibly his forth-coming election. Moreover, his appointments to the board turned out to be more liberal than he, blunting the only formal influence he had in the issue. In the event, after the first year everyone could see that the coercion had been effective in drastically altering the delivery of school services, to accord with some of the demands of a new set of contenders for city resources. Surveys by the system's Office of Desegregation after the first year reported that parents' fears were greatly reduced and minority children's learning was improving slightly—all consistent with desegregation elsewhere.[47]

Note the disposition of "the" federal government in this conflict. One of its branches, the judiciary, worked far more energetically than another, the executive, to change discrimination; for over two decades the courts have been the most reliable agency reinforcing demands for a more equitable distribution of governmental re-sources.* In San Francisco, in the face of hesitant efforts by the Civil Rights Division of the Justice Department to correct this discrimina-tion (a hesitance reflecting White House signals), it was only the courts which made a difference. Then, with the mandate in hand, the school district applied for and received from HEW special funds —the Emergency School Assistance Program—set aside by Congress to assist mandated schools. On one side, over the years of this affair, was ranged the federal district court (through required reports on progress); the USOE regional office, which placed liaison officials in the district to oversee use of ESAP funds; the state education system's Bureau of Intergroup Relations, which provided advice after 1970 under a more sympathetic state superintendent; local civil rights groups with an obvious interest in successful desegregation; the 1970–71 school superintendent; and some minority and white staff. On the other side through the important years was one branch of the federal executive, the Justice Department, reluctant to press matters; a state superintendent during the 1960s who had muffled any state effort to encourage desegregation; a newly elected local school board in 1972

---

* In a similar vein, in late 1972 a graduate of the city's schools sued the school system for failure to provide him with the twelfth-grade reading ability which his diploma implied he had.

reflecting parental opposition to the change (including Chinese-Americans and some black separatists);* Mayor Alioto, who publicly spoke against desegregation; and large segments of the teachers and administrators, who faced a system change that challenged their definitions of the standards of school service.

There is little in this school controversy that can be perceived as simply one government versus another. Rather it shares the trans-federal quality permeating most of the external operations within the city. The policy process began with hesitant negotiations during the early 1960s, but moved to coercion in the form of litigation simply because defenders of the status quo—private and public, state, local, and national—who controlled the adjustment process, refused to make real concessions. Their refusal rested not in "establishment" malevolence or sin but in their awareness that what was sought was a complete rearrangement of the standards, processes, and resources of this urban service—a total challenge to the system's maintenance.

This was thus not a politics of distribution, where challengers could be satisfied with a portion of an expandable pie, such as the addition of "new math," which federal money made possible after 1958. Rather, this had become the politics of redistribution, where for some to win others must lose. For example, integrating the faculty and the administrative staff, as the superintendent sought, meant that some white professionals would have to be replaced. When politics involves doomsday stakes and a zero-sum game, the ground exists for only one kind of conflict resolution—a fight.[48] But the main point here is that, whether the politics is one of negotiation or of fight, the issue minor or major, the resources distributed or redistributed, the federal impact operates much less to pit one level of government against another than to fragment federal resources into coalitions that contend at every level.

A TRANSFEDERAL POLITICS CASE STUDY:
THE YERBA BUENA CENTER

Pipes and schools may seem to some not representative of federal roles in city government, because the first is trivial and the second is independent of local government. While we suggest rather that they demonstrate both the minutiae and the breadth of transfederal

---

* Efforts by one superintendent in the late 1960s to sell desegregation by frequent public meetings around the city were frustrated by a traveling band of opponents, including the Chinese Six Companies, Black Panthers, and the John Birch Society.

politics, it is also true that these are areas where the federal impact has been recent. Therefore, we turn to a highly publicized transfederal policy in San Francisco, which has been developing since about 1949, and which has involved $46 million in federal grants plus other subsidies.[49] This is the redevelopment of a downtown area into a complex of a convention exhibition hall, sports arena, hotel, office buildings, and parking for 2,450 cars. The project is called the Yerba Buena Center, an ironic name to contrast with the once scraggly hamlet. Backed by the city's businessmen, unions, public officials, newspapers, and a major federal agency, this looks like other "federal bulldozer" projects, which have for several decades renovated downtown America.[50] But the bulldozer hit a stump that would not be moved, and therein lies the following account of transfederal factionalism.

The Yerba Buena Center is located South of Market, as San Franciscans term the area. Its like is found in every city, a place of retired, mostly single, workingmen, transients and immigrants.[51] Their homes are in hotels or lodging houses; their social life centers around hotel lobbies, saloons, and the streets. Their business life is a patchwork of pawnshops and secondhand stores. A neighborhood of homeless men, they were pictured by center supporters as skid row bums, and by critics as decent, retired workingmen. But a group of them were to be crucial in the Yerba Buena controversy. These retired workers found the network of cheap hotels and restaurants their only way of living on limited pensions or welfare. The San Francisco Redevelopment Agency wanted them moved so that the area could enjoy an economic revival, first in construction jobs and later in tourist and convention business and office jobs. However, these retirees pressed for the federal urban renewal law requirement that those displaced should be relocated in decent housing at prices they can afford. But the problem of relocation was greatly magnified in a city with a housing vacancy rate of around zero. It was to be a classic case of the Big Rich versus the Little Poor, but there was to be a surprising denouement—both sides won. All this took an embroilment of city officials and economic powers with a major federal agency as one cohort, arrayed against the elderly, a new kind of lawyer, and the federal courts as another cohort.

The Development Cohort

Motivating the Yerba Buena project was that vision set forth earlier of the city as part of a larger economy in which both the Big

Rich and the Little Rich participated. Three major investors in the Pacific economy were also intimately involved in the planning of the project: Del Monte and Dillingham corporations and the Crocker-Citizens Bank (see figure 8). The local hoteliers and merchants involved in the Center wanted tourist accommodations. Both categories of wealth agreed that if the city were to be the envisioned pivot, it needed space for business headquarters, a convention center, and parking for commuters and tourists. But the commercial district lacked space for such a complex. Hence, with an economic desire becoming a physical need, planners turned their eyes to the nearest and cheapest land. That was across from the commercial district— South of Market.

Behind the city's redevelopment lay economic power focused in the Bay Area Council (BAC), seen earlier in chapter 7.[52] In particular, one of its committees, chaired by magnates from the electronics and pulp and paper industries, stimulated during the 1950s the thinking that led to completed projects in the 1960s; our interest is in but one of them, the biggest—Yerba Buena Center. The organizational tool for this effort was both the BAC and SPUR, the San Francisco Planning and Urban Renewal Association. The latter had been created in 1959 as a public, but not governmental, agency dominated by business realty interests. In late 1960 SPUR was designated by the then mayor, George Christopher, as the city's official citizen group for urban renewal, as required under federal law.

Before SPUR, there had been another redevelopment campaign. In the mid-1950s business support had not existed for such projects when sought by Benjamin Swig; the reason for the later change of mind by business is not yet clear. But Swig's efforts, like those following, advanced three ideas about South of Market redevelopment. This area was the one closest to the business district that could fit the "blight" conditions that would meet federal specifications for assistance (although critics strongly challenged the evidence of "blight"); not just sections but the whole area was to be cleared; and a huge complex would be constructed there on the razed blocks.

When Washington entered the scene, it was under the auspices of the San Francisco Redevelopment Agency. Like its counterparts in other cities, SFRA is a compound of private and public powers that provides a touch of the corporate state to local government in America.[53] It can make and implement its own plans, move people from one section of town to another, arrange massive sums for financing, condemn property, and promote all its wonders. Traditional controls of public power, so endemic in American government, run a little thin with these agencies. Thus, the federal agency responsible, most recently HUD, has developed a symbiotic relationship with its local counterparts, each leaning on the other for sustenance and protection. Until 1968 the courts had given no standing to sue to those forcibly removed by such agencies, in effect freeing the agencies from major requirements of the federal law. Of course, elections of these political authorities are no control, since there is no provision for them. The structure was designed to *avoid* popular control and so enhance rational-technical concepts and values of community change.

We need not detail the match of the SFRA and these characteristics—including the seemingly unchallengeable power of its executive director through most of this period, M. Justin Herman.[54] His uses of power were little different from those in other cities and need not detain us. Suffice it to say that Herman directed a public-private organization, which combined federal and local authority and resources in order to plan and carry out the details of an important segment of the economic vision of the city. Around these efforts swirled conflicts over philosophy, material interests, selective perceptions, and plain passion—as in about every city in the nation.

Some flavor of it can be seen in the accurate statement found in an unneutral account, referring to SFRA's Herman. "In the downtown highrise office buildings, banks, and City Hall he was Saint Justin, while in prison-like housing projects of Western Addition and the rat- and roach-infested homes of the Mission *barrio* he was the 'white devil.' " [55] To one side, redevelopment is "slum clearance" and "blight removal," which should be followed by modern highrises with business and tourist facilities. But to the other side, this is a device by the "power structure" to remove the poor—particularly blacks—for reasons of profit.

While we have questioned the degree of "structure" in the city's power operations, there is no doubt that the desire for profit attracts many groups here—and elsewhere—and that this includes far more than just the Big or the Little Rich. Notice other supporters in this issue. The city's Convention and Visitors Bureau represents both the private world of tourism (mainly hotels and restaurants) and the local government, which finances its efforts through a hotel tax. The tourist forces saw Yerba Buena Center as meeting a strong need for a large convention center. Even though hotel vacancy rates in the early 1970s were high, hoteliers accepted the Yerba Buena Center hotel as a trade-off for the convention hall. Organized labor was also a later supporter of SFRA, but for different reasons: to share in the expansionist vision which entailed more jobs; to continue the mutual accommodation pattern with business which developed after World War II; and to invest union funds—as with the ILWU—in realty projects. Union support did not fully come until 1970 when the San Francisco Central Labor Council endorsed the Yerba Buena Center and even filed a brief in litigation supporting the project.[56] Within the council, the Building and Construction Trades representatives had endorsed redevelopment for much longer and may have been instrumental in switching the council's views. The BCT agents' outlook was as simple as it was clear. Redevelopment meant construction, which meant more and longer jobs for its members; "We are in favor of building with no respect to where it is and how it is." [57]

Other city elements were in this development cohort. At every stage the city's daily newspapers strongly endorsed Yerba Buena Center and opposed its challengers. Both major newspapers have headquarters adjoining the project area; the *Examiner* owns two additional lots adjoining the area. Those future interests rarely were discouraged by anything in these newspapers. There were also some politicians—indeed most—who supported Yerba Buena. Some political clubs endorsed it; significantly, these included Spanish-speaking groups in the Mission District. But ultimately, the crystallizing agent was Joseph Alioto after his election as mayor in 1967. Within days of his inauguration, he ringingly endorsed the Yerba Buena Center and later sought Washington funds, heaped praise on SFRA's Herman, and courted trade union backing for the project.

These were the main elements of the local cohort behind the Yerba Buena project through the 1960s. They chose a site which shared little of the blight that the federal law was designed to correct. But possession of land either in or near the project promised to benefit directly the finances of newspapers, utilities, banks, retail firms, individuals, and trade unions. As the campaign developed, ordinary citizens were recruited. They were told that they, too, had an interest in the Center, for it would bring in business without requiring tax monies, and would create a bigger and better city—all at the expense of a few "winoes" and "bums" in a "blighted" area.

The official project began when the board of supervisors in 1962 requested a planning grant from the Housing and Home Finance

Agency (HHFA), later transformed into HUD. That planning took until 1965, when the HHFA approved the results and set aside $19.6 million in mid-1965 for the Center. In the spring of 1966, the board of supervisors also approved the project, 9 to 2. It could do little else, for while it was flooded with detailed planning it lacked the staff to evaluate it. Also it was impressed with the SFRA insistence that the Center would not cost the city anything, for all funds would come from "the feds" or from revenue that the project would generate. Three more years—until 1969—were required to negotiate a grant and loan from HUD, even more detailed planning, a search for developers, and so forth. Even the announcement of the project design in mid-1969 was not the end, for bids had to be let to private firms to carry out the land purchase and construction projects. Not until October 1970 was the developer chosen by SFRA, but even by mid-1973 most of the smaller projects around the central blocks of Yerba Buena Center had not yet been negotiated.

The Antidevelopment Cohort

The numbers and power in this transfederal cohort seemed overwhelming; clearly there was little opposition from the local government to this stimulus arising at the federal level. If these events had begun five years earlier, the Yerba Buena Center would have turned out much the same way as innumerable redevelopment cases in other American cities. But by the late 1960s a new kind of transfederal cohort had come on the scene from the antipoverty thrust from Washington noted in chapter 10. The organizational form of this thrust was the Office of Economic Opportunity's legal aid services, and the instrument was a new idea—federal law requirements concerning the right of those relocated by urban renewal should be enforced. Such a national counterforce had borne results in 1968 when a federal court provided a breakthrough in the law of the poor; that is, it declared that displaced persons have a legal standing to contest their relocation.[58]

What happened in San Francisco was another departure, when in 1972 a federal court decided that the four thousand displaced persons must be guaranteed new housing equivalent to what they had lost.[59] This was a clear reinforcement of what the law for so long had patently required, but which had been so ignored in the national rush to urban redevelopment. To enforce this requirement, SFRA was compelled to provide quarterly progress reports of its relocation of those displaced by the Yerba Buena Center. Further, in mid-1973 both sides entered into an agreement providing a detailed pace of relocation, guarantees of satisfaction with new housing by the displaced, and financial reimbursement of these people for economic losses.

The central event was a suit in late 1969 by a few men in the South of Market area, who organized as Tenants and Owners in Opposition to Redevelopment (TOOR). They charged HUD and SFRA with failing to locate them in housing that was decent, safe, and sanitary. Their co-counsels were from the San Francisco Neighborhood Legal Assistance Foundation and the Housing Law Center at the University of California, Berkeley—both OEO-funded groups. They provided the expertise to substantiate the charges of SFRA's failure to protect the rights of the relocated under federal law. This litigation had been preceded by the vain efforts of the displaced and counsel to force HUD to review SFRA's relocation plan. They were more successful against the harassment of their clients. In December 1969 a federal court issued the first of several restraining orders against alleged harassment by SFRA agents. In early 1972, one citizen obtained $1,200 in damages as a result of injuries caused by SFRA employees.

For supporters of Yerba Buena Center, these cases seemed only niggling efforts designed to subvert a project with wide community endorsement, and the main onus fell on TOOR's lawyers. But there were really two keys in this new cohort. One of these was the presence in the late 1960s of a group of elderly persons who had not been around or involved in the earlier planning of Yerba Buena, but who found the energy to mobilize against being moved out bodily. While federal statutes had called rather vaguely for citizen participation in urban renewal, that had been provided in the early 1960s by SPUR—hardly spokesmen for the old and poor in skid row. It was the latter's determination not to be overwhelmed that gave rise to TOOR, a positive action in contrast to futilely grumbling over their bean soup in cheap restaurants.

The second key in this new cohort was the introduction to the South of Market area of new resources and personnel. VISTA volunteers carried out community organization techniques,[60] and OEO-backed legal advice focused TOOR's sense of indignity on a forum where redress was possible. These lawyers pinned down specifics of what the law required, what SFRA was doing, and the gap between the two. During the long litigation, they detailed SFRA actions that seemed to evade TOOR members' rights, and pressed the court for various relief measures. TOOR was not the tail of the OEO lawyers' kite, however. At one stage when their lawyers had worked out a compromise with SFRA, TOOR refused it, claiming that it gave away their rights. In the course of events, by holding out they achieved even more from subsequent court orders and SFRA action. These attorneys, despite their obvious professional and social commitments in the case, failed to fully reflect their clients' interests. Given the difference of status and its accompanying values, this is neither surprising nor rare, according to observers of similar cases.[61]

TOOR employed instruments other than litigation, mostly community organization and protest activities, although it was never a mass movement or given to massive disruptions of meetings. Petitions, neighborhood mobilization, media-staged events, alliances with other groups—these were much more its style. This was sensible strategy, because TOOR lacked the numbers to mount mass protests. The best strategy lay in molding its few members into a firm stance. The motto was "We won't move," even though members knew they had to move and only wanted equivalent housing. Too, their members could best use the courts to demonstrate from their collective, personal experience the degree to which federal rights had been ignored.

Federal Roles in the Yerba Buena Center

As the litigation proceeded, the federal partner in the development cohort weakened. In the fall of 1971, HUD reported to the federal court a criticism of SFRA's relocation plans. TOOR sought to use this to pressure City Hall to retain and rehabilitate several hotels in the project area for members' relocation, with some of the city's hotel tax financing this compromise. They thought the board of supervisors and the mayor had agreed upon this before the 1971 municipal elections, but amid bitter and personal recriminations, the board in early 1972 backed away from the concept. Yet a year later, this was to be the core of the settlement which the city was to accept—provide the several hundred residents desiring it with permanent low-rent housing within the project area, subsidize this relocation through the hotel tax, and give TOOR responsibility for the process.

So in parallel pressures on City Hall and the federal courts, this tiny cohort played a new game in the politics of development in San

Francisco, one which begun to appear elsewhere. The once "disadvantaged" members of TOOR contributed their determination and personal experiences. But of crucial significance in the outcome was the fact that TOOR had available federal support—from the OEO-backed lawyers, from HUD when it backed down from endorsing SFRA relocation, and from a federal court. There were others on this side. Private organizations joined TOOR, sharing a common concern for problems of the poor. Intellectual resources other than the legal were also utilized, for example, a survey sponsored by a social science research agency to challenge SFRA figures on vacancy rates and to show that the site which SFRA desired for relocation had high crime rates.

But the court action was the definitive use of power in this case. For six months after accepting the case, Judge Stanley A. Weigel sought to convince SFRA to settle the matter privately by stopping harassment and providing equivalent relocation sites. When that failed, however, in late April 1970 he issued the most sweeping injunction against an urban renewal project ever seen. It halted all demolition and relocation, and gave SFRA sixty days to provide a satisfactory relocation plan before federal funds were cut off. That crucial threat was not carried out, for other maneuvers intervened, including actions in and out of court. The court's role was not merely that of an arbitrator. Going farther than any judge had gone to date, Judge Weigel also took on planning functions by requiring that certain types of housing be built. There were numerous court skirmishes before an agreement was accepted in mid-1973. But it is clear that without the central role of the federal court in this transfederal politics, TOOR would have received little, probably none, of their rights under national law.

There was another federal contingent, HUD, whose vacillation was unusual. In San Francisco as elsewhere, it had been among the pro-development cohort. Faced with a law that sought to promote the interests of development and to protect those against whom development moved, HUD had regularly chosen the former interest as its sole clientele. Of course, implementation of law would be simple if it always contained but a single objective and clientele. Administrators have a battery of devices with which to wend their ways through such traditional conflicts.[62] Urban renewal was not a program with a single value or clientele. So its administrators have traditionally implemented objectives associated with the largest amount of power that could cause them political trouble. Their internal management problems are sufficient to hinder their effectiveness anyway, even if they were not already under a conflict of clientele.[63]

In San Francisco HUD kept to its traditional course until the court's view was clearly expressed in opposition. This administrative agency's role was extraordinarily complicated at this point by Nixon administration policy. Delays in providing funds for Yerba Buena Center would help its "hold the budget down" program. Republicans in that administration did not mind too much if court action made Democrat Joseph Alioto look bad. Too, the mayor and city agencies had just sued the president and HUD to release funds already authorized for other HUD programs. All of these acted to pull HUD from this prodevelopment cohort and onto neutral grounds; at least it did not go so far as to withdraw certification of the Yerba Buena relocation plan. But HUD did later file with the court a detailed criticism of SFRA's relocation, did demand tighter requirements in those plans, and did revise SFRA's relocation plan several times.

Federal involvement in Yerba Buena Center did not end with this litigation, however. For there was another federal court challenge when it was charged that the project had violated the National Environmental Policy Act of 1969 for its failure to file with HUD a detailed environmental impact statement. But this action was defeated in early 1973 when a federal circuit court found that the NEPA did not apply because of the date of contracting for federal funds. A second case was still before the state courts in mid-1974; citizens charged that certain financing aspects of Yerba Buena Center were devised to circumvent referendum approval of bond issues. Until settlement could be achieved, the project was halted, because bonds cannot be sold during litigation.

In the cases described in this section there are important implications about transfederal factionalism for community decision making. Given the expansion of federal activity I have sketched, local politics now involves "the feds" across a much wider scope of issues. The use of federal resources to pursue national goals at the local level has introduced new interests and new actors into local politics. These will be summarized in the concluding chapter. But I note here that the growth in breadth and intensity of the federal role means that the San Francisco story is being told in every large American city. The cases, personalities, and combination of cohort will vary, as will the frequency or influence of federal action. In that event, this transfederal process has altered the nature of community decision making across the United States. But "the feds" are not the only external elements in this alteration, so we must see the extramural influences of other governments and of private forces.

CHAPTER 12

External Influences (II):
Middle Governments and Private Power

Washington is not the only level of government that has recently altered its power relationship with San Francisco. This change is also visible in city ties to public agencies between the local and national levels, "middle governments." A nationalizing effect has also taken place in private centers of power that impinge on San Francisco. In this chapter, then, I examine the nature of the influence of the state government in San Francisco, a necessarily brief review because the extent of that influence requires a separate volume. But I do give extended attention to another middle government that is little noted in its recent emergence. This is the special-purpose, regional organization, which can impinge on urban decisions and which may well be a major metropolitan force in the next few decades.

Finally, an analysis will be made of the role of private power outside the urban scene in its effect on what transpires inside it. Of course private and public are not always neatly separable in reality. Private power can take public channels to secure its ends, while public constraints can limit private institutions in the pursuit of their goals. Because that private influence does permeate all levels of government, it will be treated separately after a review of the growth of the power of governments outside the city's walls.

THE VIEW FROM SACRAMENTO

Earlier, we saw figures on the growth of the state's financial contribution to local programs which accompanied the movement of authority from local up to state levels in many areas of policy. Of course, in constitutional theory the local has always been a creature of the state government. Yet it is still striking to note the sharply circumscribed role given the states in early days.[1] Governors were agents of the legislatures and possessed few and weak powers; legislatures met only once in two years and then but for a few months; and court sessions were brief and limited in scope. Town and city governments were also meager agencies in the early Republic, when functions of schooling, welfare, and roads had not yet been adopted; the keeping of the peace and of records and limited licensing constituted their authority.[2] The truth is that during almost two centuries all levels of government have increased the run of their writs in American lives. Probably the smallest village and state today have governments that do more than the largest equivalent during Washington's administration.

That increased scope of governmental functions also demonstrates larger state contributions to local functions. For example, the financing of roads has moved from town to county to state—and heavily to Washington after World War II. During the 1920s, a movement sprang up in every state to "get the farmers out of the mud" by constructing all-weather roads linking rural to urban places. The cost was well beyond local resources, of course; therefore, state contributions were built in from the beginning, which is not surprising, given the predominance of rural power in state legislatures. A similar process lies behind the earlier data on the state's financial share in local functions; whereas the state in 1902 had given local government one of its sixteen dollars of revenue, by 1967 it gave one in three dollars—and for roads one in two.[3] A large increase appeared after World War II, with a resulting jump in state debt; from 1950 to 1969, it rose to almost $40 billion, an eightfold increase compared with localities' fivefold increase.[4]

Behind this state-local alteration were new mixtures of inducements and sanctions designed to enforce statewide norms of service. The quality of schooling, roads, and welfare—to take the three largest cost items in all state budgets—has narrowed in its variation across the nation as a result of this state imperative. The variation among states is still considerable, of course, as a result of different mixes of resources and political culture.[5] Nevertheless, centralization has meant that state standards of service now substitute for the once proliferating local standards. The main device for this change has been the reduction within a state of multiple systems for the delivery of services into a single system, albeit often with exemptions befitting the varied character of local systems.

This can be illustrated by what happened in education.[6] A major event over this century has been the reduction of the number of school districts, even though population has increased. For every 14 school districts in the United States in 1932 there is today but 1— down from 126,000 to about 17,000. Whatever "local control" once meant in education, it must have been diluted by the mere fact of the increase in the size of the districts and the reduction of their number. There has also been an accompanying state specification affecting many aspects of local control. For example, the sources of revenue are everywhere limited to the property tax; expenditures are hedged about with mandated services and minimum spending levels; the minimum qualifications of administrators and teachers are now set by the state, with certification shifting to schools of education and away from the district; and the content of the curriculum is often also mandated by definition of "tracks," minimum course requirements, requirements of teaching materials—and in some states even the textbooks one may choose.[7] It is a curious kind of "local control" in which personnel are certificated elsewhere, curriculum purposes are set outside the district, and even local funds are constrained by the fact that at least 80 percent of most school budgets are frozen by personnel costs and even more are directed by state mandates.

What we witness here is a political victory of an earlier Progressivism, when new ideas from the university about school administration united professors, businessmen, and middle-class professionals. This cohort succeeded in incorporating their concept of school content and administration into state constitutions and statutes everywhere. Such a combination of private professional and business values, plus public authority, caused in America a "transformation of the school," as Lawrence Cremin has described the process.[8] By mid-twentieth century, the magnitude of this movement of school authority to the state has converted "local control" into a new reality.[9] The rate of centralization varies with state culture, however, for in some places as seemingly disparate as Massachusetts and Texas the ethos of decentralization still dominates school politics, while in California and New York there is much more centralization.[10] But in even the most decentralized state, the professional imprint transmitted through state law has shaped local education into vastly different forms than those the community knew decades ago. In many respects, the threat to local control has been not so much an agent of state government as the local school professional who injected more universal norms into the local value system by way of the state—and prevailed.

San Francisco in the State's Educational Culture

California and San Francisco paralleled most of these developments, although some were skipped because of later entry into the Union.[11] State supervision of schools appeared in California's first constitution in 1849, with supporting legislation thereafter which emphasized centralized responsibility for education. Although the first legislature did refuse to create free public schools, subsequent legislatures expanded state authority over local schools. In the first half-century, there came state authorization to provide financial support, examine and certificate teachers, adopt textbooks and compel their local adoptions, make all schools free, staff the teacher examining boards with professionals, investigate teacher-training schools, and require uniform courses of study. For the first half century these functions were diffusely organized, but after 1913, they were coordinated into major state structures which permitted supervision of local elementary, secondary, and vocational education. But the state's financial support decreased sharply, until the Depression compelled Sacramento to undergird collapsing local economies; after World War II, however, the state's share dropped gradually, but nowhere near to that known earlier in the century.[12]

Over this century, though, strong state pressures continued to centralize California education. Districts shrank from the many and small to the few and large; the almost 3,600 districts in California in 1932 were consolidated into about 1,200 in 1966.[13] There were state curriculum requirements of physical education and "Americanization" during the second decade of this century; in later years they would include vocational skills, driver training, drugs and alcohol, and so forth. State control over courses, textbooks, and teacher training were tightened through the instruments of minimum quality standards and mandated service.

There were other areas of new state control. School construction came to be state supervised after the Long Beach earthquake of 1933. The delegation of teacher certification to county boards was discontinued after 1945, as was issuance of emergency credentials in 1954; in 1961, the state mandated a change in teachers' undergraduate major from Education to an academic subject. By that date, too, studies "found that, even in the smallest and most remote districts, progress was being made in the use of radically new programs, but the most significant changes were being developed *for* the schools, rather than *by* them." [14] Not even a controversial state superintendent during this decade, noted for his belief in local autonomy, was immune from prescribing state-wide curricula and teaching methods consonant with his philosophy. Attending the developments briefly sketched here has been a simple indicator—state regulations of education now total about 2,300 pages.

For schools in San Francisco, then, these developments over a century have diminished local control in practice despite its symbolic maintenance. Reviewing a decade of this school system's efforts to adjust to external and internal demands on the curriculum—first to stress the three Rs after the Sputnik crisis and then to provide compensatory education—one educational scholar concluded:

> State and Federal agencies bear on local education at many points. While these governmental divisions are cautious not to impose direct restrictions on the sovereignty of the local organization, they indirectly strain already stressed organizational processes. The implicit mandate to comply with priorities set and supported at these levels often precludes in the same implication the appropriate restructuring of local processes. It must not look like higher government is forcing change. The local bureaucracy does not wish to feel that it is bending to what are really irresistible grant conditions.[15]

A more specific measure of the external influence from Sacramento which has nullified local control is seen in a simple listing of functions largely controlled through the state's educational code.[16] These include the following: teacher and administrator certification, appointment and contracts of employment, salaries, tenure, resignation or abandonment of contract and leaves of absence, liability for pupil injury, defamation of character, workmen's compensation, retirement, attendance, control of teachers' conduct, transportation, courses of study and curriculum, textbooks, superintendent activities, budget and financing, building construction and maintenance, site selection and purchase, and bidding processes for letting contracts.

Some sense of this centralization was caught when twenty-five central school administrators in San Francisco estimated the proportion of their working time allocated to meeting demands of state and federal governments.[17] The range was wide; three spent as little as 10 percent and three as much as 100 percent of their time in this fashion. While the median was about 35 percent, nine officials spent half or more of their time in the throes of federalism. But these professionals were not repelled by that involvement; rather they heavily supported this higher government role in their local schools.[18]

What is sketched for the school system of San Francisco exists to a degree hardly noticed, much less explored, for other urban policies. Some of this centralization is a natural attribute of a unitary system, inherent in the state-local constitutional relationship between state and local governments. Some of it stems from group pressure to remove policy conflict to the state forum when local resistance is obdurate. In the history of school policy, this has been the strategy of school reformers seeking changes ranging from consolidation to curriculum innovations[19] to the current drive for easing the local property tax. We have also seen this bypassing effect in the Progressive political reforms in this and other states.

There exists yet another reason for this state centralization—the rise of *political professionalism*. In the private domain, for over a century, numerous occupations have developed their own standards of training, service, and rewards. These occupations have increasingly turned to state law and constitution to protect these standards, thereafter dominating their shaping, staffing, and administration. Much of this lies behind the school developments noted above, but the process applies equally well to occupations as diverse as law and cosmetology.

The significance for this analysis is that professional norms are universalistic not particularistic, cosmopolitan not local, and hence professionals work against the localistic pressures when they occupy positions of public authority. Lawyers appointed or elected to local positions feel responsibility to those who put them in office; but the desires of the mayor or the voters are not absolute if they run against professional norms of behavior. As we have seen, engineers, architects, and firefighters have standards around which to rally against highrises in San Francisco when they deem them dangerous or ugly. Social workers can complain, even strike, against heavy case loads—as their profession defines such things. Physicians can publicly point out the efficient quality of hospitals in the city in order to resist local pressures to keep expenditures down. Accountants are responsive to professional currents about methods and ethics.

All this suggests the reverse of Philip Selznick's observations on the penetration of public standards into private organizations. It is true that we have witnessed the latter become sensitive to such governmental concerns as due process of law.[20] What is here offered, however, is that privately determined standards of ethics act to constrain, if not focus, the actions of public authorities. The interaction of private and public values requires far more exploration than can be offered here, but there is an undoubted consolidation of professional values in this process when they have the sanction of state law. State certification that one is a teacher, an accountant, a lawyer, a gynecologist, a psychiatrist, an engineer, or an architect means that his primary appeal—to expertise—is enhanced by state sanction. This combination provides yet another dimension where state action can limit local autonomy.

THE REGIONAL CHALLENGE TO LOCAL AUTONOMY

In the Bay Area, and indeed elsewhere in this and other nations, there is emerging another level intermediate between the local and higher levels. This is the regional or metropolitan government, examples of which are blooming in the Bay Area. Stanley Scott and Ora Huth have recently observed:

Nearly everybody seems to be rediscovering the metropolis simultaneously. Governmental studies in regions as diverse as San Francisco and Stockholm, Paris and London, Toronto and Tokyo, Miami and the Twin Cities agree on one thing—*The Metropolis,* that vague but familiar term, has a reality and significance that is increasingly recognized almost everywhere. . . .

In fact, many of the world's major metropolitan areas appear either to have created some form of regional government, or to be attempting to establish one.[21]

In the United States, an immense stimulus to regionalism was provided by federal laws in the 1960s. These called for regional planning bodies through which local governments had to pass federal fund proposals for review and comment before submission to Washington. A key federal requirement was that a *regional plan* must be created by a *regional organization,* a plan that could thereafter be the basis on which to judge local projects. About three hundred of these new organs, called Councils of Governments, had emerged on the regional scene by the opening of the 1970s. In addition, single-purpose regional groups appeared for special service. These large numbers and diverse activities have been phenomenal, in light of the vacuum that existed at this level a decade ago. There is still a long way to go before regional governments become a reality, but on all sides the promise is clearly expressed.

Much of this growth has been federal responsibility. Victor Jones, a close scholar of regionalism has concluded: "The most startling and far-reaching change in American federalism is the emergence of the national government as the focus for discussion of urban and metropolitan affairs. It is now the leader in formulating urban programs and in using the grant-in-aid to elicit intergovernmental cooperation among local governments in the San Francisco Bay Area." [22]

For, within ten years the regional organization has become a familiar actor in local politics. As a result, Jones succinctly notes that "the Bay Area is not faced with the question of whether it should have regional government—it already has it in the form of large and powerful single-purpose agencies. . . ." [23] One indicator of this change is found in the attitudes of local officials, who in 1960 were averse to any regional organization, even one in which they were fully represented. However, the evidence of official attitudes and of the legislative proposals for broader regional governance show that local officials have clearly lost much of their old parochialism. Again, Jones's review of this evidence is to the point:

Home rule, as an article of faith and practice, is not held as tightly now by city and county officials as it was a decade ago. This is partly due to learning from experience that many problems they deal with and that concern their constituents cannot be adequately managed by cities acting alone. It is also a pragmatic adjustment to the involvement of national and state governments in metropolitan affairs.[24]

Thus, while the closed system of decision making in San Francisco was being eroded during the 1960s by the decentralizing force of neighborhood and ethnic groups, could a similar deterioration have been at work in the centralizing influence of a new regionalism? In short, while the well of power was draining away through the bottom, was someone else taking it away overhead in buckets? The details of his politics of regionalism is already complex enough for separate analysis,[25] but some of its highlights should be sketched here to fill in the picture of the flow of external influences on San Francisco.

THE NEW REGIONALISM IN THE BAY AREA

In the Bay Area, and likely elsewhere, the starting point of this development has been the belief that some ostensibly local problems actually are regional problems.[26] In this region, such a belief was strongly pressed by early supporters of a regional transit system, who claimed that existing multiple and segmented transportation systems were insufficient to meet the needs then or later. This movement was joined in the 1960s by another, initiated by conservation groups, to "save the bay." They saw the bay in danger of being destroyed by land filling for housing and other developments.

Through the decade, recognition grew that other problems were regional in origin and that a regional mechanism was needed to handle them. The response to this recognition took the form of special-purpose regional organizations, which suddenly appeared from a state legislature under pressure from this and other California areas. By the early 1970s, when regional organizations appeared at the rate of one a year, their purposes included conservation and development planning and regulation around the bay's edge (made permanent in 1969); regional transportation planning and special transportation programs for the Golden Gate Bridge (1970); liquid waste disposal (1971); and control of air pollution (expanded in 1972). Indeed, as the number of regional organizations grew, the problem became less their creation than their coordination, and that gave rise to discussion of a further stage of metropolitan government, a multipurpose—or "umbrella"—organization. However, as Eugene Lee has observed, "In 1971 the central political issue is not the necessity for some form of multipurpose regional organization, but the question of who will control it." [27]

Thus, within about one decade, local officials moved from firm opposition to even one special-purpose regional organization to the support of a multipurpose—though still limited—regional body. One study in 1970 found that mayors in the Bay Area and in southern California endorsed an umbrella organization by 85 and 64 percent respectively; better than four in five of the northern mayors would have made membership mandatory, but only half as many agreed in the south. Bay Area officials strongly endorsed the belief that such a regional organization should have responsibility for area planning, transportation, air pollution control, and the health of the environment; but the majority of southern officials would not accept any of these.[28] The key inference here, though, is that Bay Area officials have had more experience (and started earlier) with a regional approach to most of these programs, and have found that experience not unbearable.

Illustrative of the learning possibilities of such experience is found in the Association of Bay Area Governments, or ABAG. When it began in 1961, ABAG was essentially a forum for discussion of the desirability and possibility of effective regional planning; it was later designated the area's official Council of Governments by federal action. While remaining a voluntary grouping of local officials, it nevertheless moved from skepticism about regional governance to a desire for a broader regional government. While that objective had not been achieved by 1974, experience had shaped ABAG members' views of regionalism. Thomas Cronin found that its executive committee had more regional experience, held more regional perspectives, and had a stronger preference for converting ABAG into a multipurpose organ than the rest of the delegates. All of this suggests that the characteristically pragmatic American approach to governmental forms, which has made us in certain eras adopt local reforms with surprising speed, may be at work now in the new environment of regional governance.[29]

The elaboration of the duties, organization, and operations of regional organizations in the Bay Area is not our purpose here, although a brief sketch is provided in Appendix II.[30] Note, however, that they are not all of a kind. Some reach for hundreds of miles around the bay and others can be crossed easily by a twenty-five cent bus ride. They display a variety of organizational formats, from state agencies with the mandate of regional responsibilities to a few counties or cities voluntarily cooperating. They may use only inducement or may exercise considerable coercive power by refusing permits. Their funding may involve almost literally passing the hat, or, like BART, they may administer over $1 billion and employ over 1,500 people when fully operative. They may only devise plans, which members can ignore, or enjoy much wider powers, such as reviewing a local government's plans in light of regional plans, refusing permits, or disapproving local applications for federal grants.

In all of this there is evident not only the familiar mark of American experimentation with government, but more important, a clear fragmentation of function and operation. As a consequence, no regional overview exists for a set of related problems;[31] for these regional organizations, despite the sweep of territory in which they may operate, are still single-purpose agencies. Although major efforts began in the late 1960s, large-scale work still remains to be done in such areas as transportation, solid waste disposal, water pollution, and preservation of open space. Further, the regional organizations are increasingly faced with providing a representation that is more sensitive and responsive, even though the unit may cover an enormous diversity of people spread over thousands of square miles. If even the single-purpose regional organization provides such tough problems, the coming of a multipurpose umbrella government will bring even more—particularly that of representation.[32]

REGIONALISM AND THE CITY

The spurt of regionalism occurred almost simultaneously with the emergence in San Francisco of a new politics and the new political figures analyzed in earlier chapters. We have seen how one unifying theme in San Francisco's new agenda has been the problems associated with creating the center of a regional web of commerce and commuting, of which the highrises are the most visible symbol. In that local politics, growth of population and the economy in the Bay Area was the cardinal virtue. Yet many of these new regional organizations were seeking in one way or another to *control* growth in the sprawling suburbs and central cities. That is what policies for transportation, water quality, and waste disposal are all about in social terms. But when such constraints could mean blocked land development or strangled access to the city, its officials could not ignore this new regionalism.

Regional Power and Business

One way to understand this emerging politics of region and city is to realize that two kinds of politics were actually at work, depending on whether the regional organization had only the power of inducement or that of coercion. Other analytical perspectives may be valid, but because this book is concerned with what difference the several kinds of power make in the city or between governments, it is well to focus on powers of inducement versus coercion. Of course, no regional organization uses only coercion, for there is a complex, sensitive politesse in federal relationships, where those who legally *may* compel behavior go to great pains *not* to do so. But if government at any level can only advise or recommend, if its bonds are based exclusively on cooperation, and particularly if members are of unequal size, its characteristic behaviors are negotiation, delay, persuasion, and compromise. In this case, results are possible only when all parties see a mutual gain in their obedience to the group will.

In such interactions, there is much of the coalitional impulse seen throughout this book to be at work in the city.[33] If, however, an agency possesses some legitimate power of coercion, behavior must take other patterns. The group may still take on many of the qualities of inducement agencies, but now there is always possible the use of that mandated coercion.

An understanding of San Francisco's role in regionalism must begin with the realization that in one sense it has contributed immensely to the emergence of regional governance because so many San Franciscans were active on the Bay Area Council. The council, drawing heavily from big business enterprise in the Bay Area, originated after World War II for the major purpose of developing the Bay Area's economy. Its was the vision of an integrated political economy, laid out in chapter 7, and its was the strength contributing to the politics of highrise seen in chapter 8. In this regional thrust, the council early trumpeted a theme urged by businessmen elsewhere between World War II and the 1960s. With encouragement from the Committee for Economic Development, leading national spokesman for the advantage of regionalism in overcoming the fragmentation of localism, lobbies emerged in American regions to urge new structures of metropolitan government. But these were rarely achieved, because a growing suburban population feared dominance by big city interests.* In the cities, ironically, black leadership also opposed these reforms for fear of having their emerging power diluted in a larger scheme of governance.[34]

In the Bay Area, at any rate, the Bay Area Council did little to support schemes for metropolitan federation, for it gave more effort to pressing the concept of a unified economy supported by local public policies. While the council's role has never been fully studied, there is a general belief that, despite occasional internal divisions, it has been a powerful force for regionalism. This was because it stimulated discussion of the need for regional planning and generated support for concrete efforts at devising regional structures and policies.[35]

These efforts have direct relevance for the city. I intend to provide no history of the area's regional organizations but rather to promote

* Even if representation in regional organizations were proportional to population, as with other central cities, San Francisco's weight would be relatively small and declining —down from 1950 to 1970, from 29 to 16 percent in the Bay Area's population. This has paralleled a decline in the city's representation in the state legislature.

an understanding of their potential both for benefiting a city and for restricting its autonomy, particularly in growth policy. For one thing, these organizations tend to grow in influence. There is a pattern in which these agencies begin as voluntary and cooperative units and then later find greater strength. This was ABAG's pattern, as we noted; it developed stronger powers as a result of members' decisions on difficult problems and of its designation by Washington as the area's Council of Governments.[36] Yet its early inadequacies as an instrument to "save the bay" (conservationists found ABAG's membership of local officials too sensitive to local developers' views) contributed in 1965 to the creation by the state of the Bay Conservation and Development Commission (BCDC). As a reflection of the conservationist outlook, it emerged with authority to control bay filling and shoreline development.

A similar pattern of a recent toughening up of once moribund regional organizations is seen as a result of the "environmental crisis" movement of the 1960s. The Air Pollution Control District was born in 1955 but did little until it was energized by the federal Environmental Protection Agency—and a supportive opinion by the state attorney general—to toughen its controls. Also, the state's regional Water Quality Control Board had been around since 1950 (indeed, some state controls have existed since the last century); but the board did not become effective for some years, until it obtained "cease and desist" authority. Even then it lacked power to compel local authorities to build effective liquid-waste disposal facilities, until an operating arm of the board appeared in 1971 with the Bay Area Sewage Services Agency. The purpose of this agency is to develop plans for disposal locations in the nine-county region (to be ready in 1974) and, if necessary, to construct them and charge the costs to balky municipalities.

The City Loses Some, Wins Some

So, whether it was an old agency that took on new teeth, or a new agency born with them, these regional organizations presented a new power potential in the intergovernmental relationships of the Bay Area after the early 1960s. Their impact on San Francisco cannot be fully detailed, because so many of them are new. But we have earlier seen in the United States Steel case study in chapter 8 the dramatic effect of BCDC's refusal to permit certain construction incompatible with existing law; despite the outrage of capital, labor, and officials, the building plan was blocked.

In a similar case, an order issued by the Regional Water Quality Control Board also blocked the city, whose officials had been given time to provide a plan for future control of effluents—raw sewage had regularly and casually been pumped out into surrounding waters. Under pressure from the regional board, a plan was devised for the construction of treatment facilities that would separate the presently combined sewage and storm drains. But the San Francisco voters simply refused to pass the necessary bond issues, and so the board issued a cease-and-desist order against its polluting practices and in 1970 banned future hookups to city sewer pipes. If continued, the ban would have effectively stopped future building.

The city promptly devised interim improvements in its plant structures and began to dilute insoluble wastes, so that the board believed there was enough improvement to lift the hookup ban after about six months. But the cease-and-desist order continued, requiring compliance with a detailed plan for adequate control of effluence by mid-1977; any failure to meet a scheduled improvement, however, could bring back the ban. Such cases demonstrate one of the external constraints that impinge on San Francisco, but this is not the only way in which the city reacts to regional organizations. The stance of its officials toward these agencies is ambivalent, and in most cases they have developed no clear strategy.

Part of this reflects the diversity of interests in the city, which, as we have noted, makes difficult any local coordination. Concern for regionalism is not lodged merely with businessmen. Labor, clearly threatened by some actions of regional organizations, vociferously protested the veto of United States Steel and the ban of sewage hookups; to them the issue is a simple one of more jobs. Consequently, labor spokesmen want representation on regional councils and direct election methods, whereby their numbers would ensure more delegates. There are others who are involved, however. One summary of private groups with an interest in regional organizations included city planners, engineers, home builders, the League of Women Voters, Native Americans, blacks, Asians, the Spanish-speaking, the elderly, civil rights protectors, and conservationists.[37] All of these interests at the municipal level must be focused and articulated into the few representatives which San Francisco is allotted on each regional council.

There is not yet available any analysis of what issues constitute a "San Francisco interest" before regional councils. But, observers of Bay Area regionalism summarize that interest as opposition to policies that would control growth. We noted that interest in the city's outcry against BCDC and Regional Water Quality Control Board actions. Further, when the Air Pollution Control District, long quiescent, was stimulated by the Federal Clean Air Act of 1970 to take on the power of refusing permits for construction that caused "emission of air contaminants," the reaction of municipalities was not a uniform objection. But those cities and private agencies most oriented to growth policies did react strongly. Prominent among these was the Bay Area Council, while Mayor Alioto appointed himself to the board of that council to provide a stronger outlet for the city's objection. This San Francisco perspective runs counter to the interests of many suburbs, which have become increasingly worried about the economic and population growth surrounding them.*

But San Francisco's objection to regional organizations is not to the principle but to any practice that constricts its own vision of itself; if an organization contributes to that vision, it is supported. Thus, as we have seen, the city was the most active promoter of BART. Of the three counties in a special referendum, San Franciscans voted most strongly for it. Regional transit was regarded as vital to San Francisco's continuing growth as an economic center. Even then, however, the city struck a tough bargain with BART before the referendum; BART financed the relocation, rebuilding, and redevelopment of San Francisco's municipal transit while BART subways were under construction. This move, in effect paid for by taxpayers of the other two counties, was judged by BART employees as its trade-off to get the city's official support for the bond measure.[38]

But this winning trade-off does not exhaust the kinds of city relationships with other governments. In some cases the city loses because of the new external force of regionalism, as can be seen in recent transportation politics. For example, San Francisco wanted to extend its airport out into the bay as part of its commercial growth, and also to run a BART spur line to it.† But it lost on both efforts. San Mateo County objected to participating in BART, and other counties in BART wanted extensions to come first in their territory.

---

* In one ironic respect, San Francisco itself acts as a regional organization by providing water to parts of surrounding counties; as many as 600,000 citizens depend on that water.

† The San Francisco International Airport lies in adjoining San Mateo County. San Francisco's county jail is also outside its borders, and its dead are usually buried outside the city limits, too.

Also, the airport expansion was thwarted by federal and regional planning. This had begun with the insistence of the Federal Aviation Authority that it would approve no funds for airport construction unless it fit into a regional airport plan. That plan was devised by ABAG, which recommended that, of the three regional airports, San Francisco's should grow hardly at all, San Jose's somewhat more, and the big growth should come with Oakland's, across the bay. That is, federal leverage in use of the planning function ended up with a veto of San Francisco's decision making.

Again, an even more complex illustration of this external constraint is seen in the federal preference for building up the seaport of Oakland to San Francisco's disadvantage. The federal role in the Bay Area's water transportation, stemming from its constitutional authority over navigable waters, has traditionally involved the Army Corps of Engineers in local water-traffic planning. Presently the corps has under way a $6 million study of these waters up to Sacramento and Stockton, spending more on regional planning than any Bay Area regional organization.

INTRASTATE FEDERALISM

Yet such evidence of the external influence of regional governance on San Francisco is but one side of the pattern. For that influence has been filtered or resisted according to a major theme of city policy. This has been the encouragement of the area's economic growth to which public and private leaders in San Francisco have committed their city. Pursuit of that vision is not always blocked by outside forces: those forces are not always exercised vigorously or effectively, as in the limited attention city officials have paid to ABAG, which they joined only after it was formed; in at least one case—affecting Golden Gate Bridge transportation—city officials have half the votes in the regional organization and so can block objectionable actions; and this city, like many others, can achieve much of its vision simply by ignoring outside authority—until a gun is put to its head, as with United States Steel, sewer permits, and airport expansion. If we join this set of local resistors to the division of goals and methods that are sometimes found among regional organizations and that diffuses the latter's effectiveness on the urban scene,[39] we can see that the external force of regionalism is not clear, continuing, or determinant.

In short, the complexity of this state-regional-local interaction is not captured by any simple notion that higher levels are "imposing" something on lower levels. As Jones has observed from his study of California, "Much so-called imposition by the state is actually policy developed by local groups and interests, and implemented through the machinery of state government. Frequently local officials join with other local groups to seek legislation of this kind." [40] That pattern certainly characterizes the struggles of the last ten years in the Bay Area to transform ABAG into a multipurpose regional government.

This federalism is complicated even more by the splitting of functions even within a particular program. In an effort such as environmental control, there are such functions as development of basic concepts, planning, regulation, and construction and operation of control facilities.[41] Without even considering Washington's involvement, it is clear that these four functions must be sorted out among three public agencies—state, regional, local—and one private agency —industry. Add that complexity to four kinds of environmental problems, as in table 21. Even this simplistic categorization shows that any notion of federalism as a finely woven, integrated tapestry is a poor analogy for what exists. In table 21, the California experience with environmental policies demonstrates fission of responsibilities and powers for which some integrating mechanism is necessary but not available, even when a sense of crisis motivates all levels. It is simplistic to believe that a single regional organization, if created,

TABLE 21

Diffuse Responsibility for Environmental Policy in California

| | Government Level and Environmental Problems | | | |
Policy Functions	Air Pollution	Water Pollution	Water Resources	Solid Wastes
Development of basic concepts	State	State	State	State
Planning	State Local	State Region	State Local	Local Industry
Regulation	State Local	State Region	State	Local
Construction and operation	Local Industry	Local Industry	State Local	Local Industry

SOURCE: Based on Frank M. Stead, "Environmental Problems and Government Levels," in Stanley Scott and Harriet Nathan, eds., *Adapting Government to Regional Needs* (Berkeley: Institute of Governmental Studies, University of California, 1971), p. 67.

could exclude other governments from having environmental interests and participating in their management.

Yet there is more to this account of intergovernmental behavior, which will come only in the decades ahead. The abrupt reversal of attitudes of Bay Area officials about the advantages of single-purpose regional organizations, and now of a multipurpose body, is dramatic for its speed of change and for its motivations. The main reason was the experience with the new instrument of special-purpose, regional governance, during a decade of unprecedented challenge to the cities' ability to govern at all—or, at any rate, effectively. While the regional organizations may constitute potential external influences, some of which can check local programs, it also has a local representation with a potential voice for local power and preference. If so, it can be much closer to the city than many federal and state programs (some regional agencies are actually state commissions of regional character).

It seems likely that this combination of regional resources for common local problems and greater sensitivity than is available in higher levels of government underlies the continuing debate over representation. That issue was not a minor matter at the Philadelphia Convention in 1787, it will be recalled, nor is it here.[42] Should local governments or its citizens be the basic unit of regional representation? Should the representational base provide outlet for local interests only, or should it promote wider, regional interests? Can minorities be assured of more representation under any system? Do recent Supreme Court demands for "one man, one vote" representation on governing bodies operate here, too?[43] The Bay Area is getting closer to an agreement on these matters, for converting ABAG into a multipurpose organization was defeated by only one vote in the state senate in 1971.

THE ROLE OF WASHINGTON

There is a final strand to this web of regionalism to be found in the enormous role of the federal government in Washington, primarily through the device of the regional planning and clearinghouse requirements. The federal role in encouraging city planning goes back to the 1949 Housing and Redevelopment Act, which authorized large-scale projects that first required an integrated city plan. Whether this postwar growth of city planning was attributable to Washington or to more local pressures,[44] it was certain that more plans, planners, and planning money did thereafter appear on the local scene, and that sizable federal funds did accompany them. But there was little regional coordination of such activity when laissez faire among cities had existed for so long.

But this condition began to change dramatically in the early 1960s.[45] While Section 701 of the Housing Act of 1954 had provided for the coordination of urban planning, for years it had had limited use (through fiscal 1961, $16.4 million); but in the early 1960s it increased greatly ($72.7 million through 1964). The federal thrust is also seen in the fact that the larger the metropolitan area, the larger the share of federal funds in stimulating regional planning. Another development came with the 1962 Highway Act, which held back all funds for local road programs unless they were part of a regional transportation plan; this also continued the practice of setting aside funds for such planning. Then, in 1966 the Housing and Urban Development Act provided even greater stimulus by requiring the creation of regional bodies—the Councils of Governments—to review local requests for grants for airports, sewage treatment plants, housing, and health facilities. Under a program financed by Washington, these Councils (elected officials of cities and counties), quickly grew to about three hundred, representing a large majority of the American population.[46] Then, at the end of the decade, Congress capped the movement to solve the environmental crisis by legislating programs to control air and water pollution. As we have seen in the Bay Area, these stimulated state or regional agencies to devise areal plans whose standards local environmental programs must meet if they are to receive federal funding.

What all this portends for federalism is not yet clear. Melvin Mogulof's thorough review of the federal use of the Council of Government (COG) to promote regionalism found mixed results. He concluded that Washington by late 1971 had not opted to fully support the emergence of regional government in the nation, but it did support partial programs which could lead to it. The councils have never acted to check a central city on important issues;* local governments have joined councils, expecting them not to harm them; and decision making has been primarily based on full consensus. In short, "The image of COG we mean to convey is one of a beleaguered

---

* There is an important exception to this in this area, as Victor Jones has commented to me, with the regional airport planning in which Oakland's airport was upgraded at the expense of San Francisco's (see p. 320).

organization, surrounded by unsure federal partners, unwilling local members, and a barely awakening state government." Yet this critic still sounded an encouraging tone. At a minimum, the COG was "a point of regional intelligence to guide the federal government." While these agencies had not yet made a difference in the redistribution of resources within regions (an exception may be the Twin Cities), Mogulof did find grounds for optimism about their future as agencies for the promotion of regionalism. If Washington did take seriously its authority to demand that all COG clearances of local project applications actually did fit a metropolitan plan, a regionalizing force of considerable influence would exist. As it has been, however, the COG invariably approved projects from local units whose officials sat on the council, and Washington has not insisted on a different course.[47]

But not all of the Bay Area's regionalism is expressed in the Council of Governments, which here is ABAG. State action has recently provided regulatory organizations of great potential power, and as we have seen, they have been acting as if they mean to use it. But these, too, arise from strong federal pressures, which take different forms: stimulating the creation of regional plans; requiring the regional organization to act as a clearinghouse for federal fund requests from localities; and providing some proportion of the operating costs of the organization. These are summarized in table 22 for the major Bay Area organizations with planning and control functions in at least nine counties. The major variation in the pattern is in federal support, although only for ABAG is it heavy. In the environment of these agencies "the feds" are always a participant, sometimes directly sitting in on deliberations or actually voting. But that presence is most commonly found in the requirements for a regional plan. The federal role in the Bay Area has not yet been studied in detail, but some rough sense of the scope may be seen in mere numbers; by early 1971 an estimated ninety-three federal grant programs required review by ABAG.[48]

A much finer sense of that involvement appears in a review of federal specifications for regional planning. As Mogulof has shown, federal agencies have sought to use COG's for conflicting purposes; The Department of Housing and Urban Development and the Office of Management and Budget seek social welfare rather than management goals through them.[49] Yet the degree of specification is impressive in its detail, even if it is not always insisted upon. For ex-

TABLE 22

The Federal Presence in Regional Agencies in the Nine-county Bay Area

Regional Organization	Effective Origin Date	Regional Planning Function	Federal Grant Review[f]	Federal Percentage FY73 Budget[g]
Assoc. Bay Area Govts.	1961	Yes	Yes	60.9
Bay Conservation and Development Commission[a]	1965	Yes	...	...
Comprehensive Health Planning Council	1968	Yes	Yes	34.0
Water Quality Control Board	1969	Yes[b]	Yes	...
Metropolitan Transportation Commission[c]	1970	Yes	Yes	...
Air Pollution Control District	1970[d]	Yes[e]	...	10.2
Bay Area Sewer Services Agency	1971	Yes	Yes	...[h]

SOURCE: Abstracted from "Regional Regulatory Agencies in the San Francisco Bay Area" (Berkeley: League of California Cities, n.d.). Budget data provided by agency sources.

[a] By state law, sitting on commission of 27 is one member each from Army Corps of Engineers and Environmental Protection Agency, voting on planning matters but not on permit applications.

[b] To be completed mid-1974; interim plan used meanwhile.

[c] DOT and HUD each has one nonvoting member.

[d] Created in 1955, but strengthened after 1970 federal act.

[e] In the sense of utilizing federal guidelines on pollution levels.

[f] Drawn from League of California Cities, "Regional Regulatory Agencies in the San Francisco Bay Area," (Berkeley: n.d.). Blanks indicate information not provided in this source.

[g] Calculated from figures in reports of respective organizations. Other organizations in this column did not provide author with data permitting separation of revenue sources.

[h] Formed in 1972, hence no budget for FY73.

ample, the Intergovernmental Cooperation Act of 1968 contained significantly new requirements for regional planning, which a subsequent Bureau of the Budget Circular (A-95) elaborated. One review of that single law and circular finds that they

describe the process, agencies affected, and substantive requirements that, along with other directives, require ABAG to take into account all pertinent findings and decisions by Bay Area special planning and regulatory agencies and local governments.

Applications for federal assistance are to be reviewed on the basis of the [10] following considerations listed in . . . the 1968 act. . . .

Circular A-95 lists guidelines for implementing the 1968 act. They add programs for review purposes; establish new application requirements; describe the procedure for bringing the state into the review process; and emphasize the coordination and cooperation required for the grant program. The procedures direct ABAG to cooperate with the state clearinghouse for review purposes . . . and to notify all interested agencies of each pending application, before formal application to the federal government and review by ABAG. Newly listed as subject to review are activities concerned with [8] programs. The Circular also places review of all federal development projects without exception, and acquisition, disposal, and use of federal lands, under the regional clearinghouse requirements. Federal projects are reviewed to determine their consistency with other regional plans, using the same criteria that apply to federal grant review.[50]

Much more experience is needed in the operations of regionalism to determine its impact on federalism. Its evolution is certainly a part of the despair in the 1960s over the competence of the city to deal with contemporary problems. This growth of regionalism may also be understood, in Alan Altshuler's terms, as evidence of the fact that "the values of coordination as opposed to those of laissez faire have for many years been in the ascendant in our society." [51] For the call for coordination is a central theme in the regionalist perception of "urban crisis" and its criticism of urban forms. It is also clear that, despite regionalism's centralizing pull on local autonomy, this is not a one-way flow. Local systems still possess resources that enable them to resist influences which they deem vital to community interests, and regional systems must reflect that particularism and parochialism in some fashion. It is seen in the requirements for local representation on regional councils and in state legislatures, and in the informal negotiating of COGs which works against their possessing (much less using) sanctions. As with all state and federal direct influences on San Francisco, it is well to remember that these higher levels are always conditioned by a system in which localities are not yet totally powerless. For many in the Bay Area, regional government is seen as a halfway house, which will strengthen local services without surrendering too much autonomy. The first step, the single-purpose regional organization, has been well enough received to encourage the next step—a limited, multipurpose regional government. The effort is well worth an examination by those who despair of the possibility of American government structures adapting sufficiently to new demands on the political system. For their rate of adaptation and success to date are well beyond anything thought possible when the 1960s began.

THE PRIVATE EXTERNAL DIMENSION

Entry into the local decisional context, and an influence on its agenda, can also result from decisions about capital, labor, and land made outside San Francisco's borders. It hardly seems necessary to elaborate on the existence of an increasingly nationwide, aggregative, capital structure whose decisions can sharply affect the distribution and re-distribution of resources within American communities. Gross signs of such aggregation would include the following:

—the conglomeration of private corporations;
—the growth of pension funds as capital sources for insurance companies and trade unions;
—obvious but generally ignored restraint-of-trade practices in all major industries;
—the dominance of labor by trade unions in all major industries and, increasingly, in local public services, including teachers;
—the increasingly larger share of personal wealth or corporate income accounted for by an increasingly smaller proportion of persons and firms;
—the increasingly fewer number and proportion of farmers working in-creasingly larger amounts of land—the rise of agri-business;
—the increasing concentration of national communication media in fewer cities;
—the sharp rise in the dominance of American capital in foreign indus-tries, particularly in Canada and Europe;
—the increasing reduction of the number of fuel and extractive indus-tries.

My concern is not with the origins or attendant ideological debate these developments have occasioned. Rather, it is to focus on their consequences for the decisional context of this and other cities.

Decisions about the disposition of land, labor, and money were more widespread in an earlier period when these resources were more widely dispersed. But it seems undeniable that the aggregation of re-sources that has occurred more recently must be accompanied by the aggregation of decisional power *within* the domain of such resources; more, the process reaches *outside* its institutional bounds to affect other decisional centers. The congruence of the aggregation of re-sources and decisional power is not perfect, of course, because political power can direct public authority to decisions that capital aggregates would not choose. The outcry against taxation and regulation by American business, at least since the Populist days, has not always been heard in a land where political resources can sometimes substitute for economic resources in obtaining popular objectives. But even within this matrix of political checks, many capital decisions affecting citizens can proceed with few constraints except those of market conditions or of the need for institutional maintenance and protection. As Theodore Lowi has demonstrated, capital aggregates have managed a livable arrangement with national political power. Those in command of land, money, and labor find themselves, at the end of the third quarter of this century, well buttressed in national public policy, despite—or because of—the political upheavals of the New Deal and the Great Society.[52]

The resulting oligopoly of private resources acts as a major force on the community. This seems particularly likely, given its decentralization into the suburbs and small towns of the nation. The diffusion of banks, retail stores, and industry from the core city to the outland is a basic quality of post-World War II land uses.[53] These represent new resources, and sometimes new values, operating within the local decisional context. Their representatives may choose, because of institutional policy, not to get involved in any issues except those few which directly affect their interests. The last proviso is important. That is, absentee ownership does not always opt for local participation; plant directors may be more "representatives of a foreign power than the rightful chiefs of the local tribe." [54] But the injection of these outside capital sources does affect such major decisions in local institutions of the economy and the polity as: who shall work and for what return; how such returns will be spent locally; what will be an available, but only potential, tax source to support local public services;[55] how traffic will move;[56] and what public services will be needed.[57] Further, the *withdrawal* of such resources can equally—if adversely—affect citizens' lives, as Seattle discovered when contracts for military aircraft fell off at the end of the Vietnam War. The decision to insert or withdraw business resources, then, is a decision certainly as important in scope and consequence as many others treated by students of community power.

If this movement of capital affected only suburbia or small-town America, then San Francisco would not be a typical case. But the fact is that most major central cities have been experiencing what Brian

Berry has termed "the most massive downtown office boom in the nation's history that has transformed Central Business Districts of the nation's major metropoli." [58] Between 1936 and 1950 the amount of office space in Manhattan increased only minutely, 126 to 128 million square feet; but by 1960 it was up to 160 million, and by 1970, 226 million. In the Dallas Central Business District over that period it rose even more sharply, from 4.7 to 22.5 million. During the 1960s, the valuation of just the new office space authorized for construction, in billions of dollars, was for different areas: New York, 1.66; Los Angeles, 1.22; Washington, 0.81; Chicago, 0.71; Boston, 0.39; Detroit, 0.32; Atlanta, 0.28; Philadelphia, 0.25; Cleveland, 0.17; Seattle, 0.17; and Milwaukee, 0.10. In that array, San Francisco authorized 0.60 billion dollars. The results of a decade of such effort in these American cities was to increase their collective office space by 44 percent, and, along with Pittsburgh and St. Louis, "to account for over 70 percent of the headquarters and headquarters employment of the nation's top 500 industrials, and over 60 percent of all of the nation's central administrative office employment."

This phenomenon should be taken not as a harbinger of a new concentration of Americans in central cities, but rather as an indicator of the increasingly complex definition of urban life. Indeed, urbanism may no longer be conceived only as population and industrial-commercial concentration in the center city. Rather, as Berry notes, speaking for most urban specialists:[59] "It is the spontaneous creation of new communities, the flows that respond to new transportation arteries, the waves emanating from new industrial and retail growth centers, the mutually-repulsive interactions of antagonistic social groups, the reverse commuting resulting as employment decentralizes, and a variety of other facets of social dynamics that today combine to constitute the new urban systems in America." [60]

Yet, the local power structure at best can have only marginal impact on such decisions. Communities may provide the personnel for unions, but the national union sets the conditions of work, often including wages. If the national decision is to strike all ports on the West Coast, as in the early 1970s, San Francisco workers have little alternative, despite adverse consequences for them and the local activities that depend on them. Or, communities may contain minerals or rich farmlands within their boundaries, but large-scale extractive industries or farm combines will decide whether to enter and work them, with immense effects on those communities. That has for long been the basic reality of Appalachian coal-town politics.[61]

We have seen that if a corporation decides to build a skyscraper in San Francisco, local power holders contribute to that decision only at the margins. The corporation bases its decision on such factors as the availability and cost of land and labor, regional and international connections in transportation and communication, and the physical attraction of climate. Local figures may eagerly welcome—even seek —such a relocation. But there was little evidence in the highrise study that the locals' receptivity was important in shaping the final decision. The San Francisco government's willingness to overcome legal barriers —by issuing licenses and closing streets—and to provide municipal services was regarded as a constant among *all* cities eager to attract businesses.

Having had little effect on the original decisions of corporations to move to San Francisco, the city's influential citizens seem also to have had little effect on wide-scope community events following that move. There has developed a shift in local employment into finance, now about 15 percent. Additional demands have been made on city serv- ices for public safety (costs have almost tripled since 1955), water supply, and sewage disposal. The movement into these new buildings has contributed to an increase in traffic congestion in the city, now among the worst in the nation, while the daily suburban migrants in- crease the traffic load and costs.* Certainly some of the new white- collar workers have contributed to the lack of private housing, for the vacancy rate is one of the lowest in the nation. The job-opportunity structure alters, nearby supportive businesses flourish, property values and taxes increase—and even neighborhood climates are transformed.

For little of this is there evidence that a local "power structure" has exerted its putative influence to create or modify the consequences of a basic decision made elsewhere. As we have seen, little is clear about the exact shape of the redistribution of municipal services—even whether subsequent costs are matched by increased taxes—with such extra- mural injections into the local context as highrises. It is not that such

---

* A 1969–1970 study found that the private car had generated city revenue of $29.7 million, while the city expenditures for servicing this vehicle were much higher, $42.4 million. See Douglass B. Lee, Jr., *The Costs of Private Automobile Usage to the City of San Francisco* (Berkeley: Institute of Urban and Regional Development, Univer- sity of California, April, 1972). Working Paper No. 171/Bart 6.

outcomes are uncontrollable by local groups. The point is, rather, that efforts by even the most monolithic community elite does little more than affect the margins, such as hours for parking or one-way streets, rental prices, higher salaries for city workers to attract labor, public relations programs for citizens and leaders, and so forth. This seems true even in a policy that is widely enjoyed. In the special culture that is San Francisco,[62] preservation of the famous bay view is ostensibly a widely and deeply shared attitude of its citizens. But there has been little success in efforts to stop highrises, which are effectively blocking out that view.

It is not only external capital that affects community decisions of wide scope, for national labor aggregates are equally influential. Local union chiefs are popularly thought to wield considerable influence on local decision making. Mayor Alioto has certainly appointed more of them to agencies of local government than did former mayors. But this local influence, whatever its size in this or other American communities, is markedly less than labor's national influence, which shapes and constrains the outcome of local issues.

The first of these national influences is the widespread acceptance in the last four decades of the legitimacy of workingmen's demand to bargain collectively. From that acceptance flow all the other influences and benefits which labor has since enjoyed. This national legitimation, however, facilitated the centralization of authority within each union, for maximum effectiveness requires maximum member solidarity, funneled through a cohesive leadership. There is little evidence that, once successful, this group is any more sensitive to demands for decentralization of authority or to local preferences within the union structure than corporate power has been. Like those of its companion, moreover, labor's decisions are increasingly made in forums well removed from the community scene, decisions that exercise significant influence on local life opportunities. The particulars of labor's empowerment are many and familiar, and need little elaboration here except for broad strokes. Labor became one of the major factors that nationally determined the community level of wage and price structures. Intercommunity variations do exist, of course. But the base of the variation has been shaped and built by preceding economic decisions in which both national labor and capital have played the major roles. More significant for our thesis, though, the characteristic exercise of such power finds union locals, as a result of decisions made elsewhere, seeking wage alterations and striking if they are not heard. Lateral effects also operate here. That is, one union's decision may mobilize sympathetic strikes by others, or the successful demands may stimulate the equivalent in other unions—all local effects set in motion by this private extramural influence.

Illustrative of others, note the special effect in San Francisco and elsewhere of national unionism on city employees. Successful private unions achieve rewards, particularly wage and fringe benefits, which can lure municipal workers into the private domain unless local governments match those benefits. Even more linked, some public employees, as in San Francisco, explicitly tie their salary levels to equivalent union jobs in the private economy. When the latter rise by union action, the former rise like a kite's tail. And, when city workers organize more effective public unions and mobilize their political power to nudge mayors and councils, they become irresistible.* Such lateral union effects on the local community, plus the attendant political power of the city worker, account for the increasingly large weight of personnel salaries and benefits in municipal budgets. In San Francisco, both school and municipal government personnel regularly demand and get annual increments; an occasional threatened—or real—walkout seems enough to prevent school board members and supervisors from denying them. Population growth seems little related to the increase. From 1950 to 1970, San Francisco's population declined by almost 8 percent, but school employees increased by 90 percent, municipal workers by 37 percent, and the total budget by about 400 percent.[63] Political authorities may think they are reacting merely to local power configurations in this event. But behind this visible interaction lie others, set in motion outside the city's boundaries, which create local effects that local authorities can affect only at the margins.

---

* In San Francisco, city laborers in mid-1973 received $12,000, nearly $5,000 more than a beginning teacher. The driver of a medium truck received more than the chief resident physician or a surgical nurse in the city hospital.

CHAPTER 13

The City's Decisions in Perspective

In the crosscurrents of private and governmental forces in San Francisco's decisional matrix, it is easy to lose sight of the dominant patterns, my primary concern in this book. This concluding chapter focuses on what is persistent and significant in such patterns.

THE CITY'S DECISIONAL CONTEXT AS A SYSTEM

San Francisco has been viewed in this book as if it constituted a *system of decisions*.[1] There is a wide range of *needs* in any community, some of which are transmuted into *demands* on social institutions. *Decisions* are one product of the force of these demands. Politics arises out of the mismatch between these demands and the resources available to meet them. Such politics can exist within a social institution, as in "union politics," "corporation politics," "church politics." One forum where these demands struggle for resources is the *political system,* here the governmental mechanisms and processes in San Francisco. Of the innumerable demands that impinge on that political system, some are successful in being met. But because there are always irregularities of power resources in any community, some groups win more often than not, some never win, and some win inconsistently.

At the heart of such decision making by social institutions is a varied set of *exchanges*. In the private sector, the exchange function is ever present. Exchange is what transpires between buyers and sellers, employers and employees, dispensers of religious values and supporters of the institution that makes them possible, teachers and students, and so on in an enormous exchange web of values and goods.

In similar fashion, the definitive action of the political system—the authoritative allocation of values and resources—is also an exchange function. *Political authorities,* legitimate wielders of that crucial power, may extend the resources of preference and privilege—symbolic and material—to those who return other resources, which can be votes, funds, respect, credibility, or social acceptance.

Another major aspect of this system of exchanges is how demands are organized. The number of citizens who engage in this exchange is always a crucial issue in a democracy, but the research findings on this have been consistent. The participants are always few, except for elections, although even then major segments are excluded. Much more characteristically, conflict in the political system is a group affair, for mass interests become mobilized and articulated through the intermediary of the group. Whether it is as large and amorphous as "the Democratic party of San Francisco" or as small and honed as "the Telegraph Hill Owners Association," these are the major group actors in urban politics. In sum, given the characteristic indifference of Americans toward political participation—a condition differentiated by status, of course—such politics enlists the attention and resources of only a minority of the community.

Moreover, the politics of this exchange does not take place only in such publicized forums for decision making as a city council. Decisions are made by factors that operate *after* they have been made, as much as by factors that operated *before* they were authorized. Hence the truism that all segments of the political system are the targets of politics because these segments also participate in the essential exchange qualities. What supervisors or voters may have thought they were declaring by an ordinance, referendum, or charter may not be as important in determining what policies eventuate as other actions, for example, how executives, administrators, or judges decide that the law's broad purposes fit the particulars of the present.

In all these attributes of exchange the city's decisional context partakes of a *system.* That term denotes regularity of action and reaction, specification of roles and behavior, consistency of process, and prediction of outcomes. Such qualities emerge even in the fragmented, swirling politics of decision making in San Francisco. Yet the term should not be taken to mean that such structure is unchanging, invarying, and monolithic. For all these systems are prone to major alteration from two broad sources. Although less likely, change can come from the inside, from new dreams and values, which produce new internal expectations of the system's goals. However, the defenses of those who fill the positions of authority in all systems are legion; system maintenance—not system change—comes to be the primary goal of such authority figures. The second source of system change is from the outside, of course, in the appearance of new ideas and new power, which can impose new activities—even new figures of authority.

The linkages between these broad characteristics of any community's decision making and the San Francisco account will be seen in this chapter. For we have witnessed in the preceding pages all these concepts at work—needs and demands, input activities, the political system's rewards and penalties, the role of political authorities, the cross-linkages to private systems of power—and the forces of system maintenance and system change.

THE SAN FRANCISCO POLITICAL SYSTEM

The economic and status structures in San Francisco constitute at any one time a set of resources differentially available to meet community demands. This difference generates social stress among those citizens who protect or challenge these resources. Compare the wide-open quality of such resource structures in the gold rush days—when a large new population was suddenly thrown into a community with no established patterns of winners and challengers—with the city three decades later, when railroad and other utilities monopolized the resource and value structures. But these structures did not totally freeze, certainly not that early, because of the intervention of outside forces, as we shall shortly see.

Crisis over the gap between demands and resources is transmitted into the political system by carriers. This is the function here conceptualized for parties and the "power structure." I have shown how the nonpartisan character of the city's party and election system distinctively shapes the kinds of demands that get transmitted. Nonpartisanship itself distinctively affects that transmission process, whatever the form it displays. Under that nonpartisan façade, the transmission of demands in the 1950s could advantage business and Republican cohorts. But as a result of the outside state influences that benefited Democrats, local politics here became a nonpartisanship, which advantaged the Democrats and, increasingly, the spokesmen for new minorities. But whatever its content over time, nonpartisanship has always carried out nominations, gotten out the vote, presented issues, and governed, albeit loosely. Although the participants may not bear partisan labels, these activities are necessary under any political system and they have consequences for the community. For they only selectively, not fully, transmit demands into the political system. They may not carry party names, but their labels of "liberal" or "conservative" imply that they reflect certain group demands for resources and values.

In this perspective a "power structure," whatever its shape as "elite" or "pluralist," can be another carrier of group demands. Present-day San Francisco has such a carrier, as it had at any earlier period; the vigilantes, in one sense, were little more than a tactical squad for the powerful of an earlier day. Membership changes over time, of course, as do the interests represented. This present-day carrier is far from the tight oligopoly of San Francisco's earlier days, when a few bankers and railroaders set up for the community its entire agenda of issues, determined the entry to decisional forums, and influenced every kind of public and private decisional mechanism. The ethnic base of the "power structure" has changed, too. Where once the arriving Irish or Italians were excluded from such circles, today their children and their children's children are included, and they often treat the currently arriving minorities as their ancestors had been treated. But whatever the power of this "structure" may once have been, it is now less absolute, for during the 1960s new claimants with new demands emerged. If there is one ultimate quality that distinguishes an "elite," it is that it can effectively exclude from reward all persons and ideas it opposes. But today it is very hard to find such power to exclude, judging from the groups now making demands, often successfully, on the local scene.

There is lacking not only "power" of the ultimate sort but also much sign of "structure." The coalitional principle, observed in the political institutions and cases in this book, itself exhibits little structure. As we have seen, business and labor together may be all-powerful on many issues, but that combination can lose to a larger public of neighborhood and other special-interest groups. Moreover, business and labor do not always agree, and it is uncertain which dominates when they do disagree. Nor is business itself a single entity; indeed, it was a division among businessmen that led to the Boss Ruef revelations sixty years ago. We have noted for the current era the distinction between the Big and the Little Rich, as well as that between the older, more constricted visions of "the Downtowners" and the more expansive visions of a larger city economy stemming from the Chamber of Commerce.

Yet if this carrier of demands to the political system lacks power in a full sense, the individual groups usually thought to be members of it still constitute important agencies in the local decisional context. This paradox exists because (1) some individuals possess significant group resources with which to enter local decision making; (2) they maintain an advantage that comes to those who pressure decision makers constantly instead of sporadically; (3) there are some issues that do join them mutually (particularly as in the highrise politics with its enormous popular backing); and (4) they enjoy all the benefits of having to pay lesser costs for the opportunities and information that results from their active contact with other organizations.

Such mobilized bias and resources may lose to an aroused public through the referendum or may face a new breed of local politicians. But the referenda losses are not that frequent, as was shown earlier, and the batting average is relatively high for business, particularly on the issues of enormous scope, such as highrises. As for the new political tactics and actors on the scene, since these are not entirely alien forces, links can be forged to them. Some of their leaders can be co-opted by personal rewards, such as appointment or business opportunities. Some group demands can actually be met without surrendering too much, although this is done with considerable protest. And always between the established and the challenger there are grounds of mutual interest to seek and utilize, such as keeping taxes and expenditures "reasonable," boosting the local economy, and protecting the city against external encroachments.

The object of all this activity is a political system that over time has adapted to dominant demands, primarily those from business and labor. Its adaptability to community stress has been emphasized in earlier chapters. A political system that once used its police to shoot workers in the 1934 strike has since adjusted to the new power of workers and now responds sensitively to their interests. A political system caged within a complex charter develops leaders who use the charter to protect groups. Even knowledge of the charter—maze wisdom—regularly enhances those already advantaged, such as city workers who use supervisors and elections to raise and protect their benefits, already the highest in the nation.

Despite its intricate barriers to action, this is a political system with some openness to change in its programs. Thus, a century ago, the Cato-like shout of Dennis Kearney that "The Chinese must go!" disappeared with the new century, particularly after the settling of tong wars and after the eagerness of the Chinese to assist in the rebuilding of the city after 1906. Even the political system's treatment of crime shows this sensitivity to dominant community demands. What is considered serious and how energetically it is prosecuted alter dramatically in a few years in matters of gambling and prostitution, although, again, outside forces contribute powerfully to that result. When during the 1960s the local scene was stirred by events outside its boundaries, producing new demands for recognition of arriving minorities, the political system made some adjustments. There have appeared new political authorities (even some minority members) who are sensitive to the new claims; new kinds of ordinances emerge which recognize the claims for deference; and even favorable redistribution of scarce resources begins as the ethnic character of city workers changes.

But this political system also demonstrates an openness to changing expectations concerning other values, which is one measure of the quality of the political system's performance. I have shown this altering pattern in the matter of competency and adaptability. New demands for efficiency in government or for its flexibility in handling new urban crises have been generated by dissatisfactions with such qualities of the political system. But repeatedly, structures, procedures, and personnel of that governance have altered because of new charters, ordinances, and referenda.

All of these aspects of San Francisco's decisional matrix were illuminated when the analysis was shifted from the structural to the dynamic qualities of the political system in the focus on two kinds of political conflict. The first of these, the politics of profit, examined the interface between the private economy and public governance. We have seen that ever since the gold rush days San Francisco's essential character—its location, opportunity structures, reward system, leadership—was shaped deeply by the impact of economic affairs. Gold transformed it from an obscure Yerba Buena to world-famous San Francisco, and subsequently a continuing transformation has been traceable to the economic effects of silver, wheat, fruit, wine, and railroads. The city's sense of close ties to an external economy appeared again in the political economy of the 1960s, which offered a vision of salvation in a regional economy that would feature mass transit, tourist facilities, and business centers for San Francisco. The fact that agents of government joined with other civic forces, including the voters, underscores the connection between the political and economic systems. In the process, the "old San Francisco" is disappearing (except in tourist attractions), just as in earlier eras Yerba Buena and the dominant Spanish and Mexican cultures were lost under new economic and political forces.

This politics of profit is more direct, obvious, and tangible than the politics of another kind we earlier saw—the politics of deference. I again emphasize that deference is not sought to the exclusion of more material rewards, or vice versa, in the politics of profit. Rather, the conflict over deference focuses on a kind of politics that has been as characteristic of cities as the struggle for income. This politics has been particularly important to newly arrived ethnic groups, a demand for recognition of one's own value as a person and as a group. Of course, such groups also seek material rewards from the community, but deference has first priority for the *arriving* group just as profit does for the *arrived* group. Individual and group demands get mixed, obviously, but what distinguishes the politics of deference is the demand on the political system that group recognition be extended through the process of legitimation which inheres in that system. It often takes a negative form, as in demands that the system not discriminate against group members in dispensing jobs, contracts, or permits. It may also be positive and symbolic, as in the struggle to get one's own people into official positions or to declare a holiday for Martin Luther King's birthday or for a Cinco de Mayo celebration.

That this politics of deference has been shaped by external forces, no less than for the politics of profit, has been earlier shown in events of the 1960s. But similar forces operated throughout the city's history in the migration of large numbers of Irish, Italians, and Chinese, with the resulting ethnic conflict. On one occasion in the past, it took the external intervention of the President of the United States to break up local discrimination in school policy.[2] Oldtimers insist that the power of one particularly savage tong was broken only by the intervention of the Emperor of China.* But the consistent and massive

---

* The Emperor's minister advised him that "the matter has been attended to. . . . I have cast into prison all relatives of the Sue Yops in China, and have cabled to California that their heads will be chopped off if another Sum Yop is killed in San Francisco." As the source of this account noted, "And in far-away America the war ended with startling suddenness." Herbert Asbury, *The Barbary Coast* (New York: Knopf, 1933; Capricorn reprint, 1968), p. 196.

role of the federal government in recent years has provided an external influence of unprecedented dimensions in the current politics of deference.

THE CONSTRAINTS OF ELSEWHEN AND ELSEWHERE

That phenomenon of outside forces working on community decisions is another major perspective for an understanding of this and other cities. The historical influence is one of these, but it is not special to San Francisco, despite its romantic publicity. We have seen this influence of the past at work throughout this book. Thus it is seen in the early decision to locate the city inside the Golden Gate,[3] which made it an entrepôt then and now. However, the many past decisions that resulted in moving maritime commerce across the bay to Oakland continue to weaken the port of San Francisco. Further, political conflict through sixty years has shaped the existing electoral context of the city's decision making. The corruption of that earlier era influenced the charter of government which directly and daily shapes decisions forty years later. Another earlier conflict led to decisions about organized labor that account for its present influence.

The historical factor determined how the different immigrants were —and would continue to be—rewarded. The openness of the gold rush and later days created a context for ethnic succession and success that benefited Irish, Italian, and Jew to a degree—and earlier—than was true elsewhere; it also created for the current era patterns of resistance to the claims of newer ethnic groups. How the American society once thought about the original Spanish and Mexican settlers over a century ago rather effectively wiped them from the scene. Not until the last several decades have the Spanish-speaking reemerged in any numbers. These are not descendants of the early Californios, however, but emigrants from Central America. Lacking either any niche in the city's scheme of resources or a united membership, the new members of the old Spanish culture have only recently begun to press for power. Similarly, a host of earlier and more familiar decisions by Americans about the role of black citizens continues to influence that group's status and power in the local context. There are new beginnings, of course, as we have seen. But constraints imposed by decisions years ago in the black belt in the South continue to be felt in every city in the nation.

As for the second type of major force of the outside world that influences local decisions—the extramural forces—these have been fully

TABLE 23
Accounts of Major Extramural Influence

| | Influences | | | |
Subjects	Private	State	Regional	Federal
History	x	x	x	...
Political parties	x	x	...	...
Government: History and honesty	x	x	...	x
Government: Adaptability	...	x	...	x
Political economy	x	...	...	...
Highrise studies	x	x	x	...
Arrived ethnic groups	x	...	...	...
Arriving ethnic groups	x	...	...	x
Federal government	...	...	...	x
Middle governments	x	x	x	x

noted throughout this account. The summary of these influences in table 23 indicates that no analysis of local decision making, here or elsewhere, tells us much without calculation of its private and governmental extramural force. This city actually begins with the most dramatic event in its history occurring several hundred miles away in the Sierra. Both then and later, such external economic forces have loomed large in local affairs, whether this was the Southern Pacific a century ago or corporations' recent "Manhattanization" of the landscape. This city, like any other, has reverberated to the fluctuations in a national economy—the boom and bust of mining or agriculture, the Great Depression, or post-World War II prosperity. But these were events which local "power structures" could affect very little.

Moreover, there is some doubt about how much independent influence remains on major local decisions of large scope given the new federalism laid out earlier, whether that influence comes from Sacramento or from Washington. The earlier figures about shifting federal finances and an accompanying new impetus and constraint in policies across the nation have been seen here. These are the major currents running into the city over a half-century from Sacramento and over a dozen years from Washington. This book has cited major instances of that federal influence:

—during World War II, the federal stimulus to the Bay Area economy, and the army's closing of brothels;

—the crystallizing effect of Adlai Stevenson's campaigns in the 1950s on the Democracy of California;

—the effect on the poor in the 1960s of the poverty and Model Cities programs;

—the use of federal civil rights laws against economic discrimination in public and private employment;

—the federal court challenge to school segregation and federal financial support for desegregation;

—the resort to federal courts and OEO legal assistance by the poor in order to compel adherence to federal law in the Yerba Buena Center;

—the federally backed barriers to realty growth represented by environmental protection laws;

—the access to federal resources provided by congressmen;

—the federal encouragement of a budget system which for the first time would permit coordinated assessment of urban programs and resources;

—et cetera.

That "et cetera" is important, because this book has *not* provided a full inventory of the federal, or indeed state, external influences on the city's affairs. Of course, those cases recounted here were major, in the sense of affecting large numbers of people or dollars. By themselves these cases constitute the major events since World War II, and particularly during the last ten years. Yet to be analyzed are such federal influences as

—the impact of federal tax structures on highrise development or city taxes;

—the similar impact of federal expenditures;

—the infusion of federal standards of certain values (due process, equality, rational decision making, financial accountability) into local public and private institutions.

Also not developed in this account is the depth and breadth of Sacramento's involvement in local decision making. But on both of these major dimensions of extramural power I have sought to meet the objective set forth early in this book, that is, to sketch the main contours of power in the city.

Yet in this context of local power, there is a mixed picture of who controls whom as a consequence of these external forces. It is clearly not a picture of dominance by higher political authority, nor even of dominance in those affairs in which it takes interest. After all, many resources are still available to a mayor, political party, local congressman, state assemblyman, or newspaper editor, which can mediate the influence of this intervention. Indeed, alterations in state and federal relationships with the locality are far from uniform; rather, they represent much more a spectrum in which local power and local culture can defract such external pressures, as a prism treats a light beam.

What this account has raised for consideration for San Francisco and other sites is the degree to which these external influences have altered the traditional context of local decisions. This is not a struggle of embattled local people against arbitrary higher authorities, a modern Whiskey Rebellion by City Hall. Rather, it is a complex mosaic of cohorts *across* governmental jurisdictions, who are locked in combat over distribution and redistribution of resources and values. It is that phenomenon which is new in its scope and consequences, and about which so little is known systematically in current urban affairs.

THE LOCAL GAME OF RESIDUAL ALLOCATIONS

Against this complex set of perspectives, particularly the weight of historical and external forces, it seems likely that the traditional study of community power may have had too narrow a focus. It is not that scholars had been blind to the extramural shift. After all, the Lynds discussed the new unionism in Muncie, H. Lloyd Warner the absentee corporation in Newburyport, Floyd Hunter the national corporation and state political ties in Atlanta, and Robert Dahl the federal influence on urban renewal in New Haven.[4] But with one exception,[5] none asked the question raised here: *What is the extent of this extramural transference of power to extramural forces across the total range of issues affecting the lives of a community's citizens?* Some scholars use the time dimension, but are restricted in their scope of issues, while others reach for more issues, though within a narrower time span.[6] Generalizations are too tenuous when the outside influences on a broad range of issues have not been explored.

The Segmented Context

One inference that might follow from this analysis is that an increasingly smaller proportion of the community agenda now rests autonomously in local hands. Rather, what remains is a diminished autonomy, which operates only on leftover decisions—a *local game of residual decision making*. These residuals are not unimportant in the lives of citizens, of course, nor do they deal only with small resources. *What needs to be determined, however, is the extent of the residual decision making that results from such extramural influences.* Because much previous research on community power may have dealt only with these residuals, this section sketches a broader picture of what seems to be occurring in varying degrees among American cities —and especially in San Francisco.

Whatever the controversy over whether communities are "elite" or "pluralist," research reveals that only a few "participate" in local decisions, no matter how broadly one defines that verb.[7] The more diversified the community, that is, the more it becomes like a big city, the less homogeneity is found in this small band who "run things." As the community increases in size, however, there is an increasing division of labor, which brings bureaucratization and specialization of function and service. As a result of such fission, what develops at the pinnacle (if that is the word) of urban America—New York City— is a system of public and private segmented structures, in *each* of which control over allocation of its special resources is fragmented.[8]

With apologies to James Madison, we can say that a governmental bureaucracy interest, a trade union interest, a production-distribution-consumption interest, a capital-amassing and investment interest, and a communication media interest, grow up of necessity in larger cities, dividing each into a set of multiple fiefdoms, actuated by different sentiments and views—but all dedicated to survival. Each has most of what distinctive local resource it lays claim to—authority, land, money, skills, knowledge, and access. Each resists change, of course, by defending the innovations of the previous generation. Ironically, each, in company with others, provides an astounding array of local services at a level much higher for more people than ever before in world history.*

But those services are usually rendered in a fashion which outsiders call "autocratic" and insiders "efficient." This segmentation gives the impression of a monolithic elite because each fiefdom operates in parallel on common bureaucratic principles—not the least of which is survival against competing claims to resources. Even though these principles may be arrived at separately by the imperatives of bureaucratization, they result in a delivery of services which looks remarkably

---

* The "crisis in the cities" may partly reflect in objective terms a lack of a historical framework for judgment, although in subjective terms it obviously reflects widespread dissatisfaction with the present. In either the subjective or the objective sense, however, it is well to remember the wry wisdom of the fictional Mr. Dooley, that "th' past always looks betther thin it was. It's only pleasant because it isn't here."

alike to citizens—impersonal, arbitrary, insensitive, and uncontrollable.

Each segment's interest in self-maintenance has developed within a nonpartisan coalition in the recent era of postmachine urban politics. There also exists a "new convergence" in an executive-centered coalition, headed by an elected chief executive, with clusters of local economic interests and the "professional workers in technical city-related programs." Seeking coordinated problem-solving instead of the old boosterism, this combination has the initiative for broad resource allocation, public and private. But popular contributions to this policy making, as one might think a mayor had from his base of votes, were distant and feeble.[9]

In this context, segmented decisions, whether public or private, act to reduce frictions among members of the coalition. After all, the bulk of any bureaucratic activity is routine, that is, conflict free. Such routine means that there was worked out in the past a *modus vivendi* with the resources of others. If intersegment conflict occurs, even though sharp it is rarely total, and the outcome is incorporated into later operations and the issue rarely raised again. Such a process requires the development of conflict rules—how new conflict will be conducted and accommodated, and how its outcome will be administered.

The Challenge Game: Players and Resources

This closed coalition game is not the only possible local conflict game, however. Another kind arises when demands are made on the closed game by the new local players for a redistribution of resources. Within the existing distribution of resources, change is slow and marginal, although over time these changes may collectively have an important influence on what the future political system can do. The result in time is also a substantial change in the spread of services and in the forms, processes, and policies of local government. While this long view is not convincing to challengers of the closed game, until recently they have lacked resources to enter it. Whether the game outcomes are affected little or much by external forces, whether local autonomy is more residual or less, these decisions have an intimate effect on the lives of challengers. For many of them, after all, it is the *only* game in town.

In this outlook, the players and their resources may be distinguished analytically. The old players are, ethnically, the minorities that have arrived. Governmentally, they are located in old-line agencies and in mayor or manager-council systems. Privately they dominate the structures of finance and commerce. Clusters of all of these may be found separated by ethnic or status lines, although some individuals operate across these clusters. The new players, on the other hand, are, ethnically, the arriving minorities who lack niches in the public and private structures of local resources. They are found in emergent cadres of racially and economically disadvantaged, in middle-class professionals backed by federal money, and in some social scientists consciously adopting the role of change agent. For this group of challengers to the closed game there is a sequence of problems. The first is the "ante problem" of the resourceless—how do you get into the game of resource decisions when you have no resources with which to start?

The resources of these players, new and old, are different not only in their size but in their quality. The old players have a monopoly of the old resources, such as authoritative position in the community's political and status systems; knowledge of the regime rules and of strategies by which resources are amassed; land, capital, and expertise in the economic system; direct or indirect access to the communication media for transmitting publicity about decisions of the old players. Further, they control access to such resources by familiar gate-keeping techniques, themselves a reinforcing resource. On the other hand, the resources of the new players increasingly represent a direct link to the external forces discussed earlier. The "ante problem"—how to enter the game—may be attacked with new resources. Some are derived from new public programs aimed at alleviating conditions for the poor, and some from new strategies necessitated by the old players' monopoly of the old ones.

We can see this in federal laws that have recently been redefining the national values which the American political system will reinforce. Such is the case of civil rights. When enforced, these laws provide a resource that can be used both symbolically and materially to alter a local community's standing decisions. Thus, in the South since 1954, federal intervention in voting and education has created a massive fracture in regional decisions about values and resources once widely thought to be unshakable. In San Francisco as elsewhere in the urban North, school ghettos that have existed since our cities began are likewise under attack from a combination of new players working with federal—and sometimes state—authorities. In this process, law, when enforced, emerges as a force for changing behavior by equipping those new players with a new resource.[10] Of course, when it is not enforced, or is enforced so as to add to the power of the old players, no change occurs in the new players' position.[11]

All of this has relevance for the various poverty programs of the 1960s, which sought to transfer resources directly to the urban poor. Their requirement that community organizations be developed to implement many of these programs, their provision of legal skills in order to attack the old decision-patterns,* and their encouragement of the resourceless to change their fate—all represented new and still reverberating extramural resources. This does not imply that the aims of these programs have been realized or that maximum services have been delivered. Numerous critiques have suggested that some have failed for many reasons, as reflected in the subtitle of a study of one such effort toward external change—"How Great Expectations in Washington Are Dashed in Oakland." [12] But at the very least these efforts have mobilized a new cadre for insertion into local decision making. That result will linger long in San Francisco politics.

Another and highly dramatic resource being developed is a special set of political action techniques. Under such labels as "social action" or "confrontation politics," these strategies of protest politics are the demonstrations, boycotts, violence or its threat, and so forth, of the last decade. Note that these strategies-as-resources are also available to the old players, who never use them, for they can achieve satisfaction with other resources. Protest strategies may be more successful for one kind of reallocation than for another,[13] and they may be focused either on decision makers directly or on more powerful third parties who move decision makers.[14] Some strategies represent a frustration over monopoly of local resources, a frustration so bitter that destruction of "the system" is the professed aim. Other strategies, clearly the most frequent, seek rewards within the prevailing system itself.[15] Many of the new cadres are finding their way into the crevices of this system even now, as the old protest politics gives way to acquisition of resources—particularly the resource of knowledge of how the decisional system works—all resources that once were monopolized by the old players.

Accompanying these resources of law and strategy are new visions of

---

* One technique which flowered in the early 1970s was the publication of the formal and informal rules of the game operating in the city's government. E.g., see Richard Hayes, *Understanding San Francisco's Budget: How City Hall Spends Your Money and What You Can Do About It* (San Francisco Study Center, 1973).

local decision processes. Their "newness" may be relative, for most return to Jeffersonian ideas about local control of the polity. Nevertheless, old decisions about schools, police, social welfare, jobs, and so forth, are increasingly questioned, not only because they withhold deference and rewards from new groups, but also because of the manner in which the decisions themselves are reached. Community control of schools and police, decentralization of schools and welfare, citizen advisory councils, community action boards, the ombudsman —all are aspects of the direct challenge to old modes of local decision making, as well as to the consequences of such decisions.[16] Amid the tumult of public hearings, the noisy demonstrations in streets and corridors, and the vituperation and frustration of exchanges between political authorities and citizens, there is visible a demand for a more open model of community decision making.

Central to this conflict is the old democratic problem of how groups are to be represented when decisions about society's resources are being made. The poverty program during the 1960s sought to meet objectives of both representation and redistribution, but had only partial success. The failure stemmed partly from the contradictions of these goals and partly from the way they had to be strained through existing urban political systems. Some research suggests that in cities with a history of reform distribution of *power* was more successful, but in traditional machine cities the redistribution of material *rewards* was dominant. Moreover, the way that representation of the poor was provided reflected different conditions among those represented as well as among different decision making traditions.[17]

The Diversity of Outcomes

The resources of old players of the local game have thus been confronted by new resources of extramural money, structures, strategies, and ideas about the decision process itself. Among big cities, there has developed a ferment like nothing known since urban reform early in this century. Where that earlier reformation also knew extramural penetration of the local game, it was the state capitals that were deeply involved; Washington played only a limited role.

But even a rough profile of the detailed shape this transformation is currently taking is not possible. Within one city alone, the changes wrought by new players and new resources may vary from program to program, institution to institution, and among cities the pattern may vary equally widely. Thus, where blacks form a local majority they may force the local game open much farther than where they are fewer in number. For example, cities with the largest proportion of blacks could elect black mayors in Cleveland, Gary, and Newark in the 1960s. Even here, victory required support of about one in five whites; not until Thomas Bradley's election in Los Angeles in 1973 did a majority of whites support a black candidate in a major city. Where the black and the poor are less numerous, city executives speaking for the old players strive to control the federal inflow by making their offices the gate-keepers, and not bypasses, for these new resources. This was the case in San Francisco. The new players fend off such efforts or use other resources, like the vote or threats of violence, to create new resources; they may even gain entry to the decision making system, public and private.

In this way the old decision patterns may undergo alterations, which cumulatively can either reinforce or cancel one another—we need far more intercity comparison to know which. The central question would be whether any loosening of control over the range of local issues has come about because of the appearance from the outside of new resources whose allocation cannot be controlled in the old way by "power structures." Rather than autonomy, what one finds may be much better understood in the judgment drawn by Robert Wood from his study of fourteen hundred governments in the New York–New Jersey area in the late 1950s, *before* the national influences noted here: "It may be too far-fetched—though it is certainly an oversimplification—to think of local governments as players at a roulette wheel, waiting to see what number will come up as a result of decisions beyond their direct control." [18]

These are the new patterns operating in the city of this study. Old players and old coalitional processes, which constitute a "politics of hyperpluralism," [19] felt the brunt of these extramural forces when in the 1960s the injection of private capital and public federal resources created new players and processes. Competition for election became highly factional and partisan within the context of traditional nonpartisan institutions. "Community groups" of blacks (and increasingly of the Spanish-speaking) were newly politicized by federal programs; even the once politically inert Chinese entered politics more visibly. However, these groups are but new forms of an old phenomenon in San Francisco—neighborhood groups defending a territory just as older ethnic groups once defended theirs.

Federal officials and new players in San Francisco acted in the

1960s to challenge old decisions about schooling, housing, welfare, public safety, civil service, and private jobs. The mayor attempted to control as much of this federal intervention as possible. He sought either the expansion of federal funds for jobs and housing or the funneling of authority over such decisions into his hands. The federal outreach into the community took many forms, not all antagonistic to mayors. An example is the effort in the early 1970s, here and elsewhere, by the Federal Regional Council to stimulate program budgeting techniques or to establish local clearance procedures through the executive office. These would strengthen the mayors of the country in their old battle with power centers in local government and in their recent contest with newly empowered groups.

Even local political agencies usually not regarded as being under the federal gun have shown indirect effects of this new game. Nominations, the mobilization of voters, and the presentation of issues—normal tasks of local party life—have become caught up in the new context of local politics. Thus, candidates for elective office must now assess the relative strategies of supporting or criticizing these new players and their demands; few can safely ignore them. The news media, not always a willing ally of the new players, have been captured again and again by the drama of their confrontation strategies.

The private sector is also now impacted. The large capital centers in town, which had ignored the local game in the past, still ignore it, except for providing minorities with some new jobs. The moderate-sized capital groups—merchants, bankers, and trade unions—which dominated the local game in the past, find their power increasingly shared with the new players. In short, local officials and voters could only stand by and observe this skirmish in the private sector. But the new game was most affected by a much more massive change in the private sector. That was the injection of millions of dollars into the local economy for a construction boom unknown since those of 1850 and 1906. In most cases, this particular external force was widely welcomed, to judge by the decisions both of political authorities and of voters.

In those private decisions about highrises one can read signs of a local autonomy freely exercised, if he wishes. But those decisions may also be viewed quite differently. These external resources, much like federal or state funds, overwhelmed a community sorely pressed with urban problems demanding revenue, jobs, and a healthy economy. In this way of looking at what happened, it is hard to perceive the autonomy of the local "power structure" or of the voters. Rather there was much about local support of such decisions that is reminiscent of Machiavelli's caution that "a wise man will see to it that his acts always seem voluntary and not done by compulsion, however much he may be compelled by necessity." Since the compulsion of necessity is as much a threat to autonomy as is the command of a sovereign, the city probably had little chance or will to deny the thrust of this extramural force.

Meanwhile, San Francisco remains in one respect what it has always been—a contrast of mundane life and undeniable beauty. Beauty is not typical of the American urban scene, but aesthetics aside, there is much in the city's decisional life that is indeed typical. Its citizens may not agree, of course. But then, as Oliver Wendell Holmes once observed, Americans believe that "the center of Earth's gravity goes through every small town in America."

The small-town quality is another of the contrasts here, intermixed with the cosmopolitanism its spokesmen claim. The family base of personal identity (which here is more ethnic than "old family"), the community history familiar to all, the intense publicity about social leaders, the common man's knowledge of local leaders from "way back when," the daily mingling of community leaders in homes and clubs, and even the village gossip—all are easily visible signs of the city's hamlet quality, which contrasts so sharply with its ties to the nation and the world. This is not noted disparagingly, however, for this folk-community aspect was an important factor in the city's recovery from the 1906 disaster and will succor it in the one to come.

It may no longer imbue the "best bad things in America," which Hinton Helper found over a century ago (quoted in the epigraph to Part I), although it still has too many of these even now. It can never be again what it was ten or twenty or any number of years ago, for San Francisco is a time machine, which like other cities knows in its present both a past and a future, since what it has been and will be shapes what it does. Too, despite its special aesthetic, San Francisco shares much else with the urban America of today: a time of crisis, the constraints of history and the outside world, and the coalitional processes of decision making. In these political aspects, then, this city is any city. But there are many aspects to this urban scene, as I noted in the opening, including the aesthetic. That may be much more significant to most visitors and San Franciscans. For, seeing little of what this book has revealed, they see instead with the poets "a cool grey city of love" where "at the end of the streets are stars and spars." If so, they confirm the judgment that any city is measurable in many ways, each way important to the measurer. From such multiple perspectives, we can better understand the fullness of the urban mosaic. Whether taken intellectually or emotionally, such measures enable the San Franciscan to claim pridefully but pardonably with Paul of Tarsus, that he is "a citizen of no mean city."

A Note on Concepts and Methods

Certain concepts and methods of analysis employed in this book need some-what more specification than the clarity of presentation in the text would permit. This appendix is devoted to such elaborations and to the assumptions that guided the research.

THE UTILITY OF DECISION-MAKING STUDIES

The study of community power has several utilities. Of course it helps the scholar develop more general social theory, which this book attempts in detail. But there is another reason for such study—the translation of knowledge into social uses. That is, both those inside and those outside the decision-making apparatus can use knowledge to implement their values. This utility recognizes that community actors are constantly involved in surveillance of their environment in order to protect or enhance their interests. But this surveillance tends to be very limited because its perspective is that of a special interest, necessarily narrowed to what affects it very directly; when one has a toothache, not much attention is paid to the rest of the body. Such surveillance by local actors also involves little thinking ahead. Lacking any tested general theory of how the total system responds to internal and external stresses, most interests give little attention to indirect system factors that may affect their future; a man with a toothache has little interest in his persistent cough.

However, the utility of community analysis is not restricted to those inside the subsystem but goes beyond to outsiders who necessarily become knowledgeable in decision making. The degree of knowledge, however, covers a wide spectrum. Clustered massively at one end are citizens affected by such decision making but unaware not merely of its process but often of its effects. Thus, the urban poor have shown their unawareness of resources available to them, such as social benefits, while all but the very wealthy know little of their right to appeal public decisions. Rather, most citizens' only knowledge of the local decisional context is of a vague "they" who "run this town," whether they be public or private agents. Yet further along this scale, some citizens—much fewer in number—evidence more awareness of both the process and the output of decision making. At the far extreme are only a very few citizens who are familiar with the entire scope of both process and policy. Such full knowledge is probably found only in the smallest communities, for the increase in policies with city size necessarily blurs knowledge of all decisional transactions.

Whatever the degree of such knowledge, its utility lies in an understanding of how to affect community processes and policies. Such knowledge constitutes one of the major resources augmenting an individual's power in the community, but it is obvious that many have little and few have much of this resource. As the community power research demonstrates,[1] while community policies most often reflect the interests of those with the largest variety and volume of resources, it is also true that the resourceless are not totally powerless. This literature shows that the resourceless when provoked, from either fear or hope, can sometimes triumph. Observers differ over the extent of the latter's victories and their significance in the American system. Some believe this does not occur more often because of the characteristic apathy of those without resources, while others charge it to manipulation by what is claimed are opiates or tricks. In short, explaining the condition of those without resources depends in part on the normative framework for judging the local decisional arena.

An alternative explanation of the influence of the resourceless is the "law of anticipated reactions." Those with resources, it is argued, restrain themselves because of their judgment of what "the public" will or will not endure. That is, community decision makers are alleged to be influenced by the public's past behavior so as to shape their current decisions. However, such a thesis involves serious questions, both normative and empirical, about what constitutes a "resource," about the distribution of resources and their relative power, about whether "anticipated reactions" do exist and restrain the powerful, and indeed, about how the vast number of American communities are structured in such matters.

These conflicts aside for now, however, it is enough to note that the disputants agree that it is important to understand community decisional processes. Whether one is an "inside" decision maker or an "outsider" seeking to change decisions, the common requirement of such actions is a fuller conceptualization of the interaction of private subsystems and the political system.

BASIC CONCEPTS

That utility is provided by first defining our basic concepts and terms. In this book *the basic field of analysis is the decisional life of San Francisco. The specific focus within that field is on the decisions involving major allocations of the community's resources,* that is, the "politics" which decides how most of the public and private goods and services came to be distributed among its citizens. This requires understanding the actors, structures, processes, and outcomes in such decisional patterns.

Further, this perspective includes both the public and the private sectors of community decision making, for it assumes that they impinge on one another in many areas. But it will also be important to know how each sector operates independently as well as interactively. The conceptualization treats not only those authoritative allocations of the political system as conceived by David Easton,[2] but also those private decisions which may influence the lives of San Franciscans as much as—or even more than—those made in the political system.

In such analysis, certain assumptions are employed about resources and decisions.

Resources

This study builds on the understanding of a community's *resources* provided by others' studies; their conclusions about resources become our assumptions.[3] Thus:

1. *Resources are defined instrumentally.* Whatever their base or value, they are utilized to achieve other ends. The bases and ends of power are manifold. Thus, political resources are whatever may be used to achieve political influence or objectives, and economic resources are those which enable one to achieve the good material life.

2. *Resources are only potential in their influence until activated.* The vote of one man or one ethnic group means nothing in public affairs unless the threat or reality of its exercise is evident. This resource inertness can blur the vision of the unwary who ignore the distinction between *in esse* and *in posse.* For example, possession of any single resource by different men does not mean that it will necessarily be employed for the same objective or with the same skill and vigor. Equally rich men in the Union Pacific Club of San Francisco use their wealth in different ways; some chase blondes, some chase votes, some chase profits, and some do nothing at all. It is not sufficient to say with Hemingway that "the rich are different from the poor," for one must also note that the rich differ sharply among themselves.[4]

3. *Resources are exchangable.* That is, one kind may be used to replace or acquire another kind. Thus in elections, the resource of money (of

which much is available to a few but only a little to many) may equal or exceed the resource of votes (which are available to many but may not be used.) In San Francisco, for example, one may accumulate deference by amassing such resources as money and using it for cultural or civic improvements.

4. *Resources are differentially distributed.* In any community, most of a highly valued resource is in the hands of a few. Whether these few monopolize more than one resource is a subject for research. For example, in San Francisco not all can pitch for the Giants, conduct the symphony, preside over the world's largest bank, write famous novels, and mobilize enough votes to be elected again and again to public office.

Decisions

It may also be asked what *decisions* I have in mind. Certainly not every decision made in this city; even in the narrowest time span such an inventory would be immensely difficult.[5] The inventory in this book is smaller but its consequences for the city's life seem very great, since it includes the following:

1. *Local government decisions.* Specially emphasized are those acts of urban governance involving either or both the largest effects upon citizens and the largest expenditures of money. While one may properly ask the distinction between effects and money that are largest and less large, the hope is to determine whether most major public decisions are pervaded by a common pattern. What are the common and varying patterns of such decision making? What do they tell about community values?

2. *Private allocation decisions.* Again, those involved are the largest in scope of resources and of effects upon San Franciscans' lives. To what degree do such issues operate independently of the local government? What is the relative weight on the lives of the citizens from these public and private sectors?

3. *Extra-community decisions with intra-community impact.* How do outside decisions in private and governmental sectors affect the community's decision makers, the agenda of issues, the pool of available resources, and the life opportunities? [6]

THE FRAMEWORK OF ANALYSIS

These concepts provide the components of the framework by which San Francisco's decisional context is developed in this work. A fuller description is necessary of Easton's system analysis to be applied to the decisional life of San Francisco. The central element, the political system, is affected by preceding events and by demands, thereby generating decisions that impinge on community life, thereby in time generating a new cycle of demands. One of the special emphases applied in this book is the influence of the history of prior events, while another is the influence of events outside the city's walls. These may be viewed as historical and external axes of power intersecting the city's decisional processes at any point in time. Both axes are viewed primarily as constraints on the total local system by acting to dilute its autonomy, although the operation of these axes does provide special advantages to some local cohorts.

Through these constraints, there develops within the community at a given time a set of demands generated by a special combination of economic, political, social, and psychological conditions. These conditions arise partly from local forces seeking to enhance or protect their resources and values; they are also affected by the external axis. Such conditions, moreover, are filtered and organized on a group basis before they become effective in community decisions. Private groups respond in the private decisional world of San Francisco—business, finance, labor—primarily to affect private decisions that constitute the bulk of economic activity. But these and other private groups also interact in the political system when public authority must be sought for group interest. These private groups seeking political influence may be small and based only on territory—the neighborhood group to protect property values. They may be large and fully private with only occasional political involvement—ethnic, religious, or economic groups. Or they may have a rather constant interaction in both public and private decisional arenas—the "power structure" or the news media. Finally, this group basis may be entirely public and political with diverse interests involved—political parties.

However based, they act as carriers of private demands into the political system, seeking public authority for the conversion of private preference into community policy. They, too, are influenced by the past and by the extramural world of state and nation, if not the world. Thus, past constitutions and charters shape current operations while the local political culture, a given of history, shapes attitudes and behaviors of both those demanding of the system and those operating it.

The essential process of the political system is to convert demands into policy. Not all demands are so treated, however, for some are regularly ignored, others are altered during the interplay of decisional forces and eventuate in much less than originally sought, while yet other demands overwhelm the political authorities by their inescapable force. The reasons for such differential response of the political system is a proper object for analysis. The answer promises to explain much of the value priorities within the community itself.

If all this activity is successful in its demands, a policy results—ordinance, administrative ruling, court order—which differentially distributes rewards of income, safety, or deference. These policy outputs must be implemented, however, but between the output and the outcome numerous factors can intervene to reduce the promise of policy. Whatever the implementation, though, the results return to the social environment of the community, there to affect differentially those demands and their group bases which initiated this entire policy cycle. That feedback effect, by rearranging or reinforcing existing resources in community life, can itself become the stimulus for another cycle in the decisional process. For feedback effects are potentially manifold: altering the axis of historical influence; modifying or amplifying extramural effects within the community; augmenting or blocking the demands or standing of local groups; and even affecting the tenure, outlook, and subsequent behavior of political authorities.

The stimulus of such a decisional cycle is a crisis, which, among other possible consequences, works its way into the political system in the form of demands. "Crisis" refers to a perceived threat or opportunity affecting the existing intergroup equilibrium of values and resources. The system's outputs in their feedback effect are designed to deal with that crisis, sometimes modifying or allaying it, sometimes aggravating it by inappropriate or ineffective policy. However, not all crises find outlets in the political system, nor are all crises community-shaking. When group protagonists in a crisis turn to the political system, there arises the possibility of a public decision, and when they turn to the economic, social, or religious systems, there is a private decisional possibility. But in either case, the impact on the community can be very great. In the private possibility, then, there exist quasi-public elements because of the scope of public effects of private decisions. For that reason, this book does not restrict itself simply to the political system but examines these quasi-public systems which influence the way many citizens live or whether, in Aristotle's terms, they live well.

The preceding components of the conceptual framework of this study of San Francisco are incorporated in figure I. Superimposed upon the entire local decisional process are the two major forces to be investigated in this book—the historical and the external. The historical force is represented by various decisions in the past (Time -4, -3, etc.) whose influence radiates through the sequences that constitute the next decisional event. Here is shown the model of crisis-generated demands, at Time $+1$, their group-based carriers reacting at Time $+2$, with effects on the political system (Time $+3$) that eventuate in outputs (Time $+4$). The process continues, in that the feedback effect of the first output (Time $+5$) affects the factors that gave rise to it and the community with which it must interact, eventuating in an outcome that, in turn, becomes another historical decision (Time -5). This combines with other past decisions to radiate influence through another cycle (CYCLE II) at Time $+6$, working on the next set of demands, carriers, political system, and outputs. This second set is influenced by the first as well as by the present, as noted at each stage by the subscript$_{1+2}$.

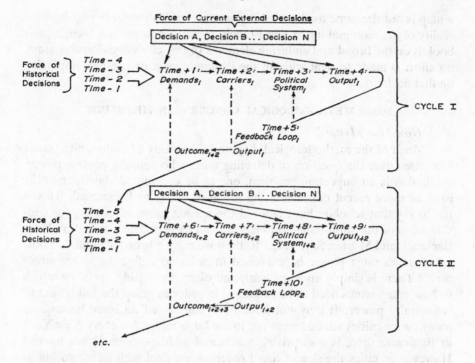

Force of Current External Decisions

Decision A, Decision B . . . Decision N

Force of Historical Decisions
Time - 4
Time - 3
Time - 2
Time - 1

Time +1: → Time +2: → Time +3: → Time +4:
Demands$_I$ Carriers$_I$ Political   Output$_I$
                            System$_I$

CYCLE I

Time +5:
Feedback Loop$_I$

Outcome$_{I+2}$ — Output$_I$

Decision A, Decision B . . . Decision N

Force of Historical Decisions
Time - 5
Time - 4
Time - 3
Time - 2
Time - 1

Time +6: → Time +7: → Time +8: → Time +9:
Demands$_{I+2}$ Carriers$_{I+2}$ Political   Output$_{I+2}$
                              System$_{I+2}$

CYCLE II

Time +10:
Feedback Loop$_2$

Outcome$_{I+2+3}$ — Output$_{I+2}$

etc.

Appendix fig. I. The interaction of historical and external forces upon community decision making.

The second force at work in the community's decision making is represented by those decisions made elsewhere. Of course, these external decisions are obviously historical forces also, as they must have existed in the near past when they began working on the local community. But they are analytically separated for this study as meaning only those large-scale and relatively recently made decisions. However, historical decisions include not only this subset, but also large external decisions made at more remote periods (such as the Progressive movement's success in the 1910s), as well as community-scale decisions made locally in the near or far past. In figure I, the lines of influence of Decision A could be duplicated for other such decisions (B . . . N), but were omitted here for the sake of clarity. Note that both major influences continue to operate at successive cycles of the process.

It is important here, however, to caution against reifying this framework. Rather, it is an abstraction designed to guide the research and analysis of this book. Like all models, this one serves to isolate major components of the phenomena to be investigated and suggests their sequence or connections; in short, it provides a heuristic organization of discrete data. Just as a map is not the same as the road it portrays, so this model is not the total reality of decision making in San Francisco. Also, because the focus of this book is on the broad and enduring elements of this city's decisional context, no effort is made to deal with all the demands, past or present, impinging on that field.

SOME METHODOLOGICAL CONCERNS IN THIS STUDY

How Many Issues?

Much of the methodological dispute in the study of community power has arisen over the question of detecting those who actually possess power. While that is an important problem, one to be considered shortly, another issue of more recent concern is the scope of issues to be studied. This is not to say that scholars have ignored the agenda issue, of course, for consideration of the "non-issue" problem was an early problem raised by Peter Bachrach and Morton S. Baratz.[7] Rather, we raise a broader point: on how many issues must power be exercised in order to define a "power structure"? There is simply no agreement, and often no consideration, on which or how many issues need to be examined in order to grasp the full nature of community power. It may not have been considered an issue because so many communities studied were not in the large range; for every New York or Baltimore there is a surprising number of middle- to small-size towns.[8] However, in cities the size of San Francisco, we deal with quantum jumps in population, which introduce new orders of demands, problems, and resources. No extant big-city research scans the full range of community decisions; indeed, even in analyses of small communities, few look for the entire inventory.[9] Attempting to review all such major decisions in even a moderate-size community is rather like painting the Golden Gate Bridge— once finished, it is necessary to start over.

Further, gathering such a complete inventory is handicapped by the possibility that the very structure of existing decisional processes constitutes a "mobilization of bias." That is, certain issues do not get on the public agenda or are viewed in only limited ways because those who captain the community institutions share common perceptions and values about the process and substance of decision making.[10] The result is that "nondecisions" tell us as much about local power as do actual (hence, publicized) decisions, but the former are rarely considered or unearthed in research.[11]

However intuitively correct such a limitation on research seems, Raymond E. Wolfinger's contention is persuasive, that "the core of the problem is the difficulty of identifying nondecisions, which seems generally to come back to determining people's 'real interests,' as opposed to what they say they want or what they are trying to get through political action." [12] As scholars have noted, there are insufficient criteria to define the entire issue inventory and hence they cannot define the criteria for even a sample of issues that would be "representative." Alternatively, to pick issues on a different basis, for example, that they are "important," merely introduces selection criteria which are inherently subjectivist and actually relativist. For it is obvious that what is important to one person may not be to all.[13]

What exists, then, are studies of highly selected sets of publicized decisions and actors, which vary with analyst, issue, era, instrument, and community. All these variations create some major problems of concept and method. Thus, as Claire Gilbert has revealed in followup analysis of scores of these case studies, time has been eroding the power context once ascribed to a given community.[14] This temporal dimension may be the most important factor working on the set of exchanges that mark community life. Further, the pattern of resource exchange for any one issue cannot be inferred as typical for other issues. The "reputational" and "decisional" methods can unearth different issues as being most "important."

These considerations provide powerful reminders that community power research lacks not only clearcut conceptualizations of its focal point but precise methods of studying its characteristics or of operationalizing its variables. It would not be inaccurate, albeit a bit blunt, to suggest that students of this subject have moved from a blissful naïveté to an awareness of major research problems and—in the comparative focus now popular—are roughly agreed on how to proceed for aggregate analysis, but not for individual case analysis. That even aggregate analysis proceeds with major uncertainties about the individual unit under study is another problem which this volume need not face.[15]

What Is Power and How Is It Discovered?

With full awareness of such problems, then, this study of power in San Francisco proceeds with certain assumptions. V. O. Key once observed laconically that it was simplest to define public opinion as "those opinions held by private persons which governments find it prudent to heed." [16] In parallel concept, we too assume that "community power" inheres in any private or public group which other groups find it prudent to pay attention to in calculating and conducting their own pursuit of resources. In these terms, the power of such a group is potential; the capability of this potential being converted into the exchange processes of community life must be reckoned with by others. The actual conversion of such a potential is what is meant by "influence," that perceived and effective use of resources to accomplish one's ends. Power *in posse* can become power *in esse,* but the transformation is not automatic, complete, or continuous.

This study is concerned far less with power than with influence. Partly this is because the potential quality of power contributes immensely to its conceptual softness and to the difficulties of detecting or measuring it in the real world of community life.[17] But "influence" has a perceptual—and hence measurable—reality about it in the decisional forums of community life. This influence is the phenomenon of persons and groups performing *visible* and *detectable* actions, for motives both professed and hidden (but *traceable*), with *overt* results. The present difficulties in conceptualizing, operationalizing, and hence uncovering purported covert behavior are beyond the capacity of social science today.[18]

The emphasis in this book upon the detectable has application also to the personal and group resources involved in the power play of San Francisco. The resources brought to bear—material and symbolic, intellectual and physical—are clearly various, but they are *there* where others, seeing them in action, can accordingly be guided in their own perceptions and behaviors. This power-in-action is the focus of this analysis exactly because it is the focus of those who engage in the transactional life of San Francisco or any other town. That is, power *in esse,* rather than *in posse,* is distinguished sharply in the lives of community actors. For them, the latter is like the fabled tree that crashes to the ground unheard; its sound is unreal and hence irrelevant to their lives. The tree that is just at hand and that is tottering uncertainly in the wind is the tree that captures their attention. For them, to recast Holmes's dictum about law, "The life of the community is not potentialities but experience."

Both critics and defenders of reputational approaches for measuring the power and influence of community actors have made contributions to an understanding of this matter.[19] Actors may misjudge, by overestimating, the potential of one group, making it out to be more powerful than it could be if it tried. This "inflation of power" may well account for some of the conservatism of political actors, particularly when they overestimate the weight of business in community power. But this illustrates not power *in posse* but power *in esse,* for it is based on past experience in a real world.

Actors may well misperceive reputation for reality, it is true, but the behavioral question is: By *what* perception do they guide their actions? No matter that their decision is not what "independent" observers claim to perceive. In this respect we must bear in mind a basic finding of social psychology that it is people's *beliefs* about reality which guides their actions, not what that reality is judged by others to be "actually." This is not to deny that there is a reality beyond the individual's perception and conception of it; to deny it is to invite the paranoia of solipsism. Nevertheless, on such matters, the elaboration of thinking can become endless and profitless.

It seems a parsimonious and initial approach, therefore, to ask as wide a range of community actors as possible how they perceive the interplay of influences in public decisions. Both their general perceptions of the total process (defining the community-wide field) and their specific perceptions of particular processes (defining issue-area fields) provide us at least a preliminary guide to the decisional context. If enough actors (holding for the while what constitutes "enough") agree on all or part of these perceptions, to *deny* that this most reliably describes what "actually" occurs is to suggest that those persons most deeply experienced have been seized by a collective madness.

None of the conceptualization urged here denies that the amount of power and influence may vary with person or group, that analysis of actual decisions provides the most useful technique for checking actors' perception, or that there are different kinds of power and influence. Indeed, these propositions are important frameworks and methods for the analysis here. But to give them empirical content always requires at some point an acceptance of the perception and judgment of community actors. For that reason, all community analysts are tied in some degree to the perceptions offered them by their subjects. The only way to escape this perceptual bondage would be to have an analyst accompany every actor in every one of a set of decisions during every waking moment.[20] That seems beyond the research capability of scholars and the tolerance of public actors.

There is a final caution against relying on the "independent" observer's evaluation of "who wins" and "who loses" rather than on the judgment of the actors. It is the almost inescapable danger which anthropologists had to face early in their discipline's history. This is the likelihood that the outside observer will apply his own values to observed behavior. The danger here is not that the observer evaluates normatively what he thinks he sees. Rather, it is that what he thinks he sees has been preordained by what, through socialization, his values have taught him to see. It is this fallacy which seems to underlie some, if not much, of the "elitist-pluralist" arguments. In some cases, ideology provided the assumptions about morality, which shaped the methods employed, which in turn generated the "reality" the analysts thereupon perceived. This is not merely ideologues arguing about the results of empirical analysis; it is ideologues divining results they expect to find. The major value of this conceptualization and method is that they maximize the chances of presenting the worlds of power and influence, of issues and values, as these are seen and felt by those most active in them. Such information provides a background against which to judge how thorough their perceptions are and what the consequences are for those in the city who do not participate in such activity.

Data Collection Techniques

Obtaining such information involved positional, reputational, and decisional methods. Those in high positions in government, law firms, banks, and business groups, news media, ethnic groups, and political parties provided one element of leaders surveyed in 1968. Another was obtained by the common process of "snowballing" names suggested by the first group and others, purportedly knowledgeable about local affairs. Decisions to be studied were arrived at by combining the judgment of these sources on issue areas most reflective of how decisions were generally made in San Francisco. Decisions in these areas were studied over several years by interviewing those involved in them and by analyzing documentary sources, thereby providing ongoing case studies, which illuminate political and social processes. Subsequent interviews in 1971–1973 of a sample of the original list of those interviewed provided information on perceptions of major changes working on these processes as the new decade opened.

While this combination of techniques incorporates many advantages of each, it also is not without faults. Not all groups with positions of possible influence were included; missing are spokesmen for neighborhood homeowner associations, organized crime, the underground press, or every religion. However, some of these were so numerous that their study exceeded available resources, some were so ephemeral that "leaders" and "structure" changed overnight; some simply couldn't be found; and some were overwhelmingly regarded by those interviewed as not visible in usual decisional forums. Nor were all positions contacted, even within a single major group. However, interviews of several major bank presidents, lawyers, and governmental officials with contacts in the banking world agree that few bankers had local interest, and even when they had, they acted much alike in motive and interests. Further extending the list of bankers interviewed would produce only minor gains.

Nor were all decisions in a given issue area studied. However, agreement among interviewees that the chosen decisional event was characteristic of the universe of how such issues were dealt with met the requirement of plumbing the perceptions of those most involved in the city's decisional life. Such selection escaped the subjectivist problem of what constitutes "important" and "representative" decisions. The issue is scanned less by the eye of the author than by those most involved in the scene. Not all empirical elements of a chosen decision may have been uncovered by this research. However, all standard research techniques for such work were employed, including experience gained in similar community study.[21] Specific instruments employed are discussed in the text.

RESEARCH DIRECTIONS

This study has emphasized the force of history and the outside in San Francisco's decisional context, and the last section suggests that such conditions prevail in other cities in varying degrees. This effort is offered as a contribution to conceptualizing urban policy and community power studies. It also has pointed out along the way that such empirical analysis raises theoretical and normative questions in which all urban studies are embedded. But a major difficulty in developing urban theory—whether about political or social processes—has been the difficulty of operationalizing subsidiary concepts in terms that permit comparative analysis.[22] While what is offered here is far from solving that basic problem, it does posit dimensions of time and social change operating in all cities, arising out of historical and contemporary events—some local, some national in scope—which differentially affect the resources, actors, and issues in the local allocational process.

Further analysis along these lines is amenable to methods of the case study or macro-analysis. The former is the genre of this book, of course, providing intimate details and nuances about the historical, internal, and external aspects of community life. But in the shift from micro- to macro-analysis, the tasks of specifying and operationalizing the variables which delimit the concepts of historical and external forces are not simple. One research strategy would be the compilation of case studies utilizing these concepts; while the usual caveats against comparing cases derived and analyzed differently still apply, such a study would permit a rough, preliminary inspection of aggregate data. Illustrative is Gilbert's secondary analysis of 166 community studies since 1900, which supports the conceptualization offered here.[23] Another strategy lies in use of a national community sample for deriving original data as in Terry Clark's work, or, with Daniel J. Elazar, in evaluating the differentiating impact of federal programs among communities within the constants of a state's constitution and politics.[24]

While these approaches would expand our knowledge of urban political processes, the maximum strategy is not yet feasible. This is the compilation of indicators of intracity transactions of a kind suggested by Deutsch for internation and intercity comparisons.[25] For example, indicators of the flow of capital, alterations in opportunity structures, and resource consumptions would put empirical meat on these concepts of "axes" and "residual allocations." That most inelastic of all resources—time—might be a surrogate for many of these interactions. As noted in the text, the amount of time that the city's schoolmen spent working out requirements imposed by Sacramento or Washington is one measure, and any growth or decay in that figure from the past would trace the historical force. Recent concern with the relationship between communities' structural features and their political and policy characteristics is a step in this direction,[26] but more use of interjurisdictional and longitudinal measures is needed. Such specification would further enhance the difficult task of systematically describing those interactions at the heart of the allocation process. Thus, cost-benefit analysis suggests ways of defining and measuring demand patterns and the costs of reaching decisions on those demands.[27] A different pattern seems likely for policies that distribute new resources and values, redistribute those that exist, or regulate the acquisition of such resources.

The differentiation in urban policies and processes implied in such grounded theory should not confuse the issue, for such local variation may well demonstrate some national commonality. That commonality most likely lies in a historical perspective that views local change as rising from national forces of bureaucratization and urbanization that affect private and public resources and institutions alike. Implicit in this perspective is a concept of urban sequence. As Richard L. Forstall has shown, American communities show structural characteristics of great variety, far beyond the limited classifications that demographers usually employ.[28] Age of community is suggestive of sequence, for Leo Schnore found that cities of similar age show remarkably characteristic attributes.[29] However, no urban theory today has the evidence to verify a sequence of urban development, like that of stellar sequences. While comparisons are misleading, social scientists do employ "prevailing metaphors." If so, the verbal linkages between stellar and urban change are interesting, for both are said to grow and explode, decay and collapse, shift and transform, and both have cores. The pessimist may note that the end of the stellar cycle is a dark, dead cinder. The optimist may note that the cycle is a very long one, however. But until we are able to specify urban *interactions* like those involved in resource allocations, instead of relying on urban *structural* characteristics, we have little data for testing a sequential model.

Along the way, scholars must return to the question of Aristotle—what difference in the life of citizens do these decision-making differences make? Some of the differences are quantitative, some qualitative, and in the effort to sort out the two, the best of contemporary social science should be dedicated. It is both a normative and a behavioral question to ask what difference a difference makes in social life. But this mixed query is the central concern of all who, in Aristotle's steps, compare social institutions and processes.

APPENDIX II

Bay Area Regional Organizations

REGIONAL PLANNING

Association of Bay Area Governments. 1961. Membership: eighty-four of the area's ninety-four cities, eight of nine* counties. The Council on Governments for the area; advisory powers otherwise.

LAND USE

Bay Conservation and Development Commission. 1965, 1969. All nine counties. Regulates all filling and draining of the bay, with some jurisdiction over developments inside a 100-foot strip inland.

California Coastal Zone Conservation Commission, which has three regional commissions touching on counties of the bay. 1972. Develops coastal zoning plan, with regional commissions issuing permits for, or prohibiting, development on coast.

Delta Advisory Planning Council. 1972. Parts of five counties bordering the Sacramento-San Joaquin River Delta. Plans for conservation and development for the delta. Cooperative, advisory agency.

TRANSPORTATION

Alameda–Contra Costa Transit District, 1956. Two counties. Public transportation system, with links to San Francisco. Tax levying power.

Bay Area Rapid Transit District. 1957, 1962. Three counties, including San Francisco. Planned, constructed, and operates rapid transit system. Tax levying power.

* The nine counties are Alameda, Contra Costa, Marin, Napa, San Francisco, San Mateo, Santa Clara, Solano, and Sonoma. The area is larger than the state of Connecticut and was the home of over 4,600,000 in 1970.

Golden Gate Bridge, Highway and Transportation District. 1928, 1969. Four whole counties and parts of two others; includes San Francisco. Provides balanced transportation system in the Golden Gate corridor. Non-taxing special district, supported by bridge tolls.

Metropolitan Transportation Commission. 1970. Nine counties. Develops regional plan for transportation system.

Skyline Scenic Recreation Route. 1970. Four counties (including San Francisco) and six cities within them. Creates and develops this recreation route. Cooperating jurisdictions.

WATER AND AIR USES

Bay Area Sewage Services Agency. 1971. Nine counties. Plans and implements regional water quality management. Financed by counties.

Bay Area Air Pollution Control District. 1955. Seven counties and part of two others. Studies air contaminants and controls air pollution by enacting and enforcing regulations. Tax levying power.

Bay Counties Water and Environmental Committee. 1954. Nine counties plus five others. Forum for discussion and cooperation in presenting mutual problem to state and federal governments. Cooperative, mutual consent agency.

Delta Water Agency. 1968. Parts of six counties lying in the delta. Negotiates with state and federal authorities on maintenance of water quality. Tax levying power.

Water Quality Control Board. 1949, 1969. Coordinates governmental and private agencies in protecting water quality. Regional agency of state agency.

MISCELLANEOUS

Health: Bay Area Regional Comprehensive Health Planning Council. 1968. Nine counties. Plans and reviews local government health care and health maintenance and protection. Cooperative agency.

Libraries: East Bay and North Bay Cooperatives. 1966, 1960. Two clusters of subregional city and county library systems. Improves use of collections, furnishes cooperative services. Cooperating jurisdictions; the latter a political entity under state law.

Municipal: Valley Community Services District. 1953, 1960. Two counties in East Bay. Gives district powers of small city, for example, sewage disposal, water, fire protection, recreation, garbage and refuse disposal. Tax levying power.

Parks: East Bay Regional Park District. 1934. Sections of two counties. Develops and maintains regional parks. Tax levying powers.

Notes

NOTES TO CHAPTER 1

1. Reflecting this historical tie are the following works: Mel Scott, *History of City Planning in America Since 1890* (Berkeley and Los Angeles: University of California Press, 1969); Constance M. Green, *American Cities in the Growth of the Nation* (New York: Harper Colophon, 1965); Peter Hall, *World Cities* (New York: McGraw-Hill, 1966).

2. D. R. Leister, *California Politics and Problems, 1964–1968: A Selective Bibliography* (Berkeley: Institute of Governmental Studies, University of California, 1969); same title and source, David Leuthold, for 1900–1963, published 1965; and W. Brook Graves, *San Francisco: A Selected Bibliography* (Washington, D.C.: Library of Congress, 1968), pp. 22–25.

3. Walton Bean, *Boss Ruef's San Francisco* (Berkeley and Los Angeles: University of California Press, 1952).

4. For depiction of these radii for Milwaukee, see John C. Bollens and Henry J. Schmandt, *The Metropolis* (New York: Harper & Row, 1965), p. 49.

5. Robert C. Wood, *1400 Governments* (Garden City, N.Y.: Doubleday Anchor, 1961), chap. 2; but see the measurement problems involved in Terry Clark, "Urban Typologies and Political Outputs," in Brian J. L. Berry, ed., *City Classification Handbook: Methods and Applications* (New York: Wiley-Interscience, 1972), chap. 5.

6. For a full development of this variety, see Oliver Williams et al., *Suburban Differences and Metropolitan Policies* (Philadelphia: University of Pennsylvania Press, 1965).

7. The analytical framework is drawn from David Easton, *The Political System* (New York: Knopf, 1953); *A Framework for Political Analysis* (Englewood Cliffs, N.J.: Prentice-Hall, 1965); and *A Systems Analysis of Political Life* (New York: Wiley, 1965). For application to a major city, Toronto, see Harold Kaplan, *Urban Political System* (New York: Columbia University Press, 1967).

8. Manfred Kochen and Karl W. Deutsch, "Toward a Rational Theory of Decentralization: Some Implications of a Mathematical Approach," *American Political Science Review,* 63 (1969), 738.

1. The following is expanded on in the extensive histories of the city and the state; for a convenient summary, see Walton Bean, *California: An Interpretative History* (New York: McGraw-Hill, 1968); Oscar Lewis, *From Mission to Metropolis* (Berkeley: Howell-North, 1966); and their bibliographies. Much of the economic analysis of the following section relies on James E. Vance, Jr., *Geography and Urban Evolution in the San Francisco Bay Area* (Berkeley: Institute of Governmental Studies, University of California, 1964); and Martyn J. Bowden, "The Dynamics of City Growth: An Historical Geography of the San Francisco Central District, 1850–1931," 2 vols., Ph.D. dissertation, University of California, Berkeley, 1967.

2. Attorney William Coblentz.

3. Vance, p. 17.

4. Ibid., p. 18.

5. Marybeth Branaman, *Growth of the San Francisco Bay Area Urban Core* (Berkeley: Bureau of Business and Economic Research, University of California, 1956), Report 8, chap. 3, and Bowden, vol. 2, provide the data used in the following sections.

6. Sam B. Warner, Jr., *Streetcar Suburbs* (Cambridge: Harvard University Press, 1962); for application of this transportation thesis to other sites, see Frederick M. Wirt et al., *On The City's Rim* (Lexington, Mass.: Heath, 1972), chaps. 2 and 3, passim.

7. Branaman, p. 26, citing San Francisco Department of City Planning, *Local Shopping Districts in San Francisco,* November 1952, p. 9.

8. *San Francisco Business,* the San Francisco Chamber of Commerce monthly magazine, provides full economic reports on this and other aspects of recent growth. See issues on construction and wholesale-retail trade, February/June 1966; June 1968.

9. Ibid., May 1966; May 1969.

10. Ibid., April 1967; May 1968.

11. Weekly Bulletin, San Francisco Dept. Public Health, Nov. 11, 1972, and Bureau of Census, *1970 Census of Population and Housing* (Washington, D.C.: Government Printing Office, 1971).

12. Robert C. Tryon, *Identification of Social Areas by Cluster Analysis* (Berkeley and Los Angeles: University of California Press, 1955); and his "Predicting Group Differences in Cluster Analysis: The Social Area Problem," *Multivariate Behavioral Research,* 2 (1967), 453–475.

13. Tryon, "Predicting Group Differences," p. 467.

14. Samuel Lubell, *The Future of American Politics* (New York: Harper & Bros., 1952).

15. One evidence of the consistency of the intercensal stability of these neighborhoods is the extraordinary degree to which they predict political behavior. Tryon found a high relation between 1940 life-styles and the vote for Roosevelt that year, not a new finding, of course. But these 1940 life-style characteristics correlated almost just as highly years later in the vote for mayor in 1947 (R = .90), a set of referenda and election with a political cast (R = .85), a series of tax referenda issues in 1954 (R = .82), and even referenda in 1954 on which there was an ethnic or religious conflict (R = .66). This work not only suggests that political attitudes are predictable from demographic features in the same time frame; it also argues that demography, because of its stability over time, makes possible surprisingly accurate predictions—in this case, fourteen years into the future.

16. Chamber of Commerce, *San Francisco Business,* March 1966, pp. 21–27, and January 1970, pp. 15–18. Jeffrey K. Hadden and Edgar F. Borgatta, *American Cities: Their Social Characteristics* (Chicago: Rand McNally, 1965), p. 79.

17. U. S. Commission on Civil Rights, *Hearings on Housing in San Francisco, May 4–6, 1960* (Washington: Government Printing Office, 1960), pp. 549ff.; Irving Babow, "Discrimination in Places of Public Accommodation: Findings of the San Francisco Civil Rights Inventory," *Journal of Intergroup Relations,* 2 (1961); reports of San Francisco Commission on Human Rights.

18. Illustrative of this literature on American class, life-style, attitudes, and policy differences are the following: Norval D. Glenn and J. L. Simmons, "Are Regional Cultural Differences Diminishing?" *Public Opinion Quarterly,* 31 (1967), 176–193; Samuel C. Patterson, "The Political Cultures of the American States," *Journal of Politics,* 30 (1968), 187–209; Daniel J. Elazar, *American Federalism,* (New York: Crowell, 1966); Ira Sharkansky, *Regionalism in American Politics* (Indianapolis: Bobbs-Merrill, 1969). On sex and income differences, see Lester W. Milbrath, *Political Participation* (Chicago: Rand McNally, 1965), chap. 5; V. O. Key, Jr., *Public Opinion and American Democracy* (New York: Knopf, 1961), chap. 6.

19. For the fullest picture of this phenomenon, see Ted Gurr and Hugh Graham, *Violence in America* (New York: Random House, 1969).

20. For development of this thesis as it applies to modern San Francisco, see Howard S. Becker and Irving L. Horowitz, "The Culture of Civility," *trans-action,* April, 1970, pp. 12–19.

NOTES TO CHAPTER 3

1. These queries, and the controversy over them, are explored in Willis D. Hawley and Frederick M. Wirt, eds., *The Search for Community Power,* 2nd ed. (Englewood Cliffs, N.J.: Prentice-Hall, 1974). See also W. D. Hawley and James H. Svara, *The Study of Community Power: A Bibliographic Review* (Santa Barbara: ABC-CLIO, 1972).

2. "We must therefore look at the elements of which the state is composed, in order that we may see in what the different kinds of rule differ from one another, and whether any scientific result can be attained about each one of them. . . . Our purpose is to consider what form of political community is best of all for those who are most able to realize their ideal of life." Aristotle, *Politics.*

3. Prototypical of this model are Robert S. Lynd and Helen M. Lynd, *Middletown* and *Middletown in Transition* (New York: Harcourt and Brace, 1929, 1937); and Floyd Hunter, *Community Power Structure* (Chapel Hill: University of North Carolina Press, 1953).

4. For a close study of this transition, see Frederick M. Wirt, *Politics of Southern Equality* (Chicago: Aldine, 1970). A broader analysis is found in Hanes Walton, Jr., *Black Politics* (Philadelphia: Lippincott, 1972).

5. Robert H. Salisbury, "Urban Politics: The New Convergence of Power," *Journal of Politics,* 26 (1964), 775–797.

6. Frederick M. Wirt et al., *On The City's Rim* (Lexington, Mass.: Heath, 1972), Part 4, case studies.

7. This smacks of "infinite regress," as cautioned against in Robert A. Dahl, "A Critique of the Ruling Elite Model," *American Political Science Review,* 52 (1958), 463–469.

8. With small change, this list was that developed by Charles Bonjean, "Dimensions of Power Structure: Some Problems in Conceptualization and Measurement," in Frederick M. Wirt, ed., *Future Research Directions in Community Power Study* (Berkeley: Institute of Governmental Studies, University of California, 1971), p. 31.

9. This seminal treatment of the problem is Peter Bachrach and Morton S. Baratz, "Two Faces of Power," *American Political Science Review,* 56 (1962), 947–952; and their "Decisions and Nondecisions: An Analytical Framework," ibid., 57 (1963), 632–642.

10. Inspection of nine persons shows how little they share even common involvement—much less agreement—on these issues. The table below calculates the number of times each possible pair of nine men were involved in at least five of the seven "high-involvement" issues seen in table 4. If there is some kind of association among like-minded men, as a minimum they should be commonly involved in such issues. That is, each pair of men in the table below should be commonly involved in most of these issues. But that condition is met in only two of the thirty-six possible pairs, both involving one man with two other men (A–D and A–H).

San Francisco Observers' Co-Involvement
on Seven Issues

Observer

	A	B	C	D	E	F	G	H	I
A	—								
B	2	—							
C	3	0	—						
D	6	2	2	—					
E	4	1	2	4	—				
F	4	1	2	3	1	—			
G	4	1	1	3	2	2	—		
H	6	2	1	5	4	3	3	—	
I	4	1	1	3	2	2	4	3	—
Total issue 63	15	5	9	15	11	6	5	9	7

11. This reflects a general trend noted in Salisbury, "Urban Politics."

12. For two decades prior to 1968, a good indicator of the chances of a proposal, according to observers, was the recommendation of the San Francisco *Chronicle*. In each of the five-year periods from 1948 to 1967, successful recommendation percentages were, successively, 77, 91, 78, and 71 percent for all issues in November elections. The paper's overall rate of success was 79 percent for 237 issues. However, the independent power of this paper to achieve these electoral results is highly problematical. A more likely explanation is its sensitivity to the prevailing viewpoints of major community groups among whom editors and reporters moved.

Another analyst has found some marginal influence of the *Chronicle* and other California papers; see James E. Gregg, "Newspaper Editorial Endorsements and California Elections, 1948–1962," *Journalism Quarterly,* 42 (1965), 532–538, and an expanded version from the Institute of Governmental Affairs, University of California, Davis, 1966. However, a Los Angeles study, looking directly at voters' ballots in a 1964 study, found little evidence of newspaper effect; see John F. Mueller, "Voting on the Propositions: Ballot Patterns and Historical Trends in California," *American Political Science Review,* 63 (1969), 1197–1212.

NOTES TO CHAPTER 4

1. V. O. Key, Jr., *Public Opinion and American Democracy* (New York: Knopf, 1961), pp. 8, 14.

2. Lucien Pye and Sidney Verba, eds., *Political Culture and Political Development* (Princeton: Princeton University Press, 1965), p. 513. The following section has relied on concepts and data from Samuel C. Patterson, "The Political Cultures of the American States," *Journal of Politics,* 30 (1968), 187–209; and for California poli-

tics, successive articles in *Western Political Quarterly* during the 1960s by Totten J. Anderson and Eugene C. Lee, *The Politics of Nonpartisanship* (Berkeley and Los Angeles: University of California Press, 1960), hereafter referred to as Lee, *PNP;* Willis D. Hawley, *Nonpartisan Urban Politics* (New York: Wiley Interscience, 1973); and sources noted in the bibliographies in chap. 1, note 2. For a brief survey, see, Joseph P. Harris, *California Politics,* 4th ed. (San Francisco: Chandler, 1967).

3. Alexander Callow, Jr., "San Francisco's Blind Boss," *Pacific Historical Review,* 25 (1956), 261.

4. George E. Mowry, *The California Progressives* (Berkeley and Los Angeles: University of California Press, 1951).

5. Callow, pp. 261–262.

6. Lincoln Steffens, *The Shame of the Cities* (New York: Hill and Wang, 1957); Harold Zink, *City Bosses in the United States* (Durham, N.C.: Duke University Press, 1930); William L. Riordan, *Plunkitt of Tammany Hall* (New York: Knopf, 1948).

7. Once, the chairman of the board of education, facing an indictment for fraud, was nominated for Congress by Buckley. What must be the oddest directive in the history of American education belongs to Buckley. Some boys had stolen a fourteen-room schoolhouse and had moved it sixteen blocks before the boss heard of it, at which time, he later wrote, "I issued an imperative order to 'bring that schoolhouse back. . . .'" All observations on Buckley are drawn from Callow.

8. See both Steffens and Zink.

9. Callow, p. 271, citing reminiscences in the *San Francisco Bulletin* by Martin Kelly, September 1 through November 28, 1917. What with the published autobiographies of their malfeasances of Ruef and Kelly among others, San Francisco's bosses were remarkably frank and sophisticated writers.

10. For a fuller history, see Mowry, *California Progressives.*

11. Full details are found in Walton Bean, *Boss Ruef's San Francisco* (Berkeley and Los Angeles: University of California Press, 1952).

12. Michael Rogin, "Progressivism and the California Electorate," *Journal of American History,* 55 (1968), 297–314.

13. We follow here Alexander Saxton, "San Francisco Labor and the Populist and Progressive Insurgencies," *Pacific Historical Review,* 34 (1965), 421–438.

14. Rogin expands Saxton's data base to cover the whole state to make this point of the labor basis of Progressivism. See also his "California Populism and the 'System of 1896,'" *Western Political Quarterly,* 22 (1969), 179–196, for the impact on Democrats here.

15. The evidence of this analysis is drawn from George H. Higginbottom, "EPIC by the Bay: A Voting Study of the Gubernatorial Election of 1934 in San Francisco," M.A. thesis, San Francisco State, 1965; Homer B. Thompson, "An Analysis of Voting Behavior in San Francisco, 1936–1946," M.A. thesis, Stanford, 1947. The former used scattergrams and the latter factor analysis (maybe the first use in election studies). For the Chicago comparison, see Thompson, p. 33.

16. Analysis of these more recent events may be found in the *Western Political Quarterly* in years succeeding each election; Francis Carney, *The Rise of the Democratic Clubs in California* (New York: Holt, 1958); Harris, *California Politics;* Robert J. Pitchell, "Electoral System and Voting Behavior: The Case of California's Cross-filing," *Western Political Quarterly,* 12 (1959), 234.

17. Eugene C. Lee, "The Two Arenas and the Two Worlds of California Politics," in Eugene C. Lee, ed., *The California Governmental Process* (Boston: Little, Brown, 1966), p. 47.

18. Totten J. Anderson and Eugene C. Lee, "The 1964 Election in California,"

Western Political Quarterly, 18 (1965), 465, show the persistence of this division from 1958 to 1964, as do Raymond E. Wolfinger and Fred I. Greenstein, "Comparing Political Regions: The Case of California," *American Political Science Review,* 63 (1969), 85–85, for later years.

19. Eugene C. Lee, *California Votes* (Berkeley: Institute of Governmental Studies, University of California, 1963), pp. 38–42; Appendix, p. 165.

20. Pitchell averages for decade. The following data are drawn from Lee, *California Votes,* and the two special reports on the city's congressmen in Ralph Nader Congress Project, *Citizens Look at Congress,* August, 1972.

21. Data from *Municipal Yearbook, 1968* (Washington: International City Managers Association, 1968), p. 58. By 1967, 65 percent of all cities had nonpartisan elections. The figures for the big versus small cities are 58 versus 88 percent.

22. Lee, *PNP,* p. 12.

23. See Lee, *PNP,* and W. D. Hawley, *Nonpartisan Urban Politics,* passim. One case study of CDC local involvement is James Q. Wilson, *The Amateur Democrat* (Chicago: University of Chicago Press, 1962), chap. 4; Wilson insightfully notes the parallel between the CDC and earlier Populist and Progressive movements, on pp. 24–28.

24. Lee, *PNP,* pp. 102–105.

25. Wilson, pp. 101–102.

26. Don Koepp, "Nonpartisan Elections in the San Francisco Bay Area," *Public Affairs Report* (Berkeley: Bureau of Public Administration, University of California, August, 1962), vol. 3, 4. See also for similar statewide findings, Lee, *PNP,* chap. 9. See also R. B. Dixon, "Predicting Voter Turnout in City Elections," Ph.D. dissertation, University of California, Berkeley, 1966.

27. Charles R. Adrian, "A Typology for Nonpartisan Elections," *Western Political Quarterly,* 12 (1959), 449–458.

28. The 65 include 22 superior court judges, 18 municipal court judges, 11 supervisors, 7 board of education members, mayor, district attorney, sheriff, city attorney, treasurer, assessor, and public defender. Of these, 18 are elected directly and at large while the other 47 are merely confirmed by the voters after appointment.

29. Eugene C. Lee, *PNP,* p. 65, found 71 percent of the incumbents victorious in his six cities in the period 1932–1955; James E. Gregg, *Newspaper Endorsements and Local Elections in California* (Davis: Institute of Government Affairs, University of California, 1966), p. 18, in a study of much bigger cities for the period 1948–1962 (including San Francisco and Los Angeles), found much higher rates: 93.4 percent for city councilmen, 96.8 percent for county supervisors, and 83.3 percent for mayor.

30. It might give him formal representation in higher state party councils, but those too were of little importance. It might influence some Democrats to hear that the committee was quietly supporting certain candidates in a primary, but this was illegal and of dubious effectiveness.

31. Major money backers in 1968 were Emmet Solomon, president of Crocker Bank; Charles de Bretteville, Bank of California; Otto Miller, Standard Oil; Donald Russell, chairman of the board, Southern Pacific; Michael Hellman, Sutro & Co.

32. See Bureau of the Census, *Congressional District Data Book, 88th Congress* (Washington: Government Printing Office, 1963), pp. 38ff. Until a redistricting in the mid-1950s, the separating line was a huge C-shape running north and south from the end of the docks.

33. *Congressional Quarterly Almanac, 1965* (Washington: Congress Quarterly, 1965), pp. 88–92, shows agreement on five of fifteen acts that year. There is little pattern in the five they agreed on. The Voting Rights Act was a mighty bipartisan effort in the House, and laws liberalizing immigration, supporting the Arts and Hu-

manities Foundation and highway beautification are very salient in San Francisco—but so then were others on which they disagreed. A subsequent voting-record study on other major issues of the early 1970s shows again Mailliard agreeing with Burton on only one-third of fifteen major acts; see Michael Barone et al., *The Almanac of American Politics—1972* (New York: Gambit, 1972), pp. 51–52, and the same source for ratings by interest groups which support the text's interpretation of their votes.

34. For closer study of this factor in California, see Edmond Costantini, "Intraparty Attitude Conflict: Democratic Party Leadership in California," *Western Political Quarterly,* 16 (1963), 956–972; Costantini and Kenneth H. Craig, "Competing Elites Within a Political Party: A Study of Republican Leadership," ibid., 22 (1969), 879–903. That this is a national phenomenon under some conditions is seen in Thomas Flinn, "Party Responsibility in the States: Some Causal Factors," *American Political Science Review,* 58 (1964), 60–71.

35. Income maps of San Francisco employed here were from Chamber of Commerce, *San Francisco Business,* March 1966.

36. League of Women Voters, *An Introduction to the City—San Francisco* (1967), p. 29.

37. Ibid., p. 28.

38. Aside from Morrison versus Tamaras and Tinney, the comparative rank order of each man's vote among the thirteen districts showed some relationship. Spearman correlations for Tamaras-Tinney and Blake-Boas of +0.87 and +0.93 showed unusually similar voting decisions in these districts.

39. His campaign cochairmen were William Coblentz (Jewish, liberal), Joseph Alioto (Catholic, Italian, moderate), and Frank Keesling (Republican WASP). As cochairmen of his executive committee, he had William Porter (old-line Democratic lawyer) and Roger Lapham, Jr. (Republican businessman, son of former Republican mayor). His vice-chairman included a Democratic women's leader with state contacts, two blacks, a national committeewoman, a Nisei civil rights figure, a Latin American attorney, and a Republican businessman.

40. Gene Geisler, "California's Sixth Congressional District, 1962: A Study in Political Disorganization," unpublished paper, San Francisco State College. His focus was on Mailliard's 1962 campaign.

41. Koepp, "Nonpartisan Elections," p. 20.

42. Lee, *PNP,* pp. 170–171, rates nonpartisanship's democratic effects much more highly for the decades prior to 1960. But of this representative quality, he too judges the outcome to be "pretty bad."

43. Hawley, p. 173. For evidence of the partisan bias of nonpartisanship, see Hawley's analysis; for his suggestions about creating a more effective and democratic local party system, see pp. 149–163.

44. Walter Dean Burnham and John Sprague, "Additive and Multiplicative Models of the Voting Universe: The Case of Pennsylvania: 1960–1968," *American Political Science Review,* 64 (1970), 471–490, demonstrate the great stability of opposing party coalitions but also the conditions of alienation that produce a Wallace movement when the parties fail to meet increasingly felt needs. On the general role of minority parties and innovation, see Theodore Lowi, "Toward Functionalism in Political Science: The Case of Innovation in Party Systems," ibid., 62 (1963), 570–583.

45. Costantini, "Interparty Attitude Conflict," Costantini and Craig, "Competing Elites," and the sources cited therein demonstrate such an orientation among party cadre in California. On the national phenomena, Herbert J. McCloskey et al., "Issue Conflicts and Consensus Among Party Leaders and Followers," *American Political Science Review,* 54 (1960), 406–427.

46. Daniel Bell, *The End of Ideology* (Glencoe, Ill.: Free Press, 1960), pp. 115–136.

47. Lee, *PNP*, pp. 170–171.

48. On the San Francisco scene, the Examiner's Dick Nolan and Guy Wright and editor Bruce Brugmann of the *Bay Guardian* have consistently illustrated and attacked such resistance to responsibility and efficiency among civil servants. An annual event is the study and report of a special Grand Jury, which regularly condemns bureaucratic insensitivity, confusion, and inefficiency. Little results from any of these efforts.

NOTES TO CHAPTER 5

1. Anwar H. Syed, *The Political Theory of American Government* (New York: Random House, 1966).

2. Charles Adrian and Charles Press, *Governing Urban America* (New York: McGraw Hill, 1961).

3. For the broader movement sketched here, see Eric F. Goldman, *Rendezvous with Destiny* (New York: Vintage Books, Random House, 1961), and Richard Hofstadter, *The Age of Reform* (New York: Vintage Books, Random House, 1961).

4. Lincoln Steffens, *The Shame of the Cities* (New York: Hill and Wang, 1957), originally published in 1904. A more detailed, scholarly analysis is Harold Zink, *City Bosses in the United States* (Durham: Duke University Press, 1930). For the acme of this phenomenon in San Francisco, see, Walton Bean, *Boss Ruef's San Francisco* (Berkeley and Los Angeles: University of California Press, 1952). It has been convincingly argued that Ruef lacked most of the attributes of the typical boss of the era; see James Walsh, "Abe Ruef Was No Boss: Machine Politics, Reform and San Francisco," *California Historical Society*, 24 (February–March 1972).

5. On the socially useful nature of graft, see Daniel Bell, *The End of Ideology* (Glencoe, Ill.: Free Press, 1960), pp. 115–136.

6. Adrian and Press.

7. Oliver Williams and Charles R. Adrian, *Four Cities* (Philadelphia: University of Pennsylvania Press, 1963).

8. Unless otherwise indicated, the following references to events prior to 1911 are drawn from Mildred P. Martin, "City Government in San Francisco: A Half-Century of Charter Development," M.A. thesis, University of California, Berkeley, 1911.

9. Ibid., p. 11.

10. Ibid., pp. 21–22.

11. For brief review of this phenomenon and evaluation of writing on the subject, see Walton Bean, *California: An Interpretive History* (New York: McGraw-Hill, 1968), chap. 12. A recent popular, sympathetic portrayal is George R. Stewart, *Committee of Vigilance* (Boston: Houghton Mifflin, 1964).

12. Martin, p. 18.

13. Ibid., p. 20.

14. School decentralization and community control of schools, publicized in the 1960s as the wave of the future, were actually our *earliest* administrative structure. See Frederick M. Wirt and Michael W. Kirst, *The Political Web of American Schools* (Boston: Little, Brown, 1972), chap. 2, for the general pattern; and for the San Francisco pattern see Lee S. Dolson, "The Administration of the San Francisco Public Schools, 1847 to 1947," Ph.D. dissertation, University of California, Berkeley, 1964.

15. This instrument of corruption is seen frequently in the analyses of Steffens and Zink (see n. 4 above).

16. Goldman, *Rendezvous,* and Hofstadter, *Age of Reform.* For accounts by lead-

ers, see Richard S. Childs, *Civic Victories* (New York: Harper, 1952); and Frank M. Stewart, *A Half Century of Municipal Reform* (Berkeley and Los Angeles: University of California Press, 1950).

17. *Report on Charter Reform,* Good Government Club of San Francisco, Publication No. 2, pp. 17–18 (Library Document Room, University of California, Berkeley).

18. Bean, *Boss Ruef's San Francisco,* and Zink, *City Bosses.*

19. This section relies on a close observer of these events, Preston Devine, "The Adoption of the 1932 Charter of San Francisco," M.A. thesis, University of California, Berkeley, 1933.

20. Ibid., p. 73. The newspapers of the time were actually split over different methods and, later, over reforms.

21. Ibid., pp. 47–48.

22. Ibid., pp. 52, 77. For the voting record on fifteen issues, see ibid., Appendix I.

23. Ibid., p. 77.

24. *Rand* v. *Collins,* 214 Cal. 168 (1932).

25. On these linkages in the three types, see Adrian and Press, *Governing Urban America,* chaps. 8 and 9.

26. For background analysis of these personnel in the mid-1960s, see San Francisco League of Women Voters, *An Introduction to City Government—San Francisco* (1967), p. 6.

27. These 65 offices are: mayor, district attorney, sheriff, city attorney, treasurer, assessor, public defender, board of education (7), supervisors (11), municipal court judges (18), and superior court judges (22). The judicial elections are a requirement of state law.

28. For the period 1958–1971, the range was 61–86 percent, but the median turnout rate for the three five-year periods in that time was, respectively, 70, 74, and 70 percent.

29. Curt Gentry, *The Madams of San Francisco* (New York: Ballantine, 1971). At the opening of the gold rush, a touring Frenchman described with sardonic detail the drab life of the plain prostitutes asking a "fabulous amount" for their services. After naming the "famous beauties" of that day, he concluded drily, "There are also some honest women in San Francisco, but not very many." See Albert B. de Russailh, *Last Adventure* (San Francisco: Westgate Press, 1931), translated by Clarkson Crane, p. 175.

30. The account is detailed in Charles Raudebaugh, "San Francisco: The Beldam Dozes," in Robert S. Allen, *Our Fair City* (New York: Vanguard, 1947), pp. 347–369.

31. Dick Nolan column, San Francisco *Examiner and Chronicle,* January 11, 1970, B30.

32. San Francisco Committee on Crime, 1969–1971, pp. 13–27 is the source for this paragraph.

33. Ibid., pp. 47–55 is the source for this and the next paragraph.

34. The author appreciates the field assistance of a student, Ronald James, in this analysis.

35. Arnold A. Rogow and Harold D. Lasswell, *Power, Corruption, and Rectitude* (Englewood Cliffs, N.J.: Prentice-Hall, 1963), p. 133.

36. However, one columnist, Dick Nolan of the *Examiner,* had by the early 1970s publicly hinted at the mayor's use of public authority—through a network of cronies —to enrich his finances. But this was never made explicit enough for others to research the innuendo. Compare contemporary newspapermen's judgments about honesty with those for an earlier era, in Raudebaugh.

NOTES TO CHAPTER 6

1. Appreciation is extended for the field work of Edward Daube, who contributed to the following.

2. Aaron Wildavsky, *The Politics of the Budgetary Process* (Boston: Little, Brown, 1964). The field work cited in note 1 explored and reinforced Wildavsky's general theses.

3. From a 1968 letter from the Finance Committee, Board of Supervisors, to all department heads.

4. Heinz Eulau, Betty Zisk, and Kenneth Prewitt, "City Councilmen and the Group Struggle: A Typology of Role Orientations," *Journal of Politics*, 27 (1965) 618–646.

5. This characteristic of many aspects of governance and politics is developed fully in Ira Sharkansky, *The Routines of Politics* (New York: Van Nostrand Reinhold, 1970).

6. League of Women Voters of San Francisco, *An Introduction to City Government—San Francisco* (1967), pp. 34ff.

7. San Francisco *Chronicle,* September 23, 1966.

8. League of Women Voters, p. 44.

9. For a sympathetic account of such a mayor, see George Dorsey, *Christopher of San Francisco* (New York: Macmillan, 1962).

10. League of Women Voters, p. 44.

11. San Francisco Chamber of Commerce, *San Francisco Business,* June 1966, p. 30.

12. Ibid., May 1966, p. 8; this is written by Thomas Caylor, chamber representative appointed to the Charter Revision Committee in 1968.

13. The preceding and the following have been drawn from these sources: "Report of the San Francisco Citizens Charter Revision Committee to the Mayor and the Board of Supervisors, First Annual Report, June, 1969," filed with both the mayor and the board; interviews with members of this committee; and Joseph Azzolino, "The San Francisco Charter Reform of 1969," M.A. thesis, University of California, 1970.

14. The League of Women Voters president, Mrs. Robert G. Bull, James Frankel, Mrs. Audrey Rogers of the CCRC, plus supervisors Leo McCarthy and Robert Mendelsohn and a few others.

15. *Examiner* columnist Dick Nolan reported this at the time, and a CCRC member confirmed it to the author later.

16. League of Women Voters, p. 46.

17. William L. Rivers and David M. Rubin, *A Region's Press: Anatomy of Newspapers in the San Francisco Bay Area* (Berkeley: Institute of Governmental Studies, University of California, 1971), pp. 43–44.

18. Illustratively, Dick Nolan of the *Examiner* has for years criticized the then director of the Public Utilities Commission and later director of the airport, while turning his column against Mayor Alioto in the early 1970's. Given the reelection of the latter in 1971, the effect is questionable.

19. E. E. Schattschneider, *The Semi-Sovereign People* (New York: Holt, Rinehart & Winston, 1960).

NOTES TO CHAPTER 7

1. Mirian Beard, *A History of the Business Man* (New York: Macmillan, 1938).

2. Carl Bridenbaugh, *Cities in the Wilderness: The First Century of Urban Life in America, 1625–1742* (New York: Ronald Press, 1938).

3. Oliver Williams and Charles R. Adrian, *Four Cities* (Philadelphia: University of Pennsylvania Press, 1963).

4. On the last, see Frederick M. Wirt, *Politics of Southern Equality* (Chicago: Aldine, 1970).

5. For two sites reflecting this, see Arthur J. Vidich and Joseph Bensman, *Small Town in Mass Society* (Princeton: Princeton University Press, 1958); Ritchie P. Lowry, *Who's Running This Town? Community Leadership and Social Change* (New York: Harper & Row, 1962).

6. This is seen in the variety of urban policy studies: Robert C. Wood, *1400 Governments* (Garden City, N.Y.: Doubleday Anchor, 1964); Warner Bloomberg, Jr., Morris Sunshine, with Thomas J. Fararo, *Suburban Power Structures and Public Education* (Syracuse: Syracuse University Press, 1963); Oliver P. Williams, et al., *Suburban Differences and Metropolitan Policies* (Philadelphia: University of Pennsylvania Press, 1965); and Frederick M. Wirt et al., *On the City's Rim: Politics and Policy in Suburbia* (Lexington, Mass.: Heath, 1972).

7. The following section relies heavily on David Rogers and Melvin Zimet, "The Corporation and the Community: Perspectives and Recent Developments," in Ivar Berg, ed., *The Business of America* (New York: Harcourt, Brace and World, 1968), pp. 39–80, and Edwin M. Epstein, *The Corporation in American Politics* (Englewood Cliffs, N.J.: Prentice-Hall, 1969).

8. The moral orientation and its political and economic consequences are seen in Eric F. Goldman, *Rendezvous with Destiny* (New York: Vintage Books, 1956).

9. Norton E. Long, *The Polity* (Chicago: Rand McNally, 1962), p. 133; Long here on "The Corporation and the Local Community" is a powerful essay asserting this withdrawal. Its substantiation appears in passing in Edward C. Banfield and James Q. Wilson, *City Politics* (Cambridge: MIT and Harvard University Press, 1963), chap. 18, and Banfield, *Big City Politics* (New York: Random House, 1965). For case studies of this development, see Epstein, chap. 8.

10. Studies in Public Affairs, *The Role of Business in Public Affairs* (New York: National Industrial Conference Board, 1968), No. 2.

11. Stephen A. Greyser, "Business and Politics, 1968: Special Report," *Harvard Business Review*, 46 (November–December 1968), 10.

12. Rogers and Zimet, p. 53.

13. Community power studies have moved into a much more comparative mode in the late 1960s, but comparative analysis of the role of one community force, such as business, among many cities, has yet to be attempted; the Rogers and Zimet and Epstein sources are an effort in that direction but far from the sophistication of comparisons of whole community systems.

More characteristic is the case study, whether a set, such as S. Prakash Sethi, *Up Against the Corporate Wall* (Englewood Cliffs, N.J.: Prentice-Hall, 1970), or a single piece, as in Floyd Hunter's seminal study of Atlanta or, more recently, Edward C. Hayes, *Power Structure and Urban Policy: Who Rules in Oakland?* (New York: McGraw-Hill, 1972). For review of the state of the scholarship, and an annotated bibliography, see Willis D. Hawley and James H. Svara, *The Study of Community Power: A Bibliographic Review* (Santa Barbara, Calif.: ABC–CLIO, 1972).

14. Epstein, 193, with these components developed throughout chap. 8.

15. Ibid., pp. 221–229.

16. See note 10 and David T. Bazelon, "Big Business and the Democrats," *Commentary*, May 1965, pp. 39–47; and Greyser.

17. Robert A. Brady, *Business as a System of Power* (New York: Columbia University Press, 1943), p. 3.

18. For a review of these in recent years, see Rogers and Zimet, pp. 68–77.

19. Ibid., p. 76.

20. Andrew Hacker, ed., *The Corporation Take-Over* (New York: Harper & Row, 1964), pp. 7–8.

21. Rogers and Zimet, p. 48, note the role of Phillips Petroleum in Bartlesville, Oklahoma; see *Wall Street Journal,* August 4, 1966, pp. 1 ff.

22. Greggar Sletteland, "Economics of Highrise," in Bruce B. Brugmann, ed., *The Ultimate Highrise* (San Francisco: San Francisco Bay Guardian Book, 1971), p. 33.

23. Bruce Brugmann, "Politics of Highrise," in *The Ultimate Highrise,* p. 85.

24. Ibid.

25. William L. Rivers and David M. Rubin, *A Region's Press* (Berkeley: Institute of Governmental Studies, University of California, 1971). Their editorializing in news columns has been analyzed over some years. See Robert Batlin, "San Francisco Newspapers' Campaign Coverage: 1896, 1952," *Journalism Quarterly,* 31 (1954), 297–303; John B. Barry and Tsurue Taniguchi, "Press Coverage of the Douglas-Nixon Campaign," and Edith Carper, "The Nixon Fund as Reported by Three California Newspapers," private mss. in the Institute of Governmental Studies, University of California, Berkeley; and Rivers and Rubin, Appendix III.

26. For a typical *Bay Guardian* attack, see the issue of December 22, 1971, pp. 1–3. For a more objective approach, but with similar conclusions, see Rivers and Rubin.

27. Brugmann, pp. 82–84.

28. Floyd Hunter, *The Big Rich and the Little Rich* (Garden City, N.Y.: Doubleday, 1965), chap. 8.

29. Hans C. Palmer, "Italian Immigration and the Development of California Agriculture," Ph.D. thesis, University of California, Berkeley, 1965.

30. Details of banking and world trade are found in *San Francisco Bay Area Report: A Study of Growth and Economic Stature of the Nine Bay Area Counties* (San Francisco: Economic Research Division, Security Pacific National Bank, April, 1971), pp. 30–31, 108–111; hereafter referred to as *SPNB.*

31. Ibid., pp. 19–20.

32. Ibid., p. 69.

33. Ibid., p. 61.

34. On the worker connections here, see Walton Bean, *San Francisco's Boss Ruef* (Berkeley: University of California Press, 1952); for a longer view, see Bean, *California: An Interpretive History* (New York: McGraw-Hill, 1968), pp. 236–238 (the Kearney statement is at p. 238). See also Peter R. Varcados, "Labor and Politics in San Francisco, 1880–1892," Ph.D. dissertation, University of California, Berkeley, 1968.

35. Bean, *California,* pp. 356–358. A full analysis in modern time suggests that Mooney was most likely innocent; see Richard H. Frost, "The Mooney Case," Ph.D. dissertation, University of California, Berkeley, 1960.

36. Herbert Resner, "The Law in Action during the San Francisco Longshore and Maritime Strike of 1934," Division of Labor Statistics and Law Enforcement, California Department of Industrial Relations, 1936, as cited in a history of the city's waterfront, William M. Camp, *San Francisco: Port of Gold* (Garden City, N.Y.: Doubleday, 1948), p. 343.

37. Bean, *California,* pp. 414–417, and David W. Mabon, "The West Coast Maritime and Sympathy Strikes of 1934," Ph.D. dissertation, University of California, Berkeley, 1965.

38. A larger framework for understanding this development is provided in Theodore J. Lowi, *The End of Liberalism* (New York: Norton, 1969).

39. In one listing of a hundred major donors to his campaign, only two union heads (firefighters and cooks) are listed; see Brugmann, *The Ultimate Highrise,* pp.

72–79. This source's listing of only donors in *winning* campaigns obscures what labor was donating to losers.

40. Dick Meister, "Labor Power," *San Francisco Bay Guardian,* December 23, 1970, p. 2.

41. Compare Brugmann, p. 70, with San Francisco League of Women Voters, *An Introduction to City Government—San Francisco* (1967), p. 46.

42. Meister, p. 3.

43. *SPNB* (n. 30 above), p. 86, for data on specific buildings.

44. See particularly, Sletteland, "Economics of Highrise" (n. 22 above).

45. Abstracted from Chamber reports: "Four Working Papers on the Economic, Social and Fiscal Effects of High-Rise Buildings in San Francisco (Gruen & Gruen, 1971); "Tall Buildings and San Francisco," (McCue Boone Tomsick, 1971); both mimeographed.

46. The literature on the 1906 quake is voluminous on this subject, but a recent description has been very popular; see William Bronson, *The Earth Shook, The Sky Burned* (Garden City, N.Y.: Doubleday, 1959). The clearest technical exposition of the general problem in the Bay Area is Karl V. Steinbrugge, *Earthquake Hazard in the San Francisco Bay Area: A Continuing Problem in Public Policy* (Berkeley: Institute of Governmental Studies, University of California, 1968); his bibliography provides the extensive geological analysis underlying his book. Sierra Club, *Earthquake Country,* is the best introduction to the regional problem. For a recent technical report, see Theodore Algernussen, *A Study of Earthquake Losses in the San Francisco Bay Area* (Washington: U.S. Office of Emergency Preparedness, 1972).

47. These are listed in Sletteland, pp. 143–145.

48. On the geological zones, see Steinbrugge, p. 24.

49. The following is from Michael J. Cussen, "Holocausts above the 35th Floor," from Brugmann, *The Ultimate Highrise,* pp. 148–155, and from interviews in the Fire Department in 1972.

50. The best single volume of text and pictures that captures this mystique is Herb Caen and Dong Kingman, *San Francisco, City on Golden Hills* (Garden City, N.Y.: Doubleday, 1967).

51. Herb Caen best transmits this sense of Shangri-La; see San Francisco *Chronicle,* April 26, 1972, 29, for a prime example of this haunting quality.

52. For a listing of over eighty of these, see Brugmann, *The Ultimate Highrise,* pp. 236–240.

53. Meister, p. 25.

NOTES TO CHAPTER 8

1. An account much more critical than mine, but one finding this vision of a regionally focused economy among decision makers, is Stephen Zwerling, "The Political Consequences of Technological Choice: Public Transit in the San Francisco Metropolitan Area," Ph.D. dissertation, University of California, Berkeley, 1972 (publication by Praeger forthcoming). I find Zwerling's account very useful but do not agree that the result represented the primacy of technical experts in the value of relieving traffic congestion. As noted earlier, the economic motive was predominant from early on, and businessmen led the program, not "experts," who mobilized extensive political support rather than seducing or misleading the public.

2. The context is developed in Richard M. Zettel, *Urban Transportation in the San Francisco Bay Area* (Berkeley: Institute of Government Studies, University of California, 1963), and Zwirling, chap. 2.

3. *Fortune,* September 1970, p. 54.

4. *Examiner* columnist Dick Nolan maintained a running criticism of the engineering design of the cars and track within the city, which was ignored.

5. Alan Lupo, et al., *Rites of Way* (Boston: Little, Brown, 1971), chap. 16, authored by Frank Colcord.

6. Ibid., figures 1–4, which present comparison of impressionistic findings based on interviews with key actors in transportation politics in eight major cities. The present research would disagree with these authors' measurements of businessmen's influence as shown in ibid., figure 1.

7. R. A. Sundeen, "The San Francisco Bay Area Council," Ph.D. dissertation, University of California, Berkeley, 1963. For business's view of its role, see the Chamber of Commerce account in *Fortune*, September 1970, pp. 40–78.

8. This last works against the thesis that material gain motivates everyone in this. As the Chamber spokesman wrote, "Despite Standard's obvious economic link to the automobile and highway construction, it backed the BART project because [its representative] and its then president . . . agreed that the project was vital to the economic and social development of the Bay Area."

9. Lupo, p. 201.

10. Ibid., pp. 205–206.

11. Ibid., p. 209.

12. Burton Wolfe, "BART's Ride to Bankruptcy," in Bruce B. Brugmann, ed., *The Ultimate Highrise* (San Francisco: San Francisco Bay Guardian Books, 1971), pp. 194–202, reports conversations with business leaders declaring this need for highrise interlinked economic activity with BART. It is also clear in the Chamber of Commerce account of BART's history in *Fortune*, September 1970.

13. Wolfe, p. 198. For a powerful critique of business activity in this whole campaign, see Zwerling.

14. The manager of this program wrote about it later; John Krizek, "How to Build a Pyramid," *Public Relations Journal*, 26(1970), 17–21. The following draws upon interviews with private and public leaders in the issue and on contemporary news accounts.

15. The following account is drawn from interviews of community leaders; analysis of press coverage; Clark H. Alsop, "Social Responsibility and the U.S. Steel Project," M.B.A. thesis, University of California, Berkeley, 1971; and Richard Reinhardt, "On the Waterfront: The Great Wall of Magnin," in Brugmann, chap. 4.

16. Reinhardt, p. 107.

17. Ibid., pp. 115–116, claims this occurred because SPUR, thinking the project unbeatable anyhow, conceded in exchange for certain conditions that would meet its aesthetic concerns. See *SPUR Newsletter*, January 1970.

18. See account by Robert Jones, environmental editor of the *Bay Guardian*, in Reinhardt, pp. 117–123.

19. Ibid., p. 122, quoting Jerry Gauthen of San Francisco Tomorrow.

20. A convenient statement of both sides appears in the booklet from the San Francisco Registrar of Voters, November 2, 1971, election, at pp. 151–158.

21. Chamber of Commerce, *San Francisco Business*, January 1972, pp. 33–36, for the chamber's view of the campaign.

22. Bruce B. Brugmann, "The Politics of Highrise," in Brugmann, *The Ultimate Highrise*, pp. 72–81. However, examining only the successes of the donors, and not their failures as well, blurs the thesis of this report.

23. The agencies were the Planning Commission, the Board of Permit Appeals, the Port Commission, and the Redevelopment Authority, ostensibly for 1971; see ibid., pp. 68–70, for the listing from which figures in the text were drawn.

24. Thus see the tally for Fall 1966, in San Francisco League of Women Voters,

An Introduction to City Government—San Francisco (1967), p. 46. Of 19 agencies with 133 appointees, 47 were businessmen, 50 professionals, 13 women organization representatives, 22 from labor and 12 from ethnic groups (2 are unaccounted for in this tally).

25. For general conditions here, see Guy Benveniste, *The Politics of Expertise* (Berkeley: Glendessary, 1972); for particular applications, see Francine F. Rabinovitz, *City Politics and Planning* (New York: Atherton, 1970).

26. Frederick M. Wirt and Michael W. Kirst, *The Political Web of American Schools* (Boston: Little, Brown, 1972), p. 138.

27. I have benefited immensely in the following from the insights expressed in Leonard Ruchelmand and Charles Brownstein, "Public Needs and Private Decisions in Tall Building Development: A Policy-Making Model," paper for the American Political Science Association's annual convention, 1973.

28. Charles N. Glaab, "Historical Perspective on Urban Development Schemes," in Leo F. Schnore, ed., *Social Science and the City* (New York: Praeger, 1967), p. 197. A fuller treatment is Sam Bass Warner, *The Urban Wilderness* (New York: Harper and Row, 1972).

29. Homer Hoyt, *One Hundred Years of Land Values in Chicago* (Chicago: University of Chicago Press, 1933), and Stanislaw J. Makielski, Jr., *The Politics of Zoning: The New York Experience* (New York: Columbia University Press, 1966), pp. 7–40, cited in Ruchelmand and Brownstein, pp. 5–6.

30. Alan S. Kravatz, "Mandarism: Planning as Handmaiden to Conservative Politics," in Beyle and Lathrop, eds., *Planning and Politics: Uneasy Partnership* (New York: Odyssey Press, 1970).

31. Dennis A. Rondinelli, "Urban Planning as Policy Analysis: Management of Urban Change," *Journal of the American Institute of Planners*, January 1973, p. 13. There are complex reasons for this result, which I must pass over but which are discussed in David Ranney, *Planning and Politics in the Metropolis* (Columbus, O.: Merrill, 1969). A recent study of Bay Area planners finds them as political as they were professional in their roles, particularly when hired by central cities; J. Vincent Buck, "The Limits to Professional Autonomy in Municipal Planning," paper for the American Political Science Association annual convention, 1973.

32. Ruchelmand and Brownstein, p. 10.

NOTES TO CHAPTER 9

1. The fullest bibliography is Bryan Thompson, *Ethnic Groups in Urban Areas: Community Formation and Growth* (Monticello, Ill.: Council of Planning Librarians, 1971). A good survey of the California experience is Anne Loftis, *California—Where the Twain Did Meet* (New York: Macmillan, 1973).

2. Milton M. Gordon, *Assimilation in American Life* (New York: Oxford University Press, 1964), develops these changes.

3. Joseph Lopreato, *Italian Americans* (New York: Random House, 1970), 86–7.

4. Carlton Beals, *The Brass-Knuckle Crusade* (New York: Hastings House, 1960).

5. Wilfred E. Binkley, *American Political Parties; Their Natural History*, 4th ed. (New York: Knopf, 1962).

6. Carl Wittke, *The Irish in America* (Baton Rouge: Louisiana State University Press, 1956).

7. On the pre-gold-rush history, see Walton Bean, *California: An Interpretive History* (New York: McGraw Hill, 1968), chaps. 1–9.

8. Earl Raab, "There's No City like San Francisco: Profile of a Jewish Community," *Commentary*, 10 (1950), 369–378. One observer noted of the Irish-Jewish connec-

tions, "We both have what the other wants. The Jews want to be good-looking like us while the Irish need a one-eyed general like theirs." Seamus Breatnac, "Should Irish Eyes Be Smiling?" *San Francisco,* August 1970, p. 28.

9. James A. Fisher, "The Political Development of the Black Community in California, 1850–1950," *California Historical Quarterly,* 50 (1971), 256–266.

10. The following draws heavily upon interviews with the city's Irish spokesmen and accredits the assistance in field work by Randall Hough and especially Patricia Gallagher.

11. Garrett McEnerny was a powerful figure for four decades in the development of the University of California at Berkeley. For a full account, see John B. McGloin, *Jesuits by the Golden Gate* (San Francisco: University of San Francisco, 1972).

12. At the time of the 1906 disaster, of the estimated 143,000 proclaimed church members, 116,000 were Roman Catholic, with about 95,000 Irish in the total population of the city; see Breatnac, p. 28.

13. Of the city's twenty police chiefs from 1878 to 1972, eleven were Irish.

14. The following analysis is drawn from interviews with Irish officials, clergy, and scholars conducted by the author and Patricia Gallagher. The most informed student of San Francisco's Irish is Professor James Walsh, History Department, San Jose State University.

15. Breatnac, p. 38.

16. Ibid., p. 28.

17. Nathan Glazer and Daniel P. Moynihan, *Beyond the Melting Pot* (Cambridge, Mass.: MIT Press, 1963), p. 229.

18. Ibid., pp. 181–216; Lopreato, and Alexander DeConde, *Half Bitter, Half Sweet* (New York: Scribners, 1971), provide the background for the following. A full annotated bibliography is found in DeConde, pp. 387–446.

19. Lopreato, pp. 102–103, reports that the parochialism is labeled *campanilismo* from the Italian words for bell or church tower. For dissection of a contemporary southern Italian village of this kind, see Edward Banfield, *The Moral Basis of a Backward Society* (Glencoe, Ill.: Free Press, 1958).

20. Lopreato, p. 103.

21. Herbert J. Gans, *The Urban Villagers* (New York: Free Press of Glencoe, 1962).

22. The loose tie of the Church is seen in the smaller proportions of priests than their absolute numbers require. See also the finding that as late as 1965, while 37 percent of Irish-American wives used contraceptive devices, the figure was 68 percent for Italian-Americans; see Lopreato, p. 93.

23. Daniel Bell, *The End of Ideology* (Glencoe, Ill.: Free Press, 1960), pp. 115–136. For evidence of the family-kinship basis of contemporary organized Italian crime, see Francis A. J. Ianni, "The Mafia and the Web of Kinship," *The Public Interest,* Winter 1971, pp. 78–100.

24. "*Governo ladro* (thief of a government) is still an everyday imprecation throughout Italy"; Lopreato, p. 114.

25. But while Italian-Americans are about one-third the number of Irish, as late as the mid-twentieth century no Italian name appeared among the twenty-one archbishops and over one hundred bishops in the nation.

26. The revisionist analysis of this experience is Andrew F. Rolle, *The Immigrant Upraised* (Norman: University of Oklahoma Press, 1968); all figures cited below are drawn from this source. Of help on the early San Francisco Italian experience, see Francesco M. Nicosia, "Italian Pioneers in California" n.d., private printing, in author's possession.

27. Rolle, p. 350, assembles 1870–1940 data for the twenty-two states. Louisiana

drew the second largest number of Italians. For a time prior to 1890, Italians in the South supported Negro causes, but the pressure of the Klan, including public lynchings of Italians in New Orleans, moved them to accept white supremacy. See G. E. Cunningham, "Italian, A Hindrance to White Solidarity in Louisiana," *Journal of Negro History,* 50 (1965), 22–36.

28. Lopreato, p. 54, tabulates the 1960 data by regions.

29. Rolle, chap. 12, provides the names and locations of origins which led to this judgment. Italian city leaders interviewed for this study first brought this significant difference to the author's attention.

30. Rolle, p. 28, lists the comparative wage scales.

31. Rolle, p. 255, for original citation.

32. Italian papers were operating extensively throughout the state as late as 1931 in Dunsmuir, Martinez, Sacramento, Stockton, and Weed; see Rolle, p. 264. *L'Italo-Americano* still published in the city in 1968, but by 1973, only the monthly periodical *Bulletin of the Italian Catholic Federation* (bilingual) remained.

33. On the Italian Catholic influence at USF, see McGloin. Late in the century, San Franciscans went into a frenzy over two divas, Luisa Tetrazzini and Adelina Patti, resulting in damaged commercial property and personal injuries. For over a century, opera has continued to thrive, with the season's opening a highly publicized "non-event."

34. On this development, see Bean, *California,* p. 494, and Hans C. Palmer, "Italian Immigration and the Development of California Agriculture," Ph.D. dissertation, University of California, Berkeley, 1965.

35. In 1879, Sicilians formed the Scavengers Protective Union, which improved and regulated their working conditions, including sick benefits and burial arrangements. Still active today, it is dominated by Italian-Americans.

36. Marquis and Bessie R. James, *Biography of a Bank, the Story of the Bank of America* (New York: Harper, 1954).

37. Rolle, p. 335–337.

38. Ibid., p. 259.

39. Charles Garrett, *The LaGuardia Years* (New Brunswick, N. J.: Rutgers University Press, 1961).

40. The problem is raised in W. S. Robinson, "Ecological Correlations and the Behavior of Individuals," *American Sociological Review,* 15 (1950), 351–357.

41. References to this change are found in Lopreato; Glazer and Moynihan; and Gans. See also Samuel Lubell, *The Future of American Politics* (New York: Harper, 1952), and Robert A. Dahl, *Who Governs?* (New Haven: Yale University Press, 1961), passim.

42. In absolute numbers which this represented in 1960–65, of the 121 candidates 32 were Irish, of whom 21 won, while 9 were Italian, of whom 1 won; from 1966 to 1971, of the 205 candidates (the increase was partly due to one more year in this interval but also suggestive of the more open electoral scene discussed in chapter 4), 39 were Irish, of whom 19 won, while 16 were Italian, of whom 10 won.

43. Brett W. Hawkins and Robert A. Lorinskas, eds., *The Ethnic Factor in American Politics* (Columbus, O.: Merrill, 1970), p. 6.

44. The critique runs heavily through the works of DeConde, Lopreato, and Rolle. See especially Rudolph J. Vecoli, "*Contandini* in Chicago: A Critique of *The Uprooted,*" *Journal of American History,* June–March 1964–1965, pp. 404–417.

45. Oscar Handlin, *The Uprooted* (New York: Grosset & Dunlap, 1951).

46. For elaboration of these factors, Humbert S. Nelli, *Italians in Chicago, 1880–1930* (New York: Oxford University Press, 1970), pp. 115–122, and Lopreato, pp. 106–113.

47. Nelli, chap. 4, provides full details on the politics of these two wards.

48. Michael Parenti, "Ethnic Politics and the Persistence of Ethnic Identification," *American Political Science Review,* 61 (1967), 717–726, provides the conceptualization which this and the succeeding chapter substantiate.

NOTES TO CHAPTER 10

1. Wilson Record, *Minority Groups and Intergroup Relations in the San Francisco Bay Area* (Berkeley: Institute of Governmental Studies, University of California, 1963), p. 4. A fuller historical account is Anne Loftis, *California—Where the Twain Did Meet* (New York: Macmillan, 1973).

2. The following is drawn from interviews in the Chinese and Japanese communities of San Francisco; Alexander Saxton, *The Indispensable Enemy* (Berkeley and Los Angeles: University of California Press, 1967); Rose Hum Lee, *The Chinese in the USA* (Hong Kong: Hong Kong University Press, 1960); and accounts in the city's press. For a good popular account, see Mary Ellen Leary, "San Francisco's Chinatown," *Atlantic Monthly,* March 1970, pp. 32 ff.

3. The following account is drawn from Ralph W. Kramer, *Participation of the Poor* (Englewood Cliffs, N.J.: Prentice-Hall, 1969), pp. 45–49, et seq.; all quotations on this episode are from this source.

4. The city's postmaster, Lim P. Lee, was appointed in 1966; George Chinn came close to election as supervisor in 1969 and was later appointed by Mayor Alioto to the board of education and then to the board of supervisors but was defeated in a 1973 supervisorial election; Philip Lum was appointed in 1971 as acting principal of a high school; his brother, Dr. John Lum, active in the Association of Chinese Teachers, achieved a Ph.D. in Education; and J. J. Choy from the late 1960s onward was a television news reporter—all firsts of their kind. For the reflections of this new generation on these changes, see Victor G. and Brett de Bary Nee, *Longtime Californ'* (New York: Pantheon, 1972).

5. See the excellent analysis of these two, and their comments, in Tom Emch, "A Question of Identity," San Francisco *Examiner and Chronicle,* December 5, 1971, magazine section, 12–23. On the background, see John Modell, "Japanese-Americans: Some Costs of Group Achievement," in Charles Wollenberg, ed., *Ethnic Conflict in California History,* (Santa Monica: Tinnon-Brown, 1970), chap. 5; other chapters in this volume are valuable analyses of the Chinese, Spanish-speaking, and black minorities discussed here.

6. "Comparative Figures, 1960–1970, Population of San Francisco by Ethnic Groups," report of the Human Rights Commission, March 1972.

7. From a special study on the Inner Mission, San Francisco *Examiner,* June 19, 1972.

8. On this and other aspects of this subculture, see the monumental work of Leo Grebler, et al., *The Mexican-American People: The Nation's Second Largest Minority* (New York: Free Press, 1970), and its eleven attendant Advance Reports. This focuses, however, on the valleys and Los Angeles in its California analysis, not on San Francisco.

9. Ibid., for a study of low support of unification with blacks for political gains.

10. Kramer, chap. 2, details this account.

11. U. S. Commission on Civil Rights, "The Spanish-American Community of the San Francisco Bay Area," Staff Report in *Hearings in San Francisco and Oakland, May 1–6, 1967* (Washington: U.S. Government Printing Office, 1967), pp. 817–825; San Francisco Human Rights Commission, "A Preliminary Report: Racial and Ethnic Employment Pattern Survey of City and County of San Francisco," 1965.

12. The following account is drawn from interviews with Mission District organizational leaders, reports of the MCO, series in San Francisco *Examiner*, June 19–29, 1972. Special assistance was provided by interviews conducted for the author by Michael Cortes and Douglas Dodds.

13. San Francisco *Examiner*, June 19, 1972.

14. Record, p. 10.

15. Ibid., p. 3.

16. Some hallmarks of that history, cited below, are found in James A. Fisher, "The Political Development of the Black Community in California, 1850–1950," *California Historical Quarterly*, 50 (1971), 256–266, and his sources. See also Velesta Jenkins, "White Racism and White Response in California History", in Wollenberg, chap. 6; Randolph Lapp, "The Negro in Gold Rush California," *Journal of Negro History*, 49 (1964), 81–98; Francis M. Lortie, "San Francisco's Black Community, 1870–1890; Dilemmas in the Struggle for Equality," M.A. thesis, San Francisco State College, 1970.

17. A 1970 school report noted a decrease in elementary school enrollments in these neighborhoods, unmatched by a similar drop in white neighborhoods; see San Francisco *Examiner*, May 26, 1970.

18. U. S. Commission on Civil Rights, *Hearings in Los Angeles and San Francisco, January 25–28, 1960* (Washington: Government Printing Office, 1960).

19. However, of the thirty largest cities by proportion of black population, San Francisco was thirtieth (smallest) but it was tied for twenty-third place for the black proportion of its police force in 1971. Five percent of the police were black, while 13.4 percent of the population was black. See San Francisco *Sunday Examiner & Chronicle*. May 9, 1971, p. A19, citing sources in *Ebony*, May 1971. The city's record of life opportunities for both races is mixed. In 1970, among the thirty largest cities in the nation, it was twenty-eighth on housing cost relative to income (very expensive), and on plumbing adequacy (very inadequate). But it was first in the decline in racial segregation, sixth in differences in cost between black and white rentals (very small), and tenth in crowding. Cited in *Washington Post*, November 11, 1973, p. 2, from report of Council on Municipal Performance, New York.

20. Preliminary and final reports of the Lemberg Center for the Study of Violence, Brandeis University, Waltham, Mass. In their reports, San Francisco is City B.

21. The rank order correlation between blacks in the population and in the police force is .45; size of the group seems to exercise some influence, through unknown processes, to provide it with city rewards. Schuman and Gruenberg (see table 17) demonstrate that both black dissatisfaction with government and belief in local discrimination decline as the proportion of blacks increases in their fifteen cities.

22. The seminal statement was Stokely Carmichael and Charles V. Hamilton, *Black Power* (New York: Random House, 1967).

23. See Walter Kintz, "The Negro and San Francisco Politics" (Berkeley: Institute of Governmental Studies Library, University of California), private ms.; the work of Linda Brown for the author showed that blacks moved from 53 to 65 to 75 percent Democratic in the presidential contests of 1948, 1952, and 1960.

24. See Kintz, and Brown, and the data reported for Detroit and Cleveland in Frederick M. Wirt, and Michael Kirst, *The Political Web of American Schools*, (Boston: Little, Brown, 1972), pp. 102–104.

25. For a study of these differential effects, see Frederick M. Wirt, *Politics of Southern Equality* (Chicago: Aldine, 1970). For a comparative study of state and municipal civil rights commissions, which finds them generally impotent to make basic changes in discrimination, as well as plagued with their own internal problems of discrimination, see Burton Levy, "The Bureaucracy of Race: Enforcement of Civil

Rights Laws and Its Impact on People, Process, and Organization," paper presented to the American Political Science Association, 1970.

26. David T. Wellman, "Negro Leadership in San Francisco," M.A. thesis, University of California, Berkeley, 1966.

27. This campaign is detailed in S. Prakash Sethi, *Up Against the Corporate Wall* (Englewood Cliffs, N.J.: Prentice-Hall, 1970), pp. 129–159.

28. San Francisco *Chronicle,* November 21, 1964.

29. Richard Young, "The Impact of Protest Leadership on Negro Politicians in San Francisco," *Western Political Quarterly,* 22 (1969), 94–111, covers some of these events, although his thesis of the effects of such protest on black politicians is not demonstrated.

30. The following draws heavily on the excellent interview studies of these leaders during the middle 1960s by Berkeley graduate students. See Wellman, and the cooperative parallel studies for degree in Master of City Planning by Natalie Becker and Marjorie B. Myhill, published jointly as *Power and Participation in the San Francisco Community Action Program, 1964–1967* (Berkeley: University of California, Institute of Urban and Regional Development, 1967).

31. James Q. Wilson, *Negro Leadership* (Glencoe, Ill.: Free Press, 1960); and Ernest Ladd, *Negro Political Leadership in the South* (Ithaca, N.Y.: Cornell University Press, 1966).

32. Wellman, pp. 120–121. An analysis of these leadership factors among community organizations across the nation, including the Western Addition in San Francisco, became available too late for inclusion here. But it does note the dichotomy between the "ideological" and the "material" strategies. See John Mollenkopf, "Community Organization and City Politics," Ph.D. dissertation, Harvard University, 1973.

33. The following is drawn from Kramer, chap. 2 et seq., and Becker and Myhill. For an insider's account of the national origins and development of this participatory requirement, see Daniel P. Moynihan, *Maximum Feasible Misunderstanding* (New York: Free Press, 1970).

34. Marjorie B. Myhill, "The Struggle for Power in the Poverty Program in the Western Addition," M.C.P. thesis, University of California, Berkeley, 1968, p. 8.

35. Kramer, p. 67.

36. Michael Lipsky, *Protest in City Politics* (Chicago: Rand McNally, 1970), provides both theoretical framework and urban experience for the strategy.

37. Matthew Holden, "Some Suggestions for Black Politicians in the Time of the 'New' Urban Politics," in National League of Cities, *The City: Its Resources, Structures, and Systems* (Washington: NLC Proceedings, 1970), p. 97.

38. Some very perceptive and close studies, employing participant-observer techniques, show that the social and psychological matrix of black community life in Hunter's Point was much like that found in other cities. See Arthur E. Hippler, "Family Structure and Social Structure: Matrifocality in Hunter's Point," Ph.D. dissertation, University of California, Berkeley, 1968, and in published form as *Hunter's Point: A Black Ghetto in America* (New York: Basic Books, 1970); Hippler used TAT tests and personality profiles to demonstrate the presence of father-absent families and its consequence for sexual roles and achievement motivations. See also Renee L. Goldsmith, "Negro Youth Culture and Identity: The Case of Hunter's Point," Master of Criminology thesis, University of California, Berkeley, 1967, which studied the origins, content and eufunctional and dysfunctional aspects of expressive life styles within the black youth subculture of the area; and Benjamin G. Carmichael, "Hunter's Point: A Participant Observer's View," Master of Criminology thesis, University of California, Berkeley, 1968, which analyzed family as well as

community structure to note the broad gap between black youth and adult cultures.

39. San Francisco *Chronicle,* February 17, 1972.

40. The following draws on the works of Wellman, Young, Becker and Myhill, and Kramer, noted above, and the in-progress dissertation research of Sy Arnstein, Berkeley.

41. This point emerges in all the cases in Howard W. Hallman, *Community Control: A Study of Community Corporations and Neighborhood Boards* (Washington: Center for Metropolitan Studies, 1969); on the San Francisco experience, see pp. 137–143.

42. See the views of Supervisor Terry Francois in opposition to black racism, San Francisco *Examiner & Chronicle,* October 5, 1969, reprinted appropriately in *Reader's Digest,* September 1969. His position should also be seen in light of his electoral constituency, the entire city, where blacks are just over 13 percent. On the other hand, Assemblyman Willie Brown, in the same period, could be more "militant" with a district that covered only part of the city and included 25 percent black; see Young, pp. 98–100, for a comparison of their styles.

43. A striking parallel may be seen in the early stages of political development of Chicago Italians and Irish; Humbert S. Nelli, *Italians in Chicago, 1880–1930* (New York: Oxford University Press, 1970).

44. The following is drawn from interviews with black group spokesmen, assistants to the mayor's office, and newspaper accounts.

45. The works of Carmichael, Kramer, and Hallman, noted above, all caught their role in studies of this area.

46. Alioto is quoted in the excellent series on Hunter's Point politics by Joel Tlumak, San Francisco *Examiner,* February–March, 1972; quotations are found in the *Examiner* for February 18 and March 29, with no emphasis in the original.

47. San Francisco *Examiner,* March 27, 1972.

48. Alioto thereafter moved one of these to direct another model cities agency at a much higher salary; one of the prime requirements of leadership is to take care of one's own.

49. See San Francisco Human Relations Commission, *Racial and Ethnic Employment Pattern Survey,* December 31, 1971, and *The Examination Procedures of the San Francisco Civil Service and Their Effects on Minority Employment.* Becker and Myhill are more sanguine about gains from the poverty programs, but they deal with the early years and do not provide data on jobs provided versus jobs needed.

50. For similar findings under these conditions in Baltimore, see Peter Bachrach and Morton S. Baratz, *Power and Poverty: Theory and Practice* (New York: Oxford University Press, 1970). A similar event transpired for Mexican-Americans in nearby Santa Clara County; see Kramer, chap. 3.

51. For a close study of the divide-and-rule strategy of the Irish against the Italians earlier in Chicago, see Nelli, chap. 4.

52. This was the conviction not merely of other minorities and of some whites, but it was the naive view of sympathetic supporters of the blacks; see Tom Wolfe, *Mau-Mauing the Flak Catchers* (New York: Farrar, Straus and Giroux, 1970).

53. Personal correspondence to author from Director of Ethnic Studies, University of San Francisco, himself a prototype of this observation. In the Western Addition Community Organization, members later became a director of the urban renewal advisory committee, a Berkeley Ph.D., an officer in the National Tenants Association, and contractors and developers under the renewal program. Cited in John H. Mollenkopf, "On the Causes and Consequences of Neighborhood Political Mobilization," paper presented at the American Political Science Association convention, 1973, p. 11.

NOTES TO CHAPTER 11

1. This concept was advanced over a decade ago by Warren, but except for an article by Walton and a book by Vidich and Bensman, its consequences for community power have not been developed fully. See Roland L. Warren, *The Community in America* (Chicago: Rand McNally, 1963); John Walton, "The Vertical Axis of Community Organization and the Structure of Power," *Southwestern Social Science Quarterly,* 48 (1967), 353–368; Arthur J. Vidich and Joseph Bensman, *Small Town in Mass Society* (Garden City, N.Y.: Doubleday-Anchor, 1960).

2. Daniel J. Elazar, *The American Partnership* (Chicago: University of Chicago Press, 1962), pp. 23–24.

3. Michael D. Reagan, *The New Federalism* (New York: Oxford University Press, 1972), p. 145. Precursers of this important work include Elazar, and Roscoe C. Martin, *The Cities and the Federal System* (New York: Atherton Press, 1965).

4. The following analysis draws heavily on Reagan, chap. 2, and Advisory Commission on Intergovernmental Relations, *Fiscal Balance in the American Federal System* (Washington, D.C.: Government Printing Office, 1967), vol. 1.

5. It is much more flexible than the major taxes of state and locality—sales and property—for the purpose of making large jumps in revenue. Its elasticity and richness are tied to the growth of national income; as the latter grows each year, an increment appears which policy makers need not ask ever-reluctant citizens to accept.

6. Reagan, pp. 46–49.

7. Ibid., pp. 55–56; 150 of these programs in 1967 were federally funded at 100 percent and about 90 at 50 percent or less. Some states got more than others, of course, but as the number of programs increased, states shared differentially in the rate of change. The key to this difference was not short-term public sentiment and socioeconomic environment but structural governmental processes, like budgetary procedures, governors' powers, and so on. See Gerald S. Ferman, "A Systematic Approach to the Politics of the Distribution of Grants-in-Aid, 1960–69," paper presented to the Midwest Political Science Association convention, 1972.

8. James L. Sundquist and David W. Davis, *Making Federalism Work* (Washington, D.C.: Brookings Institution, 1969), pp. 3–6; emphasis in original.

9. Ibid., p. 11; for a listing of all GIAs during the period 1966–1968, see ibid., pp. 279–285.

10. For criticism of revenue sharing and a strong endorsement of the 1960s pattern, see Reagan, chaps. 4 and 5.

11. For a summary of these actions, see *Congressional Quarterly,* October 7, 1972, pp. 2630–31.

12. An important early statement of this interpretation is Currin V. Shields, "The American Tradition of Empirical Collectivism," *American Political Science Review,* 46 (1952), 104–120.

13. ACIR, *Fiscal Balance,* pp. 37, 84–85. On schools, see R. L. Johns, "State Financing of Elementary and Secondary Education," in Edgar Fuller and Jim B. Pearson, eds., *Education in the States: Nationwide Development since 1900* (Washington, D.C.: National Education Assn., 1969), pp. 175–214.

14. John D. Lewis, ed., *Anti-Federalists versus Federalists* (San Francisco: Chandler, 1967).

15. U.S. Senate Committee on Government Operations, Subcommittee on Intergovernmental Relations, *The Federal System as Seen by State and Local Officials* (Washington, D.C.: Government Printing Office, 1963), Section E.

16. Morley Segal and A. Lee Fritschler, "Emerging Patterns of Intergovernmental

Relations," *Municipal Year Book 1970* (Washington, D.C.: International City Management Assn., 1970), pp. 13–38.

17. Project Head Start, *A National Survey of the Impacts of Head Start Centers on Community Institutions—Summary Report* (Washington, D.C.: U. S. Department of Health, Education, and Welfare, 1970). Most of these changes were in the educational area; half of the change came in greater educational emphasis on the particular needs of the poor and of minorities, and only one-fifth of the reported changes came from greater involvement of the poor at, or in, decision-making centers.

18. Frances F. Piven and Richard A. Cloward, "How The Federal Government Caused the Welfare Crisis," *Social Policy,* May/June 1971, pp. 40–49. For more details, see by the same authors, *Regulating The Poor; The Functions of Public Welfare* (New York: Pantheon-Random House, 1971), chap. 10. See also, Marilyn J. Blawlie, "Law and Politics of Welfare Rights Organizations," paper presented to the American Political Science Association convention, 1970.

19. Deil S. Wright, "The States and Intergovernmental Relations," *Publius: The Journal of Federalism,* 1 (1972), 7–68.

20. Ibid., p. 19. For an early review of this outcome, see V. O. Key, Jr., *The Administration of Federal Grants to the States* (Chicago: Public Administration Service, 1937).

21. Washington Research Project, *Title I: Is it Helping Poor Children?* (Washington, D.C.: NAACP Legal Defense and Education Funds, 1969). Only in mid-1973 did Washington arrive at a formula requiring erring school districts to return the funds.

22. For an intensive study of these processes, see Frederick M. Wirt, *Politics of Southern Equality: Law and Social Change in a Mississippi County* (Chicago: Aldine, 1970), and Gary Orfield, *The Reconstruction of Southern Education: The Schools and the 1964 Civil Rights Act* (New York: Wiley-Interscience, 1969). For a fuller study of the wide extent of noncompliance with civil rights legislation, see U.S. Commission on Civil Rights, *Federal Civil Rights Enforcement Effort* (Washington, D.C.: Government Printing Office, 1971).

23. Frederick A. Lazin, "The Failure of Federal Enforcement of Civil Rights Regulations in Public Housing, 1963–1971: The Co-optation of a Federal Agency by Its Local Constituency," paper presented to the American Political Science Association convention, 1972, p. 9.

24. James S. Coleman et al., *Equality of Educational Opportunity* (Washington, D.C.: Government Printing Office, 1966); Frederick Mosteller and Daniel P. Moynihan, eds., *On Equality of Educational Opportunity* (New York: Random House, 1972); and Christopher Jencks, et al., *Inequality: A Reassessment of the Effect of Family and Schooling in America* (New York: Basic Books, 1972). The author is aware of the criticisms of these studies and shares many of them.

25. Economic Development Administration, *Federal Activities Affecting Location of Economic Development—Final Report* (Washington, D.C.: U.S. Department of Commerce, 1970), vol. 1. For the reverse impact, see Charles B. Garrison, *The Impact of New Industry on Local Government Finances in 5 Small Towns in Kentucky* (Washington, D.C.: Economic Resource Service, U.S. Department of Agriculture, 1970).

26. An excellent analysis of the complex federal politics involved is B. Douglas Harman, "Public Administration and Order and Violence: Intergovernmental Politics in the Block Grant Approach to Law Enforcement Assistance," paper presented to the American Political Science Association convention in 1969. His survey of chief executives of cities and state law enforcement planning agencies, in 50 states and 582 cities, found that only about half the cities regarded the states as sympathetic or helpful, and the bigger the city the greater the antipathy.

27. See two papers by Bennett Harrison, "Model Cities as a Vehicle for Employing Ghetto Residents," and "Ghetto Employment and the Model Cities Program," delivered to the annual conventions of the American Society for Public Administration and the American Political Science Assn., both in 1972. He found that while the resident participation rate varied enormously between cities (from 0 to 100 percent), regression analysis found little to explain this variance other than those factors noted in the text. By the same author, see "The Participation of Ghetto Residents in the Model Cities Program," *Journal of the American Institute of Planners,* 39 (January 1973).

28. E. E. Schattschneider, *The Semi-Sovereign People* (New York: Holt, Rinehart and Winston, 1960), p. 71.

29. For a detailed analysis of this device and its outcome, see Frederick M. Wirt and Michael Kirst, *The Political Web of American Schools* (Boston: Little, Brown, 1972), chap. 9.

30. Sundquist and Davis, pp. 62, 77, 177.

31. Judson L. James, "Federalism and the Model Cities Experiment," paper presented to the American Political Science Assn. annual convention, 1970, p. 7.

32. Sundquist and Davis, pp. 12–13, 19.

33. The chief administrative officer, Thomas Mellon, has produced excellent annual reports for the board of supervisors on the revenue and tax picture; figures in the text are from his *San Francisco Revenue and Taxation Report—1972,* p. 18, hereafter referred to as *SFRTR–1972.*

34. Ibid., p. 8.

35. Ibid., p. 9. This source, at p. 11, shows for fiscal 1971 a total of $58.4 million in federal grants; the difference from the $44.6 million cited at p. 9 is probably going to school, poverty, and Model Cities programs. However, a state report estimates that for fiscal 1970, the federal GIAs to the city totaled as much as $87.9 million, of which only $7.3 million was for schools; see Legislative Analyst, *Federal Aid Programs in California* (Sacramento: State of California, December, 1971), p. 16. This difference indicates the difficulties of establishing even totals, much less distributions by functions.

36. See *SFRTR–1972,* pp. 69, 74, for evidence of increase of the aged and the decline of youth in population distribution (the under-five-years age categories declined from 6.8 to 6.0 percent from 1910 to 1970, while the 25–34 categories declined from 24 to 15 percent, and the over-65 increased from 4 to 14 percent) and the higher city costs (the consumer price index in every year since 1960 shows that San Francisco's was higher than that in Los Angeles, the state, and the nation).

37. Legislative Analyst, *Federal Aid Programs,* pp. 16, 41.

38. This additive effect varies by policy area, but overall in 1960, it was about 44¢ of state and local money stimulated by $1 of federal GIA; see Wright, pp. 15–18, and his sources and analysis.

39. For a six-state study of these constellations, see Joel Berke and Michael Kirst, eds., *Federal Aid to Education: Who Benefits? Who Governs?* (Lexington, Mass.: Heath, 1973); for the California context, see chap. 2.

40. This quality stems from the large share of such costs that must be raised locally. For an excellent analysis of this and other factors of welfare in San Francisco, viewed comparatively, see Sharon P. Krefetz, "City Politics and Public Welfare: The Administration of Public Assistance in Baltimore and San Francisco," paper presented to the American Political Science Association convention, 1972, based on her dissertation at Brandeis, 1972.

41. The conceptual distinctions of these conceptual modes of conflict and their applications to this and other cities are found in Ralph M. Kramer, *Participation of the Poor* (Englewood Cliffs, N.J.: Prentice-Hall, 1969), chap. 6.

42. For illustration of this framework in the urban scene, see Brett Hawkins, *Politics and Urban Policies* (Indianapolis: Bobbs-Merrill, 1971).

43. A currently developing conceptualization of this kind is found in Harvey Boulay, Betty H. Zisk, and Edward Berger, "A Bargaining Paradigm for the Study of Urban Politics: Theoretical Imperatives and Conceptual Clarifications," and by the same authors, "Urban Bargaining: A Comparison of Simulation and Field Data," papers presented at the American Political Science Association annual conventions, 1970 and 1972.

44. On this politesse concept, see Wirt, *Politics of Southern Equality*, pp. 95–96.

45. See Orfield, chap. 1, on the historical reluctance of federal administrators to use coercion, and Jeffrey L. Pressman and Aaron B. Wildavsky, *Implementation* (Berkeley and Los Angeles: University of California Press, 1973), on such barriers in a federal program in Oakland.

46. The following account is drawn from these sources: interviews with leading school officials; experience as director of the Institute of Desegregation Problems, University of California, Berkeley, 1970–1972; research papers by John and Philip Lum, Gerald Colvin, and M. G. Dan Daniels in a graduate seminar on the power context of the San Francisco school system; and John Kaplan, "San Francisco," in a special issue of *Law and Society Review* on desegregation in selected cities. For historical background, see Lee S. Dolson, "The Administration of the San Francisco Public Schools, 1847 to 1947," Ph.D. dissertation, University of California, Berkeley, 1964.

47. On the familiar experience that it takes two superintendents to get desegregation under way—the initiator is sacrificed and his successor consolidates gains—see Frederick M. Wirt, "Role Attitudes in the Desegregation Process," Occasional Paper, Institute for Desegregation Problems, 1970; same author, "On Understanding the Realities of Desegregation," private ms. For an examination of the politics involved, see Robert L. Crain, et al., *The Politics of School Desegregation* (Garden City, N. Y.: Anchor-Doubleday, 1969); David J. Kirby, et al., *Political Strategies in Northern School Desegregation* (Lexington, Mass.: Heath, 1973); T. Bentley Edwards and Frederick M. Wirt, eds., *Northern School Desegregation* (San Francisco: Chandler, 1968). For the best review of the academic effects of desegregation, see Meyer Weinberg, *Desegregation Research: An Appraisal*, 2d ed. (Bloomington, Ind.: Phi Delta Kappan, 1970).

48. For the important insight on the relevance of changing the scope of the conflict and its stakes, see Schattschneider.

49. This section draws extensively on the lengthy analysis provided by Chester Hartman, et al., *Yerba Buena* (San Francisco: Glide Publications, 1974). This was cross-checked by use of the daily press and the briefs and memoranda in the litigation described later.

50. See Martin Anderson, *The Federal Bulldozer* (Cambridge: MIT Press, 1964).

51. A history of the area is provided by Alvin Averbach, "San Francisco's South of Market District, 1850–1950; The Emergence of a Skid Row," *California Historical Quarterly*, 52 (Fall 1973), 196–223.

52. See Les Shipnuck and Dan Feshbach, "Bay Area Council: Regional Powerhouse," *Pacific Research and World Empire Telegram*, 4, no. 1 (November–December 1972): 3–11, for a recent critical account.

53. Scott Greer, *Urban Renewal and American Cities* (New York: Bobbs-Merrill, 1965).

54. Several of the SFRA publications document the building additions to the city made during his tenure.

55. Hartman, chap. 3, p. 5.

56. It seems that it is not merely the young that revolutions devour. Many of the retired residents of the area to be cleared for Yerba Buena Center "had once been active union members, organizers, and even officials, and were supplementing their Social Security with union pensions." Ibid., p. 31.

57. *Wall Street Journal,* May 27, 1970.

58. *Norwalk CORE v. Norwalk Redevelopment Agency,* 395 F. 2d 920 (2d Cir., 1968).

59. Memorandum and Order, *TOOR v. HUD,* No. C-69 324 SAW (N.D. Cal. July 11, 1972). This judicial insistence had been foreshadowed a year earlier in another SFRA constraint involving the Western Addition; see San Francisco *Chronicle,* April 2, 1971. For a systematic review of the role of federal judges in urban renewal, see Chester W. Hartman, "Relocation: Illusory Promises and No Relief," *Virginia Law Review,* 57 (1971), 756–769.

60. Others alongside TOOR were a religious settlement house, a local businessman, and graduate students from San Francisco State University.

61. Hartman, *Yerba Buena,* discusses this problem at length. See also Harry Brill, *Why Organizers Fail: The Story of a Rent Strike* (Berkeley and Los Angeles: University of California Press, 1971), pp. 112–139.

62. See Pressman and Wildavsky, chap. 5.

63. For a review of HUD's internal problems, which hinder its effectiveness, see Richard T. LeGates, "Can The Federal Welfare Bureaucracies Control Their Programs: The Case of HUD and Urban Renewal" (Berkeley: Institute for Urban and Regional Development, University of California, 1972), Working Paper No. 172.

NOTES TO CHAPTER 12

1. Charles Adrian and Charles Press, *Governing Urban America* (New York: McGraw Hill, 1961).

2. On the seaboard, though, it is surprising to note the early prevalence of the pricing of bread and setting of fees for use of public markets by local governments; see Carl Bridenbaugh, *Cities in the Wilderness* (New York: Ronald Press, 1938).

3. State subventions to localities rose from 6.1 to 32.3 percent of all local revenues between 1902 and 1967. The state share of school costs between 1919 to 1969 rose from 16.5 to 40.7 percent; for highways costs between 1922 and 1967 it rose from 21.7 to 50.2 percent. See Advisory Commission on Intergovernmental Relations, *Fiscal Balance in the American Federal System* (Washington, D.C.: Government Printing Office, 1967), pp. 3, 85.

4. Michael D. Reagan, *The New Federalism* (New York: Oxford University Press, 1972), p. 34. Note, however, that the local debt total was still larger than the states' in the aggregate, almost $94 billion; the national debt, while only doubling, still aggregated $354 billion by 1969.

5. These conclusions are drawn from an extensive literature on macroanalysis of state policy. The variation among states is far from small. Thus, local contributions to highways in 1967 varied from Alaska and West Virginia at less than 5 percent to Wisconsin at over 50 percent, with the mean at about 21 percent; ACIR, *Fiscal Balance,* 84–85. Similarly for education, the state share in 1970–71 ran from Hawaii's 89.4 percent to New Hampshire's 9.6 percent, with the average at about 41 percent; National Education Assn., *Estimates of School Statistics, 1970–71* (Washington, D.C.: NEA, 1970). For the local differences occasioned by these state differences, see San Francisco and Baltimore welfare politics in Sharon P. Krefetz, "City Politics and Public Welfare: The Administration of Public Assistance in Baltimore and San Fran-

cisco," paper presented to the American Political Science Association convention, 1972, based on her dissertation at Brandeis University, 1972.

6. A fuller account of these shifts is found in Frederick M. Wirt, *The Slender Reed: Limits on Local Education Agencies for Achieving Equal Educational Opportunities,* private ms. Enormous comparative detail to support this finding is in Edgar Fuller and Jim B. Pearson, eds., *Education in the States: Nationwide Development since 1900* (Washington, D.C.: National Education Assn., 1969).

7. For elaboration of this thesis as it applies to curriculum decision making, see Frederick M. Wirt and Michael W. Kirst, *The Political Web of American Schools* (Boston: Little Brown, 1972), chap. 10.

8. Lawrence A. Cremin, *The Transformation of the School: Progressivism in American Education, 1876–1957* (New York: Vintage, 1964).

9. For full elaboration of the details, both comparatively and state-by-state, see the two volumes of Fuller and Pearson.

10. Compare these states in Joel Berke and Michael Kirst, eds., *Federal Aid to Education: Who Benefits? Who Governs?* (Lexington, Mass.: Heath, 1973); for two regional analyses, see Stephen K. Bailey, *Schoolmen and Politics* (Syracuse: Syracuse University Press, 1962), and Nicholas Masters, et al., *State Politics and Public Schools* (New York: Knopf, 1964). See more recently Nicholas Masters et al., *Education and State Politics* (New York: Teachers College Press, Columbia University, 1969).

11. Unless otherwise noted, the following data are drawn from a full survey of the state's role in education in Pearson and Fuller (see n. 13, chap. 11 above), ch. 5, written by the California Bureau of Publications.

12. From 1900 to 1965–66, the state percentages for each decade were: 48.7, 28.1, 20.4, 25.6, 45.9, 41.3, 40.6, and 35.0. See ibid., p. 180. The later Reagan administration reduced the figure even more. But by the 1970s, new pressures for state contributions arose when the property tax base for local schools was declared unconstitutional in the *Serrano* case.

13. Robert M. Isenberg, "State Organization for Service and Leadership to Local Schools," in Fuller and Pearson, p. 147.

14. Ibid., p. 135; emphasis in original.

15. Joseph W. Erlach, "Influences on Policy Making for Urban Curriculum; a Case Study," Ph.D. dissertation, Stanford University, 1972, p. 202; a briefer version appears as "Curriculum Development for Urban Education," *The Urban Review,* May 1972, pp. 23–29, where the anonymous city referred to is San Francisco.

16. The following list was provided by the research of Gerald S. Colvin, for the author.

17. The following is the result of a mail survey of 50 central office administrators, of whom 25 responded. Results here corroborate those from a similar study in a Daly City school system by Gerald Colvin for the author, but the data are too limited for more than their suggestiveness.

18. The instrument is found in Marvin E. Shaw and Jack M. Wright, *Scales for the Measurement of Attitudes* (New York: McGraw-Hill, 1967), pp. 124–126. On a 0–10 scale, with a high score representing attitudes more favorable, thirteen of the twenty-five respondents scored 8.0 or more, only two scored below 5.0, and the mean was 7.3. The time spent and government attitude scales were not related; the correlation was −.02.

19. The highly political aspects of curriculum defense and challenge is detailed in Wirt and Kirst, chap. 10.

20. Philip Selznick, *Law, Society, and Industrial Justice* (New York: Russell Sage Foundation, 1969).

21. Stanley Scott and Ora Huth, "Who Has The Power to Decide? An Unresolved

Issue in The San Francisco Bay Area," *Public Affairs Report,* 13, no. 2 (April 1972), 2.

22. Victor Jones, "Bay Area Regionalism" (Berkeley: Institute of Governmental Studies, University of California, 1972), p. 4.

23. Ibid., p. 2.

24. Ibid., p. 4.

25. Scholarly study of the phenomenon in the Bay Area has centered on the analysis of the Institute of Governmental Studies, University of California, Berkeley, under Director Eugene C. Lee. Publications include: Jones; Scott and Huth; Stanley Scott and John C. Bollens, *Governing a Metropolitan Region: The San Franciso Bay Area* (1968); Stanley Scott and Willis D. Hawley, "Leadership Views of the Bay Area and Its Regional Problems: A Preliminary Report," *Public Affairs Report,* 9, no. 1 (February 1968); Victor Jones, "Representative Local Government: From Neighborhood to Region," ibid., 11, no. 2 (April 1970); Eugene C. Lee, "The Politics of Regional Organization," ibid., 12, no. 2 (April 1971); Stanley Scott and Harriet Nathan, eds., *Adapting Local Government to Regional Needs* (1971); Willis D. Hawley, *Blacks and Metropolitan Governance: The Stakes of Reform* (1972).

26. For this and other assumptions in the regionalist perspective, see Eugene C. Lee, "Background and Purpose," in Scott and Nathan, pp. 3–7.

27. Ibid., p. 2.

28. Jones, "Bay Area Regionalism," p. 12, citing dissertation research of Norman C. Boehm, Claremont Graduate School, 1971.

29. Ibid., p. 76, citing dissertation research of Thomas E. Cronin, Stanford University, 1969.

30. For a full listing and brief description of these regional organizations, see Ora Huth, "Regional Organization in the San Francisco Bay Area—1970," in Scott and Nathan, pp. 19–60; *San Francisco Bay Area Decision Makers; Regional and Inter-County Bay Area Agencies* (San Francisco: League of Women Voters of the Bay Area, 1973); and "Regional Regulatory Agencies in the San Francisco Bay Area," Berkeley: League of California Cities, 1972).

31. For a review of these problems, see Scott and Huth.

32. For a review of the representative question, see Lee, "Background and Purpose"; Jones, "Representative Local Government"; and papers by Jones, Scott, and Willie Brown in Scott and Nathan.

33. A recent review of these regional organizations and their politics, namely, COGs, sustains this judgment of the relationship among power, process, and outcomes. See Melvin B. Mogulof, *Governing Metropolitan Areas: A Critical Review of Council of Governments and the Federal Role* (Washington, D.C.: The Urban Institute, 1971).

34. Scott Greer, *Metropolitics* (New York: Wiley, 1963), takes the development up to the last decade. On black fears of this development, see Hawley, *Blacks and Metropolitan Governance.*

35. Jones, "Bay Area Regionalism," p. 58. Even critics of this council accept its stimulus role; see "Regionalism and the Bay Area," *Pacific Research and World Empire Telegram,* 4 (1972), no. 1, pp. 3–11, and Bruce Bruggman et al., *The Ultimate Highrise* (San Francisco: Bay Guardian Books, 1971), passim. A specialized study of this council's influence in one regional organization is Burton W. Wolfe, "BART—Steve Bechtel's $2 Billion Toy," *San Francisco Bay Guardian,* 7 (1973), 208. For an earlier examination of regionalism here, see Mel Scott, *The San Francisco Bay Area: A Metropolis in Perspective* (Berkeley and Los Angeles: University of California Press, 1959).

36. For a review by its chief consultant and historian, see Jones, "Bay Area Regionalism," chap. 3.

37. Ibid., pp. 58–60.

38. Stephen Zwerling, "The Political Consequences of Technological Choice: Public Transit in the San Francisco Metropolitan Area," Ph. D. dissertation, University of California, Berkeley, 1972, pp. 56–57.

39. For analysis of this factor, see Mogulof.

40. Jones, "Bay Area Regionalism," p. 61.

41. Frank M. Stead, "Environmental Problems and Governmental Levels," in Scott and Nathan, pp. 62–68, provides the following analysis.

42. Mogulof, pp. 81–82, believes the issue is more intense here than elsewhere.

43. These are treated in studies cited in note 32.

44. Contrasting views are found in Alan Altshuler, *The City Planning Process: A Political Analysis* (Ithaca, N.Y.: Cornell University Press, 1965), and T. J. Kent, Jr., *The Urban General Plan* (San Francisco: Chandler, 1964).

45. The following is drawn from Altshuler, pp. 425–429; for more extensive analysis, see the sources cited therein.

46. Hearings, Joint Economic Committee, U.S. Congress, *Regional Planning Issues* (Washington: Government Printing Office), Part 4, 696–698. For a full review of COG operations, see Mogulof.

47. Mogulof, pp. 14, 16, 45, 67, 73, 74–75, and 100–104 provide the quotations and paraphrasings found in the text.

48. Huth, "Regional Organization," p. 52.

49. Mogulof, chap. 4.

50. Huth, pp. 50–51.

51. Altshuler, p. 424.

52. Theodore J. Lowi, *The End of Liberalism* (New York: Norton, 1969).

53. Marion Clawson, *Suburban Land Conversion in the United States* (Baltimore: Johns Hopkins Press, 1971); a briefer treatment is found in Frederick Wirt et al., *On The City's Rim* (Lexington, Mass.: Heath, 1972) chap. 2.

54. Norton Long, *The Polity* (Chicago: Rand McNally, 1962).

55. A study of five Kentucky towns on the tax returns from welcoming new businesses reaches pessimistic conclusions; see Charles B. Garrison, *The Impact of New Industry on Local Government Finances in 5 Small Towns in Kentucky* (Washington D.C.: Economic Resource Service, U.S. Department of Agriculture, 1970).

56. A comparison of this type of politics at the city level is found in Alan Lupo et al., *Rites of Way* (Boston: Little, Brown, 1971), Part Two.

57. For analysis of the consequences for a region where such capital has newly come, see James G. Maddox et al., *The Advancing South* (New York: Twentieth Century Fund, 1967).

58. The data and statements in this and the following paragraph are drawn from Brian J. L. Berry and Yehoshua S. Cohen, "Decentralization of Commerce and Industry: The Restructuring of Metropolitan America," in Louis Masotti and Jeffry Hadden, eds., *The Urbanization of the Suburbs* (Beverly Hills, Ca.: Sage, 1973), chap. 17.

59. Ibid.

60. Harry M. Caudill, *Night Comes to the Cumberland: A Biography of a Depressed Area* (Boston: Little, Brown, 1963).

61. Howard Becker, ed., *Culture and Civility in San Francisco* (Chicago: Aldine, 1971).

62. *San Francisco Revenue and Taxation Report—1972,* by the chief administrative

officer, Thomas Mellon, pp. 8, 84. Neither this major document nor the city's annual appropriation ordinance provides a total amount for salaries and wages; rather, they are shown spread among 127 agencies.

NOTES TO CHAPTER 13

1. A fuller treatment and its sources are found in Appendix I. For an explanation of the utility of systems analysis, see Frederick M. Wirt and Michael Kirst, *The Political Web of American Schools* (Boston: Little, Brown, 1972), Part Three.

2. David Brudnoy, "Race and the San Francisco School Board Incident: Contemporary Evaluations," *California Historical Quarterly,* 50 (1971), 295–312.

3. For new light on these formative events, see Roger Lotchin, "San Francisco: The Patterns and Chaos of Growth," in Kenneth T. Jackson and Stanley K. Schultz, eds., *Cities in American History* (New York: Knopf, 1972), pp. 143–163.

4. Robert S. and Helen Lynd, *Middletown* and *Middletown in Transition* (New York: Harcourt, Brace, 1929 and 1937); H. Lloyd Warner's "Yankee City Series," Yale University Press; Floyd Hunter, *Community Power Structure* (Chapel Hill: University of North Carolina Press, 1953); Robert Dahl, *Who Governs?* (New Haven: Yale University Press, 1961).

5. Arthur Vidich and Joseph Bensman, *Small Town in Mass Society* (Princeton: Princeton University Press, 1959). But not even they raised the question of the total range of issues, even though their major focus was on the conflict between an ideology of localism and a reality of extramural decisions.

6. On the first type, see Dahl, and Robert A. Agger, et al., *The Rulers and the Ruled* (New York: Wiley, 1964). On the second type, see Roscoe C. Martin et al., *Decisions in Syracuse* (Bloomington: Indiana University Press, 1961), and Robert Presthus, *Men at the Top* (New York: Oxford University Press, 1964).

7. A definition that includes "the law of anticipated reaction" as a form of popular participation may follow logically from the ideology of representative democracy, but its empirical referents have not yet been verified. For a review of the evidence, see Normal R. Luttbeg, ed., *Public Opinion and Public Policy* (Homewood, Ill.; Dorsey, 1968), sections V and VI.

8. Wallace S. Sayre and Herbert Kaufman, *Governing New York City* (New York: Russell Sage Foundation, 1960).

9. Robert H. Salisbury, "Urban Politics: The New Convergence of Power," *Journal of Politics,* 26 (1964), 775–797.

10. The thesis of this paragraph is developed empirically in T. Bentley Edwards and Frederick M. Wirt, eds., *School Desegregation in the North* (San Francisco: Chandler, 1968), chaps. 1, 13; Wirt, *Politics of Southern Equality* (Chicago: Aldine, 1970), Part V; and Wirt and Kirst, chaps. 8 and 9.

11. For example, see Jeffrey L. Pressman and Aaron B. Wildavsky, *Implementation* (Berkeley and Los Angeles: University of California Press, 1973).

12. Ibid.

13. Michael Aiken and Robert R. Alford, "Community Structure and Innovation: The Case of Public Housing," *American Political Science Review,* 64 (1970), 843–864; David J. Kirby et al., *Political Strategies in Northern School Desegregation* (Lexington, Mass.: Heath, 1973).

14. Michael Lipsky, "Protest as a Political Resource," *American Political Science Review,* 62 (1968), 1144–58.

15. A useful review of the literature on strategies of protest politics is in ibid. See also H. L. Nieburg, *Political Violence* (New York: St. Martin's Press, 1969), chap. 6; Louis H. Masotti and Don R. Bowen, eds., *Riots and Rebellion* (Beverly Hills, Calif.:

Sage, 1968), Parts II, V; Norval D. Glenn and Charles M. Bonjean, eds., *Blacks in the United States* (San Francisco: Chandler, 1969), Part III, esp. bibliography at pp. 480–486.

16. A survey of actual developments in American cities is Howard W. Hallman, *Community Control: A Study of Community Corporations and Neighborhood Boards* (Washington: Washington Center for Metropolitan Studies, 1969). An intensive case study of the interactions in Baltimore is Peter Bachrach and Moton S. Baratz, *Power and Poverty* (New York: Oxford University Press, 1970). On school community control, see the putative advantage analysis in Henry M. Levin, ed., *Community Control of Schools* (Washington: Brookings, 1970); on the actual experience, see George R. LaNoue and Bruce L.R. Smith, *The Politics of School Decentralization* (Lexington, Mass.: Heath, 1973), and David Rogers and Willis D. Hawley, eds., *Improving the Quality of Urban Management* (Beverly Hills, Ca.: Sage, 1974), Part 3.

17. For studies of New York, Chicago, and Philadelphia, J. David Greenstone and Paul E. Peterson, "Performers, Machines, and the War on Poverty," in James Q. Wilson, ed., *City Politics and Public Policy* (New York: John Wiley, 1968), pp. 267–292; Paul E. Peterson, "Forms of Representation: Participation of the Poor in the Community Action Program," *American Political Science Review,* 64 (1970), 491–507; for Baltimore, see Bachrach and Baratz; for four cities, including San Francisco, see John Mollenkopf, "Community Organization and the City Politics," Ph.D. dissertation, Harvard University, 1973.

18. Robert Wood, *1400 Governments* (Cambridge: Harvard University Press, 1961), p. 62.

19. For a sketch of the process, see Frederick M. Wirt, "Alioto and the Politics of Hyperpluralism," *trans-action,* May 1971.

NOTES TO APPENDIX I

1. Reviews of the following propositions in the literature are found in Willis D. Hawley and Frederick M. Wirt, *The Search for Community Power* (Englewood Cliffs, N.J.: Prentice-Hall, 1974), 2d ed.; Terry Clark, ed., *Community Structure and Decision-Making* (San Francisco: Chandler, 1968); Charles M. Bonjean et al., eds., *Community Politics* (New York: Free Press, 1971); Willis D. Hawley and James H. Svara, *The Study of Community Power: A Bibliographic Review* (Santa Barbara, Calif.: ABC-CLIO, 1972).

2. David Easton, *The Political System* (New York: Knopf, 1953), *A Framework for Political Analysis* (Englewood Cliffs, N.J.: Prentice-Hall, 1965), and *A Systems Analysis of Political Life* (New York: Wiley, 1965).

3. E.g., Harold Lasswell and Abraham Kaplan, *Power and Society* (New Haven: Yale University Press, 1950), provide the conceptual bases for the following three propositions.

4. The concept is that of "slack resources" from Robert A. Dahl, *Who Governs?* (New Haven: Yale University Press, 1960). On differences of the rich, see Floyd Hunter, *The Big Rich and The Little Rich* (Garden City, N.Y.: Doubleday, 1965).

5. To say nothing of the "non-issue" problem first raised in Peter Bachrach and Morton S. Baratz, "Decisions and Nondecisions: An Analytical Framework," *American Political Science Review,* 57 (1963), 632–642, and same authors, "Two Faces of Power," ibid., 56 (1962), 947–952. But see Raymond E. Wolfinger, "Nondecisions and the Study of Local Politics," ibid., 65 (1971), 1063–81, comment by Frederick W. Frey and rejoinder by Wolfinger at pp. 1081–1104.

On the large span of issues to be inventoried, and an effort to structure such research, see Charles M. Bonjean, "Dimensions of Power Structure: Some Problems in

Conceptualization and Measurement," in Frederick M. Wirt, ed., *Future Directions in Community Power Research: A Colloquium* (Berkeley: Institute of Governmental Studies, University of California, Berkeley, 1971), pp. 19–42.

6. The first thinking on this dimension came from Roland L. Warren, "Toward a Typology of Extra-Community Controls Limiting Local Community Autonomy," *Social Forces,* 34 (1956), 338–341, and *The Community in America* (Chicago: Rand McNally, 1963). A more recent development of the concept is John Walton, "The Vertical Axis of Community Organization and the Structure of Power," *Southwestern Social Science Quarterly,* 48 (1967), 353–368, and Terry N. Clark, "Community Autonomy in the National System: Federalism, Localism, and Decentralization," in Terry N. Clark, ed., *Comparative Community Politics* (Beverly Hills, Ca.: Sage, 1973).

7. Bachrach and Baratz.

8. Bachrach and Baratz, *Power and Poverty: Theory and Practice* (New York: Oxford University Press, 1970), for Baltimore, and Wallace S. Sayre and Herbert Kaufman, *Governing New York City* (New York: Russell Sage Foundation, 1960).

9. Important exceptions are Arthur Vidich and Joseph Bensman, *Small Town in Mass Society* (Princeton: Princeton University Press, 1959), and Roscoe C. Martin, et al., *Decisions in Syracuse* (Bloomington: Indiana University Press, 1961).

10. E. E. Schattschneider, *The Semi-Sovereign People* (New York: Holt, Rinehart, and Winston, 1960).

11. Bachrach and Baratz, "Decisions and Nondecisions."

12. Wolfinger, "Nondecisions and Local Politics."

13. However, some new thinking about these limitations has been provided by Frey's comment and Wolfinger's rejoinder (see n. 5 above). For earlier comments, see Nelson Polsby, *Community Power and Political Theory* (New Haven: Yale University Press, 1963), especially at pp. 96–97; Andrew McFarland, *Power and Leadership in Pluralist Systems* (Stanford: Stanford University Press, 1969), chaps. 5 and 6.

14. Claire W. Gilbert, "Some Trends in Community Politics: A Secondary Analysis of Power Structure Data from 166 Communities," *Southwestern Social Science Quarterly,* 48 (1967), 373–381.

15. See the discussion in Nelson Polsby, " 'Pluralism' in the Study of Community Power, Or, *Erklarung* before *Verklarung in Wissenssoziologie*," *The American Sociologist,* 4 (1969), 118–122.

16. V. O. Key, Jr., *Public Opinion and American Democracy* (New York: Knopf, 1961), p. 14.

17. James March, "The Power of Power," in David Easton, ed., *Varieties of Political Theory* (Inglewood Cliffs, N.J.: Prentice-Hall, 1966), pp. 39–70.

18. The recent efforts by Frey are commendable attempts to move this factor into the realm of research; for another but related approach, see Bonjean, "Dimensions of Power Structure" (n. 5 above).

19. For an exchange along these lines, see Raymond E. Wolfinger, "Reputation and Reality in the Study of Community Power," *American Sociological Review,* 27 (1962), 841–847, and Howard J. Ehrlich, "The Social Psychology of Reputations for Community Leadership," *The Sociological Quarterly,* 8 (1967), 514–530.

20. Something close to that has been performed by congressional scholars in their study of congressional subcommittees, or by small-group analysts. For an example of the latter, with a review of relevant literature, see James D. Barber, *Power in Committees* (Chicago: Rand McNally, 1966). But in all these studies, the subject was a group possessing a formal structure, role sets, defined resources, and other attributes far from the amorphous qualities of any "power structure" reported to date.

21. Frederick M. Wirt, *Politics of Southern Equality: Law and Social Change in a*

Mississippi County (Chicago: Aldine, 1970); Wirt et al., *On The City's Rim* (Lexington, Mass.: Heath, 1972).

22. E.g., see the problems of defining the concept of "community" in Warren, *The Community in America,* chap. 2; David W. Minar and Scott Greer, eds., *The Concept of Community* (Chicago: Aldine, 1969); and Robert Nisbet, *The Sociological Tradition* (New York: Basic Books, 1966), pp. 47–106.

23. Gilbert.

24. Terry Clark's work, *inter alia,* appears in "Community Structure, Decision-Making, Budget Expenditures, and Urban Renewal in 51 American Communities," *American Sociological Review,* 33 (1968), 576–593, and is expanded in Frederick M. Wirt, ed., *Future Directions in Community Power Research,* pp. 43–94; see also Daniel J. Elazar, " 'Fragmentation' and Local Organizational Response to Federal-City Programs," *Urban Affairs Quarterly,* 2 (1967), 30–46.

25. Philip E. Jacob and James V. Toscano, *The Integration of Political Communities* (New York: Lippincott, 1964), pp. 120–142.

26. For a summary of such research findings and a test of some propositions on structure see Clark; Michael Aiken and Robert R. Alford, "Community Structure and Innovation: The Case of Public Housing," *American Political Science Review,* 64 (1970), 843–864; and Lewis A. Froman, "An Analysis of Public Policies in Cities," *Journal of Politics,* 29 (1967), 94–108. Froman's conclusions on the relationship between "segmental" policies and community heterogeneity are compatible with the thesis expressed here.

27. Robert Salisbury and John Heinz, "A Theory of Policy Analysis and Some Preliminary Applications," in Ira Sharkansky, ed., *Policy Analysis in Political Science* (Chicago: Markham, 1970), pp. 39–60.

28. Richard L. Forstall, "A New Social and Economic Grouping of Cities," *Municipal Year Book 1970* (Washington: International City Management Association, 1970), pp. 102–159. For detailed treatment of this variety, see Brian J. L. Berry, ed., *City Classification Handbook* (New York: Wiley-Interscience, 1972).

29. Leo F. Schnore, *The Urban Scene* (New York: Free Press, 1965).

Index

405

Author Index